Towards the Prophetic Church

Also by John M. Hull

Sense and Nonsense About God (1974)
Hellenistic Magic and the Synoptic Tradition (1974)
School Worship – An Obituary (1975)
Studies in Religion and Education (1984)
What Prevents Christian Adults from Learning? (1985)
The Act Unpacked: The Meaning of the 1988 Education Reform Act for Religious Education (1989)
Touching the Rock: An Experience of Blindness (1990)
God-Talk with Young Children (1991)
Mishmash: Religious Education in Multi-Cultural Britain, A Study in Metaphor (1991)
The Holy Trinity and Christian Education in a Pluralistic World (1995)
On Sight and Insight: A Journey into the World of Blindness (1997)
Utopian Whispers: Moral, Religious and Spiritual Values in Schools (1998)
In the Beginning There was Darkness: A Blind Person's Conversations With the Bible (2001)
Mission-Shaped Church: A Theological Response (2006)
The Tactile Heart: Blindness and Faith (2013)

Towards the Prophetic Church

A Study of Christian Mission

John M. Hull

scm press

© John M. Hull 2014

Published in 2014 by SCM Press
Editorial office
3rd Floor Invicta House
108–114 Golden Lane
London EC1Y OTG

SCM Press is an imprint of Hymns Ancient and Modern Ltd (a registered charity)
13A Hellesdon Park Road
Norwich NR6 5DR, UK

www.scmpress.co.uk

British Library Cataloguing in Publication data

A catalogue record for this book is available
from the British Library

978 0 334 05234 0

Typeset by Manila Typesetting Company
Printed and bound by
CPI Group (UK) Ltd, Croydon

Contents

Preface

More than 20 years ago I promised that there would be a successor to *What Prevents Christian Adults from Learning?* (Hull 1985, p. vii) As far back as 1985, I had realized that my understanding of adult Christian learning had been one-sided. I had concentrated mainly upon psychological factors such as the need for an evolving self-understanding to be accompanied by an evolving faith. I had neglected the historical and sociological problems that form the context within which modern Christians live in the West, but I had dealt only with interior aspects, not with external ones.

I had lost the last remaining traces of my sight in 1983, and the study of adult Christian learning problems was the first book I had attempted to write as a blind author. It is not surprising that in those circumstances, the problems of interiority and of the meanings of the spiritual life preoccupied me and encouraged me to project these conflicts onto other Christian adults. To understand the origin of one's opinions, however, does not invalidate them. The fact that the Christian faith we have in the postmodern West is the product of many historical and cultural influences was dawning upon me as I began to reach out toward the world again.

Twenty years later a new set of circumstances gave me a fresh impetus toward this problem. In September of 2004 I began to teach ordination candidates in the Queen's Foundation, and I have been doing this full time for nearly ten years. The experience of moving away from defending religious education, which demanded continual grappling with the problems of plurality and secularity, into a context where theology could be taught from faith to faith drew me more deeply into the life of the Church. Previously I had been in the busy high street with its crowded, competitive traffic, and from a professional point of view had viewed Christian faith from the outside, looking, as it were, into the shop window and seeing Christian faith in there. Now I had gone into the window, and found myself looking out from Christian faith toward the busy street. Training clergy took me into the back room of the shop, where the products were made. The problems of the theological education of adults took on a new urgency.

I was invited to teach a course on Christian mission, and this encouraged me to consider the nature and the vitality of Christian faith in a more strategic way. This concern for mission is expressed in the sub title of the book. Reading Paul Tillich more deeply and encountering for the first time the writings of Daniel Berrigan, Walter Brueggemann, Ched Myers, Walter Wink and many others, made me ponder on the triviality and irrelevance, as it seemed to me, of much British church life. This renewed my interest in the problems of Christian adults learning to live the life of justice and peace. The most challenging experience,

however, was when I became responsible for the development of a new forma-
tional programme in social justice. This began with the desire to make Practical Theology more practical and soon became an attempt to train ministerial
students in prophetic ministry, which we sometimes called prophetic witness.
We have thus trained future clergy in action for social justice in fulfilment of the
Fourth Mark of Mission acknowledged by the Anglican Communion worldwide and other churches.

In 2004 the Anglican report *Mission-Shaped Church* was published and
quickly became influential as new forms of congregation began to appear in the
Fresh Expressions Movement. Exciting though these trends were, the theological basis of the movement seemed to me to be weak. After having published a
short critique of this theology in 2006, I began to work steadily on the nature
and history of what I was increasingly describing as 'the prophetic Church'.
The present work is the result, and is the long deferred sequel to *What Prevents
Christian Adults from Learning?* I emphasize that the book is not entitled *The
Prophetic Church* or even *How to Mould a Prophetic Church* but the more
modest *Towards the Prophetic Church*. All I have tried to do is to examine the
biblical basis, some aspects of the history, the use of the tradition in modern
times and to put all this in a framework of Western culture and Christian ethics.
The whole thing is no more than an introduction to the practice of a prophetic
Church, something the German scholars would describe as a prolegomena,
although in view of my work at Queen's, I have added some comments about
the training of clergy and lay people. I would like to create a more practical
handbook for the use of those in the churches who want to see this aspect of its
calling revived, hopefully in less than 20 years.

The book presents positive resources for the renewal of theological education and also describes the cultural, historical and theological factors which
continue to make adult Christian learning difficult. After a brief introduction
to the various meanings of prophecy in the modern churches, Part 1 deals with
the biblical foundations of prophetic religion, the prophets of the Old Testament and the prophetic work of Jesus Christ. Part 2 continues the enquiry into
the problems of adult Christian education, explaining the origins of some of
the elements which still survive to prevent Christian renewal. I show how and
why the prophetic tradition was increasingly ignored. Chapter 4 in this second
part deals with the corruption of faith during the medieval Crusades against
Islam, Chapter 5 describes the way that Christian faith was adapted to meet
the needs of growing British power, and Chapter 6, dealing with the hymns of
Isaac Watts, argues that an imperial theology has been embedded into Christian
spirituality in Britain. Chapter 7 is a bridge, which shows that in spite of the
formation over the centuries of a shrewd, hardened, exclusive and competitive Church, the Christian faith remained porous on the edges, where poverty
could not be denied and where other forms of authentic human experience were
encountered. Part 3 offers some examples of the interpretation and the renewal
of prophetic Christian faith, showing that the ancient faith of the prophets is
still capable of energizing theological renewal. Part 4 begins with the important
Chapter 11, which offers a kind of wide perspective on the history of Christian
faith in the Western churches, seeking to show how we got to the present level
of false consciousness. It is a sort of summary of the argument of the book, and

is a contribution to the problem of understanding why Christian adults are prevented from realizing the truth of the prophetic tradition. Chapter 12 provides some insights from theological ethics to support the centrality of actions for social justice in church life. Finally, I offer a few reflections about the way theological education should develop if the prophetic Church is to be realized.

I am grateful for the patience of the British Academy, whose grants enabled me to do the research which is now reported in Chapters 5 and 11. I am also grateful to the Allan and Nesta Ferguson Trust and the Westhill Endowment Trust, whose generous support has contributed to the completion of this book. My special thanks must be to The Queen's Foundation for Ecumenical Theological Education in Birmingham. The friendship and inspiration of colleagues and students in this centre of Christian renewal have given me some of the happiest years of my life. I am particularly grateful to the work of my assistant Deanna Tyndall, and for the support of my colleagues Gary Hall, Mark Earey, Helen Cameron, Mukti Barton and the principal David Hewlett. This is why the book is dedicated to Queen's.

John M. Hull
The Queen's Foundation
Birmingham 24 January 2014

To the staff and students of The Queen's Foundation for Ecumenical Theological Education, who have explored with me the way to the prophetic Church.

Introduction

Prophetic Theology in the Church Today

The language of prophecy is a contested area. Different church traditions call upon different ways of speaking about the prophetic, and these articulate different aspects of Christian experience and, indeed, different theologies of Christian faith. In this introductory chapter, three of the most significant prophetic theologies will be briefly described. This will introduce the reader to the main distinctions upon which my own understanding of prophetic theology is based and will begin to analyse the contemporary problems of adult theological learning.

Prophecy as the ecstatic immediacy of God

Prophecy, as widely understood in the Church today, is believed to offer direct encounter with God through the Holy Spirit. Prophecy is a form of religious experience, but whereas the latter is generally experienced by individuals, prophecy takes place in the religious community; prophecy is congregational. That does not mean that there are not individual prophets in many Christian traditions but that the role of the prophet is social. Prophecy is one of the gifts given by the Holy Spirit to the Church and is exercised either by the whole congregation or on behalf of it by specially gifted individuals. Religious experience is a wider category, including mystical awareness of nature, and a sense of presence, moments of transforming insight as well as phenomena such as specific visionary or auditory occurrences. Prophecy in the Church, on the other hand, usually involves some kind of guidance or direction of the life of the community because of its meaning as revelation. The will of God is conveyed to the Church through prophetic revelation. This may include everything from ethical criticism to guided courses of action, and the congregation may respond with joyful worship.

Vivid examples of prophecy may be found in many of the African churches. A striking case is that of the Friday Apostolic Church of Zimbabwe, a denomination of 100,000 people tracing its origin back to the mid 1930s (Engelke 2007). Although people in the Church have a general knowledge of the Bible and refer to biblical models or types such as Moses and Elijah, use of the Bible itself is rejected in favour of an immediate relation with God. In pursuit of this goal, they have no church buildings. They worship God in the open air wearing white robes and singing (pp. 233–4). The prophet is the instrument through whom God speaks to them. The prophet is full of the Holy Spirit but not possessed, as might be said of an evil spirit (p. 184). The prophet is inspired rather than being possessed. In the typical church service, whenever the prophet speaks, there is an interpreter standing beside him or her. The prophets usually speak rather softly, possibly in a special form of Shona which is believed to be ancient Hebrew. The prophet does not necessarily understand what is being said through him or her, but the interpreter will shout out the meaning to the people. In general, the words of the prophet are inaccessible to ordinary human understanding, apart from the ministry of the interpreter. The prophet may be inspired by the same angel that spoke through John the Baptist, for example, so the Spirit of God, which inspired the original Bible, now speaks again to the modern Church.

When not acting in role, that is, when not speaking in the presence of the congregation through the Spirit, the prophets are ordinary people (p. 93). They may lose the prophetic spirit, may fall into sin or disbelief. God the Holy Spirit always retains the initiative. The prophet may interpret dreams or receive divine knowledge in the form of verses which are interpreted and passed on to the people who respond by singing them (pp. 200–23).

The Revival movement in evangelical Protestantism in the late nineteenth and early twentieth centuries gave rise to the Pentecostal movement, which looked for a renewal of the Pentecostal experience in modern Christian life (Anderson 2007). Prophecy, speaking in tongues and other ecstatic manifestations were typical of the Pentecostal movement, which had an important influence on the emergence of the African Independent churches, particularly in the first 30 years or so of the twentieth century (pp. 161–6). Many of these new African churches were led by inspired prophets, who often had widespread influence and attracted thousands of followers. In the early American Pentecostal movement, the pouring out of the spirit was believed to impart the gift of being able to speak in foreign languages (pp. 57–65). Armed with this belief, many Pentecostal preachers were moved to begin missionary work in Asia and Africa.

When African and Caribbean churches were established in Britain in the 1950s and 60s, the emphasis upon prophecy continued (Aldred 2005, pp. 68–112). In the Black Majority churches of today the gift of prophetic utterance may be preceded by periods of prayer and fasting, to purge the mind and open the heart to the influences of the Holy Spirit (Sturge 2005, pp. 125, 128). Leaders of the churches are, however, aware of the dangers of deception and the possibility of psychological and sociological explanations of prophecy. 'Many "prophetic words" do not have their genesis in revelation or vision, but are essentially psychological or sociological constructs' (p. 205). The prophecy of ecstatic immediacy is also common in what is sometimes called the End Times movements within Evangelical churches. The prophet Joel has said that in the last days the Spirit would be poured out upon all people so that '[y]our sons and daughters will prophesy, your old men will dream dreams, your young men will see visions. Even on my servants, both men and women, I will pour out my Spirit in those days' (Joel 2.28–9).

The early Church regarded itself as being the embodiment of this prophetic utterance, and the prevalence of prophecy was thus a proof of the end times, and its actual occurrence contributed to the belief that the Church was living in the end times (Acts 2.1–18; 1 Cor. 7.31, 10.11). This continues to be a vital influence in many charismatic and evangelical congregations. Clifford and Monica Hill, for example, think that the spread of the gift of tongues and other prophetic forms throughout the Church today is a sign that we are approaching the last days (1990, pp. 3–8, 48, 74 et passim), although they are critical of attempts to predict dates and other details (pp. 4, 52). However, Clifford Hill does give examples of revelations he has received, some of items of knowledge otherwise unknown, others of future events (pp. 29, 61–2, 67–70). In some cases actions following these revelations were instrumental in avoiding the threatened happening. The Hills also emphasize that the prophets were forth-tellers rather than fore-tellers (p. 56) and speak about prophetic judgement and of the demand of the prophets for justice (p. 168). Clifford Hill's account of the prophecy surrounding his own birth is an interesting example of the continuing influence of biblical accounts of prophetic calling (p. 85).

The role of the prophet as critic both of the Church and society is emphasized by Joe Aldred. 'Every church and context needs its own organic intellectuals to speak prophetically inward and apologetically externally' (2005, p. 28). The prophetic spirit is regarded as the attitude of Spirit inspired criticism directed inwardly toward the community of which the prophet is part. The prophet seeks for liberation of all people both in and out of the Church. However, the British Caribbean churches have only slowly accepted the idea that they were being called to a prophetic role toward the whole nation and thus to be 'involved in the fabric of society' (Joel Edwards quoted by Aldred 2005, p. 100). The need for the Church to be critical of the unjust structures of society were stimulated in the case of the Caribbean churches by the growing evidence of the social disadvantage faced by young black people. The influence of Martin Luther King and James Cone can be detected here (p. 100). Thus Caribbean Christians may exercise a prophetic role when they are minorities within largely white congregations, and the witness of the black majority churches toward their own people should also be of a prophetic kind (pp. 200–6).

Prophecy as biblical futurology

In addition to its ecstatic, revelatory sense, prophetic inspiration may be concerned with the future meaning of the biblical text. This brings us full circle from the meaning of prophecy in the Friday Apostolic Church of Zimbabwe. There, specific reference to biblical texts is considered to be a betrayal of the immediacy of the Spirit, but in this more hermeneutic kind of intellectual prophecy, the text and its interpretation become all important. The element of forth-telling, of social and ethical criticism, is less important, and the predictive aspect of the prophetic text enters the foreground. What matters now is not the immediacy of religious experience but the imminence of predicted happenings. Christian Zionism interprets the establishment of the state of Israel in 1948 as fulfilment of biblical prophecy, expecting that the conversion of Israel to Christian faith will precede the return of Jesus Christ. This is part of the End Times Movement made popular by the novels of Tim LaHaye and Jerry B. Jenkins (1995).[1] Current affairs are interpreted in the light of alleged biblical predictions and belief in the rapture is widespread, at least in American fundamentalism. Common themes in current end times literature are antagonism to the growth of the Euro-

---

1 *Left Behind* was the first of 16 novels based on the doctrine of the rapture (1 Thess. 4.17).

pean Union, the financial crisis of 2008 and the decline in the influence of the United States.[2]

In spite of the long history of such predictions in which time and again, the same biblical texts have been applied and reapplied to event after event, there continues to be a lively market for this kind of thing, but presumably from people who are unaware of the history of biblical interpretations. W. W. Meissner (1995) has studied these movements from a psychoanalytic perspective. Brent Sandy (2002), writing from an evangelical point of view, points out that '[f]or many the excitement of connecting events of the moment to biblical prophecy mutes the memory of failed predictions in previous sermons and books' (p. 156). The result is that 'the landscape of history is littered with burned-out Christian predictions' (p. 155). Sandy concludes that '[t]here is limited evidence that the Old Testament prophets generally saw the distant future and predicted it' (p. 162). He attempts to divert evangelical exegesis away from the idea that the Bible has unfulfilled prophecies that apply to the present and future of our own world:

> To those who thought that they had identified the sign that his coming would happen in their day, we express our condolences for their disappointment. But we also share in their embarrassment. Current events simply cannot be claimed as *the* sign of his coming, no matter how many wars and rumors of wars there are. (p. 174)

Sandy's brave attempt to save evangelical exegesis from further embarrassment shows that in spite of its continued popularity with the shrewd or the gullible, this kind of biblical prophecy is no longer convincing for thoughtful and widely read Christian conservatives. Nevertheless, it is unfortunate that the sensationalism and the notorious failures of biblical prediction have created an expectation that any discussion of the role of prophecy will be of this kind. I would like to reclaim the theology of prophecy for responsible contemporary use, and I suggest that attempts to discover the future from biblical texts should be denied the title 'prophecy' and should be re-designated 'biblical futurology'.

Prophetic theology in the biblical tradition

We have seen that two of the main meanings of prophecy in the Christian world today are the ecstatic immediacy of encounter with God, especially in the charismatic movements, and the attempt to find the fulfilment of predictions in a kind of exegetical futurology. There are, however, more thoughtful and responsible interpretations of the role of prophecy in the contemporary Church. Nicholas Healy takes a view somewhat similar to that of Joe Aldred. The continually changing nature of the interplay between cultures under the conditions of post-modernity gives the prophetic Church opportunity for self-criticism and for cultural engagement. This prophetic criticism cannot escape the ambiguity that is also typical

---

2 Hal Lindsey and Carole C. Carlson's *The Late, Great Planet Earth* (1970) gave enormous popularity, at least in the United States, to this kind of end times literature, which is now represented by hundreds of titles such as John F. Walvoord (2001).

of contemporary cultural complexity. 'Of course, discerning whether prophecy is true or false is sometimes extremely difficult, but such difficulties cannot be avoided; they are an inherent part of the dramatic struggle that constitutes Christian ecclesial existence' (Healy 2000, p. 179).

Prophecy functions in the Protestant churches in a way somewhat similar to the role confession has in the Roman Catholic tradition – it is an ongoing exercise of self-criticism conducted in the light of faith (p. 185). So the prophetic function is intrinsic to the nature of the Church itself, since the Church is guided by the Spirit of the risen Christ which is the spirit of prophecy. It continually exposes ecclesial practice to criticism in the light of the true goals of ecclesial life. This does not mean, according to Healy, that the prophetic Church is not also turned toward the outside; prophecy is directed to both the inside and the outside of the Church, because the distinction between the world and the Church is not hard and fast. Therefore the spirit of prophecy is not confined to one sphere or the other.

For Manas Buthelezi the Church is a prophetic sign in so far as it liberates the truth. *Letho* is the Greek word for causing to forget and conceal, hence *aletheia*, its opposite, is to remind, expose, or bring to attention that which has been concealed or forgotten. 'untruth refers to what has been blurred or covered so that it is no longer seen for what it is' (1986, p. 139). In so far as the Church does this in the world, it becomes a prophetic Church, not dependant on an individual seer or prophet, but as a whole *ecclesia* it becomes an authentic sign of abiding prophecy. Preaching and interpretation fulfils this through liberating the word of God in order to penetrate the falseness of contemporary life. A Church whose daily pursuit is self-preservation can no longer become a sign of the life of Christ in the world; '[f]or the church to be a prophetic sign means to die by pointing away from itself . . . to Christ as the rallying point' (p. 144).

Hervé Legrand points out that it is Pentecost that established the Church as a whole in its prophetic vocation. The Roman Catholic Church in its Canon Law (1983, Canon 204) explicitly includes the people within the prophetic Church. 'By baptism Christ's faithful people are made sharers in the priestly, prophetic and royal function of Christ' (1986, p. 147). Thus we may speak of the prophethood of all believers. The Church can be a symbol of the unity of all humanity as it assumes its prophetic role in the Pentecostal experience, in which the many diverse tongues found unity. The divisions of the Church along linguistic and racial lines subdue its prophetic role, but this can be recaptured as it seeks reconciliation between cultures and religions (pp. 145–8).

In the political theology of Glen Tinder (1991), the nature of prophetic hope is regarded as springing from the destiny of the human species. If we wish to understand the place of prophecy in the Christian tradition, we must understand the changing relationship between the Old Testament and the New, or between the Hebrew Bible and the Christian Testament. Put simply, the question is whether the Old Testament is to be interpreted in light of the New or whether the New Testament should be interpreted in the light of the Old. If the Old Testament is consistently interpreted in the light of the New Testament, the result is that the Old Testament is valued mainly because it foreshadows the New, because the overt meaning of the New Testament is regarded as being covert in the Old. Although the view that the Old Testament predicts current affairs is largely confined to some of the strands within conservative Christian faith, the view that the prophets are of significance mainly because they are thought to have pointed toward the coming of Jesus Christ is still a widely held assumption. This view is continually reinforced at Christmas time when, for example, the service of Nine Lessons and Carols select some of the messianic passages from the Old Testament showing how they were fulfilled in the events surrounding the birth of Jesus.[3] This way of understanding the prophets is not only authorized by the New Testament itself, but continued for many centuries to be the main way that the relationship between the Old Testament and the New was understood.

However, we have seen that efforts are being made to recapture the theology of the prophetic tradition in the Bible and to work out its significance for contemporary church practice. Religious experiences in the form of the immediate, ecstatic presence of the divine are a legitimate extension of the biblical tradition. Such experiences contribute to the wellbeing of many individuals and congregations. This tradition has links with the theology of the Old Testament prophets and of prophecy in the early Church. It is possible for this kind of religious experience to move Christians and churches into the wider responsibility of representing the justice and peace of God, but without such links religious experience can reinforce the privatized, inward spirituality that is typical of much modern Christian life and that can actually become a defence against public responsibility. I do not have the same respect for what I have called biblical futurology. This is based upon a narrow interpretation of Scripture and depends for its credibility upon ignorance of its own history. Moreover, if the ecstatic tradition can become a defence against responsible Christian involvement in the world, this is even more true of the literalism and escapism of biblical futurology. It is, indeed, a powerful and shrewd technique for preventing Christian adults from listening to the message of the prophets for today. The future of Christian faith depends not upon ancient so-called predictions but upon the recovery of the spirit of Amos and Isaiah, Jeremiah and Jesus in whom the prophetic tradition found its fullest realization. I will trace the origins of this prophetic theology in the biblical literature and will show how this tradition has been ignored, marginalized and sometimes betrayed. We will then study the attempts to recover the biblical tradition, and I will argue that this recovery offers Christian adults a powerful way of overcoming the factors that prevent learning.

---

3 The service of Nine Lessons and Carols was created by Edward White Benson (1829–96) for Truro Cathedral for the Christmas of 1880 (Benson 1900, pp. 484, 639).

Part 1

The Origins of the Prophetic Church

The biblical basis for the prophetic tradition of Christian faith is found mainly in the prophets of the Old Testament and in the work of Jesus Christ. Unfortunately, neither of these sources are without ambiguity. The society in which the prophets worked is long ago and far away from that of the modern West. It is not easy to reconstruct the beliefs and attitudes of that ancient culture and in many ways we today do not share the same assumptions.

The first chapter describes the changes that have taken place in the interpretation of the prophetic books and discusses the several ways in which these texts present serious ethical difficulties. The next chapter is more positive. In spite of the problems, there are features of the prophetic teaching which are universal and perennial. The challenge to modern society is unmistakable; they, although long since dead, still speak.

The Gospels, discussed in Chapter 3, present us with a different situation. As the Church became more powerful the prophetic work of Jesus seemed more remote. The interests of the post-Constantinian Church were not those of the Galilean villagers of the first half of the first century. Over the last several decades New Testament scholarship has begun to recover the circumstances in which Jesus of Nazareth lived and died, but as modern Christians begin to understand these insights, our own inherited assumptions make it difficult for us to turn them into action. In these chapters we will show some of the biblical problems that prevent Christian adults from learning, and at the same time we begin the long process of recovery.

I

The Prophets of Ancient Israel: Developments and Difficulties

Recent developments in the interpretation of the prophetic texts

The Book of Isaiah has been enormously influential in the formation of Christian faith. Isaiah is referred to about 250 times in the New Testament (Sawyer 1996, p. 21). If one also counts the allusions and paraphrases the number increases to more than 400 (Childs 2004, p. 5). Isaiah is referred to by name 20 times including six specific quotations in the Gospel of Matthew. Two passages were particularly significant in the early Church: Isaiah 7.14 'a young woman is with child, and she will give birth to a son and call him Immanuel', which because of the influence of the Greek Septuagint was regarded as a prediction of the virgin birth of Jesus Christ (Matt. 1.22–3). The second influential area was the various passages, mainly in Deutero-Isaiah, which refer to blessings upon the Gentiles (Isa. 42.6, 49.6). The crucial expression was 'light to the Gentiles' (Luke 2.32), which was regarded by the Church as justifying its mission to the Gentile world. Yet, other passages which are frequently referred to today did not strike the early Church as being particularly significant. Let us take Isaiah 2.4: 'they will beat their swords into ploughshares, and their spears into pruning hooks. Nation will not take up sword against nation, nor will they train for war anymore'. This passage seems to have been hardly noticed for 1,000 years. In 1263 James I of Aragon summoned a debate to test the claims of Christians and Jews. The contestants were the famous Talmudic scholar Moses Nahmanides and the Dominican Pablo Christaini, a convert from Judaism. Nahmanides claimed that the Messiah could not have arrived since the promise of universal peace foretold in Isaiah 2.4 had evidently not taken place. By way of contrast, the Dutch humanist Hugo Grotius (1583–1645) interpreted the passage not as a prediction of the Messianic Age but as a reference to the outcome of the threat against Judah from Rezin King of Syria and Pekah King of Ephraim, which took place during the reign of Ahaz King of Judah (Isa. 7.1) (Childs 2004, pp. 230–5). On the other hand, whereas Grotius gave the passage an exclusively historical interpretation, Abraham Calov (1612–86), a Lutheran Professor at the University of Wittenberg, regarded the passage as exclusively eschatological, referring to the end times, when Jerusalem would be exulted and the nations would be gathered to Zion.

The characteristic twentieth-century use of the Isaiah passage interprets it in a political sense, as an expression of the hope for reconciliation between the nations. In 1959 a bronze statue with the inscription 'Let us turn our swords into ploughshares', created by the distinguished Soviet sculptor and artist Yevgeny Vuchetich, was presented by the Soviet Union as a gift to the United Nations. The statue itself depicts a blacksmith working at his anvil, using a hammer to

9

beat a sword into the curved shape of a ploughshare. It is one of the most striking monuments in the park of the United Nations building in New York. This
powerful allegory was soon to be interpreted much more literally.

In 2002 three Dominican sisters, Ardeth Platt, Carol Gilbert and Jackie
Hudson, cut through the gateway to a military installation in Colorado. It was
a silo for the launch of intercontinental nuclear weapons. They attacked the
silo with hammers fulfilling Isaiah 2.4, where the instruments of war were to
be beaten. They then poured flasks of their own blood on it in the shape of a
cross (Nepstad 2008, p. 1; Berrigan 1997, p. 117). They were members of the
American Catholic protest organization, the Plowshares movement. The original inspiration of the group had been the social teaching of the Roman Catholic
Church and the example of the peace activist Dorothy Day, but their search for
a biblical basis soon brought them to Isaiah 2.4, which became the name of the
movement. The British Ploughshares movement, although more secular than its
American counterpart, retains the reference.

This wide range of interpretations, although rich and challenging to the imagination, presents the Christian interpreter with a problem. Is there a consistent
Christian way of interpreting the Bible? If the Church down the ages has been
guided by the Holy Spirit through Scripture, how can it yield such diverse meanings? The more one studies the reception history of Isaiah and the Prophets
in general the more pressing these questions become. Brevard Childs, one of
America's leading biblical scholars, asked:

> Can one still speak of a divine coercion or pressure exerted by the text upon
> its readers? Is there any concord between doctrinal claims regarding scripture
> and its actual effects on the church throughout its history? (2004, p. i)

The issue was made more complex not only by the diversity of interpretation
but by the radical changes in scholarly methods and approaches for studying
the prophetic tradition that have arisen in the last four or five decades. These
developments will now be described.

To what extent was biblical prophecy distinctive?

The Bible itself does not claim that prophecy was unique to Israel (Blenkinsopp
1996, p. 41). Balak, King of Moab, engaged Balaam, a well-known prophet
from the Euphrates, to prophesy against Israel (Num. 22.4–6), and the prophets of Baal were in conflict with Elijah (1 Kings 18.19). There was, however,
little independent knowledge of prophecy outside Israel in the ancient Middle
East until the excavation of the ancient city of Mari, located in modern Syria
not far from the Euphrates. The excavations began in 1933 and brought to
light thousands of clay tablets including many making reference to prophets
or actual texts of prophetic oracles (Nissinen 2003, p. 13). The city of Mari
was destroyed by Hammurabi King of Babylon in 1740 BCE, and the second
major collection of prophetic documents from the ancient Middle East comes
from a period 1,000 years later. The library of Ashurbanipal King of Nineveh

from 668 to c.627 BCE was discovered and excavated in the middle years of the nineteenth century. The library consists of about 20,000 clay tablets, but, although their significance for prophecy was recognized by the end of that century, it was not until the 1970s that their scope was realized, and not until 1977 was a scholarly edition of the neo-Assyrian oracles published (p. 3). In addition to the basic collections from Mari and Nineveh, documents of a prophetic kind have been recovered from Egypt and other parts of Mesopotamia. Nissinen concludes: 'The existing evidence of prophecy comes from all over the Fertile Crescent, witnessing to the wide distribution of prophets and proving prophecy to be a common cultural legacy which cannot be traced back to any particular society or place of origin' (pp. 40–8).

Comparing the prophetic documents in the Bible with these other ancient texts is far from simple (Nissinen 2010). But a number of interesting conclusions are suggested. Most of the texts regarded as coming from prophetic sources are relatively short and often leave us with little knowledge of the circumstances which produced them. There are some traces in the Nineveh collection of prophetic oracles being used again in later situations (p. 5). But the extended collections of prophetic oracles gathered together, edited, accumulated and re-edited over centuries, which is what we find in the biblical literature, are unknown elsewhere. Prophecy was always regarded as sacred, because it dealt with the mediation of the divine will, but only in the Bible do we find a 'canonized composition of texts of different age as the result of a centuries-long editorial process' (p. 8). The biblical prophetic books were treasured by a community for whom they had become authorized responses to an ancient covenant with God that expressed the heart of the faith of Israel.

In addition to the information yielded by the prophetic context of the ancient Near East we have the cross-cultural comparisons arising from modern anthropological studies. Thomas Overholt has compared the biblical Isaiah with the indigenous American prophet Wovoka, who operated in western Nevada in the later part of the nineteenth century. Overholt then extended his study to the prophetic figures from other cultures (1989, p. ix). The concept of the Shaman has been used to understand the nature of the biblical prophet in its own cultural context (Craffert 2008, pp. 135–68; Grabbe 2010). Overholt points out that theological discussion of the biblical prophets has tended to concentrate on what they said or the content associated with their names whereas anthropological studies have highlighted the relationship between the prophets and their audiences, recognizing the character of socially constructed knowledge (1989, p. 9). These studies have helped us to identify characteristic features of prophetic inspiration such as the spirit journey (Ezek. 8.3), visions (Isa. 1.1, 6.1) and the calling to the vocation of a seer (Jer. 1.1–7; Amos 7.15). We may conclude that biblical prophecy, although not unique, has many distinctive features, not least its status as sacred Scripture in the early Jewish/Christian communities, its incorporation into what had become by the second century CE the Christian Bible and its profound influence upon the development of all three of the monotheistic religions. These are often described as the Abrahamic traditions, but could just as well be known as the prophetic religions.

Prophecy as prediction

Almost all Christian theology until the beginning of the Enlightenment in the late seventeenth century believed that many features of the New Testament had been predicted or foretold by the prophets of the Old Testament, and this understanding of the relationship between the Old and New Testaments as being one of prediction and fulfilment dominated interpretation of the prophets for 1,500 years.[1] Although the slogan that the prophets were forth-tellers not fore-tellers has gained some currency amongst thoughtful Christians, it is doubtless still the case that many Christians believe that the prophets did predict things in the long distant future, and that some of these things are still waiting to be fulfilled. Some believe this dogmatically and others because no other meaning of prophecy has ever come their way, and it is certainly true that the Church through many of its hymns and liturgies, especially during the Advent season, encourages this view of the prophets.

Belief in prophetic predictions was first queried seriously in the Enlightenment and especially in the work of Benedict Spinoza (1632–77). The first three chapters of his *Theological-Political Treatise* deal with prophecy. Spinoza thought that prophetic inspiration is mediated through the imagination of the prophet and its content reflects whatever the prophets could reasonably imagine, bearing in mind their own context and biographies. The prophets saw things according to their temperament and their background and therefore the only certainty we can derive from their words is that of moral and spiritual truths.

> If the prophet was of a cheerful disposition, then victories, peace and other joyful events were revealed to him; for it is on things of this kind that the imagination of such people dwells . . . the visions were of oxen and cows and the like if the prophet was a countryman, of captains and armies in the case of a soldier . . . (2001, pp. 23–4)
>
> Prophecy did not render the prophets more learned, but left them with the beliefs they had previously held, and therefore we are in no way bound to believe them in matters of purely philosophical speculation. (p. 26)

Spinoza never denies that the prophets may have and actually did predict various things, indeed, from time to time he says so, but only in passing, 'Isaiah bewails and foretells the calamities, and prophesies of the restoration, not only of the Jews but of other nations' (p. 41). I describe this as a passing reference, because Spinoza's concern is not about prediction as such. He is arguing that the Jewish people have no particular privilege that was not also granted to other nations. Although the possibility of prophecy is never denied, the foibles, inconsistencies and the various personal characteristics of the prophets are described with such cool, acid irony that one feels that Spinoza is quietly mocking the true believer.

> God adapted his revelations to the understanding and beliefs of the prophets, who may well have been ignorant of matters that have no bearing on charity and moral conduct but concern philosophical speculation, and were in fact ignorant of them, holding conflicting beliefs. (p. 32)

---

1 O'Brien 2008, pp. 5–7 refers to several important exceptions to this.

To put belief in prediction in context, it is worth pointing out that this quality was not attributed to the prophetic books alone but to the books of Genesis and the Psalms and indeed to all the Scripture (O'Brien 2008, p. 3; see also Luke 24.27). It was in the nineteenth century, particularly in Germany, that it was first clearly realized that the prophetic books were more or less unintelligible unless the prophets were regarded as having spoken to the people of their own day (O'Brien 2008, pp. 11–14). Not that these insights were confined to Germany; one of the leading theologians of the nineteenth-century English Church F. D. Maurice appreciated the way that the lessons in the Anglican lectionary were designed to bring out the meaning of the prophets for their day as well as for ours.

> The compilers of the Lessons have been much more careful to exhibit the Prophets as preachers of righteousness than as mere predictors. I have felt that this aspect of their lives has been greatly overlooked in our day, and that there is none which we have more need to contemplate. (1871, pp. xiii–xiv)

It is true, I believe, that the Hebrew Bible does not represent a closed and fixed final faith, but partly because of faith in God as Lord of history it can be said to anticipate a richer fulfilment. The same is true of the New Testament. It also recognizes an element of 'not yet' in its theology and looks forward in hope to some greater and richer fulfilment. The early Christians recognized a certain fulfilment (which is not necessarily the same as a fulfilled prediction) of the Hebrew Bible, when they hailed Jesus as the Messiah, but they themselves still looked forward to a greater fulfilment when he should come again. This is the Christian hope, not that divinely given predictions would be miraculously fulfilled, but that the God of love and hope is still at work in God's creation. In Christian faith this hope is expressed through the symbols of the kingdom of God and eternal life (Tillich 1963, pp. 297–99).

The main calling of the prophet was to speak in the name of Yaweh but successful prediction was a test of the prophet's authenticity. 'If what a prophet proclaims in the name of the Lord does not take place or come true that is a message the Lord has not spoken' (Deut. 18.22). The criterion of successful prediction was, however, severely qualified by the much more important criterion of loyalty to Yaweh and to the covenant (Blenkinsopp 1995, p. 120).

> If a prophet . . . appears among you and announces to you a sign or wonder, and if the sign or wonder spoken of takes place, and the prophet said, 'let us follow other gods' (gods you have not known) and 'let us worship them', you must not listen to the words of that prophet . . . (Deut. 13.1–3)

Although prediction was an integral part of the prophetic vocation, the problem of distinguishing the false from the true prophet and perhaps the repeated experience of prophetic failure led to further qualifications in this aspect of prophecy. The book of Jonah is an ironic comment on many of the limitations of the stereotypical prophet, who was disappointed when his predictions about the destruction of Nineveh came to nothing. The book seems to be asserting the freedom of God to be gracious and forgiving in spite of predictions to the contrary (Blenkinsopp 1996, p. 242).

Another reaction to the predictive element in prophecy is found in the post-exilic books of 1 and 2 Chronicles. The role of the prophet is widened, so that army captains, Levites, priests and kings are all described as prophesying. The chronicler seems to have been keen on enlarging the category of prophecy by increasing the number of the prophets, adding anonymous ones and extending the role of prophecy to secular officers, but there is no reference to false prophets. The prophets in Chronicles do not predict the future, and do not require signs and miracles to validate what they say. Rather they are interpreters of present-day events (Amit 2006, pp. 80–101).

It is the history of prophecy and of prophetic interpretations of the Bible that has done most to discredit the concept of predictability and to move Christian opinion toward the prophets as giving messages to their own people. A striking example may be found in Ezekiel 44.1–2. Ezekiel is being shown a vision of the new temple.

> Then the man brought me back to the outer gate of the sanctuary, the one facing east and it was shut. The LORD said to me: 'This gate is to remain shut. It must not be opened; no one may enter through it. It is to remain shut because the LORD, the God of Israel, has entered through it.'

Although to the modern reader there may be no obvious connection between them, in medieval art this verse was often associated with Isaiah 7.14, both being predictions of the virgin birth of Jesus Christ. The temple was the body of Mary, and the gate, which faced the east, was her womb through which God the Holy Spirit had entered once and for all. Thereafter, the gate was to be shut. John Sawyer describes the painting by Simone Martini (c.1284–c.1344) in the Uffizi in Florence showing Isaiah holding a scroll inscribed with the words from Isaiah 7.14. Opposite him is Ezekiel holding up his scroll with the words 'This gate shall be shut' (Sawyer 1996, p. 67).[2] Sawyer concludes his discussion by saying:

> the most serious modern objection to this interpretation of Ezekiel 44.2 is not that it clearly differs from 'what the original author intended', or that it is absurd and far-fetched, but . . . it perpetuates a view of women which is biologically untrue and morally unacceptable. (2010, p. 9)

This is because, the equal contribution made by the mother to the genetic inheritance of the child being unknown, the woman's body was regarded as a mere container for the male seed. This kind of interpretation was influential in the belief which one finds referred to frequently in the apocryphal literature of the early Church, that Mary remained an intact virgin even after the birth of Christ (see for example *The Ascension of Isaiah* 11.9).

To the people of the late Middle Ages every significant public event must have been foreseen by the prophetic Scriptures. Many features of the Aztec culture discovered in the early sixteenth century were believed to be the degenerate

---

2 Sawyer has a more detailed discussion of this in 'Ezekiel in the History of Christianity' (2010).

products of the lost ten tribes of Israel and the Aztec temples were interpreted as demonic imitations of the Temple of Ezekiel (Lara 2010). This craving defined contemporary activity foreshadowed in ancient Scripture is by no means dead. Ezekiel's vision of the wheels with many eyes (1.4–28) has been interpreted as a visit from a spaceship, and the influence of this vision upon contemporary culture and science fiction is quite remarkable (see Allison 2010).

The outstanding case of prophetic prediction is to be found in Isaiah 7.14. Reconstruction of the historical crisis behind Isaiah 7–9 has enabled us to understand something of the process that led to the belief that Isaiah 7.14 was a prediction of the birth of Jesus Christ. In c.1732 BCE Ahaz King of Judah was threatened by a coalition of the kings of nearby Aram and Israel. In view, however, of the growing power of Assyria to the north Isaiah in the name of Yaweh told the king that the two small threatening states would soon be destroyed. In the meantime, a young woman showed enormous courage and hope by naming her baby 'Emmanuel' meaning 'God with us'. The giving of names, both auspicious and ominous, was a feature of the prophetic sign, and although the name Emmanuel was at first a sign of hope, in Isaiah 8.8 and 10, where the on rushing power of Assyria is described more fully, the name Emmanuel had already acquired ironic and ominous overtones. By that time Isaiah himself had given an ominous name to a prophetic child (8.1–4), but in Isaiah 9.6–7 the symbol of childhood is again used in the powerful language of religious hope to describe the restoration of the Davidic Kingdom. As Walter Brueggemann says, 'It is undoubtedly clear that a status of virginity is not of any interest or importance for the sign of Isaiah.' He adds, 'the focus is not on the birth but on the child' (1998, p. 70; see also Collins 2010).

The Bible of the New Testament Church was not the Hebrew but the Greek translation, the Septuagint, in which the Greek word 'virgin' is introduced into the quotation from Isaiah 7.14. In its search for prophetic authenticity the Gospel of Matthew incorporated this verse with its Greek translation into its version of the circumstances surrounding the birth of Jesus Christ (1.23), and the Gospel of Luke further elaborated the same theme (1.26–35). Although the passage is not referred to anywhere else in the New Testament, Isaiah 7.14 soon became the most significant verse in the Old Testament for the early Church. By the time Hebrew scholarship in the Church noticed the difference between the Hebrew and Greek texts, the belief that Isaiah had predicted the birth of Jesus had taken such deep root in Christian faith that it was impossible to remove it. Judging by the number of references to it in the sub-Apostolic period, it would seem that Isaiah became an authoritative source for the outline of the birth, life, death and resurrection of Jesus Christ even before the canonical gospels achieved that status (Sawyer 1996, pp. 49–50). The link between Matthew 1 and Isaiah 7 has distracted attention away from the political background of Matthew. The interest of those who first heard the Gospel read aloud to them would have been in their own social and political situation, oppressed by Rome, not in the sexual behaviour of a woman who lived seven centuries earlier (Carter 2001, pp. 93–107). As so often has happened in the Christian tradition, the great public issues of faith and freedom are reduced to questions of personal and individual purity.

The most searching examination of the predictive aspects of the prophetic books is to be found in the work of the former Professor of Old Testament in the University of Glasgow, Robert P. Carroll. Carroll emphasizes that prediction is only one element of the prophetic ministry and that we should not confuse prediction as we might know it today with prediction as understood in ancient Israel. The task of the prophets as messengers of Yaweh was to see society as it would be shaped by the word of God. Much that at first sight appears to be prediction is in fact conditional. Certain things will follow if society continues on its present course. Their purpose was not so much to predict the future as to bring about change in the community; it was the language of warning or of promise in relation to the keeping of Torah. The prophets were working in a world in which the transcendent dimension dominated and pressed upon every aspect of life, and this meant that when the prophet spoke about the future, it was not to satisfy curiosity but from belief in the purposes of God. Nevertheless, there is no doubt that the prophetic books encouraged certain expectations, and sometimes these expectations were disappointed. For example, the promises that the house of David would continue to occupy the throne were not fulfilled (Isa. 9.7, 16.5, 22.22), and the expectation that after the exile a restored and unified Israel would conquer and despoil their enemies (Isa. 11.12–14) did not correspond in any way to the situation after the return from exile.

How did people react to these disappointed expectations? Using the theory of cognitive dissonance (Festinger 1956 and 1957), Carroll shows how disappointed expectation was seldom simply abandoned but the meaning of the expectation was modified so as to defer the expectation, making it more ambiguous or more consistent with what was plausible for that generation. In other words, '[t]he important principle for this study is *dissonance gives rise to hermeneutic*' (Carroll 1979, p. 110). The whole of Isaiah 40–55 may be thought of as an attempt to deal with the confusion and doubt which followed the destruction of Jerusalem. However, what actually happened when the exiles returned bore little resemblance to the glowing excitement of the Isaianic proclamation. Only a few of the exiled community made the arduous journey back to the Promised Land, and when they arrived, they found a country still suffering from the ravages of the Babylonian invasion. The desert did not become pools of water (41.18), and the valleys were not elevated to become a highway (40.4). Carroll remarks: 'The proclamation of a salvation so vivid in its details and so absent in its realization constitutes the essence of dissonance arousal' (1979, p. 152). Even the famous passage about the suffering servant in Isaiah 53 can be thought of as a reinterpretation of the destiny of Israel along the lines of humility rather than triumphant domination.

The exalted promises in Isaiah 40–55 demanded a further interpretation to accommodate the disappointment, and this was the work of Chapters 56–66. These experiences of disappointment may be among the factors that led after the exile to the gradual replacement of spoken prophecy by obedience to written Torah, discovering there the prophetic word.[3]

---

3 Joseph Blenkinsopp has also made use of the theory of cognitive dissonance (1996, pp. 38–9.

For many centuries the fact that the prophets were seen mainly as pointing forward down the centuries to Jesus Christ has prevented the Church from realizing the prophetic message for today (Barton 2003, p. 131). The nineteenth-century discovery that the prophets demanded the justice of God for their own people has set the Church free to consider the impact of God's justice today. But does the Church want that freedom?

It is understandable that in its struggle for authenticity the early Christian movement had to see itself as a legitimate heir of the Old Testament that was their Scripture. This launched Christian faith into a long competition with Judaism for possession of the Bible, which at certain times was undoubtedly anti-Semitic. Christian faith today no longer needs to establish its validity by appeals to ancient prophecy; the authenticity demanded of it today is that of peace and justice. The pre-history of Christianity is coming to an end, and the Old Testament can at last participate in the renewal of God's mission to the world.[4]

From the prophets to the prophetic books

Once the decision had been made to study the prophets in their own right and not simply as predictors of Christ the question of method became urgent. It is no longer possible to read the meaning of the prophetic books from the surface of the text or through the lens of the New Testament. One has to ask about the meaning of the text, and this must include questions about its original provenance, an enquiry into the situations originally addressed and to whom their oracles were directed. There have been two major developments that have taken place over the last 150 years. German criticism reached a climax in the work of Julius Wellhausen (1844–1918), whose book *Prolegomena to the History of Israel* was published in German in 1878 and 1883. The first English translation appeared in 1885. Wellhausen believed that the real history of Israel was the reverse of that which appeared in the way the canon has been arranged. As it stands, it looks as if the giving of the law on Mount Sinai to Moses came first, and the writing prophets appeared in the eighth century. Wellhausen argued that on the contrary it was the religious genius of the eighth-century prophets that introduced ethical monotheism, which had a profound effect upon the formation of the law, which was not complete until after the return from exile. The prophets themselves emerged as great personalities, men of courage and vision whose religious faith became the climax and centre of the religion of Israel. This was the scholarly tendency that created the picture of the prophets as charismatic individuals and romantic reformers (see Clifford 2010a).

This led to an interest in the intentions of the prophets in delivering their oracles and writing their books. 'It is not enough to have the prophets in mind; we must think as if we were inside their minds' (Heschel 2007, p. ix). The same interest, of course, was given to New Testament authors (see Glover 1941; Barclay 1958).

---

4 The Book of Amos, for example, has become more prominent and influential since the decline of prediction. See Mein 2010, p. 117; Blenkinsopp 1996, pp. 31–2.

Three factors led to a decline in this emphasis, although it has not disappeared entirely. The first of these factors was a closer study of the internal evidence. The books of the prophets actually tell us very little about their lives. Sometimes they open with a heading telling us the parentage of the prophet and under whose reign or reigns he prophesied, and there are memorable stories of prophetic calling (Isa. 6.1–8). Often we cannot tell whether what appear to be biographical details are really allegories or metaphors of the teaching of the prophet. Hosea 1 and 2 are most frequently discussed. Are these chapters to be taken literally? The occasional biographical information we are given is often quite scanty and ambiguous (Amos 7.14, 15). Some of the prophetic books are anonymous and in some cases we do not know if there ever was a prophet of that name but only a collection of oracles. Other cases such as the Book of Daniel present material from later centuries under the name of an earlier prophet.

The second and more important factor rose from the historical study of the prophetic books. It became increasingly clear that most of these were collections, often gathered over the lifetimes of several generations and sometimes covering a span of centuries. The name of the prophet thus became a focus for a tradition, perhaps a group of followers who treasured the memory of that prophet and added to the tradition of his oracles.

The third and most important factor arose from a new trend in literary criticism. It does not matter very much that we know little of the life of William Shakespeare since the plays speak for themselves and are to be understood according to their own inner character and development. The work which established this point of view was by Roland Barthes published in 1957. Hans-Georg Gadamer also influenced hermeneutical theory especially through his concept of the fusion of the horizons, where the onward reach of the text meets the backward searching reach of the reader (Barthes 1977; Gadamer 1989). The method which concentrated upon the originality of the prophets themselves implied historical criticism, since if one could reach the oracles spoken by the prophet they would have greater authority than the collections added later. When attention is focused upon the text in its entirety the interest is rather in the structure of the text, its figures of speech and other rhetorical devices and the total meaning of the text. This has led to a type of evaluation called Canonical Criticism that regards the finished form of the text as available to the community of faith as the legitimate object of study. It does not much matter by what process the text was formed. However it got there, it is the word of God to the community that receives it in faith (Childs 1979). Looked at in this way, the final responsibility was that of the editors under whose guidance the book was completed. This process is clear in the Book of Jeremiah. Brueggemann remarks that the layers of interpretation and reinterpretation guaranteed that the book would continue to have a message for subsequent generations (2006, pp. 99–115). The Book of Jeremiah is no longer regarded from this perspective, as being concerned with the fall of Jerusalem but with the morale and prosperity of the community that returned after the exile, when the final text was edited (pp. 18–19). Brueggemann distinguishes between the diachronic approach to a biblical text, which seeks to interpret it in accordance with the stages of its historical development, and the synchronic approach, which deals with the final literature as a complete whole (Brueggemann 2006, pp. 60–2; Blenkinsopp 1996, p. 26).[5] Both diachronic and synchronic approaches seem to be necessary, for whatever we make of the prophetic texts, some of them are rooted in the period before the exile. Knowledge of that history would be relevant to understanding them. James Linville carries the argument further by pointing out that the construction of a prophetic literature was part of the reconstruction of meaning carried out in mainly cultic circles in post-exilic Jerusalem. 'The message or agenda of Amos, then, may be found in the religious, social and political interests of this educated elite stratum of society' (Linville 2008, p. 10). How did these scribes see their lives and problems in the light of the traditions of Amos which they were editing? What did they find in the book that was so meaningful that they carefully preserved it? Carol J. Dempsey points out that the Book of Isaiah is a poetic vision that must be interpreted as a whole regardless of 'whoever "Isaiah" may have been' (2010, p. 4). One of the most powerful recent examples of the approach through literary study is by Francis Landy (2011). Hosea, he suggests, is best understood as mystical love poetry in which the fluctuating sexual imagery reflects the 'inner dynamic of God's jealousy, rage, and cruelty' (p. 2).

This change in hermeneutical theory has led to a revision of several other assumptions of earlier criticisms. It used to be argued that there was a meaningful distinction between the non-writing prophets like Elijah and Elisha and the writing prophets like Amos and Hosea. If, however, one is dealing with the whole of the finished text as a poetic and literary production, this distinction is no longer significant. Some traditions have gathered around the name of Elijah and others around the name of Isaiah. It also used to be thought that the most active period for prophecy was before the exile, that is, from the eighth to the sixth centuries BCE. By contrast, the period after the Exile until the appearance of John the Baptist was a subdued period with little prophetic activity. This must now be radically reversed. As Michael Floyd and Robert Haak say, 'We can only know about those aspects of pre-exilic prophecy that were later considered germane to what prophecy became in the post-exilic period' (2005, p. 3).

The struggle to understand the prophets as Scripture

Now that we have briefly reviewed some of the changing features in the study of the prophetic tradition, we must return to the original question posed by Brevard Childs. In what sense can the prophets still speak to us today? We shall first consider negative factors and then go on to discuss some positive replies to this question.

God and power

It is not unusual for readers of the Bible to be critical of it. The author of 2 Peter admitted that in the letters of Paul there were 'some things hard to understand'

---

5 There is an excellent summary of the history of the interpretation of the prophetic books in O'Brien 2008, pp. 1–27.

(2 Pet. 3.16), and Martin Luther famously dismissed the letter of James as an 'epistle of straw'. It must be admitted, however, that Christian scholarship did not often find shortcomings in the prophets themselves, especially during the time when they were regarded as the founders of ethical monotheism and people of the highest moral and spiritual distinction. In the last few decades the taboo of sacredness appears to have been broken, and the following section will describe some of the criticisms which are often levelled against them.

It certainly was the feminists who began this, and a good deal of what follows will be concerned with their discoveries. But I will start with a criticism that is in a way more obvious once it has been stated. This is the attitude of the prophets toward power and its use. In much of the prophetic writings we see a God who seems to be committed to the use of violence. 'Now then, I will crush you as a cart crushes when loaded with grain' (Amos 2.13), 'I am full of the wrath of the LORD, and I cannot hold it in. Pour it out on the children in the street and on the young men gathered together, both husband and wife will be caught in it and the old, those weighed down with years' (Jer. 6.11). Isaiah 9.8–10.4 is a poem describing the anger of God. After each verse there is a refrain: 'yet for all this his anger is not turned away; his hand is still upraised'. In other words, no matter how fierce the punishment God's anger is not appeased. In Isaiah 9.11–12 we are told that God has spurred on the enemies of Israel against her, and they 'have devoured Israel with open mouth'. God will show no pity to the fatherless and the widow (Isa. v. 17); wickedness burns like a fire (v. 18) and in response Yaweh also burns like a fire (v. 19), by his anger 'the land will be scorched and the people will be fuel for the fire'. This horrible image of God burning people alive is followed by a threat that the famine will be so dreadful that the people will be driven to cannibalism (vv. 20, 21). In Isaiah 10.2 there is a protest against those who make widows their prey and rob the fatherless, but as we have seen in the previous chapter (v. 17), Yaweh himself refuses to have pity on the same people. Carol Dempsey says, 'Isaiah has offered us a picture of a God who has now become a reflection of the people. Divine justice and human wickedness mirror each other' (2010, p. 27), since God fails to defend the widows and the orphans, just as did the wicked people. The strange thing is that these terrible scenes of anger and brutal punishment against both Israel and Assyria (Isa. 9.8–10.34) are framed by some of the most beautiful passages of peaceful promise, focusing upon the image of childhood. In Isaiah 9.6 a child is born who will be called 'Wonderful Counsellor', and it is said that 'of the increase of his government and of peace there shall be no end' (v. 7). In Isaiah 11.6 we read of a peaceful earth, where 'the wolf will live with the lamb, the leopard will lie down with the goat, the calf and the lion and the yearling together; and a little child will lead them'. It is as if Isaiah is setting before us two ways of responding to injustice, one through peace and the other through violence.[6]

Amos 2 is a good example of the prophetic conception of power. The powerful classes in Israel are condemned for selling innocent and vulnerable people into slavery and for using their position to 'trample on the heads of the poor' (Amos 2.6–7). They are met, however, by an even greater power which will

---

6 Walter Wink describes the theory of 'redemptive violence', the view that violence can redeem society (1992, pp. 13–31).

crush them as a heavy cart loaded with grain crushes everything beneath it (v. 13). The same hierarchy of power is given an international perspective in the typical prophetic reaction to the great imperial nations: Assyria and Babylon. 'Certain humans and nonhumans are oppressed by those who are more power-ful than them, and the powerful are then punished by an even more powerful God' (Dempsey 2000, p. 21). God uses them to punish Israel and then they in turn are punished by the power of God, sometimes seen as working through a renewed, militant Israel. This is indeed *realpolitik*, but should we attribute the operation of this hierarchy of power to God?

Questions about the use of God's power arise in connection with justice, particularly when one considers the interpretation of natural disasters as divine punishment. The use of the earthquake in the Book of Amos is a case in point.

> There cannot be a just and individual accounting with such wholesale destruc-tion. The problem of innocent suffering as a result of natural disaster arises here – how can people believe in a God who can cause such things? (Dell 2010, p. 13)

Amos 4.1–3 describes the punishment of God upon the rich, lazy women who oppress the poor, and it is clear that, with the threatened destruction, punish-ment would fall upon both the rich and the poor. 'This is part of the conceptual framework of much of the Bible that advocates society-wide punishments for the excesses of only some of its members' (Linville 2008, p. 83). It seems to be expected in Amos 4.7–8 that the completely arbitrary and unpredictable pat-terns of rainfall would lead people in repentance back to God.

> 'I sent rain on one town, but withheld it from another. One field had rain; another had none and dried up. People staggered from town to town for water but did not get enough to drink. Yet you have not returned to me,' declared the LORD. (Amos 4.7–8)

A much discussed problem is the tension between the threats of judgement and the promises of salvation in the Book of Isaiah. Jacob Stromberg shows that the concept of the remnant resolves this tension. Isaiah suggests that it was the sin-ful mass who were judged, but God's differential justice was shown in that the righteous remnant were delivered: 'a judgment that would purge Israel of the wicked and leave a righteous remnant, a "holy seed"' (2011, 107). Of course, the distinction between the righteous and the wicked would remain ambiguous till after the event; those who survived were obviously the righteous. To the modern reader it is additionally troubling to note that animals and babies were included in the destruction (Hos. 4.3; Isa. 13.16).

God as the giver of death

In Ezekiel 23.34b God is described as the husband of Judah and Samaria by whom God had children. In 23.10b the husband describes how he will give the first of these wives over to be executed, and in verses 22–6 the second wife is to be mutilated and publicly humiliated. Gerlinde Baumann observes that in the entire Book of Ezekiel 'YHWH as a husband does not deviate from his role of imposing (and carrying out) the death penalty on his wife' (2001, p. 107). The truth is that the God of the prophets believes in the death penalty and acts upon it. Hosea experiences 'God as the agent of death' (Landy 2011, p. 10). The prophets themselves were always subject to the possibility of the death penalty, if they made a mistake about what was the true word of God spoken through them (Deut. 18.20). God may kill through natural disasters, as we have seen, or through the sword of an enemy nation, and sometimes God kills quite directly and without obvious mediation. 'I will kill all her officials' (Amos 2.3).

These aspects of the divine behaviour are dealt with most profoundly by Walter Brueggemann in his discussion of Israel's counter-testimony, speaking of the negativity in God (1997, pp. 373–99). In his essay on the nature of the demonic, Paul Tillich says demonic inspiration 'reveals the divine, but as a reality which it fears, which it cannot love, with which it cannot unite' (1936, p. 88) and 'distrust of God is demonization of God in human consciousness' (p. 95).

Violent sex

The second area of negativity which we have to consider has to do with gender. The book of the prophet Hosea begins with a strange story about the prophet being commanded to marry a prostitute by whom he had three children. The children were given ominous names to signify the breakdown of the relationship between God and Israel. It is unclear whether this is to be taken as an historical incident or whether we should respond to it as an allegorical introduction to the main part of the book. If this first chapter of Hosea is difficult, the second chapter is worse. The allegory is intensified. The marriage appears to have broken down all together, since the wife continues to be unfaithful, and the children are also rejected by their father (v. 4), although it is unclear whether these are the same children referred to in the previous chapter. God has poured out prosperity on the country, but, like a woman not realizing that the gifts she has received have come from her husband, Israel has gone off paying attention to other gods. None the less, God continues to love her (v. 14) and will reclaim her, restore her to her former position as a beloved wife and will establish a relationship of permanent justice and love (v. 19).

These chapters were often interpreted as illustrating the grace of God toward sinners (Henry 1960, p. 1108). Or in an anti-Semitic vein, showing that Israel was the faithless partner of God, but if she repented and became Christian God would restore the relationship (Luther 1975, p. 8; Henry 1960, p. 1106). However, in the past two or three decades a number of Old Testament specialists considered these chapters from the point of view of the woman. The fact is, they pointed out, that a woman reading these texts from a fresh, critical perspective, notices features which male commentators have not seen. I understand this very well and cannot but sympathize with the women, since I have had a somewhat similar experience, in the case of blindness. When I began to read the Bible in Braille and on cassette tapes after I had lost my sight in midlife, I read many of the passages dealing with blindness in a completely new way. In a sense I learned nothing new; I had, for example, studied the vocabulary of light and darkness in John's Gospel, when I was a theological student, but now it was all so different (see Hull 1990, 1997 and 2001). It is strange to think that blind Christians had been reading these same passages or listening to them for centuries, but had not, as far as I am aware, responded to them as I did. In the same way, it is no doubt true that many devout Christian women had been reading Hosea for centuries. It is, after all, quoted in the New Testament. Although historical research has uncovered some hints of feminist criticism from the past, the intensity and clarity of the contemporary approach is new. Black theology and the theologies of oppression coming from Latin America, South Korea and the Indian subcontinent are part of the same trend toward a demand for justice coming from previously marginalized groups and a recognition that the Christian tradition, including Scripture itself, has collaborated and been interpreted as collaborating in their marginalization.

Let us read Hosea 2 again. In verse 2, the faithless wife is to be rebuked and the marriage contract denied. This is followed by a series of horrifying threats. If she does not change her ways, she is to be stripped naked, and her husband will make her 'as bare as the day she was born'. This humiliating form of disgrace is to be followed by causing her to die of thirst (v. 6). Moreover, she is to be locked in with thorn bushes (still naked?) and to be 'walled in'. In verse 10 it seems that the woman is still naked, for her husband intends to expose her in the presence of her lovers, while keeping a firm hold on her. Offended and infuriated her husband now takes back all the gifts which he had given her himself because of the way she has insulted him in believing they came from her lovers, and will punish her for forgetting him (v. 12). It now appears that the tide of anger has turned, and the injured husband renews his entreaties. All the gifts are to be restored to her, the marriage covenant is to be renewed, peace is to be restored, and a new relationship of love and compassion is to be established (v. 19). Even this, however, is not quite straightforward. This pattern of ambiguity with its sudden reversals of mood is a common feature of abusive relationships: 'one who can be as cruel and pitiless toward his wife as he can be gentle and giving. He is at once seductive and menacing' (Weems 1995, p. 71). Julia O'Brien reviews the literature of domestic abuse. 'In some cases of domestic abuse, the abuser follows outbursts of physical violence with a period of tenderness and lavish attention. He promises never again to be violent and behaves temporarily as an ideal husband. These patterns are disturbingly evident in Hosea 2' (2008, p. 34). Possibly more disturbing still is the work of Drorah Setel in 1985, who surveys the literature on pornography. She applies the criteria to the Book of Hosea with alarming results. For some of those who study these images, 'the "pornographic" nature of female objectification may demand that such texts not be declared "the word of God" in a public setting' (1985, p. 95). Throughout the Book of Hosea it becomes difficult to distinguish between the words of Hosea and the words of God. Julia O'Brien draws the conclusion, 'God is like Hosea. Hosea is like God. A man is like God.' By way of contrast 'God is not like Gomer. Gomer is not like God. God is not like a woman' (2008, p. 33).

The Book of Jeremiah carries the female imagery a step further. Israel is compared to a loving and faithful bride in the early days of her marriage to God (Jer. 2.2), but this idyllic happiness did not last long. Soon the young wife became not only faithless but a prostitute. 'On every high hill and under every spreading tree you lay down as a prostitute' (Jer. 2.20). This corruption cannot be purged or cleansed (v. 22). With hot and contemptuous words the brazen sexuality of the once beautiful bride is described as 'a swift she-ass running here and there, a wild donkey accustomed to the desert, sniffing the wind in her craving, in her heat, who can restrain her? Any males that pursue her need not tire themselves; at mating time they will find her' (vv. 23–4). It is impossible for us, from such a different age and culture, to know how such words would have been heard in the seventh or sixth centuries BCE. The prophet is addressing a male audience, and his theme is the failure of Israel to be faithful to Yaweh. The savage and callous imagery is intended to shock the hearers into realizing that this is what their religious behaviour looks like to God. Perhaps the words are deliberately exaggerated to bring about a roar of laughter followed by a silence, when the point is driven home 'as a thief is disgraced when he is caught, so the House of Israel is disgraced' (v. 26).

In Jeremiah 13 the imagery moves away from the sexual appetites of animals back to the image of an offended husband. If this rhetoric was to be effective in recalling Israel back to the covenant with God, we must assume that the violent behaviour of the husband was quite understandable to the male audience, who would have sympathized with the fury of the man whose honour had been dragged in the dust by his unruly wife. In the same way, the thought goes, it is entirely reasonable for God to punish you for your sins. Nevertheless, to the modern reader, whether man or woman, the language is shocking. 'It is because of your many sins that your skirts have been torn off and your body ill-treated' (Jer. 13.22). 'I will pull up your skirt over your face that your shame may be seen – your adulteries and lustful neighings, your shameless prostitution!' (Jer. 13.26–7). The King James Version translates verse 22b as follows: 'for the greatness of thine iniquity are thy skirts discovered and thy heels made bare'. Gerlinde Baumann translates 'your heels will be violated' and comments '"heel" is another euphemism for the genitals'. She adds: 'This is the only passage in the Old Testament where YHWH himself performs the act of sexual violence against one of his own "wives"' (2001, p. 94).

The climax of this disturbing sexual imagery describing the relation between God and Israel is found in Ezekiel especially in Chapters 16 and 23. Whereas in Hosea we had a faithless wife and in Jeremiah a shameless prostitute, Ezekiel gives us the biography of Israel as a woman from infancy to adulthood. Israel was born as an unloved and unwanted baby (Ezek. 16.4–5), but God passing by saw the struggling baby and had pity. The child grew up to become a beautiful young woman. God made love to her (v. 8) and entered into covenant with her. Israel then embarked upon a brilliant career, beautifully clothed and adorned with every kind of jewellery becoming then a beauty queen famous throughout the world (vv. 9–14). However, the beautiful queen became a prostitute (vv. 15–16). Even the children were murdered by their depraved mother (vv. 20–1). Indeed, worse than a prostitute, she paid her lovers to come to her (vv. 33–34). Verses 37–41 describe a terrifying scene of brutal violence and mob rape, followed by a gracious renewal of the covenant (vv. 59–62).

Ezekiel 23 is the longest and most explicit sexual allegory in the Old Testament. We are told of two sisters, Samaria and Judah, both of whom were prostitutes, and both were wives of Yaweh. Samaria continued her prostitution, until her lovers finally murdered her (v.10) but far from learning the lesson Judah behaved even more outrageously forming illicit relations with both Assyria and Babylon (vv. 12–17). Things grew from bad to worse, as Judah began to fantasize about the sexual freedom of her days in Egypt (vv. 19–21); verses 22–34 describe the terrible destruction of Jerusalem at the hands of the Babylonians finishing up with the former prostitute mutilating her own breasts.

The story of the two sisters is now repeated, with a vivid picture of a wealthy courtesan entertaining her admirers (vv. 40–2). So their husband held them up to be treated as common prostitutes (vv. 43–44), finishing up with a terrible scene of mob violence 'that all women may take warning and not imitate you' (v. 48). The obsessive repetitions and the explicit sexual detail in this chapter have the feel of a savage neurosis, gloomy with bitterness and violent revenge.[7]

Reading these two chapters of Ezekiel slowly and carefully, one can understand why they have been described as an 'extremely pornographic, violent and cruel allegory' (Baumann 2001, p. 96). It is regrettable that the child is treated with contempt because of its mixed descent. This presumably tells us something about the hostility toward such children in ancient Israel and such features must make one wonder whether they are 'truly inspired or revelatory' (Dempsey 2000, p. 98).

For understandable reasons it was female scholars of the Old Testament who first noticed the implications for the treatment of women, both then and today. This interpretation, however, is by no means confined to female scholarship. For example, Francis Landy in his brilliant commentary on Hosea, says: 'Its use of female imagery is misogynistic; 2:4–15 is a fantasy of sadistic humiliation and bestial voracity' (2011, p. 10). Steve Moyise says that 'One of the more disagreeable features of the book of Revelation is its use of feminine imagery to characterize evil as a harlot, stripped naked and burned alive (Rev. 17.16). However, the imagery did not originate with John. He found it in Ezekiel's description of apostate Jerusalem in chapters 16 and 23' (2010, p. 51). Andrew Mein agrees that 'the language of the oracle [Ezekiel] is vulgar, shocking and as sexually explicit as the Hebrew Bible gets'. He continues: 'the text can reasonably be described as pornographic in its repeated display of the naked female body and its "misnaming" of female sexual experience' (2011, p. 160). On the other hand, some of those who write about the prophets simply ignore these passages (see Stromberg 2011; Childs 2004) or seek to minimize the criticism of them in various ways (Clifford 2010, pp. 277–9).[8] It is not surprising that writing as early as 1968 Walter Brueggemann, although referring to the sexual nature of the imagery in Hosea, does not remark upon anything particularly significant about it (1968, pp. 51–4). In his 1994 book Brueggemann does discuss the question of the sexuality of Yaweh (1994, pp. 149–73), cautiously

---

7 This becomes apparent to the English reader when various translations are compared especially of verses 3, 8, 21 and 34 (repeated references to the breasts) and verse 20, where the New Living Bible (UK) describes her lovers 'whose genitals were like those of donkeys and whose emission was like that of horses'.

8 The attempts by Clifford to avoid the feminist critique are, to my mind, unconvincing and beside the point.

concluding that 'the issue of asexuality may need to be expressed in imagery both masculine and feminine' (p. 156). His attitude to the question seems to have become a little more defensive by 1998 when, discussing Isaiah 3.16–24, an attack upon the luxurious lives of the 'daughters of Zion', he remarks:

> Now it may be that this prophetic propensity is sharply sexist and inordinately abusive of women. It is clear, however, that in verses 2–3 and 14, a vigorous critique, in a different way, is addressed against male leadership. (1998, p. 37)

It certainly is in a different way, for Isaiah 3.2–4 simply list classes of male leadership telling them that they will be governed by mere children, and verse 14 judges the elders and leaders of the people for their oppression of the poor. This cannot be compared with the description of the humiliation of the wealthy women in verses 16–24, where scabs will turn the women's scalps into baldness (v. 17), and they are to be dressed in sackcloth and branded (v. 24). In the same year Brueggemann's commentary of Isaiah 40–66 was published, and here we are told 'It is now widely recognized that the prophetic use of the imagery of marriage is profoundly sexist in that it is always the woman (Israel) who is treated as problematic, whereas the man (Yahweh) is always beyond question, even when the actions of the husband seem unthinking or brutalizing' (1998a, p. 150). In his magisterial *Theology of the Old Testament*, Brueggemann writes with interest and respect of the feminist critique (1997, pp. 55–6), although he has been criticized for dealing with such issues mainly in footnotes and seldom incorporating them into the main body of his text (O'Brien 2008, p. 41).

Of the feminist critics, Renita Weems is perhaps the most constructive in showing how the prophets, who were themselves men, spoke skilfully to the assumptions and prejudices of their mostly male hearers, confronting them with the deeply shocking thought that just as any honourable and self-respecting husband would be furious with an unfaithful wife so God was furious with faithless Israel. The interests of the prophets were social, political and religious and they used this violently sexist imagery to appeal to the sensitivities of their male audiences (Weems 1995, p. 41). However accurately the prophets may have assessed the attitudes of the men they were talking to, the question remains whether these passages have encouraged or permitted similar attitudes toward women in the history of the Church. This question has been taken up by Andrew Mein, who in a study of outstanding Christian theologians from various periods shows that all of them did apply the relevant chapters of Ezekiel to their own societies and that John Calvin stands out as using Ezekiel to justify attacks upon the Christian women of Geneva (2011). It seems wholly reasonable to suppose, as many of the feminist authors do, that these aspects of the prophetic imagery would tend to justify male superiority, dominance and even brutality.

There is another interesting aspect of this subject. We have seen how the negative imagery of women in the prophets is demeaning for women. What is its impact upon men? After all, if God is male and is like a husband, and Israel is like his wife, then presumably men in approaching God must consciously or unconsciously adopt the identity of wives. Howard Eilburg-Schwartz shows that this would involve a homoerotic relationship between male worshippers and God (1994). This might help us understand why today an entrenched male priesthood firmly rejects the possibility of woman priests and at the same time why some male Christians, who emphasize the fatherhood and are thus in unconsciously homoerotic relationships with the divine, find homosexuality abhorrent, for it externalizes and objectifies a feature of their spiritual lives which must remain concealed.

Forgiveness and reconciliation

Another aspect of the prophetic tradition that would seem to limit its relevance and usefulness today lies in the fact that it says little about human forgiveness and interpersonal reconciliation. Too often, a breakdown in relationships between individuals or communities is met either by calling upon God to intervene or by cries for vengeance. In Micah 7.1–6 there is a description of a total breakdown of society both corporate and private. One cannot trust a neighbour or a friend; even with the one who 'lies in your embrace', you have to be careful what you say (v. 5). The response of the prophet has nothing to say about healing these relationships 'but as for me I watch in hope for the LORD, I wait for God my saviour; my God will hear me' (v. 7) (Reimer 2010). The same is true of reconciliation between the nations. They 'leave the establishment of justice in divine hands . . . and do not . . . reconcile nations so much as establish divinely ordered supremacy' (p. 93). Certainly, in Malachi 4.6 we are told that the hearts of the fathers will be turned toward their children and those of the children toward their fathers, but this is done externally by Elijah and under the threat of a divine curse. Similarly, although the prophet weeps over the tragedy of the sins of Israel (Jer. 9.1–3), the only response to the lack of trust between friend and friend (vv. 4–5) is to invoke the punishment of God (vv. 15–16).

John Barton, although agreeing with David Reimer that 'the Old Testament has very little overt teaching on the need for forgiveness between human persons' points out that there are instances of forgiveness in the narrative portions of the Old Testament (2003, p. 7). For example, Joseph forgives his brothers, when he meets them in Egypt (Gen. 45.15). Perhaps this difference in emphasis between Genesis and the prophetic books is because in the narrative parts of the Bible, although there is divine intervention, the main story is carried forward by chains of human thoughts and actions (Barton 2003, p. 7), whereas the prophets are overwhelmingly concerned with relationships with God, upon whom alone rests any hope of forgiveness.

The Church and Israel

In this description of some of the factors which might make the prophetic books difficult for people today, I will finally refer to the influence of the books, particularly Isaiah, in legitimizing a supersessionalist theology in which the Church has succeeded the now redundant Israel, even leading on to outright anti-Semitism. Often, the Church adopted the role of the prophet and interpreted oracles against Israel as condemnations of the Jewish people of Europe. For example

Isaiah 6.9–10 was regarded as a curse upon Israel, which was unable to see the truth of God in Christ.

> 'Go and tell this people "Be ever hearing but never understanding; be ever seeing, but never perceiving". Then make the heart of this people callous; make their ears dull and close their eyes. Otherwise, they might see with their eyes, hear with their ears, understand with their hearts, and turn and be healed.'

It was believed that the New Testament use of these verses (Mark 4.9 and parallels) justified this use by the Church in later centuries (Sawyer 1996, pp. 100–25). We have seen that the prophets of the Hebrew Bible cannot provide a simple, immediate and uncontroversial basis for the inspiration of a modern prophetic movement. It would be all too easy to select a few of the famous sayings about justice and ignore the rest of the prophetic books. However, that does not mean that there is no inspiration and challenge to be found there. We have considered the difficulties; in the next chapter we shall turn to the positive aspects of the prophetic teaching.

2

The Prophets of Ancient Israel:
Their Message for Today

We have seen that much of the prophetic writings are half hidden in the shadows, but if half hidden, they are also half open. In spite of the problems, it remains the case that the words of the prophets are still written on the subway walls. In this chapter we will consider what they have to offer us today.

Theology is a public activity

The prophets proclaimed their message in public places. 'Stand at the gate of the Lord's house and there proclaim this message: "Hear the word of the Lord all you people and Judah who come through these gates to worship the Lord"' (Jer. 7.2). Here is another example 'This is what the Lord said to me: "Go and stand at the gate of the people through which the kings of Judah go in and out; stand also at all the other gates of Jerusalem"' (Jer. 17.19). Ezekiel mixed with the people in exile. 'I came to the exiles, who lived at Tel Abib near the Kebar river. And there, where they were living I sat among them' (Ezek. 3.15). The prophets are said to have addressed their message to leading political and religious figures, to have done their work in cities, temples and various shrines and sanctuaries. More important than the location of their work, however, was its subject matter. The prophets addressed questions of public morality, relations between social classes, economic and historical issues. Their interest extended beyond the nation of Israel into surrounding countries. They spoke about treaties and contracts, war and peace, programmes and policies (Gottwald 1964). Of course, the prophets took an interest in the attitudes of their listeners, particularly the arrogance and pride of individuals (Isa. 2.11, 2.17–18, 28.1–4), but usually it was national pride that the prophets criticized (Ezek. 32.12) or the pride of the aristocratic class (Isa. 23.9).

We learn a great deal about the interior life of Jeremiah and of his painful struggles (Jer. 20.9), but these were created by the painfulness of his public calling and the appalling nature of the messages he was required to proclaim.

The prophetic books provide a relevant and challenging model for those who seek to bring theology out of the private sphere, where it deals with the internal life of the soul or the world beyond into the public life of the community today. There are no finer examples of the significance of the prophetic books for public life today than the commentaries of Daniel Berrigan (1996, 1997, 1998, 1999). Ezekiel and Daniel, two of the most difficult books, are transformed as we see them through the work of one of the great prophetic figures of our own time.

The significance of history

The prophets perceived history as the sphere of God's activity. They believed that history was meaningful, purposeful and even in the most difficult circumstances they searched for the divine presence. Brueggemann uses the concept of history to define the very nature of prophecy. 'Prophecy in this context may be understood as a *redescription* of the public processes of history through which the purposes of Yahweh are given in human utterance' (1998, p. 2). History may be regarded as a closed system, evolving under its own laws, subject to social and economic trends which are beyond the control of human beings. An alternative view of history views it as the product of human decision, the outworking of often unintended consequences but ultimately disposable by human choice. The prophets of Israel suggest a third point of view. History is not a meaningless machine running out of control, neither is it entirely available to human manipulation. It is an open system, capable of surprise and full of ambiguity. The dramatic changes in the former Soviet Union, the relatively peaceful transition from an Apartheid society in South Africa and the financial crisis beginning in 2008 were not foreseen by specialists. Its openness does not represent the determination of history by its past but by the strange lure of the future. As Ernst Bloch puts it, 'a world as yet still undiscovered, but already somehow sensed: both these things are definitively present in the experiment of the Future, the experiment of the World' (Bloch 2009, p. 257; Brueggemann 2000, pp. 35–44). Living through the rise and fall of one empire after another, the Assyrian, Babylonian, Persian and Greek empires, the prophets of the Old Testament never failed to believe that God was working through human actions for the purpose of some greater vision. 'Woe to the Assyrian the rod of my anger in whose hand is the club of my wrath!' (Isa. 10.5)

The integrity of creation

In the prophets we find a vigorous realization that the integrity of creation is threatened because of human greed and folly (Marlow 2009, p. 135). One would expect a book like that of Amos to be expressed in images of nature, since Israel was primarily an agricultural people, and Amos himself was a farmer. The images, however, are more than rhetorical devices, they represent an intimate link between God, the natural world and human society. When God is described as a lion (Amos 1.2, 3.8) or suddenly finding God like finding a bear or a snake (5.19), the danger and strangeness of wild animals becomes a sort of window through which the otherness of God is perceived. The awe-inspiring majesty of the created world reveals the power and the otherness of God. It is God 'who forms the mountains, creates the wind, and reveals his thoughts to people. God turns dawn to darkness and treads the high places of the earth' (4.13). The stars bear witness to the divine creativity, for God made the Pleiades and Orion (5.8).

In some mysterious way nature hears the voice of God and responds. Thunder is God's voice (1.2), God calls for the waters of the sea and they respond (Amos 5.8); the very earth melts at the touch of God (9.5). There is a strange symbiosis between God and the earth such that when God is distressed or indignant, the earth itself heaves. In Amos 8.8 the land trembles and rises like the Nile. It is stirred up and sinks again like a river. This picture of the earth quaking in response to the voice of God and in reaction to human sin occurs several times in Amos (Dell 2011). Even day and night, light and darkness are confused and dislocated (Amos 5.8). Nature conspires with God against human society: the patterns of weather become erratic (4.7); the locusts swarm to devour the land (7.1–2), fire is an agent of God's will (7.4). While God uses the forces of nature to bring judgement upon human beings, nature itself is a victim of human lawlessness and injustice. The ground suffers because of human sin. 'The pastures of the shepherds dry up, and the top of Carmel withers' (1.2); the gardens and vineyards are stricken with blight (4.9). On the other hand, when peace and justice are restored the earth flourishes. 'New wine will drip from the mountains and flow from all the hills' (9.13). Amos, I think, would have agreed with the words sometimes attributed to Chief Seattle:

> All things are connected. Whatever befalls the earth befalls the sons of the earth. Man did not weave the web of life, he is merely a strand in it. Whatever he does to the web, he does to himself.[1]

I have discussed ecology only with reference to the Book of Amos, but there are many similar references in other prophetic books particularly Hosea and First Isaiah (Marlow 2009, pp. 158–243).

Society is a community

It is particularly relevant to Western society today to note that the prophets treated Israel as a community bound together in covenant and not as individuals bound together by the market. This is one of the greatest strengths of Martin Buber's classic study of the prophets, his emphasis upon community. As an example of the teaching of the prophets Buber discusses Jeremiah 7, a tremendous attack upon false religion.

> This is what the Lord almighty, the God of Israel says: reform your ways and your actions, and I will let you live in this place. Do not trust in deceptive words and say, this is the temple of the Lord, the temple of the Lord, the temple of the Lord! If you really change your ways and your actions and deal with each other justly, if you do not oppress the alien, the fatherless or the widow and do not shed innocent blood in this place and if you do not follow other Gods to your own harm, then I will let you live in this place, in the land I gave to your forefathers for ever and ever. (Jer. 7.3–7)

In the Decalogue the religious obligations come first, and the human duties and responsibilities come next. The commandments to have no other gods, to honour the name of Yaweh and to remember the Sabbath come before the commandments not to kill, commit adultery, steal, bear false witness against

---

1 http://www.ecopsychology.org/journal/gatherings2/scull.htm.

each other and not to desire the property of others (Exod. 20.1–17). In Jeremiah it is the other way around. People are to deal with each other justly, they are not to oppress aliens and the more vulnerable people in society or to commit murder. Only then do we come to the question of religious loyalty. Even the following of other gods is forbidden, because it is 'to your own harm' (Jer. 7.6b). The order is emphasized by being repeated in verse 9 'Will you steal and murder, commit adultery and perjury, burn incense to Baal and follow other gods . . . ?' Buber remarks:

> God seeks something other than religion. Out of a human community He wills to make His kingdom; community there must be in order that His kingdom shall come; therefore here, where He blames a people for not having become a community, man's claim upon man takes precedence of God's claim. (1949, p. 172)

The self-understanding of Israel first as groupings of families within tribes, had grown under the influence of the corporate demands of the covenant into a community, and beyond this to a vision of universal humanity. It was this development from a kinship society to a centralized monarchy that threatened community solidarity and provoked some of the most outspoken oracles of the prophets (Blenkinsopp 1996, p. 5; Brueggemann 1994, p. 23). The domination and exploitation associated with the monarchy were well known (1 Sam. 8.11–17). The injustice of the class system which emerged was one of the principle objectives of the prophecies of Micah. Those who have the power 'covet fields and seize them and houses and take them. They defraud a man of his home, a fellow man of his inheritance' (Mic. 2.1–2). It was the growing disparity between the rich and the poor, between the powerful and the vulnerable, which had destroyed justice in the community.

> Listen, you leaders of Jacob, you rulers of Israel. Should you not embrace justice, you who hate good and love evil; who tear the skin from my people and the flesh from their bones; who eat my people's flesh, strip off their skin and break their bones in pieces; who chop them up like meat for the pan, like flesh for the pot? (Mic. 3.1–3)

Because 'the ruler demands gifts, the judge accepts bribes, and the powerful dictate whatever they desire' (Mic. 7.3), there has been a collapse of basic community trust (7.5–6).

God's view of society, however, is that disabled people and exiles should be brought into the community (4.6–7), and with the re-establishment of real community life, international conflict will also be reduced (4.3), and every citizen will be able to lead peaceful and fruitful lives (4.4). Two features of the society described in the Old Testament were fundamental to its vision of human community. The nation was more of a nation and less of an aggregate of individuals, because it stood under the command of obedience to the covenant with God, and all that flowed from the nature of that God. Secondly, Israel became a community, because God was to be found in the works of justice and mercy extended to every personal and civic relationship. One of the most remarkable examples of this is found in Jeremiah 22, where the prophet is addressing the King of Judah Jehoiakim, son of the good king Josiah:

> Did not your father eat and drink and do justice and righteousness? Then it was well with him. He judged the cause of the poor and needy; then it was well. Is not this to know me? says the Lord.' (vv. 15–16)

Brueggemann describes this as an astonishing statement, the verse does not say

> that judging the poor and needy is the cause and knowing Yahweh the consequence; nor, conversely, that judging the poor and needy is the consequence and knowing Yahweh the cause. Rather, the two are equated. Judging the cause of the poor and the needy *is the substance* of the knowledge of Yahweh. (1997, p. 613; Brueggemann's italics)

This is a remarkable example of the way that in biblical prophetic faith the vertical dimension of trust in God is virtually collapsed into the horizontal dimension of interpersonal justice. There is no other way to create a human community.

It is true that Ezekiel speaks in forceful terms about the responsibility of the individual before God, but this is because the covenant had failed and the community with it during the Exilic period, and moreover the individualizing theology of Ezekiel also failed, since it became clear that the just and the unjust individuals perished together. It was out of this that the Book of Job arose, the most profound and agonizing study of the nature of individual suffering in the Bible (Buber 1949, p. 188).

Resisting the unjust structures of society

The Fourth Mark of the Mission of God as accepted by the worldwide Anglican Communion and in line with the mission objectives of many other churches is to seek to transform the unjust structures of society. This is a difficult and often controversial feature of mission. It is not easy to identify unjust structures and even more difficult to transform them. Unjust structures do not develop in order to practise injustice; they develop because they are in someone's interest. Those who gain profit from the structure that has developed be it political, economic or social, are either not aware of the injustice it causes to those who suffer disadvantage because of it, or they do not care because their own advantages are so comfortable. The structures are unjust not because they create wealth, but because they create wealth for a few; they develop an imbalance, a disproportionate accumulation of resources and benefits by a minority.

There are several reasons why it is difficult to expose and transform unjust structures. In the first place, most people living in the wealthy two-sevenths world are benefiting from the unjust global financial and trading arrangements. It is not in our interest to disrupt these. Second, those who have the power in an unjust structure will use their prestige, their resources and their power to defend their position. Third, the victims of the unjust structure, instead of seeking to transform the structure, may be ambitious to climb up the structure and become one of the beneficiaries of it. If they succeed, they will become keen supporters of the structure and will see success either in terms of good luck, or in terms of individual and personal achievement and will no longer attribute injustice to the structure. In the meantime, those who benefit from the structure will find ways of perpetuating it through creating means whereby a few lucky individuals will suddenly rise to the top. This is the social function of the national lottery. Those who do not succeed will blame their bad luck and will continue to live in a daydream of hope.

In a pre-analytic age, without the benefit of the social sciences, the prophets had no techniques to expose the workings of the unjust structures of their day, but they could certainly see the injustice. Because they believed in the value of the community created by the covenant and because they believed that the giver of the covenant was a just and faithful God, one who delighted in justice, they had the motivation and the insight to launch a powerful attack. Jeremiah was well aware that the moral fibre of the entire community had lapsed 'Go up and down the streets of Jerusalem. Look around and consider, search through her squares. If you can find but one person who deals honestly and seeks the truth, I will forgive this city' (Jer. 5.1). Although Jeremiah did not use the language of sociology, he was well aware of social class distinctions. 'They made their faces harder than stone and refused to repent. I thought "These are only the poor; they are foolish, for they do not know the way of the Lord, the requirements of their God"' (5.3b–4).

He soon discovered that the leadership were no better than the people: indeed they were worse, because they were manipulating the people; they had failed to protect the vulnerable as was their duty under the law and they had amassed huge wealth as a result.

Among my people are wicked men who lie in wait like men who snare birds and like those who set traps to catch men; like cages full of birds, their houses are full of deceit; they have become rich and powerful, they have grown fat and sleek, their evil deeds have no limit; they do not plead the case of the fatherless to win it; they do not defend the rights of the poor. (5.26–8)

In Hosea the call to return to the God of love and justice precedes a denunciation of the managers of the exploitative trading system.

You must return to your God; maintain love and justice, and wait for your God always. A merchant uses dishonest scales; he loves to defraud. Ephraim boasts, I am very rich; I have become wealthy. With all my wealth, they will not find in me any iniquity or sin. (12.6–8)

Evidence has been found all over the ancient Near East of an institution generally known as the Marzeah. This was a sort of social club, attended by wealthy families, sometimes associated with funeral feasts, and sometimes under the protection of a deity or dedicated to a God. The main function of the Marzeah was drinking and eating. This institution seems to have existed in Israel and was attacked by the prophets. Amos 6.1–7 is a bitter, ironic attack upon those who were 'complacent in Zion . . . you notable men of the foremost nation to whom the people come!' The tirade continues:

> You lie on beds inlaid with ivory and lounge on your couches. You dine on choice lambs and fatted calves. You strum away on your harps like David and improvise on musical instruments, you drink wine by the bowlful and use the finest lotions but you do not grieve over the ruin of Joseph. Therefore you will be among the first to go into exile; your feasting and lounging will end. (6.4–7)

Not only is this a scene of luxury, but it represents 'religion turned upside down' (Linville 2008, p. 124),[2] since the bowls may well have been the sacred utensils, and the feasting may have been upon sacrificial animals. Perhaps we could compare this to a scene in which the wealthy city friends of the senior cathedral staff have a grand dinner with plenty of wine, while the people patiently wait to offer their prayers.

It is possible that in Amos 4.1 the female members of the Marzeah are being described. 'Here this word, you cows of Bashan on Mount Samaria, you women who oppress the poor and crush the needy, and say to your husbands, "bring us some drinks!"' The reference to the cows may suggest that the feast was in honour of the Baal whose symbol was the bull, the women were being described as his cows. Whatever we think of this interpretation there is no doubt that the central feature of the text is an attack upon social class privilege in its most careless indulgent form. The same situation is described in words of scathing contempt in Amos 2.6a–8.

> They sell the righteous for silver and the needy for a pair of sandals. They trample on the heads of the poor as upon the dust of the ground, and deny justice to the oppressed . . . they lie down beside every altar on garments taken in pledge. In the house of their God they drink wine taken as fines.

This offers the same misappropriation of public property by the powerful, who regard their clients as the scum of the earth and do not hesitate to drive the poor further into poverty if they can extract from this misery the slightest financial gain for themselves. When it comes to exposing and attacking the unjust structures of society, no prophet, not even Amos, exceeds the powerful and courageous spirit of Micah (Blenkinsopp 1996, pp. 91–7). In Micah 2 the schemes of the unscrupulous land speculators are described. They can hardly sleep at night for thinking of the dodgy deals they have planned for the next day (v. 1). They search out the best land for development and think nothing of deliberately defrauding people of their property (v. 2). They are indifferent to the homelessness which they create and to the impact of destitution upon children (v. 9). They even have some of the religious leaders in their pocket who are quite happy to hold services for them provided the grants are good (v. 5), but soon they will lose any sense of spiritual vocation, if ever they had it, and

---

2 The only other reference to the Marzeah in the Bible occurs in Jeremiah 16.5, where it is often translated 'a house where there is a funeral meal'. See Moughtin-Mumby 2010, p. 73.

their ministries will become empty (3.5–7). Micah describes vividly a money mad society. The politicians are influenced by bribes, even education becomes a source of profit, and those who are specializing in predicting the future will predict whatever fills their pocket (v. 11). Therefore the city is built on wickedness (3.10). In any money society, defence becomes important, huge sums being spent on armaments. Micah's denunciation includes the military. 'In that day, declares the Lord, I will destroy your horses from among you and demolish your chariots' (5.10). The chariots were the tanks of the ancient world and horses were their attack vehicles. One day, says Micah, the nations will acknowledge that there is something greater than their own power, and then

> [t]hey will beat their swords into ploughshares and their spears into pruning hooks. Nation shall not take up sword against nation, nor will they train for war anymore. For every man will sit under his own vine and under his own fig tree, and no one will make them afraid for the Lord almighty has spoken. (Mic. 4.3–4)

The nations themselves are amongst the unjust structures that stand under the judgement of God. This is the central argument of Reinhold Niebuhr's classic study of social morality (1932). And the prophets of Israel said much the same sort of thing, but in a more picturesque and terse manner (Barton 2003, pp. 77–129).

A great deal of the prophetic writings may be read as a critique of ancient imperialism, whether of Assyria or Babylon or later empires (Blenkinsopp 1995, p. 147). This is the main theme of Brueggemann's first well-known book, *The Prophetic Imagination*, where he says: 'The task of prophetic ministry is to nurture, nourish, and evoke a consciousness and perception alternative to the consciousness and perception of the dominant culture around us' (1992, p. 13). He interprets the post-exilic prophets in the same way, and it is the central point of his interpretation of Second Isaiah. Brueggemann draws links between the prophetic mission to create an alternative reality in a world where the claims of empire were total, and our own reality, caught up in the all-pervading ideology of the consuming society with its military support (1992a, pp. 109–30).

The prophetic process against imperialism has also affected the spiritual lives of Christians today. The kingdom of God emerged as an alternative to the claims of empire, and much of the language of kingdom and empire has been included in Christian prayer and worship (Blenkinsopp 1995, p. 147). The greatest interpreter of this aspect of the prophetic tradition does not claim to be a specialist in the Old Testament, but someone who has lived the prophetic life under the inspiration of the prophetic books. I am referring again to Daniel Berrigan, and no understanding of the impact of the prophets upon resistance to unjust structures today can be adequate without reading his inspirational books.

The prophets and the worship of God

Even worship can become an unjust structure. This happened in Israel whenever the cult was carried on regardless of the covenant, and it happens in the Church today whenever worship takes place without ethics. Just as the covenant was the reason for being Israel so the mission of God is the reason for being Church. The cult was a response to the covenant just as the worship of the Church is a response to the mission of God. The cult was not the heart of Israel's faith just as worship is not the heart of the Church. The prophets, whose principal task was to call the people on to obey the covenant, saw correctly that when thousands of priests serve God day and night in the worship of the temple cult, while the fundamentals of covenantal justice were ignored, worship itself had become an unjust structure.

The tension between the covenant and the temple in Israel can be traced back to the policies of King Solomon. The question was: where was God to dwell? When Moses had dedicated the sacred tent, which was moved from place to place during the years of wandering in the wilderness, God said, 'I will dwell among the Israelites, and be their God' (Exod. 29.45). This was repeated almost as a warning, when Solomon was actually building the temple. 'And I will live among the Israelites, and will not abandon my people Israel' (1 Kings 6.13). This, however, was not the policy of Solomon. The temple had been completed, and Solomon brought up the ark, the mobile symbol of the people's God, with a most extravagant display of piety and wealth (1 Kings 8.3-5). The priests carried the ark into the inner sanctuary of the temple, into a place where even the very long poles that carried the ark could not be seen from where the people would gather outside the holy place. 'Then Solomon said, "The Lord has said that he would dwell in a dark cloud; I indeed have built a magnificent temple for you, a place for you to dwell forever"' (8.12-13). Martin Buber, commenting on this verse, remarks, 'we meet the unreserved expression of the aim of the early kingdom to confine YHWH's sovereignty within the cultic sphere alone' (Buber 1949, p. 82; cf. Brueggemann 1992, p. 35).

Perhaps Solomon was more conscious of addressing the public, when, having delivered a speech glorifying himself (vv. 15-21), he dedicated the temple in prayer. 'Will God really dwell on earth? The heavens, even the highest heaven, cannot contain you. How much less this temple I have built!' (v. 27) It was not in the mind of the king that Yaweh would continue to dwell as he had done in the midst of the people. If the temple cannot contain Yaweh, then Yaweh must be in heaven, and it is from thence that prayers will be heard. Only the name of God actually dwells in the temple.

> May your eyes be open toward this temple night and day, this place of which you said, 'My name shall be there' so that you will hear the prayer your servant prays toward this place. Hear the supplication of your servant and of your people Israel when they pray towards this place. Hear from heaven, your dwelling place, and when you hear, forgive. (vv. 29-30)

God now looks after the heavenly things, where he stays, but pays attention to earth when he is needed. There is no scope any longer for God to be the leader of the people, because Solomon will do that (Berrigan 2008, pp. 32-59). Buber regards this as 'a classic expression of the tensions between the free God of history and the fettered deity of natural things' (1949, p. 83).

The story of this tension takes us next to the conflict between Micaiah, the solitary prophet of the people, and the 400 prophets who served the royal court.

As Micaiah is being dragged off to prison, he shouts out 'Mark my words, all you people!' (1 Kings 22.28). A century later we come to the conflict between Amaziah, priest of the royal shrine at Bethel, and Amos, the farmer from Tekoa (Amos 7.10–17). Amaziah said, 'Get out, you seer! Go back to the land of Judah. Earn your bread there and do your prophesying there. Don't prophesy any more at Bethel, because this is the king's sanctuary, the temple of the kingdom' (vv. 12–13). These hot, contemptuous words express the perennial attitude of the religious officials, who, in whatever country, yesterday and today, regard it as their main business to serve 'the temple of the kingdom' (v. 13).

The sarcastic words 'Get on with your work in Judah and try to fill your belly' are reminiscent of the taunt 'Get a job' frequently shouted out at nuclear protestors by the occupants of passing cars. James Linville comments 'The absence of any mention of God in Amaziah's warning to the king is all the more striking, given the priest's admission that Amos is, in fact, a 'seer' (2008, p. 144). 'The priest cannot even tell one of God's intermediaries from another' (p. 145).

In the Old Testament scholarship of the nineteenth century, the contrast between the prophets and the cult was exaggerated, and it was the work of Sigmund Mowinckel (1884–1966) in emphasizing the role of the ecstatic prophets in the cult that reasserted the balance. Many of the prophets were associated with the temple, as the very common designation 'priest and prophet' suggests. In Isaiah and Jeremiah priest and prophet are often jointly criticized (Isa. 28.7; Jer. 2.8, 26; 5.31), but particularly in the post-exilic prophets, priest and prophet are often associated in the ministry of the temple, as if this was their normal role (Hag. 1.1; Zech. 7.3). Whether associated with the cult or independently, the prophets were critical of the way worship was often conducted. Perhaps it would be more correct to say that they were critical of the disconnection between the worship and the life of the community.

With bitter irony Amos attacks the worship at the shrines of Bethel and Gilgal. 'Go to Bethel and sin; go to Gilgal and sin yet more. Bring your sacrifices every morning, your tithes every three years. Burn leavened bread as a thank offering and brag about your freewill offerings – boast about them, you Israelites, for this is what you love to do, declares the Sovereign Lord' (Amos 4.4–5). In Amos 5.21–4, the irony has turned to anger. 'I hate, I despise your religious feasts; I cannot stand your assemblies. Even though you bring me burnt offerings and grain offerings, I will not accept that. Though you bring choice fellowship offerings, I will have no regard for them. Away with the noise of your songs! I will not listen to the music of your harps. But let justice roll on like a river, righteousness like a never-failing stream!'

Here we find a massive rejection of the whole apparatus of state religion. The whole structure of worship, although required by an ancient tradition, is rejected 'as the expression of a radically sinful way of life' (Blenkinsopp 1996, p. 80). This does not mean that Amos was proposing a purely spiritual worship without liturgy or symbol (p. 81). We see from Isaiah 1.15 that it was not only the incense and the ceremony that was rejected, but the prayers of the worshipping people were also unheard by God. The reason why the religious life of the nation has become a weary burden for God to bear is not that the liturgy was unacceptable in itself but because they were 'meaningless offerings' (Isa. 1.13). It was false worship, because it came from false worshippers. It was false, because it was not accompanied by a search for public justice (Berrigan 1996, p. 7).

Not only did the prophets attack false worship (Hos. 6.6, 8.13; Jer. 6.20), but the religious authorities fought back. Jeremiah took a clay pot, carried it to a popular place just outside one of the city gates, broke it as a symbolic gesture and denounced the government of the people at large (Jer. 19.1–13). Nothing is said about the reaction of the authorities. Returning into the city, Jeremiah 'stood in the court of the Lord's temple' (v. 14) and repeated more or less the same denunciation of the city and the surrounding villages (v. 15). The officials of the temple react with violence. One of the senior priests had Jeremiah beaten and put in the stocks (Jer. 20.1–2). Why was there such a contrast between the reactions of the secular and the religious authorities? Berrigan comments 'One thinks of the skin, thin as a gold leaf, that quivers away beneath a public pattern of religiosity and respectability' (1999, p. 85). The problem was that Jeremiah was an insider; he knew the ancient traditions, the demands of the covenant, as well as anyone, and he walked closer to God than anyone in the official establishment. Religious establishments often turn more harshly against their insiders because their words wound to the heart of the tradition. The insider is aware of the failure of religious belief and worship to act in accordance with its own ethical ideals, but the secular authorities are indifferent to this.

Idolatry

Two kinds of worship are attacked by the prophets. There is the worship directed to the living God but not supported by justice, and there is the worship directed toward false gods. Idolatry is one of the most common themes in the prophetic writers. In Isaiah alone there are dozens of references to idolatry. Sometimes their condemnation was directed towards the idols of Egypt (Isa. 19.1) or Babylon (Isa. 46.1); sometimes the attack was directed toward idols present in Israel itself (Isa. 10.11); sometimes idols of gold and silver are denounced (Isa. 2.20, 31.7). The exposure to Babylonian religion during the exile had sharpened criticism of idolatry. Second Isaiah presents some magnificent diatribes against the folly of idolatry, with mocking descriptions of how the idols were actually made (Isa. 40.19, 41.7). The climax of this polemic comes with the realization that the makers of idols represent nothing at all; they are sheer nothingness (Isa. 44.9).

Contemporary theologians have not been slow in pointing out the relevance today of these attacks upon idolatry. Brueggemann describes this as 'the battle for definition of reality' (1992, p. 74). The false reality implied in the concept of idolatry has been variously understood. For Girolamo Savonarola in the late fifteenth century, the idols were the wealth and luxury of the Italian church (Lara 2010, p. 141). For John Calvin in the sixteenth century it goes without saying that the idols were the Roman Pontiff and the Mass (Mein 2010, p. 170), and for the Puritans a century later the same was the case (p. 176).

One of the most influential definitions of idolatry from the twentieth century is that provided by Paul Tillich, for whom God from a subjective point of view is that which we take with ultimate seriousness, without any reservations whatever. If we give our ultimate concern to that which is not truly ultimate, then we are idolatrous. 'Faith in anything which has only preliminary reality is idolatrous' (1955, p. 59). Another way of expressing this is to say that to grant absolute status to anything except God is to commit idolatry. This represents an 'idolatrous confusion' of God with that which is merely human (1951, p. xliv). This is the essence of 'prophetic criticism' (p. 43). The endless preoccupation with security which is so typical of the modern West may be regarded as a form of idolatry, and the weapon of mass destruction, the nuclear bomb, is its concrete expression. Daniel Berrigan discusses the dream of Nebuchadnezzar, with the idol of the head of gold and feet of clay, which was smashed to pieces by a rock not hewn with human hands (Dan. 2.31–5). He goes on to say, 'among many Christians, such deadly idols as nuclear weapons raise not a whiff of scandal. But what a storm and scandal erupt, when a few Christians decide to launch a "rock" against these images of violence! The scandal is strangely misapplied, one thinks, when nuclear weapons are regarded as normal and civil disobedience as scandalous' (Berrigan 1998, p. 42).

This is the meaning of the commandment which forbids the making of images of God. This may be interpreted as using *'wrong* speech about Yahweh, which amounts to idolatry', faulty language for God, creating false images of God, rather than making statues of other gods (Brueggemann 1997, p. 136; Brueggemann's italics). The rich variety of names given to God in the Old Testament prevents any single image from attaining idolatrous status (p. 262).

In Christian faith the absolutizing of Jesus of Nazareth is an example of religious idolatry (p. 332). The mere name of Jesus, especially when pronounced emphatically and drawn out as long as possible, takes on a kind of fetish-like energy. What parallel can we find in Christian faith to the endless criticism of Yaweh in the Hebrew Bible? The doctrine of the Holy Trinity may be regarded as an attempt made by the tradition to prevent Jesus of Nazareth from becoming an idol, for in the Trinity Jesus Christ becomes a mode of God, God the Father and God the Spirit being the other modes. This is the reason why in Christian faith one can confess that Jesus Christ is God, but not that God is Jesus. Without the exfoliation of the divine environment, Christian faith can easily forget to worship God in Jesus Christ and instead make Jesus into an absolute God (p. 332). It is the crucifixion which prevents Jesus from becoming an idol. Paul Tillich applies his theology of symbols to the crucifixion. In order to prevent any symbol from becoming absolute, and taking the place of that which it symbolizes, all symbols must be broken (1965, pp. 135–6). As Brueggemann says, 'In living in the midst of Friday, Christians reach back as far as the command issued at Sinai against idols' (1997, p. 332).

Tillich's idea of the breaking of symbols to prevent them from becoming idols may be compared with the idea of the renewal of the knowledge of God in the theology of Karl Barth. This knowledge must continually be renewed, otherwise it becomes knowledge not of the living God but of the knowledge of human ideas, leading to 'dead gods or all too living demons' (1957, p. 23). For this reason Barth warns us against 'abstract Jesus-worship', the worship of Jesus the man; Christian worship is directed towards Jesus the Christ (1956, p. 136).

The experience of God

This expression 'The experience of God' points us both to the experiences which Israel and supremely the prophets had of the presence and acts of God, and also in some strange manner the experiences which God had in relation to Israel. In the prophets God is described as a God of pathos (Heschel 2007, pp. 1–11). Although the prophets used many images to describe God and gave God many names and titles, it is always God in action and in relationship rather than God in essence and in being that is the subject of their books. God is transcendent, dwelling in another realm, but at the same time God is intimately involved with human life. A characteristic expression of this tension is to be found in Isaiah 57.15. 'For this is what the high and lofty one says – he who lives forever, whose name is holy, I live in a high and holy place, but also with him who is contrite and lowly in spirit, to revive the spirit of the lowly and to revive the heart of the contrite.' God, however, does not hide in that high and holy place, but participates in the griefs and sorrows of human beings. Human beings are not treated merely as creatures to be disposed of, but are taken with complete seriousness by God as partners in God's plans. This takes both individual and collective forms, since God is involved in the history of Israel. In these various situations God is sometimes angry, sometimes forgiving, sometimes disappointed, and at other times hopeful.

In one astonishing passage God seems to apologize for the break in Israel's continuity caused by the exile, the destruction of the temple and the monarchy and the apparent termination of the covenant. 'For a brief moment I abandoned you but with deep compassion I will bring you back. In a surge of anger I hid my face from you for a moment but with everlasting kindness I will have compassion on you, says the Lord your Redeemer' (Isa. 54.7–8). Here the break in the continuity of the relationship with God is admitted. 'I abandoned you'. This is depicted as God speaking; it is not the people or the prophet complaining of having been abandoned; it is God who has briefly but really broken off the relationship.

Christian readers will be reminded of another moment of abandonment, when the dereliction was expressed with great pathos from the human side. 'My God, why have you forsaken me?' This intense involvement, leading even as we have seen to a breaking point, means that the God of the prophets is not a neutral, abstract concept but a God who is passionately one-sided. 'Pathos means: God is never neutral, never beyond good and evil. He is always partial to justice' (Heschel 2007, p. 11). This must not be understood as a projection into God of human emotions, as anthropopathy, but an insight into the relation of God to human beings (pp. 48–58). The intensity of God's love makes God vulnerable to disappointment and betrayal. In the Book of Jeremiah it is sometimes quite difficult to tell whether the voice of suffering is that of the prophet or of God. Perhaps this ambiguity is intended to show that Jeremiah had so deeply identified with Yaweh that he did not know, he could not tell whether the words he was speaking were his own words or the words of Yaweh speaking within him. At the same time the ambiguity indicates that so close was the identification of Yaweh with Yaweh's people that their feelings became the feelings of Yaweh, their sufferings the sufferings of Yaweh. 'Since my people are crushed, I am crushed; I mourn, and horror grips me. Is there no balm in Gilead? Is there no physician there? Why then is there no healing for the wound of my people?' (Jer. 8.21–2). As the ninth chapter opens, the question about who is speaking becomes yet more poignant. 'Oh that my head were a spring of water and my eyes a fountain of tears! I would weep day and night for the slain of my people' (Jer. 9.1). Yaweh yearns to find a place to escape, to hide away 'so that I might leave my people and go away . . . They do not acknowledge me, declares the Lord' (vv. 2–3) (Brueggemann 2006, p. 150).

The people have become thick-skinned and dull to the pain they are inflicting upon themselves and on others but the commitment of God and God's endless compassion means that God has nowhere to hide from all the pain.

In the theological imagination of Hosea the relationship between God and Israel had moved beyond the question of law, broken law and punishment into the complexities of personal relationship. We have seen how tortured some of the imagery is in Hosea; now we must realize that this tortured language came from the heart of suffering love.

This is vividly expressed in Second Isaiah. 'Though the mountains be shaken and the hills be removed yet my unfailing love for you will not be shaken nor my covenant of peace be removed' (Isa. 54.10). Third Isaiah takes up the refrain: 'In all their distress he too was distressed; the angel of his presence saved them. In his love and mercy he redeemed them; he lifted them up and carried them all the days of old' (Isa. 63.9). God speaks like a mother caring for a child. 'I led them with cords of human kindness, with ties of love; I lifted the yoke from their neck and knelt down to feed them' (Hos. 11.4). The prophet Joel cries out 'Return to the Lord your God, for he is gracious and compassionate, slow to anger and abounding in love' (Joel 2.13). Jeremiah, the most sensitive of prophets, sums it all up when God speaks through him, saying, 'I have loved you with an everlasting love, I have drawn you with loving kindness' (Jer. 31.3).

Hope

In the midst of the struggle for life, a struggle described so brilliantly, so passionately in the prophetic literature, comes the voice of hope. Emerging from its own ruin, hope is found on the far side of despair. Many symbols and images are used to express this inexpressible hope, and one of the most moving is that of the child. In Isaiah 7 a little child becomes the symbol of the presence of God; in Chapter 9 the child has now become the image of a society of justice and peace. 'To us a child is born, to us a son is given, and the government will be on his shoulders. And he will be called Wonderful Councillor, Mighty God, Everlasting Father, Prince of Peace' (Isa. 9.6). In Isaiah 11 we find a further development of this imagery. Childhood has now become the central symbol of a new world order, where even the animals are at peace with one another.

> The wolf will live with the lamb, the leopard will lie down with the goat, the calf and the lion and the yearling together; and a little child will lead them. The cow will feed with the bear, their young will lie down together, and the lion will eat straw like the ox. The infant will play near the hole of the cobra

and the young child will put his hand into the viper's nest. They will neither harm nor destroy on all my holy mountain for the earth will be full of the knowledge of the Lord as the waters cover the sea. (11.6–9)

The message of the prophets and the inspiration of the Bible

We began this study by asking with Brevard Childs about the struggle to understand the prophets as Christian Scripture for today. As we bring this chapter to a close, we can see that the struggle is very real and that it continues. The problems are deeper than those raised for many nineteenth-century Christians by Biblical Criticism. The simple confidence which many Christians had in the Bible was challenged by the discovery that the history of Israel was not necessarily as straightforward as the Bible itself appeared to indicate, and by the discovery that the books that carry their names were not necessarily written by the prophets themselves, but were composite works, accumulated in some cases over centuries. Today the difficulties are created by the realization that the world of the prophets was very different from that in which we live. Historical and anthropological research has deepened the sense of the difference. The assumptions, customs and even the language of that ancient society gave meaning to the prophetic oracles, a meaning which is difficult if not impossible for us to grasp. We have become sharply aware of the fact that our understanding of human rights and of the dignity of the person is not the same as theirs and that previously marginalized sections of society are unwilling to continue to accept their marginalized status. The remoteness of their expectations cannot be overcome by searching for their fulfilment in the contemporary politics of the Middle East, and the hermeneutical abyss between them and us cannot be bridged by appeal to some kind of external inspiration in the texts themselves. We have seen that there is much in the prophetic writings that is still of huge significance, but the mere fact that we have found it necessary to distinguish these positive from other more negative aspects creates a crisis in our understanding of the Bible.

Instead of speaking of the inspiration of the Bible, we must speak of its inspirational quality. That quality does not lie objectively in the text itself nor is it merely subjective in the lives of those who are inspired. Those who stand in the Christian tradition would not be so inspired without the witness of the prophets; indeed, it is possible that there might not even be a Christian tradition without the heritage of Scripture. The same is true in reverse: the Bible would no longer be the inspiration of the Christian tradition unless Christian people were inspired by it. There is a sort of flash point between the inspiring text and the inspired people. In Christian faith the activation of that flash point is the work of the Holy Spirit. That means that living Scripture is the product of the prophetic Spirit.

In his second letter to the Corinthian Church, Paul deals with the question of interpretation. He is discussing the validity of the ministry of himself and his closest friends. He says that to authenticate this ministry it is not necessary to have references in writing, because their own hearts and the change in their lives bore witness to the Christian faith they had received from Paul. 'You yourselves are our letter, written on our hearts, known and read by everybody' (2 Cor. 3.2). The Christian disciples were 'letters of Christ', inscribed in their hearts and lives by the Holy Spirit. This witness, Paul continues, is more reliable than that of laws written in stone, a reference to the Ten Commandments. Even the Ten Commandments are dead if not written in the hearts and lives of people. How can we be sure of this? We have this confidence, continues Paul: we ourselves have the witness of Christ as we stand before God (v. 4). This is a new kind of literary competence, competence not based upon scribal techniques or knowledge of the text, but a competence of interpretation lying in the new relationship with God through Jesus Christ. This is a competence, he concludes, not of the letter but of the Spirit, 'for the letter kills, but the Spirit gives life' (v. 6).

Paul speaks about the ministry of death, inscribed in letters of stone (v. 7), and if even such permanence could be overwhelmed by the new life of the spirit, then how much more is that true of letters inscribed upon parchment, vellum or paper? This is what Paul calls 'the ministry of the Spirit' (v. 8), and it is glorious, because it brings life. There is a veil hanging over these inscribed letters, a veil which is taken away by the Holy Spirit, who is the Lord and Giver of life, the freedom-giver (v. 17).

These are the principles which should guide the Church in the interpretation of Scripture. In the power of the Spirit we have to discriminate between those things that bring death and those that bring life, and the criterion of this discrimination is none other than life and freedom.

How does this approach to the Bible square with the traditional statements of faith? Article 6 of the Thirty-Nine Articles of the Church of England (1662) declares that 'Holy scripture containeth all things necessary to salvation: so that whatsoever is not read therein, nor may be proved thereby, is not to be required of any man, that it should be believed as an article of the Faith, or be thought requisite or necessary to salvation.'

It is important to observe that the Article is not about the text of Holy Scripture, although the extent of Holy Scripture is defined in the list of canonical books which follows, but it directs our attention to the criterion of salvation. Moreover, it is negative in the sense that it does not require a Christian person in this tradition to accept and believe everything that is in the Scripture, only that anything that is not in the Scripture cannot be thought necessary or required for salvation. The next Article, Article 7, deals with the Old Testament in particular. 'The Old Testament is not contrary to the New: for both in the Old and New Testament everlasting life is offered to Mankind by Christ.' This is precisely what Paul was talking about in 2 Corinthians 3, where Jesus Christ is the unity of Scripture. The Article concludes 'no Christian man whatsoever is free from the obedience of the Commandments which are called Moral'.

One cannot but admire the careful way this expression is worded. Reference is made to 'the Commandments which are called Moral'. As we have seen, there is much in the prophets which cannot be called moral, therefore no Christian person is obliged to believe them, otherwise we would all be committed to belief in the death penalty and in the right and duty of husbands to threaten, persecute and abuse their wives. The point is more clearly expressed in the modern version (1974), which refers to 'those commandments which may be classified as moral'.[3] The Article also says that those who regard the Old Testament as only

---

3 http://www.churchsociety.org.

providing 'transitory promises' are not to be listened to. This is what I had in mind when I argue that the message of the prophets to the Church today has been inhibited or dulled by the idea that the prophets are of interest mainly because of the way they are said to have predicted the coming of Jesus Christ. This is the veil which prevents the contemporary message of the prophets from being read in those parts of the Church where the prophets are valued mainly because of their so-called predictions. When this veil is removed, the Spirit of life and freedom will once again enable the prophets to speak out loud and clear.

When we examine some of the more recent statements about the authority of the Bible, the guidance they offer is less clear. 'The divine inspiration and supreme authority of the Old and New Testament Scriptures, which are the written Word of God – fully trustworthy for faith and conduct' (Evangelical Alliance *Basis of Faith,* paragraph 2).[4] This statement appears to attach to the written word the very supreme authority that Paul denies to it. The focus of interest has moved away from the issue of salvation or of the Spirit of Jesus Christ as the ruling norm of interpretation and fastens attention upon divine inspiration as residing in the actual written documents. Its emphasis upon the supremacy of Scripture and its fully trustworthy nature not only for faith but for conduct allows for no reciprocity between Scripture and the reader, and thus does not allow for the divine spark to fly between them. The statement does not permit the kind of discriminating awareness which our study of the prophets encourages, and if this approach dulls sensitivity to the darker parts of the prophets, as it must, it seems not improbable that the impact of the brighter and more life-enhancing aspects will also be somewhat dulled.

The Christian tradition which flows from the Bible is like a very large river. Broadly flowing down the centuries, it brings to us whether we are carried along by it or stand on the banks watching and waiting, all sorts of debris from higher upstream. It also brings life-giving water and, sometimes, being carried along in its flood, a box of treasures from former years. It is not always easy to tell what is debris and what is treasure, which is life-giving water and which is dead matter. It may be difficult to choose, but choose we must. Peter Berger (1980) has pointed out that the heretic is really one who picks and chooses, and that so great and diverse is the Christian tradition we have received, all serious Christians must be heretics, because there is no option other than selection. The situation is the same when we come to the Bible itself. This means that we have to look upon the Bible as a source of inspiration in the sense that the Bible is a highly esteemed conversational partner. The Bible occupies a privileged position in the several conversational partners of the serious Christian, but it remains a conversational partner not an autocratic dictator. We must listen with respect to everything our conversational partner shares with us, but because it is a conversation and not a monologue we have to listen to the Bible with an ear that is both attentive and discriminating. We have to recognize that our conversational partner has been in dialogue with human beings for more than 2,000 years and that in that time some of the things that were relevant to partners in previous conversations are no longer relevant to our generation. This does not mean that

---

4 http://www.eauk.org/connect/about-us/basis-of-faith.cfm. Versions of this statement, differing only slightly, may be found in Randall and Hilborn 2001, Appendices 1, 2, 3 and 6.

the Bible keeps on saying the same old things, for in our generation we pose different questions to the Bible, and in turn the Bible directs our attention to new insights. Scripture remains 'God-breathed' (2 Tim. 3.16), but, having said this, the text in question continues in what might be thought a surprisingly modest and open way. 'All scripture is God-breathed and is useful for teaching, rebuking, correcting and training in righteousness.' The word here for righteousness could also be translated 'justice', which would suggest that Scripture is breathed by God to train us in justice.[5] And the *pneuma*, the breath of God, is none other than the Holy Spirit, who breathes through Scripture in the two-way process which is the meaning of inspiration.

Conclusions

We have considered the relevance of the prophetic message under ten headings. Under each of these I have tried to show its relevance for today. This relevance is not confined to Jews or Christians, since the prophets did not always call their contemporaries back to obedience to the covenant but appealed to what might be called the universal conscience of humanity (Barton 2003, pp. 112–15).

Let us consider the following facts. At a conservative estimate the eight or nine nuclear powers spent in 2012 approximately one hundred billion dollars on researching, manufacturing and maintaining stockpiles of nuclear weapons. This sum, huge though it is, represented only nine per cent of the total military expenditure for the year. Meanwhile, more than three billion people live on less than 2.5 dollars a day, and 80 per cent of all human beings live on less than ten dollars a day. The poorest 40 per cent of the world's population accounts for five per cent of global income. The richest 20 per cent counts for 75 per cent of world income. Every day, approximately 20,000 children under the age of five die from preventable conditions such as poverty. It would take less than one per cent of what the world spends on weapons to put every child in the world into school, and yet it is not happening. In that context, let us hear again the voice of Amos. 'They trample on the heads of the poor as on the dust of the ground and deny justice to the oppressed' (Amos 2.6). Let us hear the voice of Isaiah: 'Learn to do right; seek justice. Defend the oppressed. Take up the cause of the fatherless; plead the case of the widow' (Isa. 1.17), and again Isaiah says, 'The plunder from the poor is in your houses. What do you mean by crushing my people and grinding the faces of the poor?' (Isa. 3.14–15).

Who is speaking here and to whom? Who will dare say that these statements, these questions are not relevant to us today and to our world? There is a voice here, a voice from antiquity, yet a voice speaking from the universal conscience of humanity. Is this not the word of God?

---

5 The Douay-Rheims Bible translates 'to instruct in justice'. http://Bible.cc/2_timothy/3-16.htm.

3

Jesus Christ as Prophet

More than a prophet?

When Christians are reminded that Jesus was a prophet, someone will usually say, 'Yes, but he was more than a prophet'.

There is certainly much in the New Testament and in Christian faith that would support such a response. There were many prophets, but only one Son (Heb. 1.1–2). It appears to be a long way from Amos, the farm worker, to Jesus Christ, the one in whom the fullness of God was pleased to dwell (Col. 1.19). The Nicene Creed declares that the Holy Spirit spoke through the prophets, but that Jesus Christ is 'God from God, Light from Light, true God from true God, begotten not made, of one substance with the Father; through him all things were made'. Moreover, Jesus seemed to distinguish himself from the prophetic tradition when he said that, 'Truly I tell you, among those born of women there has not risen anyone greater than John the Baptist; yet whoever is least in the kingdom of heaven is greater than he' (Matt. 11.11). When his disciples were reporting what people said about him, he seemed to be unsatisfied at the comment that he was 'one of the prophets' (Mark 8.27–30).

Nevertheless, although Christian faith affirms that he was more than a prophet, he was at least a prophet. The Galilean villages where he worked said that, 'A great prophet has appeared among us' (Luke 7.16), some of his earliest disciples remembered him as 'a prophet, powerful in word and deed before God and all the people' (Luke 24.19), and the preaching of the early Church included the affirmation that he was a prophet (Acts 3.20–22, 7.37).

But that was long ago; now that he has been hailed as Son of God, Lord and Christ, does it matter that he was also a prophet? If the life and work of Jesus matters, then it matters that he was a prophet. If Christian discipleship includes the imitation of Christ, then it matters that he was a prophet. If the mission of the Church is, as Matthew says, to teach 'everything I have commanded you' (Matt. 28.20), then it matters what Jesus said, and this includes his descriptions of his own prophetic mission (Luke 4.18–21) and of what it means to be a prophet (Matt. 13.57, 23.37; Mark 6.4; Luke 4.24, 13.34). If the sending of the Church into the world is to be modelled upon the sending of Jesus Christ by God (John 20.21), then it matters why he was sent, and what the circumstances were in which he worked. So if the response of the Church to the modern world is in some sense to be modelled upon or inspired by the way Jesus responded to the world in which he lived, then it matters that we should know what his world was like and what Jesus did in it. If in Jesus Christ God was incarnate, then it matters into what situation he was born, and what he did about it.

The implications of this are far reaching. The prophets were fully engaged in the social and political issues of their day; they were often critical of the policies of both temple and state; they were involved in conflict, and frequently the state authorities tried to silence them, even to the point of killing them. They spoke for the ordinary people against the rich and powerful, and they joined in the struggle of the people for freedom from oppressive powers, whether internal or international. Faith in the God of Israel led them to see that Israel's God loved justice and mercy, and that only when justice and mercy were characteristics of human societies could society expect to live in peace and security.

The apolitical Jesus

This, however, is very far from the apolitical and spiritualized Jesus that most British people were brought up on. One of the most popular school textbooks for teaching religious education in England in the late 1950s and 60s, and for many years later, was Bernard Youngman's *The Palestine of Jesus*. Youngman describes Jesus as one who taught 'with the gentle persuasion of love that wins men to God' (1956, p. 35). His offences, such as they were, were of a purely religious nature. Certainly, Jesus was involved in conflict, but it was always about religious doctrine. The teaching of Jesus, Youngman said, 'would not be controlled by the Law of Moses' (p. 62), and this was why the scribes and Pharisees hated him; their religious orthodoxy and material comfort were threatened. He told people about 'the kingdom of God—the rule of God in men's hearts' (p. 56). The Romans, with their 'hard discipline, firm government, [and] practical outlook on life' (p. 39) provided the 'benefits of good government' (p. 85). The tension in Palestine was attributed by Youngman to the character of the Jewish people, who 'lived in an atmosphere of hate and distrust; there were feuds and quarrels among them all' (p. 72). The Galilean countryside is described by Youngman as an idyll of rural prosperity and contentment, a land of plenty in a rich and beautiful countryside. The Romans were indifferent to Jesus; they gave in to the hatred of the Jews when it seemed expedient, but they did not consider Jesus himself to be a threat. Jesus was convicted of blasphemy, and the Romans crucified him to save themselves the trouble of a riot. This, then, was the picture of Jesus, the master of the inner life, which was widespread in those days, and it continues to be held by many Christians in Britain today.

Peasants under the rule of an aristocratic empire

Since the popularity of Bernard Youngman, scholarly views of Jesus have undergone significant changes. Studies of the anthropology and sociology of ancient Palestine have emphasized the difficulty of understanding and of entering into a culture so remote to our own. When we read that the people of Judea and Galilee were taxed, we tend to think of taxation as we know it, which is the sharing of personal and corporate funds for the common good. We expect our taxes to be used for the well-being of the country as a whole to provide roads, education and health. If we were to discover that our taxes were being wasted or diverted, we would be indignant and would make sure that there was a change of government at the next election. For us, a fundamental form of criminality is corruption, the misuse of public funds for private profit. We believe that corruption undermines democracy and frustrates the public intention in electing its representatives.

None of this made sense in the ancient world. The crime of corruption as we know it did not occur for the simple reason that there was no distinction made between general taxation and private income. Taxation was money or products taken as tribute by those who ruled and had power for the sole purpose of increasing their wealth and power. Taxation was the extraction of surplus value from a conquered people, who were then left to survive at a subsistence level. The right to collect taxes from a group of villages could be sold or given by one ruling family to another.[1] The overwhelming proportion of the population worked in order to maintain a tiny minority who lived in luxury and did not work.

It has been estimated that under the Roman Empire, the wealthy elite were no more than one to three per cent of the population. They were served by a class of retainers: clerks, administrators, cooks and architects, poets and tax collectors, police and torturers, and by an all-powerful army. This retaining class would perhaps have been between eight to ten per cent of the population.

At least 80 per cent of the population would have been peasants living for the most part in tiny villages of between 100–500 persons. They would have been almost entirely illiterate, working as agriculturalists either on traditional family land or as day labourers if the family had lost its land through debt. If a day labourer was ill, suffered injury or became old, and his family were unable to keep him, he would drift down into the expendable class, the robbers and bandits that infested the hills and the multitudes of beggars, who crowded the gates of the wealthy. Slaves were to be found at every level of society, and were often better looked after than the day labourers. It was in the interests of their owners that slaves should be able to work and to be sufficiently well-fed to maintain their health, but when a day labourer had received his wages the overlord had no more responsibility, and if work was hard to find, he and his family would sink more deeply into poverty.

In order to extract wealth from a conquered people, the Romans found that a large armed presence was not always necessary. The conquerors in all aristocratic empires found 'aristocrats exploiting peasants' (Kautsky 1997, p. 15). It was relatively easy to create alliances between these local rulers and the central power of Rome. It was of mutual benefit. This had happened in Palestine, as in other parts of the Mediterranean world, when the Romans formed an alliance with the Herodian family. Although an additional burden of taxation was now imposed upon them, the fact that their lords were now subjected to an even more remote set of overlords would have made little difference to the people in the villages.

Herod the Great reigned from 37 BCE to 4 BCE and displayed all the cruelty and ostentatious wealth that was typical of aristocratic families. He engaged in a huge programme of what we would call public works, building cities, castles and palaces, and especially the temple in Jerusalem. These building operations

---

1 Josephus describes a case in Ptolemaic Egypt when 'all the principal men and rulers went up out of the cities of Syria and Phoenicia to bid for their taxes. For every year the king sold them to the men of the greatest power in every city'. They were bidding for the right to farm taxes from certain cities. *Ant*, XII, 3.4.

would have been carried on with a mixture of hired and forced labour. Herod was hated by his people and gave orders that at his own death, a number of leading people were to be executed to make sure that at least somebody mourned. Herod had domesticated the high priestly office, requiring such office bearers to be appointed by himself. It was in the interests of a small group of wealthy priestly families to collaborate with him. After Herod's death the country was divided into a number of smaller areas, each ruled over by a member of his family. His son Herod Antipas was given Galilee (reigned 4 BCE–39 CE). He followed the example of his father in undertaking huge building programmes, including his capitals at Sepphoris in upper Galilee and later Tiberius on the western shore of Lake Galilee. None of this building was for the sake of the public; they were not 'public works' as we know them. They were built to enhance the prestige and greater glory of the ruling families.

In Judea another of Herod's sons, Herod Archalaus, was dismissed by Emperor Augustus in 6 CE, and that part of the country was placed under direct Roman rule administered by a series of procurators, including Pontius Pilate (26–36 CE).

The people of Palestine were thus subjected to several layers of taxation. First, there would have been the Roman poll tax, or tribute, demanded from every adult male between the ages of 18 and 60, Roman citizens themselves being exempt. Then, there was the temple tax, which was expected of every Jew throughout the Empire. In areas where the Herod family continued to reign, there would have been additional taxation demands. The temple in Jerusalem had become extremely wealthy. Josephus tells us that when the Romans destroyed the temple in 70 CE, there was so much gold that its price throughout the Middle East was halved. There are various estimations of the taxation burden, ranging from 29–40 per cent.

Moreover, one must remember that each of the ruling authorities, including the temple, had its own military forces, and the Romans regarded any refusal to pay the tribute as an act of rebellion. This was reinforced through a reign of terror, the principal instrument of which was crucifixion, a form of torture leading to death, which was never imposed upon Roman citizens but was used to ensure the subjection of conquered populations.

How did the temple and the aristocratic families who ran it and profited from it maintain their control over the population? This was done mainly through various techniques of mind control. A significant element within this dominating ideology was the demand for ritual purity in accordance with certain aspects of the Torah. The scrolls of the Law would have been rare and costly and may not often have been found outside Jerusalem. In any case, most of the people were illiterate. A class of scribes was employed by the temple authorities to teach the law and to enforce it. The purity code is mainly found in the books of Exodus, Numbers and Leviticus and was based upon the concept of holiness that had to be protected from profane contamination. If somebody or something holy came into contact with something that was not holy, the resulting uncleanness would have to be put right through means of the sacrificial system. This involved a presentation of livestock, such as a sheep or a goat if the sinner could afford it, and a pair of doves or a portion of the finest flour in the case of poor people. These were all agricultural or farming products, and must have been an additional burden upon the hard-pressed people.

The very architecture of the temple enshrined this ideology of separation. The outer court could be entered by everybody, including people who were not Jewish, but only Jews could go into the next court, and only Jewish men into the one after that. Priests were more holy than other Jewish men, and the next court was for them. The high priest was most holy, and he alone could go into the sanctuary itself, and even that only under certain conditions. Jerusalem was holy because the temple was in it, and the land as a whole was holy because Jerusalem was in it. Beyond the borders of the land, holiness was completely overtaken by 'uncleanness'. To enter the house of a non-Jew would make a Jew ritually unclean and one would be ritually contaminated by sharing a meal with someone who was not ritually pure. It was hard for the villagers to pay the temple tax on top of all the rest, but if they did not pay, thus breaking a commandment of Torah, they were in danger of becoming ritually impure. Indeed, the divine guarantee of rainfall and good crops depended upon keeping the law, and this was something that peasant farmers would not like to risk.

Galilee itself was a place where people of many backgrounds mixed. It had been settled by the Assyrian conquerors centuries earlier, and was a crossroads for trade. It was thus generally regarded as inferior to Judea.

What would Elijah and Elisha have done in such a situation? They were figures of great repute who had worked in the north of what was then Israel and was subsequently known as Galilee. They had defended the people against an alien and vicious ruler who had polluted the land with idolatry. They provided food and healing for the people, and defended the traditional land rights of the peasantry (1 Kings 21.1–26).

One must remember that it was not merely the occasional act of contact which might have rendered an individual unclean, but the whole country was polluted by the Roman soldiers, whose standards carried the images of their gods. Certainly, they were discreetly garrisoned in Caesarea, a Hellenized Roman city on the coast built by Herod. Roman troops were seldom seen in Galilee, and not often in Judea except at Passover time when additional troops were brought from Caesarea to provide added security. The Roman coins were circulated throughout the land with their idolatrous images and blasphemous inscriptions. One of the functions of the money changers in the temple was to protect its sanctity by changing the secular coinage for the sacred money recognized by the temple.

The prophetic protest

What would Micah have done in such a situation? How would Jeremiah have behaved? A number of prophets in the first century gave various answers. One led a party of his followers up Mount Gerizim in Samaria; another took his followers to the banks of the Jordan River, expecting its waters to roll back as they had done for Joshua; another brought a crowd of at least 3,000 disciples to the Mount of Olives outside Jerusalem, telling them that the walls would fall down just as the walls of Jericho had done. None of these expectations were fulfilled, and the Roman procurators had no difficulty in sending detachments of cavalry to scatter, arrest or kill them.

Among these prophets, perhaps the most famous because of the place given to him in the Gospels, was John the Baptist. In a society where the poor were suffering from austerity, he recommended that people should share; he even instructed the soldiers of Herod Antipas not to exploit the people. In offering a baptism for the forgiveness of sins, he must have known that he was setting up a form of purity different from that of the temple. As Robert Webb says, 'John's baptism provided an alternative to the temple's sacrificial system as a means of forgiveness' (Webb 1991, p. 203). In criticizing the private life of Herod Antipas and in describing the Sadducees and scribes, who came from Jerusalem to hear him, as a nest of vipers, John had challenged both the religious and political authorities. The account of his execution in Mark 6 gives us a rare glimpse into the wealth, luxury, arbitrary government and sexual degradation which was typical of the way elite classes lived (vv. 17–28).

All this must have been very clear to Jesus. As he grew up, he would have been told of the terrible cruelty of the Romans, who had executed thousands of his fellow countrymen only a few years earlier. Instead of leading a public revolt, Jesus attempted to create a renewal movement in the Galilean villages. He himself was of peasant stock and would have had a vivid, first-hand experience of conditions in the villages. Very quickly his work attracted the attention of the temple authorities, who began to hate and fear him as he undermined the purity laws and ignored and bypassed their status as gatekeepers of the divine forgiveness and blessing.

When he touched the man with the skin disease (Mark 1.40–5), Jesus instantly lost his own ritual purity. As a person faithful to the law, he should have gone straight to the temple himself and offered a sacrifice for his transgression, which was very serious, since it was not the result of accident or ignorance. However, the flow of the sacred energy, if we can speak like that, went the other way. The unclean man was purified. No wonder Jesus was angry at this example of the way that the purity law led to exclusion and isolation for the sick man (Lev. 13.45–46). The instruction to go and show himself to the priests was tantamount to a direct challenge, since the man had already been healed. The reports of this incident would have made Jesus notorious, and this is probably why he had to avoid the larger towns and confine his work to the more remote villages.

When Jesus pronounced the forgiveness of the sins of the man lowered through the roof in Mark 2, he was not committing blasphemy. In using the passive form of the verb, 'Your sins are forgiven' (2.5), he did not personally claim to forgive sins but declared, as the broker of the new kingdom, that the man had been forgiven. When he said that 'the Son of Man' had authority to forgive sins, it is not clear that he was referring to himself. His general approach had the effect of humanizing and simplifying life, and it is possible that the saying simply means that it is a truly human action to forgive sins. It is also possible that he was referring to the eschatological Son of Man, who would one day offer forgiveness. In any case, the idea that he was challenging the prerogatives of the temple had already occurred to the scribes (2.6–7). The representatives of the purity code, the scribes, found it shocking, because it violated the accepted channel of forgiveness, the sacrificial system, and opened up new levels of freedom for the people.

This is nowhere seen more clearly than in two stories, both of which are found in all three Synoptic Gospels. In the first one, the outer garment of Jesus is touched by a woman with a menstrual flow. According to Leviticus 15.19–30, anyone who touches even the bed upon which such a woman was sitting would be unclean. The woman must have known that in touching even his outer garment, she would render Jesus ritually unclean, and she tried her best to minimize the damage by touching only the tassel of the garment (Matt. 9.20; Luke 8.44). Nevertheless, the 'purity knowledge' was awoken, and as in the case of the leper, it flowed the other way. If Jesus was made unclean, he showed no awareness of it, but the woman was instantly cured. Most significant of all is what happened next. Leviticus 15.28 declares that 'if she shall be cleansed of her discharge, she must count seven days, and after that she shall be clean'. Then 'on the eighth day, she shall take two turtle doves or two pigeons and bring them to the priest . . . who shall use one of them for a sin offering . . . and the priest shall make atonement for her before the Lord for her unclean discharge' (vv. 29–30).

Jesus ignored all that. Turning to the woman, he immediately accepted her into the family of God by calling her not an unclean woman but a 'daughter', and simply told her that her faith had made her whole, not the turtle doves or the priest, but her trust in the mercy of God.

As if that was not enough, according to Mark, Jesus goes on almost immediately to break the purity code again by touching a dead body (Mark 5.35–41; c.f. Num. 19.11). Again, he is undamaged, but the little girl is restored to life.

I am not suggesting that Jesus set out to deliberately break the purity code; he simply ignored it in the interests of the immediate relief of human misery. This is nowhere seen more clearly than the exorcism of the man who lived among the tombs (Mark 5.1–13). Here we find an accumulation of factors which were unclean: the man was possessed, he lived among the dead, in a non-Jewish territory further contaminated by the presence of pigs, which were unclean animals. Breaking through all these considerations, Jesus went straight to the afflicted person with the question, 'What is your name?' (v. 9).

There was probably little the temple authorities could do about his activities, as long as he remained in the relative safety of Galilee, where he avoided the larger towns and moved frequently from village to village. However, when he was determined to take his message and his actions to Jerusalem itself, the very centre of the powers hostile to him, he knew full well that he was entering a dangerous situation (Mark 8.31, 9.31, 10.33). His dramatic entry into the city accompanied by crowds of admirers was the last straw as far as the authorities were concerned. They soon found an opportunity to arrest him, and before the following day had come to an end the prophet from Nazareth had been executed.

The work of the prophet and the renewal of the kingdom

The Gospel of Mark contains the oldest memories of the prophetic work of Jesus. He is described as the Christ in the first verse of the Gospel, but that title is not heard again until Mark 8.29, when Peter recognizes him. The intervening sections are best understood as an account of his messianic practice, marked, so to speak, at both the beginning and the end by the use of the messianic title.

Mark 9.2–8 puts the stamp of approval upon his prophetic work by associating him with the two greatest of the old prophets, Moses and Elijah, and we do not come upon the messianic title again until Mark 14.61, where it is used in a hostile sense by the high priest. The rest of the Gospel is really an extended account of his journey to Jerusalem and its outcome.

Fernando Belo (1981), in his ground-breaking study of Mark's Gospel, exaggerates the distinction between what he calls the purity code and the debt code, the latter being essentially the ethical requirements of the law, as distinct from its ritual observances. He remarks that traces of the debt code are found in Leviticus. In fact, Leviticus 19 is entirely devoted to what we would call ethics, and Jesus quotes from verse 18 the commandment to love the neighbour.

Mary Douglas (2000), however, argues for the unity of the book, which is modelled upon the structure of the Tabernacle, the dwelling place of God in the wilderness. It was divided into three sections: the court of the people, from whence the sacrifices offered by the priests were visible, which corresponds to Chapters 1–7; the court of the priests, which deals with the obligations of the priests as opposed to those of the ordinary people; and finally the holy sanctuary, the ethical instruction of Chapter 19. The book of Leviticus is set out as a sort of imaginative guide through these various parts of the Tabernacle, each part being divided from the next by a chapter acting as a sort of barrier. Now, if we think of Jesus as seeking to renew the ancient demands and promises of the covenant, it is as if he does not bother about the two preliminary areas, but goes straight into the holy place, the place where love of the neighbour becomes the very heart of faithful obedience. He shortcuts the way to forgiveness and the way to God.

The message of the prophets was the same: 'For I desire mercy, not sacrifice, and acknowledgment of God rather than burnt offerings' (Hos. 6.6).

In Matthew's Gospel, Jesus refers to this verse twice (9.13, 12.7), and on both occasions, it is in connection with food, always the main preoccupation of impoverished people. Several times in Mark's Gospel we are told that Jesus preached 'the word' (2.2, 4.13–20, 4.33), but we are never given any details about what this consisted of. We may infer that 'the word' refers to the actions which occupy Chapters 1–8 of the Gospel.

However, we are given a hint in Mark 1.14. The text says that Jesus went into Galilee 'proclaiming the good news of God'. The fact that what follows is not what he proclaimed, as it were, on that occasion, but what he 'was proclaiming', indicates that what follows is a summary of his message: 'The time has come . . . The kingdom of God has come near. Repent and believe the good news' (1.15). In these verses, twice we are told that what he announced was 'good news', and the content of the good news was that 'the time has come', and the kingdom of God 'has come near'.

As we saw at the start of this chapter, the meaning of the prophetic work of Jesus has been obscured by later Christological developments, and the original meaning of the kingdom of God has become something of a Christian cliché, a heading in books of systematic theology and, consistent with the view that Jesus was a spiritual teacher, has become interpreted as a spiritual kingdom: the reign of love in people's hearts. Let us, however, ask ourselves what those who heard this message would have understood by it. We need to ask what the temple authorities would have heard Jesus saying, what Herod Antipas would have heard, and what the Romans, when they finally heard it, would have thought. Above all, we must try to feel what the ordinary people would have thought when they heard this.

For the temple authorities, the Sadducees and their scribes, the expression 'kingdom of God' would have carried all sorts of traditional meanings. It would, perhaps, have reminded them of the roughly 500 years when Israel and Judah were monarchies, but at the same time, it might also have been understood as implying a criticism of the monarchs. The very idea that it was the kingdom of God, and not the kingdom of Herod or of Solomon, or even of David, might have suggested a certain reservation. This becomes more likely if we consider the situation in ancient Israel before the monarchy was founded, i.e. from about 1250 to 1050 BCE. During this period of 200 years, Israel, simply known as 'the people of Yahweh', had no monarchy. Indeed, there was a powerful strain of hostility towards the very idea of monarchy. We see this, for example, in the refusal of Gideon to become a ruler on the grounds that Yahweh alone was the ruler of Israel (Judg. 8.23), in the fiercely ironic parable of how the thorn bush became king of the forest (9.8–15), and in the graphic description of the tyranny which would be the effect of creating a monarchy, spoken by Samuel when the people wanted him to appoint a king (1 Sam. 8.10–18). In fact, it was Yahweh himself who was strongly against the creation of the monarchy: 'it is not you they have rejected, but they have rejected me as their king' (1 Sam. 8.7). Israel would cease to be the kingdom of God, when a human king was chosen.

It seems likely that the various groups who became known as the people of Yahweh were refugees, who had escaped from the domination of the Canaanite cities and made their way into the hill country, where they were joined by rebels, runaway slaves and bandits who were already living in those more remote areas. Here they formed a sort of alliance, a loose affiliation of agriculturalists with no central government. They were also joined by a number of other escaped slaves who had passed through the desert on their way from Egypt, where they had suffered from the cruel exploitation of Pharaoh. This exodus group brought with them a new ideology centred upon the God Yahweh, who had delivered them from Egyptian slavery. Whereas the gods of Egypt and the Canaanite cities were aristocratic deities, projections of royal power who offered legitimation to the powerful dynasties, Yahweh was a friend of slaves, a freedom-loving God, a God of the people instead of a god of the aristocracy. It seems to have been faith in Yahweh as the liberating God that created the ideology and the social structures which bound the diverse hill people together in a covenant of loyalty to each other and to Yahweh. Samuel had told the people that if they were to have a king, they would 'become his slaves' (1 Sam. 8.17).

During this interlude of about 200 years, poised, as it were, between a freedom lost in the past and one soon to be lost again, there are few signs of what was to become classical Hebrew prophesy. In common with other cultures of the ancient Middle East, there were seers, mediums and diviners (Josh. 13.22; 1 Sam. 9.9, 28.3), but the characteristic features of the prophetic tradition do not appear until the conditions of the covenant with Yahweh were blatantly ignored. The roots of the prophetic tradition lay in military charisma (Judg. 4.4–9), Samuel being an intermediate figure, both seer and prophet (1 Sam. 3.20, 9.19), as was Gad (2 Sam. 24.11), but not until the injustices of the tenth century BCE do we find the classical Hebrew prophet in Elijah and Elisha. It is as if in such figures, and even more so with the eighth century BCE prophets Amos and Hosea, the nature of the kingdom of God had to be reasserted against the political regimes of both the northern and the southern kingdoms. In other words, it was oppression that stirred up the spirit of prophetic criticism in order to protect the freedoms of the people and to insist that the kings and queens should observe the terms of the covenant between Yahweh and the people.

An essential feature of this covenant related to the land itself. The whole of the territory of Israel belonged to Yahweh, its King.

> The idea is essentially to achieve justice and righteousness in the land. Freedom means that no one can be permanently enslaved, debts are to be cancelled, and land returned to its original owners in the jubilee year. To be able to promise this Leviticus has to insist that the land belongs to God, he is the owner, and the people are his tenants using it by right of a divine grant or contract. (Douglas 2000, p. 243)

This was the famous Year of Jubilee, which was prefigured in the Sabbath, the seventh day, when the people were to rest and not work. This tradition, that there could be no genuine ruler of Israel or Judah except God, had persisted down the centuries and was very much alive in the first century of our era.

It is against the background of God as the owner of the land that we must understand the agricultural parables of Jesus. The farming land described in Mark 4.3–8 would yield abundant crops when it received the word of God, but would otherwise be relatively barren. We are reminded of the land where the seeds grow in secret (4.26–9), where the mustard plant grew (4.30–2) and where the treasure was hidden (Matt. 13.44). Agricultural labourers would have been sensitive to the implications of the story of the land, the vineyard of Yahweh (Isa. 5.1, 7), which had come into the possession of alien, absent landowners, and to the violence of those who may well have been owners of the land before the vineyard was created (Mark 12.1b–9).

The land, as it was in the first century, was very far from being the kingdom of God, conquered by a brutal and alien enemy and reigned over by a cruel family, only part Jewish. The land had become corrupted with idolatry, statues of the Greek and Roman deities and images of the so-called divine emperor even on the coins. This helps us to understand the contemptuous dismissal of the profane and blasphemous Roman coins, when Jesus said that the people of Israel should give the Roman coins back to the people who had made them and the revolutionary nature of the comment about giving to God what belonged to God, i.e. the land itself (Mark 12.17).

The monarchs of the Herodian dynasty would have been well aware of the implications of the expression 'kingdom of God'. Herod the Great was extremely sensitive to the question, 'Where is the one who has been born king of the Jews?' (Matt. 2.2), and had the star gazers from the East been aware of it, the very asking of that question could have led to their execution. Only Herod's anxiety to discover the new born king saved them. Herod's announcement that he wanted to pay homage to his successor must have struck them as odd. It was in a dream that they were warned to escape (v. 12), although the expression on Herod's face might have been enough (v. 3)!

We can also understand the desire of Herod Antipas to silence Jesus and to prevent him from carrying out his messianic practice of liberation (Luke 13.31) and the extraordinary risk taken by Jesus when he replied by insulting Antipas and insisting that he would go on doing exactly the same as before, knowing full well that in so doing he was doomed to meet the fate of the prophets (13.32–3). Another example of Jesus' mockery of royal wealth and power is when he suggested that Antipas was like a reed swaying in the wind and was one of those who wore expensive clothes in palaces and indulged in luxury (7.24–5), contrasting this with the life of a simple prophet (7.24–6).

The coins of Herod the Great carried the inscription 'Kingdom of Herod' together with symbols indicating that he claimed the titles of both king and high priest. The reed and the palm branch on the coins of Herod Antipas might perhaps have reminded people of the saying of Jesus about the reed swaying in the wind and of the palm branches used at his entry into Jerusalem. By the way, speaking of coins and of taxation, the strange little story about the coin in the fish's mouth (Matt. 17.24–7), suggests that Jesus regarded both the Roman tribute and the taxation demands of the temple authorities as being alien, from which the children of the kingdom were free. There is a hint of amused contempt for the taxation system when he tells Peter to find a coin in the fish's mouth to pay the tax, lest offense should be caused.

Turning now to the Romans, Jesus was certainly aware of the Roman power and of the threat it posed to the very existence of the nation. News had evidently penetrated Galilee about the atrocity committed by Pilate, who had mixed the blood of Galilean worshippers with the sacrifice they were offering, and it seems possible from the context that the collapse of the Tower of Siloam was a similar atrocity (Luke 13.1–5). When Jesus said that they would all suffer in the same way unless they repented, he was not referring to inward conversion of a Christian kind, but to the ever present threat of Roman brutality. The repentance that was demanded was the same repentance which Jesus called for at his first proclamation of the kingdom of God (Luke 13.1–5; cf. Mark 1.15). The warnings about the need to be armed (Luke 22.36) and about those who use the sword dying by the sword (Matt. 26.52) seem to express the same sense of imminent danger. It is widely agreed that Mark 13, sometimes known as 'the little apocalypse', does not only refer to some approaching apocalyptic event beyond history, but to the impending destruction of the country by Rome. The sanctuary would be violated (v. 14) and everyone in Judea would become refugees (v. 14–16). The whole chapter breathes an ominous spirit of crisis, which would fall upon this present generation (v. 30). The authorities of the temple state were well aware that the actions of Jesus might bring down upon the country the wrath of Rome (John 11.47–8). Jesus seems to have regarded his own crucifixion as a mere preliminary to the more widespread horrors that would occur later (Luke 23.26–31). Josephus tells us that during the Roman siege of Jerusalem in 70 CE, thousands of people were crucified.

Perhaps the clearest indication of Jesus' prophetic foreboding is found in his lament over Jerusalem (Matt. 23.37–8; Luke 13.34–5). Jesus says, 'Look, your house is left to you desolate.' Many versions translate 'house' as 'temple'. While it would be natural to think that the house of God in Jerusalem would be the temple, it is also possible that the reference is to the whole of the temple state. The covenant people as a whole were described as the house of Israel; in Exodus 40.38, for example, the 'house of Israel' is distinguished from the tabernacle. So it is possible that the lamentation is not only over the temple, but over the country as a whole. One is reminded of the sayings of the prophet Jeremiah in the last days of Jerusalem lamenting over the fall of the city (14.16–17, 15.5).

The Roman reaction to Jesus and to his proclamation of the kingdom of God is seen quite clearly in the question which Pilate asked: 'Are you the king of the Jews?' (John 18.33). He was unimpressed by the reply of Jesus that 'My kingdom is not of this world' (v. 36), hence his exclamation: 'So you are a king, then!' (v. 37). Jesus did not unambiguously describe himself as a king, but his references to 'the kingdom' were enough for Pilate. It was not the Roman custom to stand idly by when peasants from the provinces started to talk about their kingdoms. Pilate believed Jesus was a real threat, just as Herod the Great all those years before. This is why the Romans put him to death with other similar troublemakers, describing him as 'the king of the Judeans' (v. 38).

We have considered the negative way the teaching of Jesus about the kingdom of God would have been heard by the temple authorities, the Herodian dynasts and the Romans. The common people, on the other hand, received his teaching with gladness (Mark 1.27, 2.12, 7.37; Luke 7.16, 8.40). When the people heard him attack the royal pretensions of the house of David, they 'heard him with delight' (Mark 12.35–7). They were delighted because he was one of them and was taking on the temple officials, playing their own game and beating them.

The living God and the money-god

An important part of Jesus' prophetic mission was his approach to the problems of taxation and debt, and his attitudes toward poverty and wealth. Money was the rival to God (Matt. 6.24). Jesus said that it would be hard for rich people to enter the kingdom of God, and at this comment the disciples were amazed (Mark 10.23–4). When Jesus followed this up by saying that it would be easier for a camel to go through the eye of a needle than for a rich person to enter the kingdom of God, they were 'even more amazed' (vv. 25–6). Sometimes this blunt saying is moralized or spiritualized, so that it is said that the camel had to get rid of its burden or lower its head to pass through the tiny side gate in the wall, but whether the 'eye of the needle' was a tiny gate or a metaphor from sewing, the meaning is clear. It is ludicrous to suppose that a camel could pass through it, and it is just as preposterous to think that humanly speaking, rich people can enter the kingdom of God; not only so, but their place would be taken by the poor (Luke 6.20–4). The small number of rich and the large number of poor are separated by a great abyss. It divides these two social classes from each other in this present life and will continue into the next where it will be equally impassable, although in reverse (16.19–31). This reversal was not confined to the next life, but was the demand of the kingdom of God here and now. The property owner who asked Jesus about eternal life understood this clearly, which is why 'he went away sad because he had great wealth' (Mark 10.17–22). Jesus had no doubt struck a note when, to the usual commandments, he shrewdly added 'you shall not defraud' (10.19).

Jesus set out a kind of manifesto for his forthcoming work when he spoke in the synagogue at Nazareth (Luke 4.16–19).

The Spirit of the Lord is on me, because he has anointed me to proclaim good news to the poor. He has sent me to proclaim freedom for the prisoners and recovery of sight for the blind, to set the oppressed free, to proclaim the year of the Lord's favour.

Jesus here, according to Luke, combined two passages from the final chapters of Isaiah, the work of the prophet of the restoration. The exiles had returned from Babylon and a new priestly state was being created. This unknown prophet believed himself to be an anointed one (i.e. a Messiah or a Christ), calling the people back to the central features of the ancient covenant with the God of freedom and justice. It is striking that he included in this message a warning about the coming 'day of vengeance of our God' (Isa. 61.2), words which his successor, the anointed one of Nazareth, omitted. Jesus finished his quotation with the words 'to proclaim the year of the Lord's favour' (Luke 4.19), stopping suddenly before the reference to judgment. It seems likely that both Jesus and the anonymous prophet of the late sixth century BCE were referring to the Jubilee Year, when, as we saw above, the original equality of the people was to be restored in a gracious act of levelling.

The first prophetic task of the anointed one is 'to proclaim good news to the poor' (Luke 4.18). The idea of 'good news', or 'the gospel', was not originally religious, and perhaps we today misconstrue it, if we think of it as primarily religious. It became a technical expression in later years for the essential message of Christian faith, but before this, its meaning was more secular and more ordinary.

The English nouns 'evangel' and 'gospel' have identical meanings; 'gospel' originates in the northern European languages and 'evangel' from the southern European languages. Evangel (verb to evangelize) comes from the Middle English *evaungel*. This is derived from the Late Latin *evangelium*, which in turn comes from the Greek *euangelion*, comprising a noun *angelos*: a messenger, an angel plus a prefix *eu* = good, hence one who speaks of what is good.

Turning now to the northern European languages, 'gospel' comes from the Old English *gōdspel* in which *gōd* means good and *spel* = news, speech, tale. This comes from the Old Norse *guthspjall* and the Old High German *guotspell*. Note that the modern English word 'spell' can mean words that charm or break an enchantment or induce a trance-like state.

These are not religious words but purely secular indications of favourable speech or good news. This is consistent with its use in ancient Greece where 'to evangelize' was used to announce a victory in battle or any communication whether private or public which was a message of joy, such as the birth of a child or a promotion.

The identity of gospel and evangel can be seen in the fact that the authors of the four Gospels are known as the four evangelists. Hence to evangelize with the gospel would be to express a truism.

The biblical background to the New Testament concept of 'good news' is found in Isaiah 40.9: 'You who bring good news to Zion, go up on a high mountain. You who bring good news to Jerusalem, lift up your voice with a shout.' In Isaiah 41.27 God says: 'I was the first to tell Zion, "Look, here they are!" I gave to Jerusalem a messenger of good news.' In Isaiah 52.7 he proclaims:

> How beautiful on the mountains are the feet of those who bring good news, who proclaim peace, who bring good tidings, who proclaim salvation, who say to Zion, 'Your God reigns!'

The good news was the intervention of God into a situation where a refugee people had been kept in captivity. It may be thought of as applying to all dislocated people. As its use in Isaiah shows, the context was historical and political as well as religious. It was religious, because the ancient Israelites did not distinguish between religion and politics the way we tend to do in the modern West. Because we separate them, it is the social and political meaning which tends to disappear and only the religious remains.

Compare this with Mark 1.14, 'After John was put in prison, Jesus went into Galilee, proclaiming the good news of God.' We have the same conjunction of a captivity followed by the good news of divine intervention. Jesus now took the expression 'good news' from Isaiah, and applied it to the poor people of Galilee. This involved 'freedom for the prisoners and recovery of sight for the blind' (Luke 4.18). Both these expressions were probably intended in a literal sense, as is indicated by the restoration of sight by Jesus to blind people, although the idea of opening the eyes of the poor people so that they have a better insight into their social situation should not be ruled out. However, one thing was lacking from Isaiah 61. Jesus, or Luke's interpretation of Jesus, wanted to emphasize the current oppression which the people were experiencing. In order to strengthen this emphasis, a little snippet from Isaiah 58.6 was taken: 'to set the oppressed free'. The context of Isaiah 58 is just as significant in understanding the prophetic work of Jesus as Chapter 61. It reads:

> Is not this the kind of fasting I have chosen: to loose the chains of injustice and untie the cords of the yoke, to set the oppressed free and break every yoke? Is it not to share your food with the hungry and to provide the poor wanderer with shelter – when you see the naked, to clothe them, and not to turn away from your own flesh and blood? (Isa. 58.6–7)

We are reminded of the saying 'my yoke is easy' (Matt. 11.30) and of the breaking of the oppressive yoke in Isaiah 9.4 and 10.27. We are also reminded of the feeding of the hungry, the welcome to strangers and the clothing of the naked of Matthew 25.35–45.

Similar emphases are found in the prayer which Jesus taught his disciples at their request (Matt. 6.9–13; Luke 11.2–4). This must be seen as relevant to the work of Jesus among the Galilean villagers. There is a concrete, human quality about it. We are not told to pray for blessings or for God's grace, but for bread, the basic need of daily life. The expression 'forgive our sins' does not refer to moral shortcomings or offenses committed against God, but to release from debt. The verb *aphiēmi* means 'to get rid of, to send away or to cancel'. The same word is used in the proclamation at Nazareth (Luke 4.18): the release *(aphesis)* of the captives probably means cancelling the debts of those who were in prison as debtors. It is relevant to note that many of the occasions when the Gospels refer to imprisonment, it is because of debt.

Both Matthew and Luke use the verb *aphiēmi* in their versions of the prayer, and Matthew specifically uses the word for debts. Hence, 'cancel our debts' would be a perfectly legitimate translation of the Matthean version. Problems of falling into debt were widespread in Galilee where a village farmer might have to buy grain for the harvest, only to find that if the rains failed, the harvest would not be plentiful enough for him to repay the debt. People must have been borrowing from each other, and perhaps this was causing the breakdown of many friendships. In his work for the renewal of community life, Jesus goes straight to the economic heart of the problem: 'Cancel our debts just as we cancel the debts of our neighbours,' The prayers for both the bread and the debt fall within the meaning of the coming of the kingdom, which is the principle purpose of the prayer as a whole.

Many of the stories which Jesus told offer critical insights into the way that Palestinian society was functioning. There is a powerful description of the lives of the day wage labourers in the parable of the workers who were employed at different hours of the day (Matt. 20.1–16). These men would probably have become day labourers through the loss of their traditional land, perhaps through debt or some form of confiscation. No longer able to work as subsistence agriculturalists, they would have been forced to seek employment from the owners of the large estates. If work was not available, the workers and their families would go to bed hungry. In the story, the owner is careful not to employ too many men. He waits to see how the harvesting proceeds before going back to the market place to employ more workers. Having decided to pay all the men the same, he could have avoided trouble by paying first those who had worked all day, so by the time it became clear that he was paying everybody the same wage, those who had worked all day would have taken their money and gone. To pay them in reverse order was provocative. Not only was the inequality obvious to everybody, but the implication was that the labour of those who had worked longer was worthless. The perfectly natural protest is met by the owner's astonishing claim that he can do what he liked with what he owned. There is no sense here of stewardship or of community responsibility, although the money must have been gained through the labour of workers in previous years. The patronizing comment, 'Take your pay and get out' (20.14) sums up the situation of working people on these estates. It is against this kind of situation that we can understand the meaning of the prayer: 'Your kingdom come, your will be done on earth as in heaven. Give us our daily bread, and cancel our debts.'

Another picture of the sensitive relations between the rich and the poor is found in the story of the money lender and the shrewd peasant (Matt. 25.14–30). When the overlord rewarded the two successful entrepreneurs by putting them 'in charge of many things', he probably meant to promote them into higher positions in his own financial affairs or even, perhaps, to give them the right to collect taxes from certain areas. And so the cycle of extraction would continue.

The third man had the courage to resist. He broke the cycle by putting the money back into the ground, the only source of true wealth. He confronted the principle moneylender to his face, telling him the bald truth, which was that he was trying to make profit where he had not worked. One is reminded of the essential difference between the aristocrats and the peasants: The peasants worked but did not enjoy the fruits of their labour, while the aristocrats enjoyed the fruits of others' labour and did not work themselves.

The temple was a major centre of financial power. In considering the attitude of Jesus toward the temple, one must remember that the temple was not a purely religious institution. It was a major employer, not only of priests but of scribes, of stone masons and workmen of all kinds, of security forces, moneychangers and of those who provided the animals for the sacrificial system. It also owned extensive landed estates and, most important of all, it was the centre of control over the hearts and minds of people from Galilee and Judea. It was the focus of the identity of Israel. Jesus realized that the wealth of the temple mostly came from the gifts of poor people, many of whom could not afford to give (Mark 12.42). In other words, the temple functioned, like most temples in the ancient world, as a form of social control through coalition with God. It was the temple authorities who had most to lose if new relationships with God were opened up. Jesus was aware of the legalism and the superficial morality of much that went on in the temple (Luke 18.10–14). The temple was the fig tree that had not produced any fruit, and its cursing was symbolic of the destruction of the whole place (Mark 11.12–21). Jesus was critical of the Temple not only because of its market activities, but because it represented exclusion. It reinforced the difference between 'us' and 'them', when it should have become a place of prayer for all the nations (11.17).

It was widely believed that Jesus had threatened to destroy the temple, or at least that the temple would be destroyed. This was claimed by the 'false witnesses' at his trumped-up trial (14.57–58), and was the impression left by his ominous prediction that not one stone of the temple would be left standing upon another (13.1–2). Indeed, the whole of his public work could be described as an attack, direct or indirect, upon the authority of the temple state. Although his onslaught upon the temple was carried out in broad daylight, as the week went on, he and his disciples preferred to move around in secrecy, no doubt aware of the increasing hostility that he had aroused.

The prophetic mission: failure or success?

What the next stage in the prophetic work of Jesus might have been, it is impossible for us to tell. The campaign which had begun in Galilee reached its climax in Jerusalem, but then was brought to a heart-wrenching halt. The exact circumstances surrounding his death remain a mystery. It is possible that the bystanders were correct in thinking that he had called upon Elijah to help him (Mark 15.34–6). It was Elijah who had followed him throughout his work in Galilee, had discussed his death on the mountain of transfiguration, but who had now apparently abandoned him. At any rate, it seems that while the heavens which were split open to acknowledge him as the divine Son (Mark 1.10) were now closed, the veil of the temple was split in two (Mark 15.38).

Had the prophetic mission failed? This seems to have been the view of the disappointed disciples who walked the road to Emmaus on that lonely Sunday (Luke 24.21), and there was also a trace of disappointment in the last question the disciples were able to ask him: 'Lord, are you at this time going to restore the kingdom to Israel?' (Acts 1.6). Mark's Gospel ends in a profound and terrified silence (16.8). Matthew's account of the resurrection is full of noise and activity: A mighty angel descends, the stone is rolled away, the petrified guards must have cried out, and we imagine the crash of their armour as they fell to the ground. In Mark, on the other hand, it is strangely quiet; the young man clothed in white, sitting in the empty tomb, tells the startled women that Jesus has gone ahead of them into Galilee where they will see him. The Galilean work was to continue. From that day until now, wherever his disciples gather to renew his prophetic work, he rises again and again.

Prophesy, Christology and discipleship

The prophet from Nazareth left behind him an indelible memory, and that memory was subversive. Although Paul never describes Jesus as a prophet, the subversive memory of the one who had deceived the authorities and the powers and had made a fool of them, seemed to grow more powerful. The Roman cross, the symbol of the final defeat of the prophetic hope, soon became the only thing Paul really knew. As he identified himself with that symbol of shame and apparently futile protest, Paul's own mission to subvert the values of Rome became both more insistent and more subtle. It took more than 300 years to bring that mission to completion. By that time, the Christ, who had opposed the Empire, had himself become an imperial figure. The Church began to suppress the disturbing character of the eschatological hope, and the prophetic work of Jesus was almost forgotten. It proved to be more convenient to worship him as Christ, Son of God and Lord, then to follow him as prophet. In a profound and lasting sense, Christology has proved to be the enemy of prophesy. Jesus is remembered as having said that no prophet is without honour except in his own country and among his own people. The Church of today believes that it represents his people, and the prophetic saying of Jesus has once again been fulfilled.

Part 2

The Betrayal of the Prophetic Church

In my previous study of the factors which prevent Christian adults from learning (Hull 1985) I dealt mainly with the nature and role of faith in the human development of individual adults. I considered problems like the desire to retain infantile security and the need to allow faith to change and mature as we ourselves do so. However, I also discussed faith as an ideology created by the values of our monetized culture and the false consciousness which is produced by the distortions of power. In this second part of the book, I deal in greater detail with the way that the faith of the Western Church has been profoundly changed by its social and political context. In other words, although Christendom has long since passed away, the Christian faith it generated still lingers on, sometimes in the innocence of an accepted tradition, but sometimes in the shrewdness of a religion that has learned how to resist its own prophetic roots.

Chapter 4 presents a case study of the Western Church at the height of its power. While we no longer sing 'Onward, Christian Soldiers Marching as to War', the assumptions of aggressive power lie just beneath the surface. Chapter 5 describes the oldest Atlantic colonies of Britain and shows how Christian faith had to be adapted in order to become the ideology of Empire, and Chapter 6 on the hymns of Isaac Watts argues that these values have permeated Christian spirituality and theology. In spite of this, the generosity and compassion of the prophet of Nazareth were never entirely lost. There have always been moments when the hardness of the self-interested Church has come face to face with its true self. Such encounters usually took place in some situation of extremity, when faith had been shaken from its normality by the approach of otherness. Three such encounters are described in Chapter 7. The factors that prevent Christian adults from learning can be overcome.

4

The Christian Crusades of the Eleventh to Thirteenth Centuries

We have seen how in the demand of the prophets for justice, and in the life and work of Jesus Christ, the prophetic tradition became the mission of prophetic love. We must now consider some of the ways in which that failed.

[A] religion, which breaks radically with particular and idolatrous conceptions of the meaning of life, can never carry through consistently what it has established in basic principle. Even a Christian missionary enterprise can never completely overcome certain imperialistic corruptions which arise from the historic relation of the missionary enterprise to particular powerful nations and cultures. (Niebuhr 1949, p. 28)

Love and power in the missionary enterprise

In the history of the Christian mission, we see a religion of love in the midst of the ambiguities of history. The two central ironies of Christian faith are that the redeeming love which made this world its home found nowhere to lay its head, and that those who submitted to this love began to force others to submit to power. This was, perhaps, inevitable because the Christian story 'portrays a love "which seeketh not its own". But a love which seeketh not its own is not able to maintain itself in historical society' (Niebuhr 1943, p. 75).

These characteristics of prophetic love will be illustrated with three case studies. The first will discuss the theology of the Crusades in the eleventh to the thirteenth centuries. We shall then study the transformation that came over Christian faith in the early years of the British Empire, and we shall see how prophetic love was adapted to meet the requirements of expanding colonialism. The third example will be taken from the hymns of Isaac Watts (1674–1746), widely regarded as the founder of the English hymn. Three remarkable encounters will then summarize the ambiguities of prophetic love, the first from England in the seventeenth century representing the encounter between the Church and poverty, the second from America early in the eighteenth century illustrates the ambiguity of the Christian mission in its contacts with other religions. The third encounter will illustrate the competition between Christian faith and the rain makers of south Africa in the work of David Livingstone.

Against this background, an attempt will be made to understand the weaknesses of much contemporary theology and strategy of mission, and it will be claimed that a new search should now be made for the fullness of the mission of prophetic love.

Bernard of Clairvaux

In preparation for the Second Crusade (1146–49), Bernard of Clairvaux (1090–1153) wrote an open letter to the people of England. 'The Lord of heaven', he writes, 'is losing his land, the land in which he appeared to men, in which he lived amongst men for more than thirty years; the land made glorious by his miracles, holy by his blood; the land in which the flowers of his resurrection first blossomed' (1953, Letter 391, p. 461). That land is now threatened by 'the enemy of the Cross', and 'if there should be none to withstand him, he will soon invade the very city of the living God, overturn the arsenal of our redemption, and defile the holy places which had been adorned by the blood of the immaculate lamb'.

Bernard reminds his hearers of 'the time when these holy precincts were cleansed of pagan filth by the swords of our fathers'. He is referring to the remarkable success of the First Crusade (1096–99) in recapturing Jerusalem from the Muslims, and setting up Christian kingdoms in the Eastern Mediterranean. If Jerusalem were to fall again into the hands of the Muslims, it would be an 'endless shame for our generation'.

But why does the omnipotent Lord require our assistance?

Is the hand of the Lord shortened and is he now powerless to work salvation, so that he must call upon us, petty worms of the earth, to save and restore to him his heritage?

Would not a single word from God be sufficient to save God's own land? In reply Bernard begins to unfold his theology of crusading. Certainly, God could restore the land at God's command, but the truth is that 'God has pity on his people and on those who have grievously fallen away and has prepared for them a means of salvation'. 'Look, sinners, at the depths of his pity, and take courage.' If God had intended to punish the people for their sins, 'he would not have asked of you this present service'. A way has been prepared whereby you can satisfy your obligations toward God. God 'puts himself in your debt so that, in return for your taking up arms in his cause, he can reward you with pardon for your sins and everlasting glory' (p. 462). How blessed are we to be alive in this generation! Now the whole world 'is flocking to receive this badge of immortality'.

The English, continues Bernard, are known to be great fighters but now they are being offered 'a cause for which you can fight without danger to your souls; a cause in which to conquer is glorious and for which to die is gain'. In England there are many merchants, 'men quick to seek a bargain'. Bernard offers them a great opportunity too good to miss. 'Take up the sign of the Cross and you will find indulgence for all the sins which you humbly confess. The cost is small, the reward is great.' If this call is taken up in the spirit of devotion, it will become 'a sign of salvation' (p. 462).[1]

---

[1] For the impact of the Crusades on life in England see Tyerman 1988.

Similar letters were sent to the bishops, clergy and people in many parts of eastern France and Germany. The Crusade was expected to pass through parts of eastern Europe and Bernard wrote to 'the Duke of Wladislaus, and the other nobles, and to all the people of Bohemia' (1953, p. 463, Letter 392). This time is, Bernard says, a remarkable time, a day of grace:

> This time is not like any time that has gone before, new riches of divine mercy are descending on you from heaven, and happy are we to be alive in this year of God's choice, this year of jubilee, this year of pardon. (p. 463)

God in his mercy and pity, 'places himself in need of you, or pretends to do so, in order to help you with the riches of heaven' (p. 464).

Insults are being offered to Jesus Christ our king, in that 'they charge him with pretending to be God when he was not'. Therefore those who are loyal to Christ must arise and defend him against 'the shame of such an imputation'. To all who have confessed their sins with truly contrite hearts and who take up the cross of Christ the Supreme Pontiff 'offers a full pardon' (p. 464).

Although Bernard had a practical end in view in his letters and sermons on the Crusades, the recruitment of Crusaders, he also intended to provide a spiritual and theological motivation for them (Tyerman 2004, pp. 96–7). This took the form of a mystical theology of the cross expressed in pilgrimage on the way to holy war (Tyerman 1988, p. 2). As they travelled through suffering to the land which Jesus Christ had hallowed with his own humanity, they would share in his incarnation, visit Jerusalem made sacred by his presence and perhaps share in his death. In this way they would show their gratitude to Christ, receive the forgiveness of sins and inherit eternal life (Cole 1991, pp. 59–60).

Although crusading was primarily a way of Christian discipleship for lay people, the formation of the military orders lifted crusading spirituality to a new height (Forey 1992). The knights were already living in community under the traditional vows of poverty, chastity and obedience, and when they fought for Christendom, they were particularly auspicious. Bernard admired the Knights Templar, who had been recognized by the Holy See in 1129. He addressed a treatise to them encouraging them in their devotion.

> The Knights of Christ may safely fight the battles of their Lord, fearing neither sin if they smite the enemy nor danger at their own death; since to inflict death or to die for Christ is no sin, but rather, an abundant claim to glory. (Bernard, *In Praise of the New Knighthood*, Chapter 3)

Pope Urban II

Although he deepened the theology of its discipleship, Bernard did not create this understanding of taking the cross and following Christ. On 27 November 1095 Pope Urban II (1088–99) concluded the Council of Clermont with a speech in which he called the faithful of Europe to regain the Holy Land, in what was to become the First Crusade. Five versions of his speech have survived. It is difficult to be sure of what the Pope actually said but the interest for us lies in what he was thought to have said, and how this reflects the theology of the Crusade movement (Cole 2013, pp. 1–36). People are not to be deterred from the dangers of the journey, by love of family, for Jesus said, 'he that loveth father or mother more than me is not worthy of me' (Robert the Monk 2005, p. 81). Those who go on pilgrimage are to place the sign of the cross on their forehead or on the breast, and when returning, the cross was to be placed on the back between the shoulders. The pope is said to have referred to the saying of Jesus: '[h]e that taketh not his cross, and followeth after me, is not worthy of me' (p. 82). Another version says that the cross was to be made from cloth and to be sewn onto the right shoulder: 'they followed with one accord the footsteps of Christ by which they had been redeemed' (*Gesta Francorum*).

The object of the pilgrimage was the recovery of Jerusalem. '[T]he holy sepulchre of the Lord our Saviour . . . is possessed by unclean nations . . . and the holy places are now treated with ignominy and irreverently polluted with their filthiness' (Robert the Monk, *Gesta Francorum*). The 'royal city at the centre of the world is now held captive by her enemies and enslaved by those who know nothing of the ways of the people of God' (Robert the Monk 2005, p. 81).

'This very city, in which, as you all know, Christ Himself suffered for us, because our sins demanded it, has been reduced to the pollution of paganism' (Baldreic, *Gesta Francorum*). Jerusalem is the very source of the Christian faith and the origin of its holiness. '[G]lory is indivisibly fixed to His Sepulchre . . . If you reverence the source of that holiness and if you cherish these shrines, which are the marks of His footprints on earth', then pilgrims should 'cleanse the Holy City and the glory of the Sepulchre now polluted by the concourse of the gentiles' (Guibert of Nogent, *Gesta Francorum*).

The Church is the inheritor of the promises of the Old Testament, and the battle for the Holy Land is the continuation of the history of Israel. The conquest of the Holy Land by Joshua has now been undone. Once again, it has been invaded by the pagans, but 'the Holy Church has reserved a soldiery for herself to help her people'. Therefore 'under Jesus Christ our leader may you struggle for your Jerusalem, in your Christian battle line, most invincible line, even more successfully than did the sons of Jacob of old – struggle, that you may assail and drive out the Turks, more execrable than the Jebusites'. Meanwhile, it shall be the duty of the priests 'to pray, yours to fight against the Amalekites. With Moses, we shall extend unwearied hands in prayer to Heaven, while you go forth, to brandish the sword like dauntless warriors, against Amalek' (Balderic, *Gesta Francorum*). The example of the Maccabees proves that it is legitimate to use arms against such oppression (Guibert of Nogent, *Gesta Francorum*).

The sacredness of the expedition is guaranteed not only by its context in the sacred history of the past, but also as pointing toward the promised future. The Antichrist will attack Christians in Jerusalem, and it would be appalling if there were no Christians there to oppose him. 'Jerusalem shall be trodden down by the Gentiles until the times of the Gentiles be fulfilled', thus it is vital that 'the Christian sway be renewed in those regions' (Guibert of Nogent, *Gesta Francorum*).

The success of the First Crusade was regarded as a complete vindication of this theology and was an encouragement to make further efforts. Robert was a monk in the Benedictine abbey of Remi in Reims and had been present at the

Council of Clermont. In 1106 or 7 his abbot instructed him to prepare a history of the First Crusade, which would inspire people with the belief that it was the will of God to launch a second Crusade (Robert the Monk 2005, pp. 1–2). Robert begins his account with a description of the speech made by the pope at Clermont, as we have already seen, but he adds an epilogue to the speech in which the pope praises Jerusalem. 'Our Redeemer dignified it with his arrival, adorned it with his words, consecrated it through his Passion, redeemed it by his death and glorified it with his burial' (p. 81).[2] It is characteristic of this theology to regard Jerusalem as having been glorified not so much by Christ's resurrection as by his burial. Relics are of great importance for the medieval Church, as they are seen as providing a link between the believer and the object of faith. So the Holy Sepulchre, having been touched by the crucified body, was such a relic. Indeed, Jerusalem itself and the entire Holy Land upon which the feet of Christ had walked was itself a kind of geographical relic, still glowing with that sacred contact between earth and heaven. Just as the sick woman had clutched the hem of Christ's garment, which became the conduit for saving power, so now Christians are to clutch at the sacred remnants of the saviour so as to grasp salvation.

The Crusades as penitential pilgrimage

Jonathan Riley-Smith has done more than any other modern historian to emphasize the Crusades as a penitential pilgrimage (2009, p. 3; Tyerman 2004, p. 112). The nineteenth century had romanticized the Crusades as heroic exploits of chivalry (Tyerman 1988, p. 6), and unfortunately these images persist in many of the nineteenth-century hymns (such as 'Onward Christian Soldiers' or 'Soldiers, who are Christ's below'), still sung in some churches. In the twentieth century economic motives were often attributed to the Crusades, or they were regarded as the first overseas colonies created by western European imperialism. Louise and Jonathan Riley-Smith speak of 'generations of historians who have been extraordinarily reluctant to face up to the implication that it [the Crusade] was motivated by genuine piety. So repugnant has been the idea of Christians engaging in war as an expression of devotion that they have clung to the explanation of a general economic motivation' (1981, p. 11).

It has now become clearer that very few Crusaders gained material benefit from their activities (Tyerman 1988, p. 18). Indeed, on the contrary, many individuals and families made considerable sacrifices to fulfil what they came to see as their religious duty to go on armed pilgrimage. Many people still think of the Crusades as expeditions aimed at the recovery or defence of Palestine, but it has become clearer that crusading was a far more general phenomenon. 'It is now clear that the fourteenth century, like the thirteenth, was one in which there was hardly a year in which a crusade was not being waged somewhere' (Riley-Smith 2009, p. x).

---

2 For discussions about the theology of Robert, see Carol Sweetenham's introduction to her translation (2005, pp. 48–59) and Riley-Smith 1993, pp. 135–55.

The recovery of the Iberian Peninsula from the Moors, which began in a significant way with the Battle of Tours won by the Franks in 732, and was not complete until the fall of Granada in 1492, occupying nearly 800 years, was again and again blessed by the popes and given the status of a Crusade (Riley-Smith 1981, pp. 15–16). The Northern Crusades fought against the Baltic and eastern European countries between the twelfth and fourteenth centuries in which the military orders played a prominent part, were given the status of Crusades from the time of Pope Celestine III in 1193 (Christiansen 1997). There were Crusades against secular authorities and against fellow Christians in southern Germany and in south-western France.

In understanding this we must consider the prevailing political philosophy in which Christendom was 'seen not merely as a society of Christians but as a universal state, the Christian Republic, transcendental in that it existed at the same time in heaven and on earth' (Riley-Smith 2009, p. 24). This universal state had been established by Christ for the benefit of all humanity. It was not only a Christian republic; it was a monarchy of which Christ was the King (p. 25).

In a society where great importance was attached to the status of land, and where there were continual conflicts about the rightful possession of land, it was the duty of Christian citizens to go to the support of their King where his lands had fallen into alien hands. Feudal society was bound together by oaths of loyalty, whereby vassals were bound to their lord, to defend his rights and to avenge him. Similarly, the vassals of Jesus Christ were obliged to defend his rights and to restore his lost inheritance (p. 25).

A major influence upon the Christian theology of violence was that of Augustine of Hippo. His writings on the just war had become more generally available since about 1083, when Anselm of Lucca issued a collection of the writings of Augustine on love and war, which was followed by similar collections (Riley-Smith 1993, pp. 5–6). These had considerable influence at a time when the Gregorian reforms of the period 1150–80 were inspiring many Christians to greater obedience to the Church.[3] Augustine had shown how God could command violence not from cruelty, but from God's justice and righteous anger. Christ had commanded his disciples to take two swords with them, and in the garden of Gethsemane, when Peter had tried to use his sword, he had been told to return it to its sheath, but not to get rid of it altogether (Riley-Smith 1981, p. 5). The central feature, however, was love. There is very little reference in the crusading literature to love of Muslims, but rather love for the Christians of the eastern Mediterranean, and one showed one's love for Christ by attacking those who, it was believed, had insulted him. It was all too easy for this to turn into a kind of vendetta or vengeance, and in much popular thought the Crusades were regarded as taking vengeance upon the enemies of Christ (Riley-Smith 2009, p. 9). The appalling results of this can be seen in the attacks upon the Jewish communities of southern Germany, while Crusaders were passing through to the Balkans.

Devotion to the cross of Christ was a central feature of crusading spirituality. Those who were recruiting were described as converts and as having been recruited for Christ's service (Cole 2013, p. 60). This preaching reached its climax during the Pontificate of Innocent III (1190–1216). It was the moral duty

---

3 For the influence of the concept of holy war in England see Tyerman 1988, pp. 9–14.

of every Christian to participate in the Crusades. Only in this way could Christians repay their debt to Christ. It is Christ who is really suffering in Jerusalem. The Holy Land, which Christ trod with his own blessed feet, is now occupied by the Infidel; Christ himself is in exile (pp. 80–97).

Martin, Abbot of the Alsatian Abbey of Paris, concludes his sermon on crusading with a stirring appeal. 'Therefore now, brothers, receive with joyful minds the victorious sign of the cross so that by carrying out faithfully the cause of him who was crucified, you may obtain for this brief and modest hardship great and eternal payments' (p. 95).

Innocent III announced the details of a new Crusade at the Fourth Lateran Council in 1215, publishing a detailed set of instructions for those who were to preach it throughout western Europe. 'When Christ cries out to men, "If any man will come after me, let him deny himself and take up his cross and follow me", it is a summons to crusade' (p. 104). Refusal to go on the Crusade would bring damnation on the day of judgement. First, people must turn to Christ in penitence, proving their sincerity by taking up the journey to the Holy Land or paying for somebody else to go. Much crusade preaching was based upon a massive appeal to the guilt over the crucifixion of Jesus Christ. Christ died because of human sin, and the Crusade is given by God as a means to expiate this guilt. By going on Crusade they would show that the death of Christ had not been in vain. The outward actions must be accompanied by genuine inner penitence, because the Crusade is ultimately a spiritual warfare against demonic powers. When the Crusades failed, the participants were locked into an inescapable vice of guilt. The only reason for the failure could be God's just punishment for their failing to inwardly repent and in their continuation in sin (Nicholson 1997, pp. 23, 63). Any victory would alleviate the guilt but in the end victory against the Muslims was impossible (Jackson 2009, pp. 165–77). One can see how this type of theology demanded a revival of spirituality in the Church in order that crusading might be successful (Cole 2013, pp. 100–1).

Dominicans and Franciscans

One of the most remarkable features in the history of crusade preaching was the role played by the mendicant orders, Franciscans and Dominicans (Maier 1994). It was Pope Gregory IX (1227–41) who first used the mendicant orders to provide an efficient preaching service (p. 4). From about 1230 the Dominicans preached the Baltic Crusades, and from that time on both Dominicans and Franciscans preached the Crusades to the Holy Land. There was little or no tension between this development and the ideals of the great founders, Francis of Assisi (1181/2–1286) and Dominic (1170–1221). The famous incident when Francis crossed the enemy lines at Damietta to preach before the Sultan of Egypt Melek al-Kamil has been widely regarded as a notable exception to the theology and practice of violence and has become a centre piece of missionary iconography. It is often claimed that Francis was advocating peaceful persuasion and the preaching of the word of God as an alternative to holy war. However, Christoph Maier argues that 'such a view can no longer be justified' (p. 9). The earliest references to the event are very vague, sometimes not even mentioning

Francis by name, and, as is not uncommon in the development of hagiography, later chronicles supplied the incident with more and more detail. After carefully examining all the sources Maier concludes: 'Francis thus accepted the crusade as both legitimate and ordained by God and he was quite obviously not opposed to the use of violence when it came to the struggle between Christians and Muslims' (p. 16).

It is unclear what the motives of Francis were in visiting al-Kamil, but it seems most probable that he intended to demand 'total submission to the Christian faith' (pp. 409–10), fully expecting to be murdered for this insult. We know that Francis had been seeking martyrdom from time to time at Muslim hands ever since 1212 (p. 9), and there are several well-attested cases where Franciscan brothers both in Morocco and in Spain had in fact been executed for their outspoken insulting language against Islam (Armstrong 1988, pp. 109–10). David Burr remarks: 'Twice he attempted to seek martyrdom at the hands of the Moslems, and when five Franciscans actually achieved it in 1220, Francis was reported to have exclaimed "Now I can truly say I have five brothers!"' (2001, p. 2). There is no reason to think that Francis would have used insulting language, but it seems that he was in agreement with the current ideology of crusading in so far as, short of their conversion to Christ, Muslims could only expect to receive an appropriate penalty for their stubbornness.

One of the purposes for evangelizing Muslims, and, if necessary, vilifying their faith, was precisely to secure martyrdom and thus to ensure divine judgement upon Muslims. In 1227 seven Franciscans tried to preach Christ in the streets of the Moroccan city of Ceuta. '[I]n their letter from prison they wrote that "the death and damnation of the infidels" was one of the objectives toward which Christ had directed them' (Kedar 1984, p. 126). Kedar concludes that none of the sources for the life of Francis indicate any hesitation about crusading and certainly no criticism of crusading (pp. 126–31).

The actions of Dominic between 1205 and 1215, when he was a member of the papal legation in Languedoc, have been interpreted as missions of peace. Certainly, Dominic wanted to restore the so-called heretics by means of debates and preaching, but as early as 1208 the preaching was supported by a huge and extremely violent crusading army. It appears that, like Francis, Dominic regarded the proclamation of the word of truth and the fact of the righteous anger of God as complementary methods for the conversion or at least the disciplining of those who were disloyal or openly opposed to Catholic truth (Maier 1994, pp. 8–9).

The Dominican order was approved by Pope Innocent III in 1217. Gregory IX became pope in 1227, and in the following year he canonized Francis at Assisi. By this time both mendicant orders were acting legates and delegates of the pope. The two orders were unique in being able to supply networks of teachers and preachers in many parts of western Europe. Their obedience to the pope was unquestioned. By 1230 they had become the principal preachers, representatives and supporters of the Crusades (p. 32).

A major function of the preaching by this time was to raise funds by permitting people to redeem their vows, if they could not go on armed pilgrimage. This was undoubtedly one of the reasons why unauthorized preaching of the cross was strictly forbidden. The official crusade preaching often took place on great feast days, especially those dedicated to the cross (p. 107). Devotion to the crucified was stimulated, leading to a commitment to the spiritual and physical discipline of crusading. Another popular time for preaching the Crusades was during Lent because of the demand for penance. Crusading was the highest and most noble form of penitential exercise available to lay people in the thirteenth century. The crusade sermon handbook of Humbert of Romans, probably compiled between 1266 and 1268, lists no less than 138 biblical passages upon which a crusade sermon might be based (p. 115). If penitence did not succeed in securing commitment, then anger would be stirred up against the enemies of the cross, and this had the same effect. It was probably because of their vows of personal poverty that the mendicant orders were entrusted with the collecting of the crusade revenues, together with their proven obedience to the pope. Innocent IV expanded the scope of the collection by authorizing the friars to gather up money that had been acquired by means of usury, theft or any other illegal activity (p. 125). Because they could not pay, poor people seemed to be excluded from the benefits of crusading, and those who could pay but could not go, like older people or the sick and disabled, were required to redeem their vows with cash.

There was no fundamental criticism of the redemption of vows from within the Church throughout the whole of the thirteenth century.[4]

Mission to the heretics

The study of medieval heresy gives us another insight into the mission of the Medieval Church. As with the Crusades our starting point shall be the teaching of Bernard of Clairvaux. In his sermons on the Song of Songs, three sermons (Numbers 64, 65 and 66) are devoted to the problem of heresy. The text for all three is 'Catch us the little foxes that destroy the vines, for our vine has flowered' (Song 2.15). The vines, says Bernard, represent the various Christian congregations, and the little foxes are the heresies. Bernard points out that the little foxes are not meant to be destroyed or driven away, but to be caught. 'They are to be caught, I repeat, not by force of arms but by arguments by which their errors may be refuted' (Sermon 64, para. 8). Sermon 65 deals in greater detail with the same theme. In ancient days, the heretics spoke openly and boldly, but at present is it not true that the heretics 'would rather inflict injury than win a victory in open fight?' (Sermon 65, para. 2) The trouble is that the heretics are invisible. 'How shall they be caught, when they do not even allow themselves to be seen, but prefer to creep about like snakes?' They prefer to hide away in secret 'for it is said that they practice unspeakable obscenities in private; just so the hinder parts of foxes stink' (ibid.).

The heresy that Bernard is so concerned about is not false teaching. It is something more insidious, like a hidden disease, corrupting the body internally. It is not so much their teaching as their way of life that Bernard finds objectionable. They refuse to take an oath, following Scripture literally. 'For men like you assert that they are the only followers of the true gospel' (Sermon 65, para. 3).

---

4 On the redemption of vows see Siberry 1985, pp. 150–5 and Maier 1994, pp. 135–60.

There is worse to come. The heretics welcome women as their companions, but '[t]o be always in a woman's company without having carnal knowledge of her – is this not a greater miracle than raising the dead?' (Sermon 65, para. 4) The wickedness of these people is evident from the fact that 'if you question him about his faith, nothing could be more orthodox; if [you question him] after his way of life, nothing could be more irreproachable; and he proves his words by his deeds . . . As far as his life and conduct are concerned he harms no-one, distresses no-one, does not set himself above any-one' (Sermon 65, para. 5). The only important thing that can be said against the heretics is that they live and work with women, but this is a scandal and against the practices of the Church. 'If he does not remove the woman, he does not remove the scandal; if he does not remove the scandal, when he can remove it, he is clearly disobedient to the Gospel' (Sermon 65, para. 7).

There is no denying the fact that the heretics appear to be good, but this itself is deceptive. 'They only desire to appear good that they may not be alone in their evil . . . It is to cause the downfall of the good that they strive to appear good' (Sermon 66, para. 1). The heretics refuse to name the founder or leader of their heresy. The implication is clear to Bernard. They cannot or will not name a man as their founder; therefore it cannot be from men. It must therefore be 'a deceitful suggestion of demons' (Sermon 66, para. 2).

Bernard now comes back to the theme that seems to trouble him most, the sexual lives of the heretics. The trouble is that they take vows of chastity and live, they say, celibate lives. The only way to maintain such a life would be for men and women to live in separate monastic houses, as was the practice of the Church. To take vows of celibacy and yet continue in each other's company is simply to invite immorality.

The diet of the heretics illustrates this profound hypocrisy, for they avoid milk and everything made from it. So great is their horror of the body and of sexuality that the heretics refuse to eat anything that is the product of sexual intercourse. There is no doubt, Bernard admits, that the heretics do face death with joy, but '[t]he obstinacy of these men has nothing in common with the constancy of the martyrs; for they were endowed by their piety with a contempt for death, whereas these others are prompted by their hardness of heart' (Sermon 66, para. 13). Although the suffering looks the same, the intention is very different.

There is only one way to save all this Bernard thinks. You must 'require the women to live with others of their sex who are under similar vows and similarly men with men of the same way of life'. If they will not accept this, then they should be expelled from the Church because of their 'blatant and illicit co-habitation' (Sermon 66, para. 14).

The people that Bernard was so fearful of appear to be part of a movement of spiritual renewal in which lay people rejected the wealth and ceremony of the Church and tried to follow the gospel by living in Christian communities. The unsatisfied sexuality of so much medieval life is apparent on both sides. Bernard cannot believe that such common life is possible and concludes that it must be a cover-up for promiscuity. The simple gospel Christians, on the other hand, take their chastity so seriously that they refuse to eat anything that is the product of animal sexuality. Indeed, their search for spirituality, as they understood it, leads them into a rejection of materiality as such. The so-called heretics offered a threat to the permanence of the boundaries upon which medieval privilege was based. 'The fear of pollution protects boundaries, and the fear of sexual pollution, social boundaries in particular' (Moore 1987, p. 100). In the case of the Church, we see 'the fear that the privileged feel of those at whose expense their privilege is enjoyed' (p. 101), and in the case of the communities of simple Christians we see both a desire to break the social boundaries of privilege as well as a deeply ingrained fear of sexual impurity due largely to the association in the medieval mind between sex and sin.

The first secular legislation against heresy since Roman times is to be found in the Assize of Clarendon of Henry II of England in 1166:

> Moreover the lord king forbids that any one in all England should receive into his land or jurisdiction or any house of his, any of the sect of those apostates who have been excommunicated and branded at Oxford. And if any one receives them he shall be in the mercy of the lord king; and the house in which they were shall be carried outside the vill and burned. (para. 21)

One of the intentions of the king was to transfer power from the ecclesiastical courts to royal jurisdiction. The heresy in question was the *populicani*, a movement originating in Germany as an expression of the popular piety, one of the consequences of the impact of the Gregorian Reforms of the eleventh century. But 'the legislation reflected the vigour not of the heresy, but of the legislator' (Moore 1987, p. 111). These people had been examined by a synod of bishops at the request of the king late in 1165 and then passed over to the secular arm for punishment at the command of the king. The movement was typical of many that appeared in north-west Europe at around this time. It was anti-sacramental and anti-clerical, consisting mainly of poor and illiterate people. The reasons for their persecution were more political than religious. It was not merely that an offended Church passed the heretics over to a largely indifferent state for punishment, but the extension of its judiciary served the interests of the growing power of the centralized European states as part of their own aggrandisement.

Until the end of the twentieth century most accounts of heresy took quite seriously the descriptions of the heresies and accepted them at face value. It has now become clear that many of these accounts are constructions created retrospectively, often at a much later date. A new understanding of heresy as a mythological creation of the powerful has emerged.[5]

The phenomenon of heresy began to disappear from Europe after the conquests of Clovis early in the sixth century. The Arianism of the Germanic tribes seemed to gradually disappear as the tribes were slowly included in the culture of the late Roman world. One of the earliest outbreaks of heresy in medieval Europe took place in Orleans in 1032 under the jurisdiction of Robert I of France (Moore 1987, p. 8). In the eleventh and twelfth centuries western Europe was slowly changing from a kinship society to one based upon the bureaucracies of central power. It was in the light of increasingly efficient authority that resistance

---

5 For the process whereby similar events were developed into mythology, see Kamen 1998, pp. 305–20.

to it emerged, just as the powers of the state to interrogate the lives of its citizens in greater detail also increased. The religious doctrines of the heretics of Orleans, and they were probably no different from most of the other so called heretical movements of the eleventh century, seem to have amounted to little more than a rather simple and literalistic adherence to the ethical teachings of the Gospels. This tended to make people more sceptical of the more complex teachings of the Church. Many of them denied the significance of baptism, arguing that it was pointless unless accompanied by good works, and they all seem to have agreed that the Church needed to be reformed. Reactions to the Gregorian Revolution varied from those who believed it did not go far enough in purifying the Church to those who resented the growing power of Rome.

Bernard of Clairvaux had been especially concerned with the work of Henry of Lausanne (died c.1148), who was active in the Toulouse area of south-western France. In 1146 Bernard and a group of senior clerics visited the city and managed to secure the condemnation not only of Henry, but of all who sympathized with him. Henry appears to have been a fiery reformer, who rejected much of the authority of the Church in favour of the authority of the Gospels, but he was sentenced to permanent imprisonment by the Bishop of Toulouse soon after the departure of Bernard. The offences of Waldes of Lyon (c.1140–c.1218), who was excommunicated in 1161, seem to have been no more than the fact that he insisted upon his calling to preach with or without the authority of the Church. Preaching had become a closely regulated activity somewhat similar perhaps to the control of the press in modern totalitarian societies.

It was in the Toulouse area that the outstanding example of medieval heresy, that of the Albigensians, arose. This has been given its own name, the Cathar heresy, and is often regarded as having been a significant organized movement with its own clergy, diocese and bishops. It was believed to have taught the ancient Manichaean heresy that was supposed to have come from the Balkans.[6]

This picture has been subjected to devastating criticism by Mark Pegg. In trying to identify heretics, articles of clothing were often significant. The Valdensians were accused of wearing sandals in imitation of the apostles. Those accused were often quite simple, unsophisticated people, who were described with metaphors of disgusting food. They were said to be 'festering', and metaphors taken from disease were common. Southern France was described as 'a damnable region, which is like a great cesspool of evil, with all the scum of heresy flowing into it' (2008, p. 21).

Examining the honour and kinship society of south-western France, Pegg shows how the role of religion and morality in this region came to be thought of as heretical. Social and economic conditions tended to encourage a less coherent and more informal faith. The people in this area did not consider themselves to be heretical, but were not sufficiently informed or interested in the official theology of the Church to know or care whether they were heretical or not. Crusaders summoned by Innocent III gave no indication of thinking that they were fighting against an alternative church nor against the local people. They were fighting rather for the purity and integrity of Christendom. As with the Crusades to the

---

6 For the usual older interpretation see Sumption 1978. Hindley (2003, p. 167) accepts a modified version of this.

East, the Albigensian Crusade was a deeply religious activity. During the attack on Carcasson on 6 August 1209, the priests sang *Veni Sancte Spiritus*, while the troops attacked (p. 82). This combination of violence and sacred liturgy was a standard technique that was terrifying to the besieged city. There was also a political factor in these Southern Crusades. South-western France was linked both with the Iberian Peninsula and to France, which consisted of northern France, the area around Paris. With the Treaty of Paris in 1229, when the Count of Toulouse offered loyalty to Louis IV, who was then a boy of 14, the political objectives of the Albigensian Crusade were secured (p. 179). This was followed by the inquisition led by the Dominicans. Pegg comments 'the inquisitions into heretical depravity persecuted a heresy of pessimistic sentimentality only two decades old' (p. 187). The old courteous society of the south had been virtually destroyed and

> the Albigensian crusade ushered genocide into the West by linking divine salvation to mass murder, by making slaughter as loving an act as His [Christ's] sacrifice on the cross. This ethos of redemptive homicide is what separates the crusade massacres from other great killings before the thirteenth century. (p. 188)

Pegg concludes that the trouble was that the pestilential heretics of the Languedoc area, as it came to be known, looked like Christians and thought they were Christians. That made them all the more dangerous since it illustrated the perfidious deception of heresy (p. 191).

This assessment is vividly verified in *The Song of the Cathar Wars* by William of Tudela. The fascinating feature of this text is that it falls into two sections. The first, about one third of the total, is by William himself. It is staunchly Catholic and hostile to the so-called heretics; the (longer) second part is by a different author, an anonymous poet who fiercely defends the area and was opposed to the Catholic military leader Simon Demontford (*Song of the Cathar Wars* 1996, pp. 1–2). William tells us, from his point of view, why people were so keen to join the Crusade. 'Then, once they knew that their sins would be forgiven, men took the cross in France and all over the kingdom' (p. 14). 'Every man came flocking because the pardon offered to crusaders was so generous' (p. 17). The crusading army went forward in the faith that 'against the host of Christ, the judge of all, no high rocks, no steepness may avail, no mountain fortress hold out' (p. 33).

This is typical of many such expressions in the work of William. Every battle won is attributed to Christ and the Blessed Virgin, while the heretics are described as fools who reject the call to surrender, but nothing is said about what they believe or why they should have been regarded as heretics. William emphasizes both the political motivation of the conquest and the role of the clergy in sanctifying it. 'May the Lord God never forgive me my sins, if while they were fighting, the clergy did not at the same time sing the *Sanctus Spiritus* in a great procession, so that you would have heard it half a league away' (p. 57).

In the second part of the poem, the conflict is described as being between the men of Provence and the French or the Northerners, and now the clergy are described as supporting the Southern resistance.

The chaplain, Sir Abert, addressed them briefly [the supporters of the Count of Toulouse]: 'My lords, in the name of God and the count I tell you that every-one who helps to build this dry-stone wall will be richly rewarded by God and by Count Raymond. Upon my holy orders, I promise each one of you salvation' (p. 89).

There were protests against this sort of thing from some leading lay people, who regarded such promises as a kind of religious bribery. 'It amazes me that you clerics give absolution where there is no repentance . . . I do not and will not believe, unless you can prove it better, that any man who dies unshriven deserves salvation' (pp. 94–95). This is reported as having been said by one of the supporters of Simon Demontford after a defeat by the provincial forces. It is clear that each side in the conflict claimed divine authority. 'Pride and glory have been flung out of Toulouse . . . and clearly it is God who has given the place back to him' [the Count of Toulouse], (p. 126), his forces having defeated the Normans and the French. The cardinal, who was speaking, went on to instruct the Crusaders to utterly destroy every person, men and women, because they had disobeyed Rome. The anonymous author goes on rather bit-terly 'the clergy are praying to Saint Mary and the true Trinity to protect the town by damning it, to defend right and their loyalty, to cherish the Count de Montford' (p. 132).

Far from being described as an attempt to extinguish heresy, although this is mentioned from time to time, the war is usually described by the anonymous poet as a military contest between the Count of Toulouse and the Count Simon Demontford. The longest statement describing the faith of the people of Toulouse shows them to have been completely orthodox, at least in the opinion of this sympathetic observer. 'Jesus Christ directs us, he gives us good or ill, and we must thank him' (p. 150).

Contemporary criticism of the Crusades

To what extent was there contemporary criticism of the link between crusad-ing and faith or of crusading itself? This question is carefully considered by Elizabeth Siberry (1985). There certainly was criticism from the Troubadors, the poets and singers who flourished in many parts of Europe between about 1150 and 1250. It must be noted, however, that most of these, particularly the ones in Germany and south-western France, came from areas where there was considerable sensitivity about the extension of papal power. Other criticism came from the School of St. Auburn, headed by Matthew Parish, but they were motivated more by the wish to protect their monastery from outside power and resentment of the papal taxes imposed upon the area. Humbert of the Romans, whom we met earlier in connection with guidance given to the crusade preach-ers, minister general of the Dominicans (1254–63), wrote four treatises discuss-ing various criticisms of the Crusades. Humbert divided the critics into seven groups and after reviewing his comments on each group, Siberry concludes that it is not true to claim as some have done that 'almost from the beginning there was a significant body of individuals who condemned the military conquest of the Holy Land and advocated peaceful conversion of the Muslims through a programme of missionary work' (p. 17). Even Peter the Venerable (c.1092–56), the abbot of Cluny, although he commissioned a series of translations of the Qur'an as early as 1140 and wanted to approach the Muslims in the spirit of love, did not reject the use of force as a means of maintaining and defending the Holy Land. Far from regarding crusading as an obstacle to the conversion of Muslims most writers of the period seem to have taken the opposite view. They appealed to the Muslims to convert because of the greatness of the forces arrayed against them. It was agreed that it would be wrong to force Muslims to convert, but at the same time it was thought that the conquest of the Holy Land 'would create the right political conditions for them to enter the Christian fold of their own volition' (p. 18).

It is also quite unjustified, Siberry insists, to hold that the thirteenth-century Crusades met with opposition from the newly formed Franciscan and Dominican Orders. They did accept that the Muslims should be converted by peaceful means, but at the same time they were the principal advocates and preachers of the Crusades. Not until the 1260s do serious critics emerge, such as Roger Bacon, who argued that the Crusades actually hindered the conversion of Muslims, advocating nothing but preaching and teaching.

There were some people who did not go on Crusades because, in the light of contemporary attitudes, it suggested that they were impenitent; there was also a great deal of criticism of the sins of the army, for which God had denied them victory. The heavy taxation increasingly demanded by the popes to support the Crusades met with widespread resentment. The practice of allowing those who had taken the cross to redeem their vows with cash, often on the same day, was widely criticized.

The German expedition against the Wends in 1147 was the first officially recognized crusade against north-eastern Europe, and it was followed by many others. Such campaigns had been accepted as part of the mission to expand Christendom ever since Charlemagne had converted the Saxons at the point of the sword. There was criticism of many of the campaigns against fellow Christians and against lay rulers. But in spite of this thousands of people continued to flock to join the various Crusades. As a matter of fact much of the criticism came from the fact that the Crusades against the Christian heretics were distracting resources away from the more important struggle in the Middle East. Early in the eleventh century there seem to have been small groups of pacifists, who did object to the use of force against the Muslims, but our knowledge of them is confined to the writings of those who supported the Crusades and whatever their influence may have been was limited (p. 16).

Elizabeth Siberry concludes that in the Middle Ages most critics were concerned with aspects of crusading rather than crusading itself; their intention was to improve crusading.

Crusades and Christian mission

We must now discuss the question of the relationship between crusading and mission, first in the thought of the Middle Ages and then as seen by missiologists today. During the eleventh to thirteenth centuries, Latin Christianity was at war on virtually all of its frontiers. The reclamation or the expansion of territory was part of what lay behind this. The Northern Crusades in particular were associated quite explicitly with mission (Riley-Smith 2009, p. 10). However, that does not mean that the Crusades to the Holy Lands were regarded by most of its participants as a mission. 'The crusaders seem to have believed, in accordance with Canon Law, that land once Christian belonged thereafter to Christendom by right' (1993, p. 108). Does that mean that the Crusaders thought that their activities in the various theatres of war were intended to bring about conversion? Many of the attitudes were not far from this idea, although this seldom meant the conversion of individuals. Riley-Smith concludes:

> I have tried to explain them, and there is little doubt that when combined with a contempt for the validity of pagan rule the idea of a war for the expansion of Christendom manifested itself in attitudes not far removed from those in favour of forcible conversion, even if they could be technically distinguished from them, being concerned with the nature of government rather than with proselytism. (p. 109)

On the other hand, the attacks on the Jews in Germany seem to have been motivated by both revenge and the desire to convert. One must also remember that Crusaders often found it difficult to distinguish between Jews and Muslims. They were both enemies of Christ and therefore victims of divine judgement. The Crusaders believed that they were chosen by God to fulfil a task long prophesied in Scripture. They saw themselves as united by their common love of God and of their Christian brothers. 'Christendom itself was seen as an extended family while its members saw themselves as extended families occupying time and eternity' (Hindley 2003, p. 4). This same love of the Christian family led to a desire for vengeance upon those who had harmed it. It also led to the conviction that those who died for the love of God and neighbour had earned the martyrs' crown (Riley-Smith 2009, pp. 65–6). The Crusaders then believed in a certain sense that they were on a mission sent by God; they were performing God's work.

The attitudes of modern missiologists are often ambiguous. Jean Comby restricts his study of missions to the 'history of evangelization' (1996, p. xiii) directed at non-Christians. For this reason the question of Crusades against fellow Christians is outside the scope of his enquiry. His description of the mendicant orders is interesting in dealing with the Eastern dimensions of Catholic Christianity, but he does not refer to the fact that very soon after their foundation Franciscans and Dominicans became the principle advocates of crusading. Indeed, Comby makes no reference to the preaching of the cross in western Europe, although this might surely be thought of as a form of evangelization. Because it was directed at church people, Comby does not deal with it. His emphasis upon literal evangelization means that he does not deal adequately with the self-understanding of Medieval Christianity in its fanatical search for homogeneity. Medieval evangelism, whether directed toward Christians or non-Christians, was driven by the desire to eliminate diversity.

Comby, however, is more radical than the last paragraph suggests. Practically confining his study of mission to the evangelization of non-Christian people, he concludes by showing that the expansion of Christianity was almost always accompanied by force or pressure of some kind, 'we have to concede that Christianity has a real chance of becoming a majority religion only when it addresses cultures in process of development under the pressure of outside events' (p. 174). Since the Christian churches are no longer in a position where they can manage these pressures, evangelism and mission must be reinterpreted as witnessing to the kingdom of God. Moreover, '[t]he historical Church does not have a monopoly of signs and realizations of the kingdom' (p. 176).

David Bosch regards Luke 14.23 'Go out on the highways and along the hedgerows and compel them to come in; I want my house full' as summing up the paradigm of the mission enterprises of the Medieval Catholic Church. While the explicit use of this verse became less frequent, Bosch believes that 'the sentiment behind it persisted well into the twentieth century and some of its missionary encyclicals' (1991, p. 236). He points out that it could not easily be otherwise, as long as it was believed that there was no salvation outside the Catholic Church 'and it was to the eternal advantage of people to join' (p. 237).

Bosch agrees that his use of the word 'mission' to describe the expansion of Christianity before the modern period is an anachronism, because that activity was never called mission during the first 1,500 years. It was sometimes described as 'planting the Church' and 'illuminating the nations'. 'The new word, "mission", is historically linked indissolubly with the colonial era and with the idea of a magisterial commissioning' (p. 228). Mission thus refers to the way in which the structure of the Catholic Church was extended in modern times to all parts of the world. Consequently, mission manifests itself as the 'self-realization of the Church' (p. 275).

It is significant that Bosch's self-imposed anachronism in describing the self-realization and expansion of the Western Church as mission means that he underestimates the significance for the character of Christianity of the Crusades. He highlights the fact that very few leading figures advocated conversion by force, but he makes no reference to the preaching of the cross, although this gave crusading a significance far beyond the meaning of the modern conception of mission. Although Bosch realizes the impact upon the self-understanding of the Church on its theology of heaven and hell, he does not seem to appreciate the way that the theology itself was a by-product of the possibilities of domination opened up for the Church under the control of monarchical papacy. It was not only the theology that produced the powerful actions; it was equally the use and the enjoyment of power that required such a theology to justify it.

Bosch refers briefly to the conversion of pagan peoples under the rule of Charlemagne and his successors, but concludes: 'These aggressive and frequently brutal "direct missionary wars" remained the exception' (p. 224). The old ambiguity of the Church's attitude to war restrained it from encouraging it as a normal practice. There was, Bosch suggests, 'an internal contradiction' between the attitudes required by warfare and those required by missionary preaching such that 'no army can ever be inspired by a vision of evangelical service' (p. 225). Bosch concludes 'in light of this, it is really impossible to consider the crusades of the eleventh to thirteenth century as "missionary wars", even if many ordinary Christians saw them in this light' (p. 225). In view of the research conducted into the religious crusading since Bosch wrote it is now impossible to continue to hold his view. There certainly was a profound tension between the teachings of Jesus and those of the just war, but the Medieval Church overcame that tension by assimilating the demands of the gospel into the political and psychological requirements for the Christian exercise of power.

Stephen Spencer agrees that Medieval Catholicism attempted through the use of military coercion 'to force peoples into baptism and membership of the Church' (2007, p. 102). A number of examples are mentioned but Spencer concludes 'these remained the exception' (p. 103). 'The crusades might be thought to provide another example, but, as Bosch points out, they were not launched to convert Muslims but to defeat and overwhelm them, and so cannot be seen as direct expressions of Christian mission' (p. 103). Spencer does not discuss the Crusades himself but takes Bosch's word for it and so falls into the same mistake of acknowledging that the concept of mission is a modern one, without noticing the implication that it is an inappropriate designation of the purposes of the Church in earlier centuries. Spencer does refer to the mendicant orders but makes no reference to their role as advocates of the Crusades, and he is dependent here upon the work of Stephen Bevans and Roger Schroeder. Spencer makes no reference to the Northern Crusades in spite of the fact that nobody denied that their intention was to conquer and convert. No mention is made of the Albigensian Crusade and the other Crusades against heretics all of which fall outside Spencer's anachronistic definition.

The most substantial contribution to the history of missions since the foundational work of David Bosch is that of Bevans and Schroeder (2004). Once again, however, we find that the implications for the self-understanding of Christian faith of its history of violence and power is not dealt with. They recognize that Charlemagne used force to convert the Saxons, but this is referred to quite briefly (p. 126). No details are given and no attempt is made to understand why Charlemagne did this or whether he believed it was incompatible with his Christian profession. As for the monasteries, their role as frontier settlements is recognized, but there is no hint of their importance as fortresses, centres of conquest and resources for domination (Christiansen 1997, pp. 82–92; Fletcher 1997, pp. 451–82). Now and again reference is made to the conversion of a monarch, but the class orientated character of religion and conversion is not discussed. In order to cope with the wide diversity of Christian mission down the ages, the authors trace various theological continuities, called 'constants', against changing environments, which are described as 'contexts'. The problem with this methodology is that the constants are not always seen as being in sufficient tension with their contexts and the result is sometimes a description that is too bland. Christian faith is seldom perceived as enigmatic, nor is it seen as being as responsive to its contexts as the methodology would seem to require. For example, why is not the emergence of Islam itself regarded as a context which enabled Christian faith to realize its inner nature? This adaptation to context happened again and again, according to Bevans and Schroeder, in the period of the Acts of the Apostles. Why is not the encirclement of the kingdom of Charlemagne by hostile forces regarded as a context for the toughening up of theology so that force would become not exceptional but normal?

Turning to the period of the Crusades, Bevans and Schroeder remark that while they were 'religious in intent', they were 'marked by cultural insensitivity, wanton violence and ultimate defeat' (2004, p. 137). These features of the Crusades are contrasted with contemporary religion, as if the religion should have been a mitigating factor or at least a restraining influence upon the Crusades. Our authors fail to see that religion itself had undergone changes and had become a causal factor. Bevans and Schroeder agree that '[d]espite the originally high religious intentions, the behavior of the crusaders . . . often contradicted the very Christian values they came to defend' (p. 139). This is true, up to a point, but it is also true that crusading did not contradict the values, but was an expression of them. It is not recognized here that crusading had become a form of discipleship; it was the way of the cross in imitation of Christ.

The conventional iconographical portrait of Francis of Assisi before al-Kamil is repeated with no reference to the ambiguity of the original records, nor of Francis' support for the Crusades (pp. 143–4).

The description of the Cathar Church is equally conventional. It is described as a 'movement of lay preachers . . . who had organized a counter-church movement by the beginning of the thirteenth century, they were considered heretical and so demanded the urgent attention of the church' (p. 153). Bevans and Schroeder do not indicate what the character of this urgent attention was.[7] The reader is left mystified about the sudden appearance of heresy not mentioned previously. The only hint of doubt is in the expression 'what was considered heresy', but questions such as whether it was really heresy and why heresy mattered and what the supposed heretics actually taught are left unanswered. Concerning the mendicant orders, it is remarked: 'Being "children of their times", both orders were involved to some extent in crusade preaching, but on the whole they offered alternatives to the "sword approach" to Islam' (p. 159). This seriously minimizes the scope of mendicant support for the Crusades and the extent of their preaching on its behalf. There is no reference to the preaching of the cross, nor any reference to the mysticism of armed pilgrimage. Bevans and Schroeder present many insights into the theological and spiritual renewal movements of the twelfth and thirteenth centuries and offer lively accounts of the spread of Christian faith. However, there is little insight into the character of the self-understanding of the Church as it became militant in the form of Christendom.

The centre of power

The legend of the Donation of Constantine gave credibility to the claims of the medieval popes to possess monarchical power. The legend is first referred to in a forged document of the eighth or ninth centuries and was inserted into the twelfth-century compilation known as the *Decretum Gratiani*. In gratitude for his conversion to Christian faith, the Emperor Constantine was supposed to have granted Pope Sylvester I (314–35) and his successors dominion over Rome and the western Roman Empire. The walls of the Lateran Palace in Rome, the official residence of Pope Innocent III, were adorned with pictures illustrating

---

7 For the duty to kill heretics, see Edbury 1998, p. 102.

the papal authority (Sayers 1994, p. 11). One of these showed the emperor bowing before the pope granting him supreme power in the West.

The most famous statement of the principles upon which Gregory VII based his power is the *Dictatus Papae*, which probably dates from 1075. Dictate 2 declares that 'The Roman Pontif can alone with right be declared universal.' 'He alone may use the imperial insignia' (Dictate 8). Dictate 9 says that 'of the pope alone all princes shall kiss the feet', and Dictate 12 says that 'it may be permitted to him [the Pope] to depose emperors'. Dictate 19 grants the pope judicial immunity for 'he himself may be judged by no-one', and Dictate 22 declares that 'the Roman Church has never erred; nor will it err for all eternity'.

This tendency reached a climax in the reign of Pope Innocent III (1198–1216). He was the first pope to proclaim publicly that he was the Vicar of Christ (Sayers 1994, p. 16). Previously that title had been used informally and privately. The proper role of kings and emperors according to Innocent III was that they were there to assist the papacy in its work of extending the Christian religion. The idea of a papal state had emerged very early and definitely by the ninth century, but it was with the reform movement of the eleventh and early twelfth centuries that the notion of an independent papal state 'really took hold'. By the late eleventh century popes were regarding their lands as 'the Patrimony of St Peter' or 'the patrimony of Peter' (pp. 32, 65). Many towns and cities around the area of Rome itself were transferred from imperial to papal supremacy under the energetic rule of Innocent III. By the eleventh century there was a papal banner that by the thirteenth century flew on the papal castles. Economic and military power was necessary for the maintenance of this religious state. The papacy employed troops, mainly mercenary, to garrison its castles, defend its borders and protect its property. Central to the power of the pope was his authority to excommunicate, which invoked the statement attributed to the risen Christ in John 20.23: 'If you forgive anyone's sins, they are forgiven; if you pronounce them unforgiven, unforgiven they remain.' This was, however, addressed to the assembled apostles. Even more influential was Matthew 16.29, addressed to Peter: 'What you forbid on earth shall be forbidden in heaven, and what you allow on earth shall be allowed in heaven.' Excommunication was the first step toward releasing vassals from their oaths of loyalty, and thus it weakened the cement of society (p. 78). An excommunicated king or bishop could not rule his domain or diocese. It would be impossible to baptize babies, to authorize weddings and to bury the dead according to the ceremonies of the Church. One can see the development of all these powers and assumptions in the territorial ambitions of the Crusades and the need to silence those 'heretics', who denied the spiritual necessity of taking part in the sacraments and refused to accept that only the Church could authorize the Christian preacher.

The Fourth Lateran Council in 1215 was the climax of the powers of Innocent III. In its 70 canons the character of Latin Christianity as a totalitarian society under papal rule was strengthened. Canon 1 says that 'there is one Universal Church of the faithful, outside of which there is absolutely no salvation'. The nature of the Eucharist as the transformation of the body and blood of Jesus Christ into the elements is emphasized, and this sacrament 'no-one can effect except the priest who has been duly ordained in accordance with the keys of the Church, which Jesus Christ himself gave to the apostles and their successors', (Canon 1). Canon 3 excommunicated and anathematized all heretics 'under whatever names they may be known, for while they have different faces they are, nevertheless, bound to each other by their tails, since in all of them vanity is a common element'. We note here the vagueness of the definition of heresy, and the suggestion that to oppose the Church or to think for one's self was vanity. The secular authorities are to 'exterminate in the territories subject to their jurisdiction all heretics pointed out by the Church' (Canon 3). Secular authorities who refrained from doing this are to be punished. The spiritual privileges of crusading against Islam are to be extended to those who seek to cleanse the land from heretics. 'Catholics who have girded themselves with the cross for the extermination of the heretics, shall enjoy the indulgences and privileges granted to those who go in defence of the Holy Land' (Canon 3). There was to be no preaching of any kind without the express authority of the bishop or of the Holy See itself. Payment of Church tithes is to take preference over the payment of secular taxes (Canon 64). Canon 68 requires different religious groups to be identified by their clothing 'in some provinces a difference in dress distinguishes the Jews or Saracens from the Christians, but in certain others such a confusion has grown up that they cannot be distinguished by any difference'. This sometimes leads to sexual intercourse between Christians and Jews or Muslims and this is denounced. During the last three days before Easter, especially on the Friday, Jews and Muslims are not to be seen on the streets.

> This, however, we forbid most severely, that anyone should presume at all to break forth in insult to the Redeemer. And since we ought not to ignore any insult to Him who blotted out our disgraceful deeds, we command that such impudent fellows be checked by the secular princes by imposing upon them proper punishment so that they shall not at all presume to blaspheme Him who was crucified for us. (Canon 68)

It is with no surprise that we find the Canons of the Council followed by rules for the conduct of a new Crusade against the East. Because prompted by '[our] ardent desire to liberate the Holy Land from the hands of the ungodly' against those who refuse to assist the Crusade, the Holy See

> firmly protests that on the last day they will be held to render an account to us in the presence of a terrible judge. Let them consider with what security they can appear in the presence of the only begotten Son of God, Jesus Christ, into whose hands the Father has given all things, if in this matter they refuse to serve Him who was crucified for sinners, by whose favor they live, by whose benefits they are sustained, and by whose blood they were redeemed. (*Fourth Lateran Council*, Holy Land Decrees, para. 2)

This then was the theology that formed the self-understanding of the Medieval Latin Church, which emerged in its theology of mission. So far had the Church abandoned the prophetic vision. Did the churches of the Reformation throw off this theology, or did they assimilate it and adapt it for the demands of their own times? In the next chapter, we examine this question.

5

Prophetic Theology and Imperialism: The Colonial Sermons of the Early Seventeenth Century

Much has been written about the impact of Christian faith upon the formation and development of the British Empire,[1] but less has been done to understand the way that Christian faith itself underwent changes in the course of its utilization as the ideology of empire. Patrick Collinson, for example, discusses the impact of the Reformation upon the rise of a sense of English nationalism and concludes: 'If it really was the case that England was thought to be God's peculiar place, not just *an* elect nation but *the* elect nation, and if that idea was born out of the experience of the Protestant Reformation and its immediate consequences, then we have unearthed in protestant religious consciousness a root, perhaps even the tap root, of English imperialism' (1988, p. 5). Christian faith was thus providing the ideology of national identity, but this could not happen without corresponding changes in faith itself.

By the end of the sixteenth century there were about 20 British possessions in the Atlantic, and this was the continuation of a policy of expansion that can be traced back several centuries (Armitage 2000; Canny 1998).

Sacred monarchy and the rise of empire

In the course of this development the Old Testament had become increasingly prominent in the British imagination. The New Testament was the literature of a small movement scattered around the eastern Mediterranean, but the Old Testament was the literature of a nation state. Like Britain, ancient Israel had its monarchy, its laws and its dreams of expansion. When the Roman Empire became Christian in the fourth and fifth centuries, there was another imperial antecedent that the expansionist hopes of the British crown could look back to. However, the literature which grew up around the divinely appointed destiny of Constantine could not be compared with the sacred revelation of the Old Testament (Eusebius 1999; Kee 1982). The missionary energies of Christians for 1,000 years had almost always been based upon a top-down policy in which the conversion of a royal family was followed by the baptism of the subjects. Although this policy did much to create Christendom, it also led to a change in which the values of patient suffering in the resistance to

---

1 One of the first studies is Wright 1943.

demonic power gave way to the royal virtues of majesty and domination (Fletcher 1997). Charlemagne had been crowned Holy Roman Emperor by the pope in 800, and throughout the early Middle Ages the English kings had taken from France the myth of divine kingship exemplified, for example, in the royal healing touch (Block 1973; McKenna 1982). It was understandable therefore that as they read the Bible the political classes were attracted more to the ideals of the Hebrew kingdom than to those of the suffering Messiah.

The description of England as 'an empire sufficient unto itself' arose from the desire to throw off the control of the Bishop of Rome and to assert the independence of the English monarchs. Christopher Hodgkins says, thus, 'to Elizabethans and Jacobeans the renewed "British" identity promised not only a rationale for a unified island kingdom but also a sphere of international influence that could counteract the Vatican and unify Europe (and newfound America) under a non-Roman catholicity' (2002, p. 11). As the Reformation developed and friction with Roman Catholicism became more intense, affirmation of the independence of the monarchy was supported by the idea of England as an elect nation (Collinson 2002). The mission of ancient Israel to bring light to the nations became the mission of a revitalized England, bringing its own people and as much of the world as possible out of the darkness of Rome into the light of the gospel. Roman Catholic power had taken possession of the Caribbean, Central and South America and was steadily expanding into North America through Spanish and French colonizing and evangelizing. This had to be brought to a halt, and Protestant Christian faith was called upon to provide the ideology of this expansion. It is in the trading sermons of the early seventeenth century, particularly those associated with the Virginia Company, founded in 1606,[2] that we find the clearest expressions of the theological changes which this development involved. Anglicanism was to become a powerful foil to Romanism. The voyages of exploration and the establishment of the trading companies were always associated with the Church of England. Chaplains were provided for the voyages and a sermon was normally preached at the annual meeting of the Company. Nearly 20 of these sermons have survived, and more than half a dozen of these deal with the Virginia Company. There were precedents in the voyages of Martin Frobisher in 1576–78, of Francis Drake from 1577 and Walter Raleigh's voyage to Guyana in 1595 and the establishment of the Roanoke Island settlement in 1585. The planting of settlements in Ireland became the model for similar plantations in the New World (Canny 1998a; Ohlmeyer 1998).

---

2 Original sources include John Smith, *A true Relation of such Occurrences and Accidents of Noate as hath hapned in . . .* , London, 1608; Robert Johnson, *Nova Britannia: Offering most excellent Fruits by Planting in Virginia. Exciting all such as be well affected to further tha same*, London, 1609; and Part 2, 1612, The Virginia Company, *A true and sincere Declaration of the Purpose and Ends of the Plantation begun in Virginia, of the Degrees of which it hath received and Means by which it hath been advanced and the Resolution and Conclusion of his Majesty's Council of that Colony for the constant and patient Prosecution thereof, until by the Mercies of God it shall Retribute a fruitful Harvest to the kingdom of Heaven and this Commonwealth*, Set forth by the Authority of the Governors and Councillors established for that Plantation, London, 1610; John Rolfe, *A true account of the state of Virginia*, 1615. For discussions of the sermons see Fitzmaurice 2000 and Parker 1978.

The first theme which we shall consider is the way that biblical interpretation fastened upon the Old Testament and upon the Hebrew monarchy in particular. The identification of the English monarchy with the kings of Israel enhanced the sense of a divine mandate for the expansion of the country. The publication of *The Faerie Queene* in 1592 set out an idealized Elizabeth as the source of a new, radiant authority. 'Elizabeth's cult would become the most successful Protestant version of sacred kingship in the English Reformation' (McCoy 2002, p. 59). So Elizabeth became the new David and James I became the new Solomon. In 1609 there was a cluster of sermons in defence of the Virginia Company, including one by the Reverend George Benson (1609) of Worcestershire preached at Paul's Cross in London. Benson identifies royal persons with biblical royalty.

> After a David we have a Solomon. After a David, the youngest of Jesse's sons and a shepherd, Elizabeth the youngest of King Henry's daughters not a shepherd, but one that desired to be a milkmaid in Woodstock park, we have a Solomon . . .

Richard Crakanthorpe (1567–1624), born in Westmoreland and a fellow of Queen's College, Oxford from 1598, was a well-known Puritan preacher and teacher. He was invited to preach a sermon celebrating the accession of James I, in which the king is hailed as a worthy successor of King Solomon. He claimed that just as the kingship of Solomon was obtained directly from God so was that of his own King James. Crakanthorpe speaks of 'both these Solomons' and of James as 'our Solomon' (Crakanthorpe 1608, images 6 and 8). A parallel is also drawn between James and both David and Josiah. Elizabeth was the monarch of action and turbulence and was followed by James the King of wisdom and peace, just as David preceded Solomon. By the divine wisdom given to him King James had penetrated the secret plans of the Gunpowder Plot and so saved the country (image 12).

Little is known about Robert Gray, who describes himself as a 'preacher of the Word of God'. Two of his sermons, both preached in 1609, have survived, and we know from the second one that he was one of the 'morning Lecturers' at Saint Antholines, a church in the city of London destroyed in the Great Fire of 1666. In his sermon on the Virginia Colony Robert Gray compares King James to Joshua:

> and so stands our case, whereupon they repair to have his warrant and direction to enlarge their borders, and so have many of our Noble men of honourable minds, worthy knights, rich merchants, & diverse other of the best dispositions, solicited our Joshua, and mighty Monarch, that most religious and renowned King James.

The comparison with Joshua was appropriate, because Joshua had conquered the heathens, who inhabited the Promised Land.

Thomas Cooper in a work addressed to the Lord Mayor of London and the Commissioners of the Irish and Virginia Plantations says:

> Still hath it pleased our gracious God to visit us from on high, with his saving health: and by the ministry of our gracious sovereign, James (whom the Lord in mercy prospers in this holy work that he may enlarge the bounds of his glorious kingdom far and near) . . . So blessed be the name of his majesty for ever, that

hath hereby sanctified these portions unto you (Right Honourable, worshipful and my dear Countrymen) that your hearts and purses are enlarged plentifully. (1615, image 3)[3]

The parallels between English monarchs and their biblical antecedents not only glorified Elizabeth and James, but as the power of Christian Europe grew, a number of biblical passages were read in the light of these developments. Thomas Cooper in the same work we have just been considering regarded the prophecy about the sons of Noah (Gen. 9.25–7) as being fulfilled in those events. Noah had said that God would extend the boundaries of his son Japheth, and for centuries this had been regarded as being fulfilled in the growth of the Christian Church. Cooper, however, gives it greater emphasis:

> Namely, that the believing Gentiles shall also be enlarged far and near upon the face of the earth, as rulers and conquerors of the world, and of all the enemies of the church. And let Canaan, (that is) the posterity of the wicked, for ever, be subject unto the servants of Jesus Christ . . . the Gentiles, confined especially in this part of the world which we inhabit, called Europe; and extending to all those nations, in all parts of the world, that are not either properly Jews, or of that cursed race of Ham; scattered towards the South in Africa. (image 6, p. 3)

But how best would God be glorified in the use of this power? Some of the advocates of imperial expansion showed a keen awareness of the responsibility this entailed. George Benson drew a lesson from an incident recorded by Herodotus about the Persian King Cyrus. When the white horses of Cyrus were drowned in the river, the king threatened to divide the water into many branches, depriving the river of its depth and force. So,

> if those floods and great streams of God's blessings upon us, drown and overthrow not our white horses but our souls, which should be white and spotless, God can divide that worldly pomp of ours, into many channels, convey it into many hands, dispossess us both of the name and glory that we had by those things; and therefore it was not without cause that God gave the people of Israel a caveat, that they should not forget him when they came 'into a land of corn, a land of wine, and a land of oil'. (Benson 1609, image 27, p. 46)

Benson reinforces his warning about the abuse of power with a further example:

> Those that are filled with God's blessings, should be like the full end of an hour glass, they should empty and evacuate themselves into those that want, that those who have wanted, may be raised up. (p. 47)

---

3 This work is sometimes attributed to Thomas Cooper 1517–94, who was Bishop of Lincoln, but the references to King James make it much more likely that the author was the other Thomas Cooper who flourished in 1626.

Benson even found in the story of the defeat of Benhadad by the Israelite armies (1 Kings 20.23–8) a suggestion that God had a bias to the poor.

> Benhadad was deceived when he said, the God of Israel was the God of the mountains, and not of the valleys, as though the Lord cared for the high and mighty and not for the lowly and dejected ... because of the deep sighing of the poor I will up (saith the Lord) and when he ariseth, who is able to resist? (image 44, p. 76)[4]

This prophetic denunciation of the rich for their exploitation of the poor is found in a number of the sermons including 'Saul's Prohibition Stayed' (1609) by Daniel Price D.D. (1581–1631). Price, born in Shrewsbury and an Oxford graduate, became Dean of Hereford in 1623. He had a reputation for being an excellent preacher, a warm supporter of the English crown and an evangelical Calvinist (McCollough 2004). He says:

> [I]f there be any one that viper-like hath eaten out his birth, building upon the ruins of broken poor citizens eating up his brethren like bread; the stone out of the wall shall cry against thee, and know it, that thy house is Golgotha's, the place of dead men's skulls, and thy possession ... is the field of blood: the bread thou eatest is the flesh of man, the wine thou drinkest is the blood of man, thou art a cannibal, thou art a Saul, thou dost persecute Christ. (Price 1609, image 20)

Reflections of this kind, however, were not sufficient to deter imperial progress. They applied only to the poor of England and did not seem to extend to the people in the country about to be colonized, in spite of the fact that these were frequently described as 'poor savages'. The rights of the poor abroad gave way to the rights of God's faithful people. Thomas Cooper argues that entitlement to the kingdom of heaven carries with it a similar right to possess the earth.

> The kingdom of heaven being bestowed, interests also the faithful, in the possession of the earth. The true believer alone is the right owner of all God's blessings. He that first seeks the kingdom of heaven, shall have these things also cast upon him (Matt. 16.33). So profitable is godliness, as well for this life, as that which is to come (1 Tim. 4.8–9). So Christ being ours, who is Lord of all in heaven and earth, (Matt. 28) all with him is ours, both in heaven and earth. (Cooper 1615, p. 20)

Sometimes the thought that God resists the proud and gives grace to the humble could be turned to the believer's advantage. Thomas Cooper presents a shrewd, contractual spirituality of poverty and renunciation. We are to demonstrate our worthiness to possess all the goods of the world by our readiness to discard them and by not setting our hope of salvation upon them. 'Shall not he which

---

4 Since 1601 the local parishes had been responsible for the relief of poor people. See Slack 1990.

thus leaveth house or lands have recompense a hundred fold? Shall not he find his life, that thus is willing to lose it?' (p. 20) This developed into a sort of theology of prudential humility. We are continually to have a sense of our unworthiness and by this means

> renewing our right in Christ, and disavowing confidence in the greatest [of our possessions] by submitting the blessing thereof unto our God, that so giving God the glory of his mercies, he may enlarge himself unto us, to the making of us meet to be vessels of glory: thus are the saints lords of the earth. (p. 20)

The ambiguity of colonization

The theologians whose work we are considering realized that the planting of colonies was not without moral ambiguity.[5] This was particularly acute in the case of overseas plantations, where the intention was to occupy the land already possessed by other people. Activities in Asia did not require the same legitimation, since they were not regarded as establishing settlements (Pagden 1998, p. 37). To some extent, this was mitigated by the sacred purposes of the settlement.

Patrick Copland (1572–1648) was born in Scotland. His father was a merchant in Edinburgh. He became a preacher to the East India Company in 1612 and tried to reconcile the English Company with its Dutch rival (Copland 1619).[6] In his sermon of thanksgiving he says that the grace of God is displayed in the Virginia Company

> to mollify the hearts of savages, and to make some of them voluntarily to remove from their own warm and well seated and peopled habitations, to give place to strangers, whom they had never before seen . . . to sell to the English and their governor Sir George Yeardley the right and title they had to their possessions? yet all these hath the lord done, and are they not wonderful works indeed? (1622, pp. 25–6)

Copland insists upon a direct connection between faithfulness to religion and profitable return from colonial investment 'so as when you advance religion, you advance together with it your own profit. Neglect of this hath made your hopes in your long looked for returns . . . to be frustrated' (p. 28). Examples are offered of how God's people were blessed, when they built the temple.

In spite of its noble intentions and attractive outcomes the colonization of the New World presented a number of moral dilemmas. It implied taking the land occupied by the original inhabitants. How could this be justified?

> The first objection is, by what right or warrant we can enter into the land of these savages, take away their rightful inheritance from them, and plant

---

5 For a general commendation of the policy of colonization from the same period see Richard Eburne 1624.

6 For comments on the missionary significance of the work of Copland, see Canny 1998, p. 18.

ourselves in their places, being unwronged and unprovoked by them. (Gray 1609, image 11)[7]

It is possible that the savages have 'no particular proprieties in any part or parcel of that country, but only a general residence there, as wild beasts have in the forest' (image 11). Gray comments, however, that this claim whether true or not is irrelevant since the natives are willing to give the settlers by contract or sale more land than they can possibly plant or sow, and so it is unnecessary to supplant the natives. In any case, the theology of the just war, as described by no less an authority than Augustine of Hippo, would permit the use of violence if necessary to bring the savages into the blessings of civilization.

A Christian king may lawfully make war upon barbarous and savage people, and such as live under no lawful or warrantable government, and may make a conquest of them, so that the war be undertaken to this end, to reclaim or reduce those savages from their barbarous kind of life, and from their brutish and ferine manners to humanity, piety and honesty. (image 11)[8]

Gray concludes 'we might lawfully make war upon the savages of Virginia' (image 12), but every adventurer must

examine his whole heart, and if he find that he is drawn to partake in this business, is to draw the savages from their brutish kind of life, to a merciful, honest and Christian kind of life, let him not doubt of the lawfulness of it. (image 12)

The idea that making war could be justified provided that it was done with a pure heart is a familiar example of aggressive self-deception. We noticed it in our study of the theology of the medieval Crusades. Apart from the troublesome question of war there was also the difficulty about the apparent stealing of property.

William Symonds D.D. (1556–1616), a well-known clergyman and a specialist in the interpretation of biblical prophecy, spent some time in the Virginia colony himself. He was one of the first clergy invited to preach to the members of the Virginia Company in London. He was aware of the fact that some people had doubts about the ethics of colonization.

[O]ne scruple, that some, that think themselves to be very wise, do cast in our way; which is this in effect. The country, they say, is possessed by owners, that rule, and govern it in their own right: then with what conscience, and equity, can we offer to thrust them, by violence, out of their inheritances? (1609, p. 10)

---

7 There is a discussion of this theme in the Virginia sermon of John Donne in Lim 1998, p. 78.

8 For a searching analysis of the violence implicit in Puritan rhetoric see Kibbey 1986.

Whatever doubts the colonial adventurers might have had about violence and property, they were quelled by the glorious spectacle of empire. Gray considers that the colonization of North America will be comparable to the extension of the Roman Empire. He is 'hoping to see their expectation satisfied, and the glory of England as much increased by this their honourable attempt, as ever was the Roman Empire by the enterprise of her greatest Emperors' (Gray 1609, image 15). According to William Symonds the conversion of Constantine and the founding of the Christian Empire brought to an end the first period of conflict between Michael and the Devil, which had taken place during the period when, although the gospel was proclaimed throughout the Empire, there was persecution against the Church (1605, p. 20). According to Symonds, Christian kings were emblems of Christ the King and ruled over their territories just as Christ rules over all.

> As Jesus Christ, the Lamb is King of his Church, he warreth by civil princes, in whom is a lively type of the glorious kingdom of Christ, possessing both land and sea, in such sort as none can take it from him . . . By these Christ Jesus, both taketh possession of the land and sea; and also delivereth the Word of God . . . (p. 76)

In other words, when a Christian nation conquers a non-Christian nation, it is really Christ who is the conqueror, and the kingdom of Christ is accordingly enlarged. We shall find the same argument in Chapter 6, when we come to consider Isaac Watts' Christian interpretation of Psalm 72.

By the time he preached his sermon of encouragement to the recently-formed Virginia Company, Symonds had developed this idea into a detailed theology of Christian imperialism. In the first place there is biblical authority for imperial expansion even when carried out according to the will of God by non-Christian kings. God called Cyrus to go and conquer. 'Then who can blame Cyrus, and keep himself from blaspheming the Almighty' (1609, p. 11). Moreover, many of the biblical heroes of faith were conquerors. Symonds addresses Joshua and David with the following questions: 'Joshua, where is thy virtue, to set thy feet upon the necks of princes, in their own kingdoms . . . David, how wilt thou answer for the blood thy sword hath shed' (p. 12). Even Solomon, the 'true type of Christ' is told by his father King David to 'enlarge thy borders'. Is this, Symonds asks ironically, to be regarded as a 'sinful prayer'? In Psalm 72, traditionally addressed to Solomon, the king is told 'that thine enemies should lick the dust'. In view of such illustrious examples how can anyone say 'that it is not lawful, by forces to invade the territories of other princes' (pp. 12–13)?

Symonds now turns his attention to the history of the English monarchs, who trace their origin to the Norman conquest. If conquest is illegitimate, then the present king has no claim to the crown '[f]or he hath his title from the conqueror' (p. 13). But the history of invasion is much older than the Norman Conquest of England, the Romans had colonies, and the English people are also descended from the Saxons, who came to England as invaders (p. 15).

Finally, Symonds points out that however legitimate and even obligatory violent invasions may be there is no need to get excited about it in the case of Virginia. There is 'a difference between a bloody invasion, and the planting of a peaceable colony, in a waste country, where the people do live but like deer in herds . . . where they know no God but the devil, nor sacrifice, but to offer their men and children unto Molech' (p. 15).

The need to interpret Christian faith in the interests of empire was not confined to the Virginia sermons but was a common feature of colonial expansion. John Featley (c.1605–66), who is also known as John Fairclough, was born in Northamptonshire and graduated from All Souls College, Oxford in 1624. After his ordination in the same year he went to St. Christopher's in the West Indies (Beckles 1998). The island of St. Christopher's, renamed later as St. Kitt's, became an English colony in 1624, and Featley was the first preacher in the colony. He was a royalist during the Civil War, and after the defeat of the royalists in 1642 he went to St. Christopher's for the second time, taking his wife and children. Following the restoration of the monarchy he was appointed chaplain to Charles II. Several of his writings have survived including a sermon preached in 1629 at the farewell of an expedition about to set sail for the West Indies. Once again the inspiration comes from Joshua, the chosen text being Joshua 1.9, the commission given by God to Joshua who was about to invade the promised land 'Have not I commanded thee? Only be strong, and of a good courage: be not afraid, neither be dismayed: for I will be with thee, whithersoever thou goest.' Featley then presents a kind of theology of power as a basis of imperialism because 'Earthly authority derives itself from the omnipotency, and ceases to be imperial when it forgets the author thereof' (Featly 1629, p. 4).

Reference is made to the power of the gospel, of Christ and of the Holy Spirit leading to the thought that

[w]e, whose intent it is (with God's assistance) to plough up the foamy billows of the vast ocean; whose resolutions have commanded to visit another world (as geographers have termed it) we (I say) must first be sure that our commission runs in the words of my text 'Have not I commanded thee?' (p. 17)

The possession of the Caribbean Islands was thus commanded by God, and this could be received with great confidence, because it was part of God's plan to lift up the humble and to bring down the proud. The island of St. Christopher had been settled by the Spanish and the French, but God 'punishes rebellion with extirpation; and makes religion inherit, where spotted vice seeks its subversion'. The success of the expedition about to set out was guaranteed in the light of a kind of Deutoronomic philosophy of history, according to which there would be a series of reversals, pride and luxury inevitably leading to punishment. So 'The Canaanites, which lived in the height of sensuality, must be humbled now in the depth of misery.' England, which had 'suffered the slavery of bondage' (to Roman Catholicism) would now 'inherit a Canaan, to encourage them in their integrity' (i.e. their Protestantism). 'The Israelites [the English] which were exposed to the tyranny of injustice under the Egyptian Pharaoh [the Pope of Rome], must be comforted again with milk and honey', but lest their 'sudden liberty' should cause the Israelites to forget God, the discipline of a 'tedious journey' was imposed upon them as they pass through the wilderness. In the same way, the colonists should regard the tedious voyage in front of them as a restraint upon their new found freedom. For John Featley as for so many biblical commentators, Scripture meant whatever was necessary to justify the matter at hand (pp. 23–4).

Daniel Price suggested a kind of happy equality between the benefits of colonization to both the newcomers and the original inhabitants.

> To the present assurance of great profit, add this future profit, that whoso-ever hath a hand in this business, shall receive an unspeakable blessing, for they that turn many to righteousness, shall shine as the stars forever and ever: you will make . . . a savage country to become a sanctified country; you will obtain their best commodities, they will obtain the saving of their souls, you will enlarge the bounds of this kingdom, nay the bounds of heaven, and all the angels that behold this, if they rejoice so much at the conversion of one sinner, O what will their joy be at the conversion of so many. (1609, image 22)

The superiority of the faith of the English

The growing confidence in the destiny of the English people and the sense of being the elect of God was accompanied by increasing hostility toward foreigners in general, and to the people of the other colonizing powers in particular. George Benson, for example, was worried lest the manners of the young English gentlemen going abroad might be corrupted by the folly and extravagance of continental manners, 'Else what means this revolution of fashions, when men that should be mere English are not themselves; but compounded men, Spanish, Dutch, Italian and what-not?' (image 17, p. 27).

On the other hand, Thomas Cooper gloried in God's choice of England, and thought that a helping hand could be extended to less favoured nations.

> This little flock is as dear unto the Lord, as the apple of his eye. It is his glory, his delight, here will he dwell for ever . . . Hath the Lord begun to enlarge us far and near to Virginia, and Ireland . . . Hath not God wonderfully pre-served this little island, this angle of the world? That in former ages was not known, or accounted to be any part of the world? Hath it not been the sanc-tuary of all the Christian world? Have not all the neighbour-nations taken hold of the skirt of an Englishman? Have they not joined themselves to us, because the Lord is with us? . . . So may the desire of all nations be unto us, that our desires may be enlarged to all nations, for their comfort and conver-sion. (1615, p. 34)

Robert Gray takes a slightly different perspective. He is critical of the English for not being as alert as other nations to colonize the new world.

> This hath always been reported of the English, by those that have observed the nature of nations . . . that the English were always accounted more war-like, valorous, and courageous, than the French, but the French went always beyond them in prudence, and policy. (1609, image 5)

All were agreed that the English displayed more humanity in their imperial expansion than did other nations. The contrast between English culture and Spanish cruelty is often referred to and was one of the conditions of the covenant bestowed upon England by God.

> [B]ut I hope our English are of that mettle, that having in their hands the key of the kingdom of God, they will not keep those weak ones out, but rather make way for the gospel (as I hope they may) by their gentle and humane dealings. (Benson 1609, p. 52)

The same point was made by Robert Gray:

> [B]ut far be it from the nature of the English, to exercise any bloody cruelty amongst these people: far be it from the hearts of the English, to give them occasion, that the holy name of God, should be dishonoured among the infidels, or that in the plantation of that continent, they should give any cause to the world, to say that they sought the wealth of that country above or before the glory of God, and the propagation of his kingdom. (1609, image 10)[9]

Exclusion, uniqueness and dichotomies

The contrast between Protestantism and Catholicism on one hand and the competition between English imperialism and that of other European nations tended to encourage the theologians of the early seventeenth century to read the Bible in black and white terms and to emphasize potential dichotomies in Christian faith. George Benson, for example, in his commentary on Hosea 7.7–12 said:

> The language of the prophet is all and none, all are like an oven, none call upon God, they went all with one accord down the stream: they were either possessed by a dumb spirit; they did not call; or with a frantic spirit, if they called, they called not upon God: they did not, but we must call, and call upon God. (1609, pp. 11–12)

It is clear that the reason Benson made so much of this relatively small aspect of the text of Hosea was the nature of his own attitude towards plurality and uniqueness.

> It is remembered of a certain sultan which died at the siege of Zigetum, that being persuaded by the mufti (who holds the place of a bishop or patriarch among the Mahomedan Turks) not to suffer so many religions as were in his dominion; he answered, that a nosegay of many flowers smelled more sweetly than one flower only: which I confess to be true, but the case with religions is neither the same, nor the like: for in a nosegay they may be all flowers, but

---

9 For early descriptions of the native people of North America see Berkhofer 1978, pp. 12–16.

among religions they must be all weeds, all heresies, except one only flower which is the truth. (pp. 30–1)[10]

This policy of exclusion is supported by references to the letters to the seven churches. They were rebuked for not maintaining the purity and the integrity of their Christian faith 'the same mouth that speaketh the language of Canaan, why should it speak the language of Ashdod?' (p. 31). Benson supports his policy of exclusion by pointing out that during the Reformation, some of the German cities had made a grave error in allowing their citizens to choose between religions two of which had been permitted to exist side by side. But 'the consequence had like to have been bloody' (p. 32).

Indeed, such mixing is contrary to the commandment of God, as Benson shows by referring to the purity code in the book of Leviticus.

[N]o ground should be sown with two seeds, that no garment of linsey and woolsey should be worn, that no ground should be ploughed with an ox and an ass together: all which were shadows of two religions, whereof there ought not to be a mixture. (Benson 1609, p. 31)

Further illustrations from Genesis and the Psalms show that 'he knew how well it pleased the holy Trinity, to see the union of the godly, and their loathing of the ungodly'. Benson concludes 'happy are we then, in whose lands Popery is not enfranchised and made free denison' (p. 33).

A good example of dichotomous thinking is found in Thomas Cooper's contrast between the true Church and the malignant Church. This contrast is traced through much of the Bible and is consistent with the Calvinist theology of election unto both salvation and damnation. So for an Abel there is a Cain, for a Japheth and Shem, there is a Ham, whose destiny shows that '[t]he malignant Church shall be in subjection to the true' (1615, p. 57).

Even for Jesus there is a Judas, and so a 'malignant Church there hath been, and must be to the world's end'.

And therefore, vain is that dream, that all shall be saved and vainer their conceit, that though in their daily practises, they are hastening to destruction: yet still they are confident, their estate is as good as any: their hearts are good, they mean well: they are but flesh and blood: the Lord is merciful. And will the Lord be merciful to presumptuous sinners? (Cooper 1615, p. 58).

Those who believe that all shall be saved are vain in this belief for scripture predicts that there will be a malignant church that will remain unrepentant. The parable of the wheat and the tares shows that this distinction is a feature of the church itself, and so it will be until the day of judgement. Nevertheless, it is the will of God that there should be such a dichotomy, for the good reveals the character of the bad, and the bad are a continual challenge and warning to the good.

---

10 The concept of natural religion and the possibility of a universal religion of morality did not emerge in England until much later in the seventeenth century. See Harrison 1990.

Doth not the admirable power and wisdom of God appear, in ordering these two contraries in the same fold, that each may further other, to their contrary end? (p. 59)

Robert Tynley D.D., Archdeacon of Ely, preached a sermon at Paul's Cross in London on 5 November 1608, the fourth anniversary of the failed Gunpowder Plot. In the course of a diatribe on the hostility of the Roman Catholic Church, he gives a striking description of the sectarian and oppositional character of religion:

[I]f there be anything in the world that doth provoke a man and kindle his affections, it is religion which maketh him not only defend to the uttermost of his power, and with his best endeavours, what he concieveth to be pure, but also to prosecute with all might and fury, the contrary sect, to the utter extinguishing and rooting up of it, supposing that in so doing, they fight God's battle. (Tynley 1609, pp. 16–17)

To some extent this powerful sense of conflict can be attributed to the fear of English Protestantism following the Spanish Armada of 1588, the well-known brutality of the Spanish Inquisition and the Gunpowder Plot itself. There is more to it, however, than that; the policy of the government of King James was for mediation and toleration, which makes the sharp intolerance more striking in the writings of the theologians we are discussing (Okines 2004). Moreover, the sense of exclusion and difference was not only directed toward Catholics, but also toward the inhabitants of Virginia of whom William Symonds says: 'Their God is the enemy of mankind that seeketh whom he may devour' (1609, p. 25).

Mission as a motive for colonization

A much discussed feature in the history of Christian mission is the absence of an interest in foreign missions on the part of the Protestant churches. It is often said that between the Reformation in the first half of the sixteenth century and the publication of the famous book by William Carey in 1792 the English Protestants did not engage in missionary expeditions (Robinson 1915, p. 42; Glover 1924, p. 68; Neill 1986, pp. 187–9; Bevans and Schroeder 2004, pp. 195–6). An exception is made in the case of John Eliot (1604–90) of the Massachusetts Colony who seems to have been the first to begin a systematic programme of Indian conversion (Tinker 1993, pp. 21–41). Another exception, however, is to be found in the sermons of the Virginia Company, most of which were preached and published before the Plymouth Colony was founded in 1620. It is true that the emphasis upon evangelizing the indigenous people of North America is part of the justification for the creation of the plantations, and to that extent may be considered secondary to the main purpose. This does not mean, however, that the theologians whose work we are considering were superficial or insincere. Evangelizing the new world was an important aspect of the calling of England to be an elect nation and a light to the world. Moreover, not all the preachers were satisfied with words; several of them went to one or more of the colonies to explore their calling to mission. Alexander Whitaker (1585–1616) was known by his contemporaries as the 'Apostle of Virginia'. He went to the colony in 1611 and founded two churches there (Whitaker 1613).

The belief that the end of the world was near drew the attention of many preachers to Matthew 24 and in particular to verse 14 'And this gospel will be proclaimed throughout the earth as a testimony to all nations; and then the end will come.' The evangelization of the world was sometimes undertaken in order to hasten the return of Christ. On the other hand, in George Benson's sermon the fact that the ends of the earth are already being evangelized is an indication or a sign of the coming end. We do not know when the portents in the heavens will appear but we do know that the Virginia Colony is already carrying out the mandate of Christ:

> [W]hen the sun will be darkened, and the moon turned into blood, we cannot tell: but for the publication of the Gospel over the world, it may be proved by many instances. One most pregnant, most fresh, is that of Virginia which now (by God's grace) through our English shall hear news of Christ, the gospel of Christ shall be published, no doubt the sound of the preachers will go out into that corner of the world, and make it as a well watered garden. (Benson 1609, p. 92)

Another critical sign of the approaching end was to be found in Romans 11.25, where Paul speaks of the time when 'the gentiles have been admitted in full strength', or, as the older translations say the 'full number of the gentiles' has been included. Not until then will the Jews be converted to Christian faith (v. 26). This would be another sign of the coming end. It is this sequence which Thomas Cooper sees unfolding by means of the Virginia Colony.

> And is this obstinacy any other but in part till the fullness of the Gentiles be come in, so that the remnant of the election shall certainly be gathered in? Shall not this restoring of the Gentiles be the reviving of the world, restoring new glory and beauty unto the same: when as the Jew and Gentile shall join together, in the pure worship of God? (1615, p. 54)[11]

The expectation that the indigenous people would be evangelized is very clear in the sermon by Patrick Copland, who thinks that the failure to carry out this evangelical task is one of the reasons why God has not blessed the Virginia Colony. Copland quotes from a letter he has received from Virginia

> That you have not as you ought . . . preferred God's glory by your serious endeavours of converting the Natives, who . . . do live so peaceably amongst us, and round about us, as they do even seem to groan under the burden of the bondage of Satan, and to want nothing but means to be delivered. (1622, p. 28)

---

11 For the Protestant Reformation as a search for the restoration of Christian purity see Hughes and Allen 1988, p. 2.

As previously noted, Copland had been chaplain to the East India Company and he now draws upon this experience to enforce his point.

> I might hear speak something touching my own experience, of the willingness of the heathens in general in all the Eastern parts of the world, where I have travelled, how ready they are to receive the Gospel, if there were but preachers amongst them that could and would instruct them by their doctrine and life. (p. 29)

He illustrates this by describing how he had instructed and converted someone he had brought back to London from India and who was baptized in the presence of the East India Company.

Christian civilization and the heathen

The expansion of empire into the New World led to a new way of understanding the meaning of Christian civilization, which an emphatic contrast between Christianity and the dark savagery of the non-Christian world made more vivid. In dedicating his work to the Lord Mayor of London and the commissioners for the plantations of Ireland and Virginia, Thomas Cooper gives thanks to King James because 'by his gracious Authority it hath been, that the barbarous and desolate places of the Land are now replenished, with the power of the Gospel. Yea, the rude & savage nations far & near, in Ireland and Virginia, have had this blessed light conveyed and enlarged unto them' (Cooper 1615, image 3). By contrasting ourselves with these 'foolish and forlorn nations', we ourselves may be renewed in 'our first love, by extending it to our brethren' (p. 22).

The contrasts are emphatic in the sermon of Richard Crakanthorpe:

> The Virginia colony is an happy and glorious work indeed, of planting among those poor and savage, and to be pitied Virginians, not only humanity, instead of brutish incivility, but religion also, piety, the true knowledge and sincere worship of God, where his name is not heard of: and reducing those to faith and salvation by Christ who as yet in the blindness of their infidelity and superstition, do offer sacrifice, yea, even themselves unto the Devil. (1608, image 14)

The result will be 'to see a new Britain in another world', while our own society is made glorious by the wisdom of King James.

The darker the character of the society of the indigenous peoples, the brighter shone the invading culture and the stronger the case for imposing Christian and British lordship. Psalm 115.16 distinguishes between the heavens which belong to the Lord, and earth, which God has given to human beings. This enables Gray to distinguish between worthy recipients of the earth and those whose brutality made them unworthy.

> [A]lthough the Lord hath given the earth to the children of men, yet this earth which is man's fee-simple by deed of gift from God, is the greater part of it

possessed and wrongfully usurped by wild beasts, and unreasonable creatures, or by brutish savages, which by reason of their godless ignorance, and
blasphemous idolatry, are worse than those beasts which are of most wild
and savage nature ... So may man say to himself: The earth was mine, God
gave it me, and my posterity, by the name of the children of men, and yet I
stay and take it not out of the hands of beasts, and brutish savages, which
have no interest in it, because they participate rather of the nature of beasts
than men. (Gray 1609, image 5)

The argument is simple. God has given the earth to human beings, but the
native peoples of North America are not human; they are mere beasts. Having
dehumanized them, any objection to their colonization is void, and the way is
cleared for Christian Britain to follow the example of Joshua. In the response to
their complaint about the smallness of the land allocated to them, the tribes of
Manasseh and Ephraim are told by Joshua to take more land for themselves and
to drive out the local people (Josh. 17.14–18).

[W]e are to note the direction of Joshua, upon the aforesaid complaint of the
children of Joseph, which is to enlarge their territories, and dilate their borders, by destroying God's enemies the Perizzites, and Giants, which inhabited
the valleys, bordering upon mount Ephraim, which were most abominable
idolaters, and had no knowledge of the true and only God: from whence we
may learn, how odious those people are, in the sight of God, which having
no knowledge of him and his worship, give that honour to the insensible and
unreasonable creature, which is only due to the omnipotent and almighty
Creator. (1609, image 8)

It is thus a duty in the presence of God to conquer, but that duty does not necessarily extend to exterminating the local people. Only in cases where the Christian invaders encountered a wilful determination to persist in evil and idolatry,
were they to be destroyed. Not only was this in their own interest, to secure the
reformation of the rest but would be consistent with Scripture and the divine
will.

[I]t is every man's duty to travel both by sea and land, and to venture either
with his person or with his purse, to bring the barbarous and savage people
to a civil and Christian kind of government, under which they may learn how
to live holily, justly, and soberly in this world, and to apprehend the means to
save their souls in the world to come, rather than to destroy them, or utterly
to root them out: for a wise man, but much more a Christian, ought to try all
means before they undertake war: devastation and depopulation ought to be
the last thing which Christians should put in practise, yet forasmuch as every
example in the scripture as I said is a precept, we are warranted by this direction of Joshua, to destroy wilful and convicted idolaters, rather than to let
them live, if by no other means they can be reclaimed. (image 9)

In case there should be any remaining doubt Gray concludes his theology of domination by emphasizing the utter degradation of the people about to be colonized.

> The report goeth, that in Virginia the people are savage and incredibly rude, they worship the devil, offer their young children in sacrifice unto him, wander up and down like beasts, and in manners and conditions, differ very little from beasts, having no art, nor science, nor trade, to employ themselves, or give themselves unto, yet by nature loving and, gentle, and desirous to embrace a better condition. (image 10)[12]

Robert Tynley describes the miracles of grace which accompany the expansion of the Protestant faith, whereas the Catholic Church can only claim physical miracles. His argument about the nature of this miracle of conversion is somewhat similar to that of Robert Gray. The purpose of the Virginia Plantation is

> for the gaining and winning to Christ his fold, and the reducing unto a civil society (as hope may justly conceive) of so many thousands of those silly, brutish, and ignorant souls, now fast bound with the chains of error and ignorance, under the bondage and slavery of the devil. (1609, p. 67)

John Featley uses similar arguments to encourage the expedition to the West Indies.

> Occasions command us to take leave of our native soil, that we may possess the land of the Hittites and Amorites, the habitations of savage heathens, whose understandings were never yet illuminated with the knowledge of their maker. (1629, p. 3)

Featley's hope is that the upright behaviour of the colonists will demonstrate their god-like stature, and he concludes this part of his sermon in a mood of dry humour.

> Our equal steps, and upright behaviour thus inflaming the hearts of the ignorant, it may peradventure prove in a short space, a greater task to dissuade them from believing us to be gods, than to persuade them to believe that there is a God. (p. 22)

The requirements of power and the interpretation of the Bible

Throughout this chapter we have drawn attention to the way that the requirements of imperial expansion exerted an influence upon the interpretation of the Bible. The English monarchs became the ideal Israelite kings, the blessings

---

12 Contrary to European impressions, most Native Americans were not nomadic but seasonal agriculturists. They tended to become nomadic when their land was taken by Europeans. See Gustafson 2000, p. 80, n.8.

of the covenant with God had been inherited by the faithful English, whose mission was now part of the purposes of God for the world, and the relation between England, other nations of Europe and especially the inhabitants of the New World were construed in similar terms to the relation between Israel and its pagan neighbours.

For Robert Gray the taking of Virginia is not theft, because the land is already the rightful possession of the English nation. He justifies this by reference to 1 Kings 22.3, where Ahab King of Israel said to his servants, 'know ye not that Ramoth-Gilead was ours, and we stay and take it not out of the hands of the King of Aram?' (1609, image 5).

Any biblical incident could become a precedent for a proposed course of action. In this use of Scripture, the preachers of the early seventeenth century were not unusual; the Bible had been found to give this kind of specific advice down the centuries, and examples may be found in the use made of the Old Testament by the New. Nevertheless, the use of Scripture to justify colonization was comparatively new and was demanded by the circumstances of England at the time. Robert Gray suggests that the solution for the overpopulation and unemployment, which were said to be typical problems of his time, could be relieved by encouraging emigration. This was just what the Patriarch Jacob had told his family, when they were starving in Israel:

> Why gaze ye one upon another? Behold, I have heard there is food in Egypt, get ye down thither, and buy us food thence, that we may live. Even so may it be said to a company of people in this land, which doe nothing but gaze one upon another, destitute of counsel, advice, and means, how to provide justly and honestly for their maintenance. (image 8)

A favourite passage in several sermons is the Song of Deborah, particularly Judges 5.23. After the Israelite victory the judge and prophet rebukes those who had not come to the support of the army. Symonds uses this example to reproach those who did not come forward to take part in the noble gospel expedition to Virginia.

> And who is wanting in this blessed expedition? Surely, not any tribe, praise ye the Lord, for those that offered themselves so willingly. For who can withdraw himself from concurrence in so good an action: especially when he shall but read, or hear, that one sentence which Deborah did sing: Curse ye Meroz, said the angel of the Lord curse the inhabitants thereof: because they came not forth to help the Lord. (1609, images 3 and 4)

For many modern readers, the biblical descriptions of the brutality of ancient warfare are disconcerting or at best of little relevance. The early colonial preachers, however, take quite a different view.

Robert Gray quotes with approval the commandment of David who 'doth promise a blessing upon those that shall take the children of the idolatrous Babylonians and cast them against the stones' (Ps. 137.9). Similarly, 'Saul had his kingdom rent from him and his posterity, because he spared Agag, that idolatrous king of the Amalechites whom God would not have spared: so acceptable a service is it to destroy idolaters whom God hateth' (image 9). Gray explains that such verses give permission to destroy as a last resort. God rejoices not over the death of a sinner but over their repentance, so it would be preferable, if possible, to convert the heathen, but the final solution was never far away.

The preachers who addressed the Virginia Company were fond of insisting that the divine mission of the human race was to spread and fill the earth. This applied to the created order but also more particularly to God's own chosen people. So William Symonds refers to the general rule of creation 'that man should spread abroad . . . and inhabit the earth and fill it' because God says, 'let them rule over the fish of the sea' (1609, p. 6). The same commandment was given to Noah after the flood when he was commanded to bring forth plentifully and to replenish the earth. We see then, says Symonds, that there is a general law of replenishing the earth. This is applied to Abraham and to all his descendants by faith. 'The same doth bind all his sons, according to the faith, to go likewise abroad, when God doth not otherwise call' (p. 8). The call of Abraham is now applied to the preaching of the Christian faith. 'Neither can there be any doubt, but that the Lord that called Abraham into another country, doth also by the same holy hand, call you to go and carry the gospel to a nation that never heard of Christ' (p. 9). The argument is concluded with a comforting promise 'as I was with Abraham, so I will be with you. I will bless you, to wit, with the blessings of this life and of the kingdom of heaven' (p. 36).

Although the Old Testament provided most of the material necessary for reconstructing Christian faith for the imperial adventure, the New Testament was also read through the lens of empire.

The success of the colonies depended upon persuading people to go there, and this involved persuading the rich that there was profit in the enterprise. An example was provided by the converted slave Onesimus of whom Paul said that he was 'once so useless to you, but now useful indeed, both to you and to me' (Philem. 1.11). In the same way, many of the unemployed people, 'being before their sending over like to unconverted Onesymus, unprofitable unto all'; were 'now by their being there, like unto the same Onesymus, but truly converted, profitable to the Plantation, and to the City' (Copland 1622, p. 32).

The critics of the Virginia Company had claimed that the colony was a waste of money and people, but Copland reminded his hearers of the way that Judas had criticized Mary, when she poured out the ointment on the head of Jesus:

[S]ome sons of Belial malign this worthy work, as Judas the Traitor, and son of hell, maligned that act of Mary's anointing of Christ, pretending the good of the poor, but intending it as much as his own salvation, which was little or nothing at all. (p. 33)

William Symonds refers to the New Testament theology of the Church as the bride of Christ, playing upon the title of the colony, 'Virginia'. No doubt he is thinking of 2 Corinthians 11.2, when he says that the colony named after the virgin Queen Elizabeth is to be added to the Christian world. So he prays:

Lord finish this good work thou hast begun; and marry this land, a pure virgin to thy kingly son Christ Jesus; so shall thy name be magnified: and we shall have a Virgin or maiden Britain, a comfortable addition to our Great Britain. (1609, image 4)

The requirements of power and Christian doctrine

Just as the expansion of Britain overseas influenced the way the Bible was read, it also brought about similar interpretations of Christian doctrine. In 1615 when Thomas Cooper's *The blessing of Japheth* was published, puritanism was still dominant in English Protestant theology (Tyacke 1987, p. 5; MacLure 1958, pp. 92–5). The central feature of Calvinistic or reformed theology, which had been vigorously adopted by the English Puritans, was the doctrine of the majesty, grace and freedom of God. From a sinful mass of fallen humanity God had chosen some for salvation. These were the elect, and on one interpretation of the doctrine the number of the elect would be the same as the number of the fallen angels. In any case, during the period of the Church the number of the elect was being made up and one day would be complete. This gave the colonization process a special significance, because it was God's method for making up the number of the saved. 'Hath the Lord begun to enlarge us far and near to Virginia, and Ireland, and are not their hopes in vain, that seek to root God's church out of England?' (Cooper 1615, p. 34)

But what right had the Church of England to be anywhere else but in England? Cooper's colonization rationale suggests to him a new way of understanding the Church. According to the prophecy of Noah, Japheth was to dwell in tents. Japheth represented the Church, the elect of God, and therefore the Church was to dwell in tents. But tents are the dwellings of a people who intend to migrate. The Church 'is not tied locally to any certain place, but removable, for the contempt of the Gospel, from one nation to another' (p. 10). So the idea of the vulnerable and transient Church, so popular in ecclesial tent imagery today, was for Thomas Cooper an inspiration for domination on the far side of the Atlantic.

In these two chapters we have seen how the desire for domination, whether of the medieval Church or of the English Church of the early seventeenth century, had encouraged a shift in the very meaning of Christian faith itself. This is not to suggest that the theology which we have seen in the trading company sermons was widely accepted. Nicholas Canny reminds us that the overseas adventures which were started in the early seventeenth century had very little impact on the ordinary English people:

> The reality was that, before the 1630s, the English colonies in America hardly impinged upon the consciousness of most English people. The sermons that marked the launch of the Virginia Company are proof, not of widespread interest, but of the desperate need for publicity that would attract migrants and investments. (1998, p. 164)

Moreover, western imperialism in the New World had its critics, whereas, as we have seen, there was little if any criticism of the principle of crusading in earlier centuries. The prophetic attack of Bartolome de Las Casas (1474–1566) was directed against the Spanish colonization of Central and South America (de Las Casas 1992), and the Scottish humanist and poet, George Buchanan (1506–82), criticized the European exploitation of its colonies (Williamson 1996). Conscientious objections to imperialism from the sixteenth century to the mid twentieth century are discussed by Christopher Hodgkins (2002). In spite of these reservations, the theological justification of early colonialism marks the continuation of the tendency to modify Christian faith in the interests of power. In Chapter 6 we will see how the same influences were at work a century later in the work of Isaac Watts, often regarded as the most important figure in the evolution of the English hymn.

6

Imperialism Replacing Prophetic Theology: The Hymns of Isaac Watts

Isaac Watts is generally regarded as the founder of the modern English hymn. He wrote approximately 650 hymns, of which some half dozen are still in the repertoire. This chapter will examine his hymns in their social and political context, interpreting Watts as a key figure in the formation of a British theology that was in partnership with the growth of Britain as an international power. In the first part of this chapter, two of his most significant hymns will be studied so as to indicate the political and economic sub-text concealed beneath the more superficial piety on the surface of the words. It will be argued that Christian adults who have inherited this tradition of spirituality need to undertake this kind of critical analysis in order to be freed from the ideological implications of British imperial theology. In the second part of the chapter, the theology of the hymns will be studied against the wider context of the other writings of Watts.

The life of Isaac Watts

Isaac Watts was born on 17 July 1674 in Southampton. His father, also called Isaac, was deacon of the Southampton Independent Meeting. The religious climate into which the young Isaac was born can be judged by the fact that at the time of his birth his father was in Southampton gaol and received a second sentence the following year. Ten years later, in 1685, Watts Senior fled from Southampton to avoid further imprisonment and spent two years hiding in London. These events occurred as part of the repression of dissenters following the Restoration of the Monarchy in 1660 and the 1662 Act of Uniformity that required all ministers and school masters to swear allegiance to the Book of Common Prayer (Grell, Israel and Tyacke (eds.) 1991). The notorious Five Mile Act of 1665 forbade clergy, who had not conformed three years earlier, from going within five miles of a town or parish in which they had previously ministered. This period of persecution lasted into the Toleration Act of 1689. By this time, the young Isaac was 14 years old, having grown up in the Puritan tradition of Dissent and worshipping regularly in a meeting house the very existence of which was illegal.

The great days of the Puritan Reformation were over. At the time of the Westminster Assembly (1643–53) it had seemed probable that the Church of England would be reformed along Presbyterian lines. With the execution of

King Charles I in 1649 and the establishment of the Protectorate in 1653, it looked as if a holy Commonwealth would be established, and the rule of the saints would prevail. By 1662 those hopes were in ruins, and by the time young Isaac Watts was growing up, the once powerful Puritan tradition had become inward-looking, pious and wealthy.

Refusing to renounce his dissenting principles, Isaac Watts declined an offer to have his fees paid to go to the University of Oxford and received his higher education in the Stoke Newington dissenting academy. Stoke Newington was then a village on the outskirts of London, inhabited by a coterie of wealthy dissenting families. It was a 'stately and learned society' and 'the almost arrogant patriotism of much of Watts' verse reflects the temper of this society' (Escott 1962, p. 19). The religion of the circles of which the young Watts moved 'was that of men of wealth, rank and learning and these acquisitions, material and mental alike, were conceived as signs and seals of the favour of God' (p. 20).

When he had finished his studies at Stoke Newington, he returned to his home in Southampton, where for two and a half years he continued his studies and in the context of the congregation there, began his first experiments in the writing of hymns. Returning to Stoke Newington, he became tutor to Sir John Hartopp and in 1699 he became assistant pastor to the Mark Lane Independent Chapel. He became Principal pastor three years later. In 1712 he relinquished most of his pastoral duties and took up residence in Theobolds, the estate of Sir Thomas and Lady Abney. Isaac Watts remained a house guest of the Abney family until his death in 1748. The summer residence of the family was at Theobolds in Hertfordshire and the manor house of Stoke Newington, Abney House, was their second home. Thomas Abney was one of the founders of the Bank of England (1694) and was knighted by King William. He had been Lord Mayor of London and had represented the City of London in Parliament.[1]

Jesus shall reign where e'er the Sun

Psalm 72 marks the end of a series of royal Psalms. In this final one of the series, the political functions of the Hebrew monarchy are set forth and celebrated. Three principle functions are evident: justice, prosperity and domination. The first part of the Psalm is mainly concerned with the first and most important function of the monarch, which was to execute justice and to defend the poor, and Watts wrote a separate hymn on this part of the Psalm.

> God, endow the King with your own justice, his royal person with your righteousness, that he may govern your people rightly and deal justly with your oppressed ones . . . May he give judgement for the oppressed among the people and help to the needy; may he crush the oppressor. (vv. 1–2, 4)

---

1 For biographies of Watts see not only Escott 1962 (which is easily the best), but also Davis 1948.

It was also the duty of the King to ensure the prosperity of the land.

> May the hills and mountains provide your people with prosperity in righteousness . . . May there be grain in plenty throughout the land, growing thickly over the heights of the hills; may its crops flourish like Lebanon and the sheaves be plenteous as blades of grass. (vv. 3, 16)

The last part of the Psalm is mainly concerned with the duty of the King to extend the kingdom and to secure dominion over the surrounding lands.

> May he hold sway from sea to sea, from the Euphrates river to the ends of the earth. May desert tribes bend low before him, his enemies lick the dust. May the Kings of Tarshish and of the Isles bring gifts, may the Kings of Sheba and Seba present their tribute. Let all kings pay him homage, all nations serve him. (vv. 8–11)

As in the other Psalms in Isaac Watts' collection, the powers of the Hebrew monarch are transferred to Jesus Christ and by implication, if not always directly, to the British King. However, whereas the Psalmist prays that the King has long life: 'May he fear you as long as the sun endures, and as the moon throughout the ages' (Ps. 72.5), it is unnecessary to pray that the life of Jesus Christ might be prolonged, since of his kingdom and power there will be no end. Thus when the Psalm is Christologized, the longitudinal expectation becomes a lateral one. The prayer for long life becomes a prayer for universal domination. Thus the hymn does not begin 'May Jesus live on whilst the sun shall his successive journeys run', but rather 'Jesus shall reign where're the sun doth his successive journeys run'. The desire for long life has become the desire for empire. The same is true of the references to the moon. In verse 7 the Psalmist prays that '[i]n his days may righteousness flourish, prosperity abound until the moon is no more'. In other words, the idea of prolongation is here applied to the perpetual administration of justice, but in the hymn what is to endure as long as the moon is not so much the justice of the monarch as his sheer dominion. An interesting modern extension of the political theology of the Psalm is to be found in the motto of the Dominion of Canada: 'From Sea to Sea', thus transposing the original references, presumably to the Mediterranean Sea and to either the Red Sea or the Arabian Gulf, to the Atlantic and Pacific Oceans.

The universal sway of the Christian faith is hinted at in verse 3 of the hymn.

> People and realms of every tongue
> Dwell on his love with sweetest song
> And infant voices shall proclaim
> Their early blessings on his name.

There is little in the Psalm that corresponds to this. The reference to the children is probably taken from the story about the children crying Hosanna in the temple (Matt. 21.15). It is significant that the title which Watts gives to this hymn is 'Christ's Kingdom amongst the Gentiles', whereas in the Psalm although foreign kings pay tribute to the Hebrew monarch, there is no suggestion that they would share in the faith of the king.

Already, however, before this verse, Watts had inserted a few additional lines in which the political theology of the Psalm was made more contemporary.

Before the Islands with their Kings
And Europe her best tribute brings
From North to South the princes meet
To pay their homage at his feet.

There Persia glorious to behold,
There India shines in eastern gold
And barbarous nations at his word
Submit and bow and own their Lord.

These two verses appear in brackets in the eighteenth-century editions of *Psalms of David*, because they are too remote from the words of the Psalm. However, they are important in an attempt to interpret the hymn, because the political implications of the rest of the hymn break through into the surface at this point. In 1708 the value of imports from India into England was about £500,000, but was growing rapidly. By 1758 the value of annual imports had reached more than £1,100,000 (Dodwell (ed.) 1929, p. 108). In 1708 the annual dividend paid by the company to its stockholders was 5 per cent; by 1711 it had risen to 10 per cent p.a. and fluctuated between 10 and 12 per cent for the next 10 or 15 years (p. 109). St. Anne's Church in Calcutta, the first Christian place of worship in that part of the subcontinent, was consecrated in 1709 (p. 113) and a Bank was founded in Bombay, also held by the British in 1720 (p. 114), the year after the publication of the *Psalms of David*. So the rich merchants of Stoke Newington, to say nothing of their brethren in the commercial trading port of Southampton, were certainly familiar with India's gold.

These two verses dropped out of the repertoire early in the nineteenth century. By that time the incorporation of Christian faith and empire had become thoroughly spiritualized, and the crude reminder of its economic base had become a little tasteless.

Watts, as I have explained, did not intend to create an imperial theology. He intended to make the Psalms meaningful for Christian worshippers. However, there was, if we may put it in this way, an intention deeper than his conscious intention. The theology of Christian Britain in covenant with God to spread the Protestant Christian faith throughout the world was part of the spiritual and theological world into which Isaac Watts was born. He took it for granted, which is why at the age of 20 it was fully formed in his poetry, just as it emerged in his Psalms when he was 45. To find the origin of the idea of God's special covenant with England, we would have to go back 200 years, to the covenant theology of William Tyndale (McGiffert 1981).[2] The intention beneath the intention continued to influence generations of English-speaking Christians for a further 250 years, and has created the subconscious contours of British spirituality today.

---

2 Although the theological conception was that of Tyndale, the Covenant theology achieved its specific application to the destiny of Britain (or England) in the historical philosophy of John Fox (1516–87) and William Perkins (1588–1602).

When I Survey the Wondrous Cross

The most famous of all the hymns of Isaac Watts, translated into dozens of languages and familiar throughout the Christian world, is 'When I Survey the Wondrous Cross'.

It first appears in *Hymns and Spiritual Songs* (1707), where it is number 7 in the third book, which is mainly a collection of hymns for the Eucharist. The art of surveying had developed rapidly during the seventeenth century. *Tectonicon, briefly showing the exact measuring and spe[d]ie reckoning all manner of land* by Leonard Digges (d.*c.*1571) went through many editions from 1556 to 1634. The graphometer, one of the basic instruments used by the surveyor, was invented in 1597 (Guye and Michel 1971, pp. 277, 283). A report on the survey of Cornwall was published in 1602 by Richard Carew and an enlarged survey of London in 1633 by Anthony Munday and Humfrey Dyson. Surveying had become increasingly important in the enclosures of the common land, and in the rapidly developing real estate market. To survey is to measure exactly, usually with a view to estimating the value of an estate or property. To survey also means to carry out an inspection of an area from a vantage point, or to offer a comprehensive description of something or other. The important feature which all these meanings have in common is that the one who conducts the survey is superior to that which is surveyed. The one who surveys is the owner, or master of that which is measured, inspected or laid out. So in the first line of the famous hymn Watts is about to carry out a survey upon the wondrous cross. It is as if one's attention has been attracted by a jewelled cross, displayed in the window of an antique shop. The cross is glowing with gems and golden filigree. As you draw closer to estimate its value, the truth of what happened there dawns upon you. This is the wondrous cross 'On which the prince of glory died'. We notice the shimmering radiance of the words 'wonder', 'prince', and 'glory'. It is these words which suggest the enormous value to be placed upon the object, and this is why we propose to survey it. If Watts had written instead 'When I behold the sacred cross/on which the son of Mary died', it would not have been the same.

As the contrast between the radiant treasure before us and the stark reality of its history dawns upon us, we suddenly find our values reversed. That which we set out to survey now surveys us.

> My richest gain I count but loss
> And pour contempt on all my pride.

These are the dynamics upon which this hymn turns: gain and loss, pride and contempt, death and life. One imagines a merchant seeking to make tremendous gains. We remember that Isaac Watts was born in French Street, which ran straight down to the port in Southampton. Many a time, coming out of his front door on his way to school, young Isaac must have glanced down the street and seen the great vessels anchored in the harbour, or billowing in from distant lands, from the West Indies or from India itself, laden with precious goods. These had to be counted and stored. Their value had to be assessed, which is why surveying, pouring and counting are such important words in this verse. As I estimate the value of my goods, I am full of pride. But suddenly, I have something which I did not expect, something which turns me upside-down. My bargaining, my profit margins, my rich gains, everything of which I had been so proud, is now become the object of my contempt. My counting, which previously had been the way I had measured the value of the wonders, had suddenly run into a terrible deficit. I count but loss.

As we move into the second verse, the mood changes. I remember my competitive boasting with dismay.

> Forbid it Lord that I should boast
> Save in the death of Christ my God.

I no longer boast about the rich jewels in the wondrous cross, but I boast about what the cross signifies: the death of Christ my God. Why should I boast about it? Because it is now the only thing in the world of which I am proud. I am proud of it, because of the grace and mercy extended to me through the self-giving love of God. I am not proud of it as of something in my possession, but as something which has come to possess me, and in the presence of which I feel transformed and enriched.

> All the vain things that charm the most
> I sacrifice them to his blood.

Still I remember those vain things that charmed me. Notice the magical hint in the word 'charm'. I was under a spell, but the things that charmed me were vain. I now recognize that there is indeed a competition, not between myself and other entrepreneurs, but between these vain things that charm me and the transforming enchantment of the love of God. Therefore I sacrifice them. I began by seeking for a gain; now everything I've had is loss. Now that I have lost everything, I can see more deeply into the wondrous cross. I notice the detail. I see indications of emotions, love and sorrow, quite different from the emotions I had felt before, emotions of contempt and pride, of boasting of vanity and enchantment. I no longer survey, but I see.

> See from his head, his hands, his feet,
> Sorrow and love flow mingled down.
> Did e'er such love and sorrow meet,
> Or thorns compose so rich a crown?

Again the theme of wealth and riches are here, the hint of royalty and of glory. There is indeed a crown, but the theme of the reversal of values continues even more poignantly. The richness of the crown is made up not of jewels and fine gold, but of thorns. The thorns, almost like a work of deliberate art, compose themselves. It is a composition, like the artwork of the cross, but now mingled not with boasting and counting but with sorrow and love. Once again, there is a pouring. At first I was compelled to pour contempt on my pride; now I see that sorrow and love are pouring down for me. To the paradoxes of gain and loss, richness and poverty, we now add a contrasting pair of values which completely transcend those of the commercial world: sorrow and love.

The fourth verse is usually omitted from the modern hymn books. Perhaps it is thought to be gory. When the hymn as a whole is correctly understood, however, this fourth verse is essential to the imagery.

His dying crimson like a robe
Spreads from his body o'er the tree.
Then I am dead to all the world
And all the world is dead to me.

It is not usually realized, but the first line contains a pun upon which the imagery of the verse depends. Dying can mean that one's life is terminated by death. It can also mean that cloth undergoes a dyeing process, whereby it is stained with colour. The crimson dye referred to in the first line of the verse was a particularly costly one, which only the wealthy could afford.[3] This is also suggested by the use of the word 'robe', which is what a prince of glory would indeed wear, but in this case the robe becomes his shroud. The cross or tree is compared to a robe which, as it were, wraps him round.

Although there were scarlet dyes known in antiquity and in the medieval period, coming from a small insect which inhabits certain trees growing around the Mediterranean basin (Robinson 1969, p. 25), the crimson dye imported from Mexico from about 1518 (Crace 1878, p. 207) was both more brilliant and more costly. The dye is obtained through crushing the *coccus cacti*, an insect which lives on a certain cactus which grows in Mexico. In order to obtain a pound weight of the crimson liquid (cochineal), it was necessary to crush about 7,000 of the insects (Wolf 1997, p. 140). These were gathered from the plants and crushed by the native people of Mexico under the direction of the *alcaldes mayores*, the wealthy Spanish officials (Chance 1989, p. 45). No doubt Southampton was one of the ports where this luxury item was imported.[4] In order to fix the colour into the cloth, it was mixed with ammonia (Crace 1878, p. 217). One can imagine the young Isaac Watts, watching fascinated but choking from the ammonia fumes, as a length of woollen cloth was lowered into the tub or tray containing the liquid that would spread steadily up the cloth, turning the white wool to scarlet, until the whole cloth was coloured. The deaths of so many thousands of little insects, the deaths of the native labourers, the choking and coughing as the pungent process took place, and the appearance, like blood, of the cloth as the stain spread through it, must have made a vivid impact upon the lad. 'Then am I dead to all the world.'

But would the boy have had an opportunity to visit one of the dyeing establishments? Certainly, because his father, Isaac Watts Senior, was in the cloth trade. We do not know the exact nature of his business, but doubtless he would have visited the factories, where the cloth was dyed and prepared for sale. One must remember that the woollen industry was concentrated in Southern England and that Southampton would have been one of the major ports for

3 The comparative costs of dyed and un-dyed cloths in Southampton are described in Vellacott 1908, p. 485.

4 Improved techniques of dyeing had been introduced from the Continent to Southampton in 1567 and there was a Guild of Dyers (Vellacott 1912, p. 485).

the export and import of these products. By the late seventeenth century this industry was already in decline (Vellacott 1912, p. 487), since it was tending to move towards the north of England.

This was not the only occasion when Isaac Watts used this powerful metaphor.

Ye perishing and naked poor
Who work with mighty pain
To weave a garment of your own
That will not hide your sin
Come, naked, and adorn your souls
In robes prepared by God
Wrought by the labours of his Son
And dyed in his own blood.
(*Hymns and Spiritual Songs*, Book 1, No. 7 'Let Every Mortal Ear Attend', v. 6)

This verse reflects Watts' knowledge of the clothing industry as practised in the homes of the poor. They made their own clothes, in considerable labour and hardship, but they obviously could not afford to have their clothes dyed. They are invited to strip off these mean garments of their poverty, and to accept the crimson robes of salvation, dyed by the blood of Christ. Although the picture is so vivid, it is significant that Isaac Watts neither here nor anywhere in his writings shows much interest in and concern for the actual situation of the poor. For Watts, it is no more than a convenient metaphor to describe the transformation from the sinful state to the redeemed state.

Returning to 'His dying crimson like a robe' we notice how the theme of the paradoxical reversal of values is expressed. Instead of the beautiful robes giving me life and glory, I am killed. Jesus Christ is like one of the *coccus cacti*, crushed to death, in order to yield the crimson dye, and when I identify with him, through accepting the values of his cross, I also die. I am no longer sensitive to the world of gain and loss, the world of surveying and counting. At the same moment, in another reversal of roles, it is the world which has died. It has been sacrificed to his blood and can charm me no more. I am now alive, to respond to that amazing love, which when blended with sorrow, has transformed my life.[5]

Were the whole realm of nature mine
That were an offering far too small.

We return to the theme of the first verse. Once again we are surveying. We are in the world of possession, of royal estates and of glory. I began by surveying the wondrous cross; now I survey the whole realm of nature. I have made the cross

---

5 The verse arises out of a meditation on Galatians 6.14, which in the version which Isaac Watts would have used, reads 'But God forbid that I should glory, save in the cross of our Lord Jesus Christ, by whom the world is crucified unto me, and I unto the world.' Another reference to Galatians is to be found in the second verse of the hymn, which is inspired by Galatians 3.1 'O foolish Galatians, who hath bewitched you, that ye should not obey the truth, before whose eyes Jesus Christ hath been evidently set forth, crucified among you?'

my own; now I imagine that the whole realm of nature has become mine. But what happens to this immense possession? It is not enough; it is 'far too small'. Previously I had sacrificed to his blood 'all the vain things that charm me most', but now even the offering of the entire realm of nature is insufficient. The cross which once I ventured to survey now looms up, larger than the cosmos.

> Love so amazing, so divine
> Demands my soul, my life, my all.

The exchange of values has now become total. I am stunned by the amazing inversion. Previously I loved to survey, to count, to pour out and become rich. Now I have nothing left with which to bargain (Hull 1999). What I stand before now is no longer a cross, or even a Son of God dying on a cross, but a living, amazing divine love.

Hidden transcripts

We have now examined in some detail two of Isaac Watts' best loved hymns. In each case, we have discovered a significance which lies beneath the level of the surface meaning. In the case of 'Jesus shall Reign' we saw that the values of empire were affirmed, but concealed beneath a layer of Christianity. The Christian surface had disguised the underlying imperial values and had created a kind of political theology, all the more dangerous because the association between Christian faith and political domination was disguised.

In the case of 'When I Survey' we also discovered a deeper text, so to speak, running beneath the surface. Far from affirming the values of commercial domination, the hymn is actually a statement of a radical opposition between the meaning of Christian faith and the meaning of the market economy. This implied radicalism has been overlain by a kind of Christian mystic piety, in which the cross of Christ has been separated from its commercial antithesis. Its challenge to ethical life has been glossed over, a varnishing which was all too natural in the self-enclosed Independent Churches of the early eighteenth century, when the challenge to commercial life which the hymn implies had become too challenging to hear.

Was Isaac Watts himself aware of the contrast between the surface and the depth in these two hymns? In the case of 'When I Survey' I believe that he was not conscious of it. This is indicated by the fact that nowhere in his poetical writings is there any sense of genuine concern for the poverty and squalor of many of the working people of his day. They become convenient and emotional symbols for the poverty of the sinner, but are never observed and taken seriously in their own right, except as a warning to children (1715). The middle-class fear of falling into poverty on the one-hand and the attraction of a de-politicized, internalized faith on the other encouraged this narrowing of the Christian consciousness. One wonders if Isaac Watts had ever read Abiezer Coppe's stunning account of his meeting with a poor beggar, in which Christ is heard speaking out of poverty itself (1987, pp. 39–41). It is noticeable that in all of Watts' hymns and Psalms there is not a single one which speaks of the mission of the Church to the marginalized and suffering people of his own society or of the world. Here we find the local congregation comfortably adoring its own belief system. Instead of being an instrument dedicated to an object, the Christian faith has become its own object. However, for the Christian of today, who wishes to make the cross an instrument of redemption and no longer a fetish of devotional abstraction, this rich and beautiful hymn can still vibrate with power. Its significance and relevance are increased when its social implications are realized. It is noticeable that in this hymn there is no reference to the penal and substitutionary theory of the atonement, which was to become so important in the Victorian period (Hilton 1988).[6] By then, the cross of Christ, far from challenging the commercial and market values of society, had become the very epitome of reification of them. We may contrast the words of 'When I Survey', with its negation of commercial values, with the hymn 'There is a Green Hill' with its frank acceptance of commercial values and its crude moral comparisons leading to a heightened sense of exclusivity.

There was none other good enough
To pay the price of sin
He only could unlock the gate
Of heaven and let us in.

It became fashionable to criticize 'When I Survey' for its apparent advocacy of what is sometimes called the moral theory of the atonement, because it does not describe the cross of Christ as a bargain or a device, but merely allows the cross to engage with our commercial values. One suspects that this superficial criticism comes from a Christian faith in which the tension between the cross of Christ and the values of money has become entirely lost.

We have seen that the hymns of Isaac Watts represent a vital point in the formation of an introverted ecclesiastical spirituality, in which the Christian faith becomes its own object. We have also seen the convenience of this process of spiritualization, since it left European economic and political power more-or-less free to follow its own internal logic. We are the inheritors of this spirituality, carved into the very foundations of our understanding of faith through the continual repetition of the hymns in an atmosphere of collective emotion. To put it bluntly, the Empire has gone, but the theology lingers on, now made the more irrelevant by the need to contest the domination of money in the globalized market.

Christian education with adults and young people must exorcise this inherited spirituality and must do it by attacking it at its roots, in some of its most beautiful and popular statements. Through this process of critical archaeology, Christians will become aware of the purposes of the tradition which encloses them. It is particularly important to realize that both these hymns were formed in the creative imagination of their author, not through meditating upon the place of Britain in the world, or on the conflict of values between Christian faith and money, but as expositions of biblical passages. As the poet interpreted Psalm 72 and the letter to the Galatians his own geopolitical and economic context intervened, and so Scripture was mediated through the author's social context. This mediation was veiled

---

6 For a study of the contemporary implications of this doctrine, see Selby 1997.

by piety, and the piety must therefore be regarded as a form of false consciousness. As we exorcise our faith, there will be losses as well as gains. It is possible
that some will no longer be able to sing 'Jesus shall Reign' with a clear conscience,
and it is equally possible that 'When I Survey' will be sung with renewed meaning.
The first hymn points to the past; the second still points to its future.

The formation of a political theology

Although as we have seen the principal intention of Watts was to render the
singing of the Psalms more relevant to the daily lives of the dissenting congregations, examination of the *Psalms* in the context of the sermons and other writings of Watts reveals a more comprehensive social and political outlook. In the
light of the growing significance of the British Empire and of the conscious and
unconscious influence of such power upon later generations of Christians, Isaac
Watts may be regarded as an influential figure in the creation of a faith attuned
to the needs of empire. This legacy may be traced in many Christian attitudes
today, on both sides of the Atlantic.

The Act in Restraint of Appeals (1533) of Henry VIII declared that 'this realm
of England is an empire' (Armitage 2000, p. 11). Between 1536 and 1543 Wales
was incorporated into the English crown, and the Irish Kingship Act of 1541
passed by the Irish Parliament declared Henry of England to be King of Ireland
(p. 21).[7] With the union of the crowns of England and Scotland in 1604 and the
union of the two states in 1707 this process of consolidation reached a certain
maturity, and the foundation was laid for the emergence of Great Britain as a
major actor on the European stage following the Treaty of Utrecht in 1713.[8]

In 1584 Walter Raleigh obtained the Queen's Patent for the establishing of
a colony in America, and the following year a settlement was founded on Roanoke Island off the coast of Virginia (Lim 1998, p. 18). In 1581 Elizabeth I had
granted a patent to the trading company of Osborne and Staper and their asso-
ciates to trade in the Levant, and in 1583 the first English expedition set out
via the Mediterranean for the Muslim lands of the Near East. Three members
of this party were the first English people to reach India (Locke (ed.) 1930,
pp. 1–11). As we have seen, the Virginia Company was founded in 1606 and
other British colonies in North America and the Caribbean were established in
the following years.

Historians of the British Empire emphasize the influence of the Roman Empire
as a model, not only for Britain but for all the European empires of the sixteenth
to eighteenth centuries (Richardson 1998; Pagden 1995, pp. 11–28), but the biblical heritage is, perhaps, less widely recognized. Colin Kidd draws attention to the
influence of the Pentateuch upon early European identities (1999, pp. 9–33), but
a study of the English Psalter from the mid sixteenth century up to the work
of Watts in 1719 reveals the power over the English imagination of the Hebrew

---

7 For the significance of Ireland in the growth of British imperialism see Canny 1998.

8 The wars with France between 1689 and 1713 had prepared for this, and the victories of
Marlborough (1704–08) had already increased the military prestige of Britain (Hatton 1978,
p. 111). For the rise of Britain as a financial and military power, see Brewer 1989.

kingdom. Jesus was the Son of David before he became the *Kurios* of Graeco-Roman political mysticism, and the English monarchs had for centuries been regarded as occupying the throne of David. In the Psalms, Israel is seen as the people of God, looking to its faith in God to bring victory and prosperity, and often surrounded by hostile powers. The sharp distinction between us and them, and the glorious sense of divine protection that kept Israel alive was attractive to a Protestant people, whose theology of election was forming the national consciousness of mission. J. R. Watson remarks, 'Throughout the psalms, there are references to the sharp division between good and evil. The psalm singer knew that he was surrounded by "wicked men" . . . It is possible to see the creation of a vivid myth of the saints and their opponents' (1999, p. 53).

The Psalms and Christian Britain

By 1535, and possibly earlier, some of the Psalms had been translated into metrical verse for singing. The oldest extant version seems to be that of Miles Coverdale (1535), a collection that included 15 Psalms, but the first complete Psalter was that of Robert Crowley in 1549. After many additions and revisions, the version by Thomas Sternhold and John Hopkins was published in 1562, and this was to remain the standard Psalter for more than a century. In 1696 the version of Nathaniel Tate and Nicholas Brady appeared and was to pass through many editions, becoming known as 'the new version' while that of Sternhold and Hopkins became 'the old version' (Watson 1999, pp. 42–56). In the preface of his own version, Isaac Watts tells us that he had read about 20 renditions into English of the Psalms for singing (1719, p. 5).

Although it is well known that in Christianizing the Psalms of David, Isaac Watts included several references to Britain and to Great Britain, the significance of this for the formation of religious consciousness in Britain has seldom been explored. *The Dictionary of National Biography* describes the application of the Psalms to Britain as 'grotesquely bad taste' (*DNB* 1909, p. 980), Bernard Manning says they are full of 'sound political doctrine' (1942, p. 99), whereas A. P. Davis thinks that 'the pious reader was probably shocked' (1948, p. 199). Harry Escott remarks that they are relevant to 'the growth of the British-Israel idea' (1962, p. 160).

The first mature Psalm of Watts to include the notorious reference to Britain is Psalm 47. John Patrick renders the opening line 'O all ye People clap your Hands' and his second stanza goes:

By him o'er warlike Nations we
Our Conquests do advance:
And he this happy Land has chose
For our Inheritance.

A later verse reads:

He makes the Heathen feel his pow'r,
And him their Sovereign own;

He seats himself upon the Ark,
As on his holy Throne. (Patrick 1698, Psalm 47)

Tate and Brady present the verses as follows:

Your utmost Skill in Praise be shown;
For him that all the World commands.
Who sits upon his Holy Throne,
And spreads his Sway o'er Heathen Lands.

and verse 9:

Our Chiefs and Tribes, that far from hence
T'adore the God of Abr'am came,
Found Him their constant sure defence.
How great and glorious is his Name! (1696, Psalm 47)

Sternhold and Hopkins' version is more than a century earlier.

For us the heritage he chose
Which we possess alone:
The flourishing worship of Jacob,
His wel beloved one.

God on the heathen reigns and sits
Upon his holy throne:
The princes of the people have
Them joyned every one. (1649, Psalm 47)

When Isaac Watts deals with this Psalm in 1719, he provides a heading: 'Christ's Ascending and Reigning'.

O for a Shout of sacred Joy
To God the sovereign King!
Let every Land their Tongues employ,
And Hymns of Triumph sing.

Jesus our God ascends on high;
His heavenly Guards around
Attend him rising thro' the Sky,
With Trumpets joyful Sound.

While Angels shout and praise their King,
Let Mortals learn their Strains;
Let all the Earth his Honour sing;
O'er all the Earth he reigns.

Rehearse his Praise with Awe profound,
Let Knowledge lead the Song,

Nor mock Him with a solemn Sound
Upon a thoughtless Tongue.

In Israel stood his ancient Throne,
He lov'd that chosen Race,
But now he calls the World his own,
And Heathens taste his Grace.

The British Islands are the Lords,
There Abraham's God is known,
While Powers & Princes, Shields & Swords
Submit before his Throne.

This being the first time in his Psalms that Watts refers to Britain specifically, he feels it necessary to add a note at the end: 'The Ascent of Christ into Heaven is typify'd in this Psalm by the Ark brought up to Zion. 2. Sam. 6.15, and the Kingdom of Christ among the Gentiles is here represented by David's Victory over the Nations.'

We should distinguish the intentions of Watts as author from the message and influence of the texts themselves.

No doubt Isaac Watts was motivated not only by the wish to relate the worship of the independent congregations to contemporary life, but also to affirm the loyalty and indeed the patriotism of dissenters, who were suspected of sharing the disloyalty of which Catholics and Quakers were often accused. 'Churchmen detected something as devilish as Rome in the forces of protestant dissent' (Claydon and McBride 1998, p. 17). The horizon of the works of Isaac Watts fuses with our own horizons in ways that go beyond the author's intentions (Gadamer 1989, p. 273). In order to demonstrate this it is necessary to interpret the prose and poetry of Watts against the world behind them (the growing vision of worldwide British power) and the world ahead of them (the realization of worldwide British power in the eighteenth and nineteenth centuries) and to trace the long shadow of the imperialistic theology down to its present influence upon the religious life and the foreign policy of Britain and the United States.

Watts was dissatisfied with the earlier translations of the Psalms. They all have a common defect: they presented the meaning of the Hebrew Psalms in an English which was as close as possible to the original Hebrew, maintaining the imagery and outlook of the original Psalm. Of course, there are a number of Psalms the piety of which is so general that they can stand this literal interpretation. Psalm 1 is a good example: 'Blessed is the man who walks not in the counsel of the wicked.' There are many others, however, where the interests of the Hebrew monarchy or the concerns of the Psalmist are paramount. Watts admires the work of Dr Patrick who has, says Watts, 'succeeded here and there in abandoning the Hebrayisms and using Christian language'. Watts now proposes to take up the principle of Christianization adopted by Patrick, and to pursue it more thoroughly. Christian singing of hymns cannot be confined to the Psalms. Where would one find a hymn to accompany the Lord's Supper, unless we are to sing Psalm 23 again and again. The ancient

Jewish people celebrated their national deliverances through their Psalms, and we today should do the same. How can our modern congregations sing of praising God upon the harp when in fact we use the organ? As for the places where the coming of the Messiah is foretold by the Psalmist, why should the dark and misty language of prediction be retained, when we stand in the full light of that coming?

Watts was thus acting as a pastor, and as an educator of his people when he Christianized the Psalms. For example, in Psalm 20, to which Watts gives the heading 'Prayer and hope of Victory: for a day of prayer in time of war' verses 5 and 6 read as follows:

> Let us sing aloud in praise of your Victory, Let us do homage to the name of our God! May the Lord grant your every request! Now I know that the LORD has given Victory to his anointed one: he will answer him from his holy heaven with the victorious might of his right-hand. (RSV)

Watts interprets this in the light of the military life of the seventeenth century by introducing a reference to troops and navy.

> In his salvation is our hope
> And in the name of Israel's God
> Our troops shall lift their banners up,
> Our navy's spread their flags abroad.

In verse 8 the Psalmist describes how the armies of Israel put to flight the forces of the enemy. 'They totter and fall, but we rise up and stand firm'. This, together with the prayers, becomes:

> Oh may the memory of thy name
> Inspire our armies for the fight
> Our foes shall fall and die with shame
> Or quit the field with shameful flight.

This identification of the armies of the Lord with the British army was to have profound consequences for the future of Christian faith in Britain and became particularly prominent during the Victorian period (Wolffe (ed.) 1997; Tamke 1978; Adey 1988). In Psalm 45 we have a glorification of the military might of the Davidic monarch.

> Gird your sword on your side, you warrior King, advance in your pomp and splendour, ride on in the cause of truth and for justice. Your right hand will perform awesome deeds: your arrows are sharp. (vv. 3–5)

The king is identified by Watts with Jesus Christ, and there is no mistaking the political and imperialistic tendencies of the result.

> Dress thee in arms, most mighty Lord!
> Gird on the terror of thy sword!

In majesty and glory ride
With truth and meekness at thy side
Thy anger like a pointed dart
Shall pierce the foes of stubborn heart.

Psalm 67, which begins 'May God be gracious to us and bless us, may he cause his face to shine on us', becomes:

Shine, mighty God, on Britain shine
With beams of heavenly grace
Reveal thy power through all our coasts
And show thy smiling face.

The coincidence between the spread of British arms and the spread of the Christian faith which was to become such a pronounced feature of the Empire (Goulder 1990), is foreseen particularly in the fourth verse of Watts' hymn:

Sing to the Lord, ye distant lands
Sing loud with solemn voice
While British tongues exalt his praise
And British hearts rejoice.

In later verses Britain is described as God's 'chosen Isle'. In a footnote Watts remarks that he has 'translated the scene of this Psalm to Great Britain'.

The second occurrence of specific reference to Britain is found in Psalm 60, which is headed 'On a Day of Humiliation for Disappointments in War'. The Psalm begins:

You have made the land quake and caused it to split open; repair its ruins, for it is shattered. You have made your people drunk with the bitter draught, you have given us wine which makes us stagger. (Ps. 60. 2, 3)

Watts renders this as follows:

Lord, hast thou cast the Nation off?
Must we for ever mourn?
Wilt thou indulge immortal Wrath?
Shall Mercy ne'er return?

The Terror of one Frown of thine
Melts all our Strength away;
Like Men that totter drunk with Wine,
We tremble in Dismay.

Great Britain shakes beneath thy Stroke,
And dreads thy threatening Hand;
O heal the Island Thou hast broke,
Confirm the wav'ring Land.

Lift up a Banner in the Field
For those that fear thy Name;
Save thy Beloved with thy Shield,
And put our Foes to Shame.

Go with our Armies to the Fight
Like a Confederate God;
In vain Confederate Power unite
Against thy lifted Rod.

Our Troops shall gain a wide Reknown
By thine assisting Hand;
'Tis God that treads the Mighty down,
And makes the Feeble stand.

The early development of a political theology

The first volume of Isaac Watts' poetry was published on 28 December 1705 under the title *Horae Lyricae* (1706). Here we see the early development of Watts' theology of Britain which was to become so prominent in his 1719 *The Psalms of David*. For example, the opening verse of this earlier version of Psalm 100 which is entitled 'Praise to the Lord from all Nations'.

Sing to the Lord with joyful voice
Let every land his name adore
The British Isles shall send the noise
Across the ocean to the shore.

One of the most interesting poems in this early collection entitled 'An hymn of praise to the God of England' was re-titled 'A hymn of praise for three great salvations' in the 1709 edition of *Horae Lyricae*. The three salvations were the destruction of the Spanish Armada (1588), the discovery and overthrow of the Gunpowder Plot (1605) and the Glorious Revolution; the arrival of William of Orange in England to restore the Protestant monarchy in 1688. The poem begins with a kind of geo-political meditation on the providential arrangement of the British Islands with their protective surrounding seas and rocky cliffs.

Infinite God, thy counsels stand
Like mountains of eternal brass
Pillars to prop our sinking land
Or guardian rocks to break the seas.

Within that providential arrangement of sea and land, the British Church occupies a particular place within God's historical providence.

Part of thy Church, by thy command
Stands raised upon the British Isles.

'There' said the Lord 'To ages stand
Firm as the everlasting hills.'

This providential arrangement of geography with the special mission of the British Church now culminates in God's saving acts.

In vain the Spanish ocean roared
Its billows swelled against our shore
Its billows sunk beneath thy word
With all the floating war they bore.

The arrival of William of Orange, the Protestant deliverer and hero, is surrounded by angelic bands, rejoicing at the victory of the Protestant faith.

Brigades of Angels line the way
And guarded William to his throne
There ye celestial warriors stay
And make his palace like your own.

Here we see the identification of the British monarch with the throne of God.

The ideas of divine patronage, leading to military victory in the name of God, could hardly be expressed more clearly, and we may trace the development of such a theology in the writings of Watts from his early twenties. Hymn 92 in part ii of *Hymns and Spiritual Songs* (1705) is entitled 'The Church saved and her Enemies disappointed', and unusually it is dated. The date of composition is 5 November 1694, and it celebrates the anniversary of the discovery of the Gunpowder Plot.

Shout to the Lord, and let our Joys
Through the whole Nation run;
Ye British Skies, resound the Noise
Beyond the rising Sun.

Their secret Fires in Caverns lay,
And we the Sacrifice:
But gloomy Caverns strove in vain
To 'scape all-searching Eyes.

Their dark Designs were all reveal'd,
Their Treasons all betray'd;
Praise to the Lord, that broke the Snare
Their cursed Hands had laid.

Almighty Grace defends our Land
From their malicious Pow'r:
Let Britain with united Songs
Almighty Grace adore. (1790 edition)

The national theology of Watts, like so many Protestants of his period, was moulded by the providential delivery of the country from Spanish aggression and papal plots.

What lies behind Watts' interpretation of the political events which were shaping dissenting identity was not a conscious political theology, but a biblical hermeneutic springing mainly from the pastoral and educational concerns of Watts to present the congregations with a relevant faith. The typological interpretation of the Hebrew Bible made it possible to discern a parallelism between the testaments and between Judaism and Christianity as religious systems.

> As the church or nation of the Jews, was a type or figure of the whole invisible church of God, so the ceremonies of their religion, were typical and figurative of gospel times, and spiritual things under the great Messiah; and even many of the common and natural circumstances of action prescribed in that religion, *viz.* times, places, etc. were also designed, to be types of evangelical affairs, and heavenly things. (1810, II, p. 450)

The typological interpretation led Watts into a practical application based on the evangelical demand for personal involvement.

> Though I will not assert it unlawful to sing to God the words of other men which we have no concern in, and which are very contrary to our circumstances and the frame of our spirits; yet it must be confessed abundantly more proper, when we address God in a song, to use such words as we can for the most part assume as our own. (1810, IV, p. 277)

However, sometimes the parallelism between the times of David and our own times breaks down (p. 278). The battles of Israel against Aamon can hardly be regarded as a type of the Battle of Blenheim. In such cases, one simply removed the antiquated detail and replaced it with some contemporary reality.

> I think the names of Aamon and Moab may be as properly changed into the names of the chief enemies of the gospel, so far as may be without public offence: Judah and Israel may be called England and Scotland, and the land of Canaan may be translated into Great-Britain. (p. 278)[9]

This practice, innocent enough at first sight, tended toward an uneasy compromise in which not only the names of nations but the ethical demands of biblical faith were modified to suit the requirements of a rapidly developing acquisitive

---

9 Such sacralization of the British state was a striking contrast with the attitudes of many Puritans and dissenters in the period following the Restoration of 1661. 'Far from regarding England as divinely chosen by God and blessed by God, anointed for a worldwide mission, we find dissenting, non-conformist and Quaker tracts attacking the Restoration powers and by implication the English state, as being a monstrous, Satanic power'; England was also often compared with Egypt. See Keeble 1987, pp. 253–4.

society.[10] The philosophy of possessive individualism (Macpherson 1964) took the place of the social solidarity of the Hebrew community. Watts continues,

> And when a Christian psalmist, among the characters of a saint, Psal. xv.5, meets with the man that 'puts not out his money to usury,' he ought to exchange him for one that is no oppressor or extortioner, since usury is not utterly forbidden to Christians, as it was by the Jewish law. (Watts 1810, IV, p. 278)

Here are a few final examples of Watts' method.

> The heathens know thy glory Lord,
> The wondering nations read thy word,
> In Britain is Jehovah known,
> Our worship shall no more be paid
> To gods which mortal hands have made;
> Our maker is our God alone. (Ps. 96)

* * * * * * * * * *

> He sits upon the eternal hills,
> With grace and pardon in his hands
> And sends his covenant with the seals,
> To bless the distant British lands. (*Hymns and Spiritual Songs* 1782, I, no. 52)

* * * * * * * * * *

> Ye British isles who read His love
> In long epistles from above,
> (He hath not sent his sacred word
> To every land) praise ye the Lord! (Ps. 53)

* * * * * * *

> This northern isle, our native land, lies safe in the Almighty's hand
> Our foes of victory dream in vain,
> And wear the captivating chain.

> He builds and guards the British throne
> And makes it gracious like his own;
> Makes our successive princes kind
> And gives our dangers to the wind. (*Hymns and Spiritual Songs*, 1782, II, no. 1)

---

10 Kendrick, Brewer and Plum (1983) trace this development back to the 1690s when 'The economic advantages of competition, envy, emulation, vanity and fashion were more and more explicitly stated' (p. 15).

Theological geography and national calling

If we were to restrict our discussion to *The Psalms of David*, we might find no more in the theology of Watts than the concern of a gifted educator to draw those who sang his hymns into a richer experience of the meaning of faith in their own day, but if we consider the Psalms in the context of the other writings, we may further discern the outlines of an imperial theology. My intention is not to trace the development of Watts' theology chronologically, but to indicate the imperial context and influence of his works as a whole.

Let us begin with Watts' theological geography. In a sermon entitled 'God in Christ is the saviour of the ends of the Earth' (1810, II, pp. 46–54), Watts reflects upon Isaiah 45.22 'Look unto me and be ye saved, all the ends of the earth.'

The 'ends of the earth' refer to Britain and thus it is people in Britain who are addressed. Watts explains, 'The British islands have been reckoned by the ancients to be the ends of the earth' (p. 46). Judah was situated in the middle of the earth, in the sense that 'the land of Canaan is near the borders of Asia, where it joins to Africa, and not very far off from the limits of Europe; which three were the only known parts of the earth in that day' (p. 48). From the point of view of the biblical authors, therefore, the British islands would have been the most distant parts of the earth. He refers to England especially. The conclusion is that 'This voice of compassion is therefore eminently sent to us in England' (p. 49).

Watts now uses the expression 'ends of the earth' in a more spiritual and metaphorical sense: those living in Britain but estranged from the sound of the gospel, particularly those in remote parts.

The theological geography is developed into a view of providence involving several degrees of blessedness (1810, I, pp. 131–42). The first stage of blessedness is to be living in a land called by God, and England is such a land. In order to claim the blessing, one must live close to a church, be brought up in a religious family and pay attention to the ordinances of God (p. 132).

The second stage of blessedness is being forgiven by God through the blood of Christ; the third is the blessedness of the angels; the fourth is the blessedness of the Son of God in the presence of God; and the fifth is the blessedness of the glorious Trinity. Thus the call of the nation is the least of the blessings, yet it is the first rung on the ladder leading to ultimate blessedness.[11]

> Happy Britons in our age! Though we are involved, with the rest of mankind, in the common ruins of our first defection from God, yet we are not left in the darkness of heathenism, on the very confines of hell . . . Blessed England, whom he hath chosen, and caused to approach thus far towards himself! (p. 132)

Although individual responsibility in responding to the call of the gospel is not denied, Watts is clear that the election of God concerns entire nations and races, both for salvation and for rejection. It is this sense of selection, and the awful fate of other peoples, that gives national providence its peculiar intensity.

---

11 Rivers (1991) discusses the characteristics of the affective psychology of religion developed by Watts (pp. 164–204).

And why was not the polite nation of China chosen too? And why not the poor savages of Africa, and the barbarous millions of the American world? Why are they left in a dismal estrangement from God? Even so, Father, because it pleased thee, whose counsels are unsearchable, and whose ways of judgment and mercy are past finding out (p. 132).

Within Christian Europe, the election of God is equally favourable. Protestant England has been chosen and called out from the decadent Catholic Mass. 'Blessed be the name of our God, who has delivered our nation from this bondage of iniquity . . . We are ready to look on popery now as lying afar off, a-cross the seas, as being an evil thing at a great distance' (1810, I, p. 394).

Political theology and affairs of state

The theological geography is combined with the providential view of history to form a political theology. Foreign policy during the reign of Queen Anne (1702–14) was dominated by the Wars of the Spanish Succession, a European-wide conflict intended to limit the growing power of Catholic Spain and France.[12] Anne herself was regarded by Watts as a hero of the Protestant cause and was identified with Moses (1810, II, pp. 753–68). 'Blessed be God, we have a Moses in the midst of us on the top of the hill, a queen of a manly soul upon the throne of our British Israel: She has by her royal proclamations given order to fight with Amalek, to oppose and suppress the armies of iniquity' (p. 755). The authority of Queen Anne is that of God, since she is God's hero in 'his quarrel' (p. 755). The battles of Blenheim (13 August 1704) and Ramillies (23 May 1706) are 'wonders of rescue for the German empire, and wonders of liberty for mankind' (p. 755).

In an elaborate allegory, Watts goes on to identify Aaron with the various ministers who are close to the Queen, while Joshua represents 'the inferior magistrates'. Thus Britain's political, military and civil authorities are mythologized as Israel fighting the battles of the Lord.

The same religious ideology is used to interpret the Hanoverian monarchs.[13] In 'A Sermon preached at Berry-Street on 18 June 1727', Watts comments on the death of George I and the accession of George II. The late King George was 'one of the greatest men upon earth: A king whose dominion was spread from sea to sea, and who reigned over several nations' (1810, II, p. 776). The reference to 'from sea to sea' is a quotation from Psalm 72.8 'May he have dominion

---

12 This, at any rate, was how Isaac Watts and most vigorous Protestants saw it. For a more political interpretation in terms of the resistance of many nations to French hegemony, see Pincus 1998, p. 95. For qualifications of the extent to which British identity was based upon Protestantism, see Claydon and McBride 1998, pp. 10–14.

13 Hatton sums up his more sober view of the religious significance of George I with the comment 'By accepting the Act of Settlement, the house of Hanover had taken on a responsibility for the Protestant succession which George did not think it right to abandon. Though not of a religious temperament, he held it a "point of honour" to maintain this succession for himself and for his descendants' (1978, p. 166). Hatton notes (p. 173) that the dissenters had received the accession of George I with jubilation.

from sea to sea', which as we have seen, Watts had used several years earlier in his version of the Psalm to celebrate the expansion of the Christian dominion. Just as God had extended the life of George I 'to answer wise purposes in his own government of the world' (p. 780), so the coronation of George II and Queen Caroline on 11 October 1727 was greeted with religious rapture. In his Ode celebrating this event, Watts says:

> Lo, the majestic form appears,
> Sparkling in life and manly years:
> The kingdom's pride, the nation's choice,
> And heav'n approves Britannia's voice.

Let Britain's golden ages run:

> In circles lasting as the sun. (1810, IV, pp. 561–2)

In an ode celebrating the birthday of Queen Caroline, Watts plays upon the idea that 1 March was also St. David's Day. David, King of Israel, St. David of Wales and George II are combined in this eulogy.

> Now, Britain, let thy vows arise,
> May George the royal saint assume!
> Then ask permission of the skies,
> To put the favourite name in David's room:
> Fair Carolina join thy pious cares
> To train in virtue's path your royal heirs,
> And be the British crown with endless honour theirs. (p. 562)

In his version of Psalm 75 Watts makes explicit reference to the Glorious Revolution of 1688 and 'the Happy Accession of King George to the Throne' under the heading 'Power and Government from God alone'.

> To Thee, most Holy, and most High,
> To Thee we bring our thankfull Praise.
> Thy Works declare thy Name is nigh,
> Thy Works of Wonder and of Grace.
>
> Britain was doom'd to be a Slave,
> Her Frame dissolv'd: her Fears were great;
> When God a new Supporter gave
> To bear the Pillars of the State.

Verse 6 probably has the Jacobite movement in mind.

> No vain Pretence to Royal Birth
> Shall fix a Tyrant on the Throne;
> God, the Great Sovereign of the Earth
> Will rise and make his Justice known.

Otherworldly inwardness

There are two aspects to the formation of the imperial theology of Isaac Watts, one external and the other internal. We have seen how through his theological geography, his Calvinistic history of providence and his identification of British political and military policy with the kingdom of God, Watts had created an ideology of British Israel. Corresponding to this rhetoric of public life, there is a withdrawal of faith and spirituality into the inner life. The sacralization of public life is accompanied by a retreat into Christian interiority. In his sermon 'Flesh and spirit; or, the principles of sin and holiness' (1810, I, Sermon 4), Watts discusses the psychology and spirituality of the Christian life. He is well aware of the metaphorical character of the Pauline distinction between flesh and spirit. 'Flesh' refers to human evil, whether in the body or in the mind, and 'spirit' refers to goodness or holiness. However, the flesh is also our human nature as embodied. The body is the location of the senses which are the occasions of temptation (p. 37), although sin is only occasioned by the body. Sin cannot be caused by the body since the body is material and lacks moral intention. The twin principles of good and evil are thus within the person and create a continuous struggle.

By means of the internalization of this dichotomized anthropology, the Christian struggle against oppression and injustice is distracted into introspection (p. 44).[14] The various ways this struggle is met with give rise to a kind of typology of character – some have a wrathful temperament, some a more wanton or a melancholy nature (p. 46). The psychic energies of the Christian are to be entirely devoted to this struggle, which involves a severe repression of desire. This leads the Christian to long for the next life when the body of corrupting flesh will be left behind.[15] We shall then be 'Absent from this traytor, this vexing enemy, that we constantly carry about with us! Absent from the clog and chain of this sinful flesh, the prison wherein we are kept in darkness, and are confined from God!' (p. 47). Thus death is 'the best time, is the time of our release from this sinful companion . . . Thus at the day of our death is derived a glorious liberty, and thence we date our joys' (p. 48). 'Is the body such a foul and wretched spring of sin? Then what a heaven of purity and pleasure is provided for the children of God at their death' (1810, III, p. 166). The meaning of the resurrection of the flesh is that at that time the flesh and the spirit shall no longer be in conflict with one another.

In one of his earlier poems, Watts goes so far as to wonder at the creation of such an anomaly as a human being.

How meanly dwells the immortal mind!
How vile these bodies are!
Why was a clod of earth designed

---

14 John Hoyles (1971, p. 208) suggests that one of the most significant contributions of Isaac Watts to English poetry was his development of introspective egoism. Keeble (1987, pp. 186–93, 205) attributes dissenting introspection to the political withdrawal of the Restoration period.

15 This longing for death as promising an escape from the weakness of bodily life is a prominent theme of Puritan and dissenting thought prior to Watts, and is, indeed, typical of much pre-modern Christian theology. For typical seventeenth-century examples see Baxter (1662) and Howe (1863).

To enclose a heavenly star?

Hark! From on high my Saviour calls!
I come, my Lord, my love!
Devotion breaks the prison walls
And speeds my last remove. (1810, IV, pp. 363–4)

The result of this kind of spirituality is that the Christian doctrine teaches us to condemn both the good and evil things of sense and time, by the expectation and prospect of the invisible and eternal world, where both the good and evil things are of infinitely greater importance (1810, I, p. 14), and the Christian has 'a holy superiority' over the things of this world while at the same time being wholly committed to his duty (p. 15).[16]

The privatized Church and the providential state

The view of the Christian life as being entirely preoccupied with a struggle against instinctual desire, plus a sense of duty towards the keeping of the divine commandments, is further clarified by Watts' theory about the relationship between the Church and the state. Civil government is ordained by God to secure the order and security of society, but if civil government intervenes in the religious life of citizens, it goes beyond its prerogative. There is thus a clear distinction between the civil realm and the religious realm, public order and private belief, which has the effect of confining religion within extra-terrestrial concerns, with only a few exceptions. The state needs the divine sanction to guarantee the taking of oaths, and to intimidate would-be wrongdoers. However, religion as such 'relates to the salvation of our souls and a future world of happiness' (1810, IV, p. 141).

There is no scope for a prophetic Church scrutinizing the policies of the government, and in the case of Great Britain, where the religion of civil government is Christian, there is no need for such prophetic ministry. Of course, Isaac Watts was a dissenting clergyman, and his congregations had suffered persecution from the established Church in the not so distant past. His own father had been imprisoned for non-compliance with the legal requirements of the established Church before the 1689 Act of Tolerance. The political philosophy of Watts was aimed at securing religious freedom for dissenters. Nevertheless, the general approach that flows from his thought has been influential beyond the limits of the situation he addressed. The Church becomes a private enclave, focusing not upon this world but upon salvation in the next. Its members are to spend their energies struggling against their desires, a struggle only terminated by the release of death. In the meantime the national and international purposes of God are worked out through the Christian monarchy, the Christian Parliament

---

16 Cohen (1986, pp. 46, 98) describes the Puritan religious experience of the seventeenth century as being a psychological transformation of weakness into power. Helpless sinners became powerful saints. My view is that the political theology of Watts was able to preserve the power of individual conversion whilst also seeing the power of God in the imperial power of the British state.

and the Christian armed forces, supported by the Church in prayer and praise. Isaac Watts' version of Psalm 67 is a classic example of the political theology we have been describing. Some of the verses were referred to earlier, but the remaining verses are as follows.

Amidst our Isle exalted high
Do thou our Glory stand,
And like a Wall of Guardian-Fire
Surround the Favourite-Land.

When shall thy Name from Shore to Shore
Sound all the Earth abroad,
And distant Nations know and love
Their Saviour and their God?

Earth shall obey her Maker's Will,
And yield a full Increase;
Our God will crown his chosen Isle
With Fruitfulness and Peace.

God the Redeemer scatters round
His choicest Favours here,
While the creation's utmost bound
Shall see, adore and fear.[17]

The internal response of the Church to the grace of God, and the providence of God in securing the Protestant monarchy, led Watts to a sense of the international mission of the Christian faith, with British power as its principal agent. There are two aspects of the mission: domination and conversion.

But Nations that resist his Grace
Shall fall beneath his iron Stroke;
His Rod shall crush his Foes with Ease,
As Potter's Earthen Work is broke.

Now ye that sit on earthly Thrones,
Be wise, and serve the Lord, the Lamb:
Now to his Feet submit your Crowns,
Rejoice and tremble at his Name. (Ps. 2.7–8)

The oldest of the Anglican missionary organizations, the Society for Promoting Christian Knowledge (SPCK), was founded in 1698, when Watts was aged 24, and the Society for the Propagation of the Gospel in Foreign Parts was founded in 1701. Although the work of these societies was mainly confined to the provi-

---

17 Psalm 67 'The Nation's Prosperity and the Church's Increase'. Watts adds a note, 'Having translated the scene of this psalm to Great Britain I have borrowed a devout and poetical wish for the happiness of my native land from Zaccharia 2.5 . . .' Watts is explaining the second verse which does not come from Psalm 67.

sion of chaplaincies to overseas colonies and trading posts, the vision of a universal mission resulting in the conversion of heathen lands is present and was celebrated by Watts (Stanley 1990, p. 55).

> The Heathen Lands that lie beneath
> The Shades of overspreading Death
> Revive at his first dawning Light,
> And Desarts blossom at the Sight. (Ps. 72.5)

Competitive Christianity

Beneath the increasing power of the Protestant nation and its worldwide mission to convert the heathen lies the thought that Christianity is involved in a competition with other religions. Watts regards the Christian religion as one of a series of comparable religions (1810, I, pp. 1–10, 11–19 and 20–33). The purpose of the sermon, 'The Inward Witness to Christianity', is to deal with the doubts that this situation gives rise to. Christianity is 'the noblest religion', but, asks Watts, 'How do you know that Christianity is the true religion?' (p. 2). The reply that Christianity is the religion of the country into which we were born is unsatisfactory. Such an argument would place Christianity on the same plane as the religions of the Jew, the Turk and the heathen, since each would be merely a local family or territorial tradition. It is necessary to find proofs for the truth of Christianity emerging from a direct comparison with other religions.

One of these lies in the character of the Christian experience of forgiveness.

> Other religions, that have been drawn from the remains of the light of nature, or that have been invented by the superstitious fears and fancies of men, and obtruded on mankind by the craft of their fellow-creatures, are all at a loss in this instance, and can never speak solid peace and pardon. (p. 6)

A second argument has to do with the saintly lives produced in various religions. It is true, Watts admits, that some of the other religions can produce people of great holiness, but they are few in number. The Christian faith, on the other hand, can show hundreds of thousands of other worldly saints, 'So that whatsoever religion pretends to a competition with ours, it falls vastly short in this respect, in raising the affections above the world, above the joys and fears of the present life' (p. 14).

Watts concludes that in this competition Christianity is bound to emerge victorious. '[H]ow glorious is the gospel of our Lord! How preferable to other religions! Those which men have invented are not to come into competition with it; let none of them be named' (p. 30).

A similar thought is found in the *Hymns and Spiritual Songs* of 1705:

> What if we trace the Globe around,
> And search from Britain to Japan,
> There shall be no Religion found
> So just to God, so safe to Man.

> Not the feign'd Fields of heath'nish Bliss

Could raise such Pleasure in the Mind;
Nor does the Turkish Paradise
Pretend to Joys so well refin'd.

Should all the Forms that Men devise
Assault my Faith with treach'rous Art,
I'd call them Vanity and Lies,
And bind the Gospel to my Heart. (Hymn 131 of part ii)

This competitive policy was to be urged upon children in the charity schools.

They [the children] should be put in mind frequently of the excellency of the
christian religion in distinction from that of Turks and Jews and heathens:
and of the excellency of the protestant religion in opposition to the papists,
with all their idolatry and superstition, their cruelty and wicked principles,
their mischievous and bloudy practices. (1810, II, p. 720)

Just as the constant crushing of fleshly desires is the internal counterpart of the
crushing of his enemies by the Christian monarch, so the external competition
between Christianity and other religions has an interior representation in the
competition between earthly and heavenly love which plagues the human relations of Isaac Watts and the Christians for whom he wrote. However attractive
human love may be, there is always a hidden danger in it.

Souls whom the tie of friendship binds,
And partners of our blood,
Seize a large portion of our minds,
And leave the less for God.

Nature has soft but pow'rful bands,
And reason she controls;
While children with their little hands
Hang closest to our souls.

Thoughtless they act th' old serpent's part;
What tempting things they be!
Lord, how they twine about our heart,
And draw it off from thee! (1810, IV, p. 370)

If consciousness is to a large extent a product of social environment, we may
interpret this heightened sense of competition, whether in its globalized form as a
competition between religions or in its privatized form as a competition between
human and divine love, as the reflection of the trade competition between nations
which was such a feature of the early eighteenth century. The old imperialism
of conquest and settlement was giving way to a new imperialism of trade and
commerce which had the effect of throwing nations into competitive relations
(Armitage 2000, p. 148).

Conclusions

Isaac Watts was not the founder of imperial theology. In the *Church History* and the *Life of Constantine* by Eusebius of Caesarea (*c.*260–*c.*340) we already find such an interpretation of Christian faith (1989; 1999; Kee 1982). As far as Christian faith in Britain is concerned, many of the Protestant theologians of the later sixteenth century emphasize the calling of God to Britain as modern Israel, and the trading sermons of the early seventeenth century show the way in which Christian faith was becoming an ideology of colonization. Watts, however, occupies a position of unique influence as the principal creator of the modern English hymn. Classics such as 'Our God, Our Help in Ages Past', still sung at Remembrance Day services, and the beautiful 'When I Survey the Wondrous Cross' testify to his enduring influence. The more explicit references to Great Britain and its imperial Christian mission have long since disappeared from the hymn books but the attitudes remain submerged in national conscious-ness. Speaking of his school days at Eton College, Michael Goulder remarks, 'It was in some way known to the School authorities that Her Majesty's favourite Psalm was no. 68, an ancient Hebrew war song of great power and obscurity; and whenever the royal party attended we sang Psalm 68' (1990, p. 7).

> May God arise and his enemies be scattered,
> And those hostile to him flee at his approach.
>
> You disperse them like smoke;
> You melt them like wax near fire.
> The wicked perish at the presence of God. (Ps. 68.1–2)

Goulder describes how puzzled he was about the meaning of these strange words. Why should they be sung during Christian worship in the presence of the Royal Family? The theology of Watts is at least partly responsible for the sense of uniqueness, superiority and destiny which remains as a mainly subconscious resi-due influencing the attitudes of British Christians toward people of other nations and other faiths. If in Britain such attitudes are little more than half-forgotten traces, the same is not true of much Christian consciousness in America.[18]

We have now completed our selected studies of the modification of Christian faith under the conditions of power. In these circumstances the older, prophetic theology was almost lost. From time to time, however, on the edges as it were, of that powerful theological identity, a dialogue took place which revealed the limits of such false consciousness. In the next chapter we will consider three examples of such dialogues.

---

18 Imperialistic theology was a strand in the earliest settlement of North America. The influence of such beliefs on the growth and expansion of English-speaking North America is described in Hughes and Allen 1988; Drinnon 1980 and Berkhofer 1965. For the impact of imperial theology in Australia, see Swain and Bird-Rose (eds.) 1988.

7

Mission on the Edges of Christianity:
Three Conversations

In previous chapters we have seen some examples of the way the prophetic tradition, based on love and justice, was distorted by wealth, exclusion and competition. The energy of that prophetic voice and that all embracing love, however, was never entirely lost, nor did it lose its critique of power and its character as being good news to the poor. These aspects survived often only as background, while wealth, exclusion and competition remained in the foreground. Sometimes it is the contrast with the background that renders the foreground visible. These moments of contrast often emerge on the edge of power, in places where Christian faith suddenly recognized itself in contrast.

In this chapter we will illustrate the contrasts that became visible on the margins by listening to three conversations. The first of these is found in the work of Abiezer Coppe and will illustrate the edges of wealth.[1] The second will come from the diary of David Brainerd and will illustrate the edge of exclusion. However, a third conversation from the journal of David Livingstone shows just the opposite, illustrating the edges of competitive power and how the competitive nature of falsified faith is quickly re-awakened when challenged. Many other examples could have been selected, from other centuries and other cultures, but these three from the seventeenth, eighteenth and nineteenth centuries respectively highlight the development of modernity in the Anglo-Saxon Christian world.

Abiezer Coppe (1619–72): The comfortable Church and poverty

On Sunday 13 September 1649 the thirty-year-old preacher and scholar Abiezer Coppe was making a journey on horseback, probably somewhere in the English Midlands. Coppe had been born in Warwick and educated at Warwick School, where he was a star pupil (McDowell 2003, p. 18). The Headmaster used to

---

1 Both in his own day and in some of the historical writing of today Abiezer Coppe is regarded as a member of the so-called Ranters, who were supposed to be a group or even a movement of revolutionary protest. The expression 'Ranter' was used as a term of abuse, and has drawn attention away from Coppe as an author to be taken seriously in his own right. The article about him by A. L. Morton (1982) is an example of the results of subsuming Coppe under the label 'Ranter'. A number of modern studies question whether the so-called Ranters ever had any reality beyond the imaginations of those who found such radical writing unacceptable (see Bradstock 2011, p. xxi).

call him in to read to him the works of Homer in the original Greek (p. 92). An intensely religious person he had begun at the age of 13 to make a daily record of his sins and to memorize much of the Bible (Coppe 1987, p. 73). In 1636 and the following year he had spent time at All Souls and Merton colleges in Oxford. Here he added Hebrew to his Latin and Greek.

The year 1649 was a time of dramatic social and political upheaval in England. Coppe was firmly in the Puritan tradition and served for a while as chaplain to one of the Puritan regiments. He was also becoming well known throughout the Midlands as a fiery gospel preacher in the radical tradition of the Protestant Reformation, and it may have been for this reason that he had already served a prison sentence in 1646.

On 30 January 1649 Charles I had been executed as a traitor to the people. The Levellers, among the most radical of the English revolutionaries, advocating democracy and human rights as the basis of a free people's republic, were at the height of their influence. However, they were oppressed by the parliamentary government of Cromwell. A number of the leading figures were imprisoned and on 17 May several of them were shot and killed (Bradstock 2011, pp. 27–50). In the meantime Coppe had published a brilliant satirical attack on the obscurity and irrelevance of grammar school and university education.[2]

As he rode along Coppe's attention was drawn to a pedestrian, 'a most strange deformed man, clad with patched clothes' (1987, p. 39). When he saw the poor man, Coppe says that 'my heart, or the day of the Lord, which burned as an oven in me, set my tongue on flame to speak to him' (p. 39). Stopping his horse, Coppe addressed the stranger:

'How now friend, art thou poor?'
'Yea, Master,' replied the other, 'very poor.'

As if he were not able to take this in or find anything else to say, Coppe repeated the question. 'Poor?' 'Yea, very poor.'

Poverty had been increasing in England in the late sixteenth and seventeenth centuries. There were many causes of this including the breakdown of the monastic system, which had been one of the principal providers of charity, and the practice of enclosing the common land, which had been used for grazing and for small-scale subsistence agriculture, turning it into the production of more profitable crops by the wealthy land owners (Slack 1990; Carroll 1996, p. 128). This had thrown many poor farmers off their fields, but there was very little understanding of the connection between economic development under early capitalism and the place of surplus labour. They 'could not yet realize the complex and necessary links between the formation of wealth and the formation of an entire class of expendable workers' (Carroll 1996, p. 7).

The concern of English society in the late sixteenth and early seventeenth centuries was not so much to do with understanding the causes of poverty as with keeping it under control. Beggars were vagrants, moving from place to place without respecting boundaries or restrictions; beggary was often associated with

---

2 *Some Sweet Sips of Some Spirituall Wine, Sweetly and Freely Dropping from One Cluster of Grapes* (Coppe 2011 [1649]).

protest and rebellion; the beggar was thus a threat to social stability (p. 6). The beggar was also associated with infectious disease and with madness. Bridewell and Bedlam hospitals in London, intended for the support and reformation of the poor, quickly became places of correction for those who rejected the normal conventions of society, whether through poverty or insanity (p. 98). A distinction was often recognized between the situation of the weak, disabled, sick and elderly, who could not work and were entitled to charity, and that of the strong rogues who found begging more profitable than doing a hard day's work. The fraudulent beggar is a popular figure in Elizabethan and Stuart drama and prose, where the beggar turns out to be a rich lord in disguise, or somebody living on the gullibility of the public. Only slowly was it being recognized that there might be a third category of poor people, those who could work and wanted to work but could find no employment. Perhaps the very last play before the closing of the theatres in 1642, staged in 1641/2 but not published until 1652, was Richard Brome's *A Jovial Crew*. This represents a number of gentry in the form of beggars, along with some real beggars, but even those have fallen from high positions. 'The play never investigates their real suffering in any way' (Carroll 1996, p. 211). Carroll concludes his discussion by saying that '[t]he available historical evidence in fact suggests that poverty was indeed counted a "vice", a moral failing more than an economic or a systemic one' (p. 214). The stage showed them either as noble frauds, or as living a jovial, free pastoral life.

Coppe could not deny, however, the reality of the poor man beside him on the road. Something inside him said, 'It's a poor retch, give him two-pence' (1987, p. 39).Then he had a second thought:

> It's a poor retch give him sixpence and that's enough for a Squire or Knight, to give to one poor body. Besides, [saith the holy Scripturian Whore] he's worse than an Infidel that provides not for his own family. (p. 39)[3]

Here Coppe is thinking about the balance between the duty to give charity and the responsibility of caring for his own family. He was also considering what was appropriate for a person of a certain class to give in such a situation. While he stood debating with himself, the inner voice continued.

> True love begins at home. Thou, and thy family are fed, as the young ravens strangely, though thou hast been a constant Preacher, yet thou hast abhorred both tythes and hire; and thou knowest not aforehand who will give thee the worth of a penny. Have a care of the main chance. (p. 39)[4]

Thus Coppe considered the fragility of his own family finances, arising from the fact that as an itinerant preacher without a definite parish he had no access to the normal means of support for clergy. He never knew when he would get any pay himself.

---

3 1 Tim. 5.8. Coppe describes those who used such texts to protect their own self-interest as prostituting the Scripture.

4 His family were fed miraculously by the hand of God like Elijah in the wilderness (1 Kings 17.4–6).

Suddenly, Coppe seemed to make his mind up. 'Give me six pence, here's a shilling for thee' (p. 40). He has now realized that he has no small change and cannot afford to give as much as a shilling so he asks the poor man for change. He is somewhat taken aback when the stranger replies, 'I cannot, I have never a penny.' At this point it is clear that Coppe is about to bring the conversation to a close but before parting he adds rather lamely, 'I would fain have given thee something if thou couldst have changed my money.' To which the poor man simply replies, 'God bless you.'

Coppe says that then 'with much reluctancy, with much love, and with amazement . . . I turned my horse head from him, riding away'. He had not gone far before something in him forced him to return and tell the man that if he called in at a certain place in the next town, Coppe would leave sixpence for him, on the supposition that he would have changed his shilling but as he rode slowly away again, the story of Ananias and Sapphira came flooding into his mind. They had sold their property and claimed to have given the proceeds to the Church, without letting the Church know that they had held back something for themselves. By now, Coppe is clearly thinking that the whole of the shilling really belongs to the stranger and that he like Sapphira is keeping back a portion of it for himself. He remembers that Sapphira was struck dead by the Lord, and he felt as if he himself had been struck down dead.

> And behold the plague of God fell into my pocket: and the rust of my silver rose up in judgement against me, and consumed my flesh with fire: so that I, and my money perisht with me.

The impact upon the imagination of Abiezer Coppe of those years of memorizing the Bible is now very clear. He had brought together Acts 5.1–11 with James 5.1–3, where the 'rich men' are told to

> weep and howl for your miseries that shall come upon you. Your riches are corrupted, and your garments are motheaten. Your gold and silver is cankered; and the rust of them shall be a witness against you, and shall eat your flesh as it were fire.

Coppe then pauses to consider his situation. He had ridden about eight miles not having had anything to eat, not so much as a mouthful of bread that day,

> and had drunk but one small draught of drink; and had between 8 or 9 miles more to ride, ere I came to my journeys end: my horse being lame, the waies dirty, it raining all the way, and I not knowing what extraordinary occasion I might have for money.

But, he continues,

> the rust of my silver did so rise up in judgement against me, and burnt my flesh like fire: and the 5. of James thundered such an alarm in mine ears, that I was fain to cast all I had into the hands of him, whose visage was more marr'd than any mans that ever I saw.

To his references to the Acts of the Apostles and the letter of James, Coppe had now added a quotation from Isaiah 52.14 where the reference is to the appearance of the suffering servant of God. 'His visage was so marred more than any man, and his form more than the sons of men.' These songs of the servant in Isaiah were applied by the Church to the sufferings of Jesus Christ. Coppe is now suggesting that the poor stranger on the road reminded him of the suffering servant of God, or might in some strange way represent Jesus Christ himself.

Having now given the poor man all the money he had on him, Coppe rode away at last, 'being filled with trembling, joy, and amazement, feeling the sparkles of a great glory arising up from under these ashes'.

But once more he turned around and saw the stranger looking earnestly after him. Coppe then turned around, alighted from his horse, took off his hat and bowed deeply to him seven times. He rode back toward 'the poor retch' one more time and said, 'because I am a King I have done this, but you need not tell anyone' (p. 41).

In Chapter 3 of his *Second Fiery Flying Roll*, Coppe had introduced this encounter by saying that under it was 'couched that Lion, whose roaring shall make all the beasts of the field tremble, and all the Kingdoms of the earth quake' (1987, p. 39). The lion is clearly the lion of Judah, one of the titles of Christ, and the beasts of the field are those who plunder their fellow human beings, since all the kingdoms of the earth are based upon such expropriation and plunder, their whole structure is shaken.

Coppe's expectation about the reception which his *Flying Roll* would receive turned out to be pretty accurate. The work was published on 4 January 1649. Only four days later the Council of State issued a warrant for the arrest of Coppe 'for writing of some blasphemous truths' (p. 9). By 1 February the *Flying Roll* had come to the attention of Parliament, who denounced it as containing 'many horrid blasphemies, and damnable and detestable opinions, to be abhorred by all good and godly people' (p. 111). The book was to be burned in public by the state hangman, any individual possessing a copy of the book was to surrender it for burning. Coppe himself had been arrested and placed in Coventry Jail by 13 January and by March had been moved to Newgate Prison in London. Coppe was no doubt correct in believing that the Blasphemy Act of August 1650 had his works in view, and by 1651 he had issued a defence in which he explained the intentions of his writing (pp. 57–62).[5]

No doubt Coppe's bold insistence upon freedom, and his belief that to the pure all things are pure, encouraged him to express himself incautiously. When, for example, he says, 'I can if it be my will, kiss and hug Ladies, and love my neighbour's wife as myself, without sin' (p. 44), the tone is more of truculent defiance rather than serious intention, he only says that he could do it, not that he had done it. It seems far more probable that what really offended Parliament was Coppe's insistence upon '[t]he author's strange and lofty carriage towards great ones, and his most lowly carriage towards beggars, rogues, prisoners, gypsies' (p. 20), and his declaration that the base things of the earth would overthrow the rich and powerful. Coppe was turning the world upside down and the world struck back at him.

---

5 For the text of the Blasphemy Act see Andrew Hopton's Introduction in Coppe 1987, pp. 6–7.

Sometime between the encounter with the poor stranger and the end of 1649, Coppe had experienced a vision which was the climax of a trance-like state which had lasted four days and nights. In the vision he saw three hearts or, as he says, '(three appearances) in the form of hearts' followed by a huge company of such hearts filling every corner of the room (p. 17). The hearts were variegated and diverse and yet 'folded up into unity'. He interpreted the vision as meaning that judgement would fall upon everyone who refused to bow down to universal love, whose service is perfect freedom. He was then commanded to write and 'lo a hand was sent to me' (p. 18). This seems to mean that he saw his own hand writing in response to the revelation. He wanted to publish the text immediately, but it was taken out of his hand and thrust into his mouth. A remark he makes in chapter eight of the second roll suggests that he had intended to include an account of his imprisonment in 1646, but on second thought he decided to remove this from the text (pp. 51–2).

The *Fiery Flying Roll* of Abiezer Coppe is now recognized as an outstanding example of seventeenth-century prose. Nicholas McDowell describes it as an 'unsettling mixture of prophecy, sexuality, and social radicalism' (2003, p. 89). Its author quickly became the 'most notorious radical prophet of the 1640s' (p. 18). The tract, a tirade of prophetic exclamations and denunciations and appeals to the God of love, comes to a climax in its last chapter with a stunning attack upon conventional religion, whether Catholic, Anglican or Anabaptist, in which doctrine and liturgy had become disassociated from Christian ethics. The tumultuous imagery finally emerges into the clear light of day.

> He that hath this worlds goods, and seeth his brother in want, and shutteth up the bowels of compassion from him, the love of God dwelleth not in him; this man's religion is in vain. (Coppe 1987, p. 53; 1 John 3.17; James 1.26b)

Before we leave Abiezer Coppe, his encounter with the stranger and his experience of hearts folded in upon hearts in the spirit of universal love, we should pause to consider the sources of his inspiration. Nicholas McDowell shows how Coppe's writing can be interpreted against the background of seventeenth-century literary conventions, which are mocked by Abiezer. For example, 'even the bibliographic conventions of publication are undermined' (2003, p. 115). McDowell continues:

> The division of the contents of 'A Second Fiery Flying Roule' is printed on the same page as that of A Fiery Flying Roll, and the 'separate' pamphlets are printed as one, despite having individual title pages. Coppe plays with authorship and anonymity, but not with any apparent purpose of self-protection. (p. 115)

No doubt this is a correct analysis of the style of Abiezer Coppe, but there is another source of his inspiration, which seems to have been hardly noticed by the literary commentators: the prophets of the Hebrew Bible.

In the symbolism of biblical prophecy, the roll always has a negative meaning. In a culture like ours today of social networks and bloggers, communication through words is so easy and widespread that it has become an everyday thing.

In the ancient world, writing itself was a memorable action. To write something was to declare that a decision had been made, a law pronounced, or something definite had been done. Something like this may be observed when pre-literate people encounter the art of writing.

> Writing is to the natives here a profound mystery. There is nothing like it in the sphere of their knowledge. There is nothing with which we can compare it in order to give them an idea of it. They always look upon it as something supernatural, and expect the *lokualo* [a local word for 'writing'] to tell us things at a distance, or that we see in it things happening at a distance. (Livingstone 1960, p. 133)

This quality in the context of the judgements of God gave the biblical roll an ominous, even a threatening aspect. The prophet Isaiah was instructed to give his child an ominous name, anticipating the destruction of Israel by Assyria. 'Moreover the LORD said unto me, Take thee a great roll, and write in it with a man's pen concerning Maher-shalal-hash-baz' (Isa. 8.1). The finality of the judgement was indicated by the fact that the name was given before the birth of the child and was written in 'a great roll' in the presence of witnesses (vv. 2–3).

When Jeremiah was under house arrest in Jerusalem, the word of God came to him: 'Take thee a roll of a book, and write therein all the words that I have spoken unto thee against Israel, and against Judah, and against all the nations' (Jer. 36.2). The words written in the roll would move about freely even when Jeremiah was constrained.

Another example of ominous writing is found in the Revelation of John. A mighty angel is seen with a little book in his hand followed by the sounding of seven thunders (Rev. 10.1–3).

It has been suggested that in introducing the title page of the second *Fiery Flying Roll* immediately after the contents page of the first one that Coppe was making fun of the literary pretensions of contemporary authors, perhaps by suggesting that there was nothing at all worth reading in the first volume. It is far more likely, I think, that the reference is to the experience of Jeremiah in Jerusalem already mentioned. Baruch wrote down everything that Jeremiah told him, and read the words to the people. When King Jehoiakim heard the words of the scroll he had each page cut out and threw it into the fire until the whole scroll was consumed (Jer. 36.21–23). Then Jeremiah was instructed by God to write out all the words again in a second book

> Then took Jeremiah another roll, and gave it to Baruch . . . who wrote therein from the mouth of Jeremiah all the words of the book which Jehoiakim king of Judah had burned in the fire: and there were added besides unto them many like words. (v. 32)

Coppe, in adding the second book, immediately is giving us a hint that the first book will be disregarded and destroyed. He anticipates this by already adding a second book. The first book would be burned in the fire but a second one, also on fire, comes hard on its heels.

Why did Coppe describe his *Rolls* as flying through the air? He is referring to Zechariah 5.1 'and then I turned, and lifted up mine eyes, and looked, and behold a flying roll'. The roll was full of curses upon the houses of the thieves and liars, 'and it shall remain in the midst of his house, and shall consume it with the timber thereof and the stones thereof' (5.4).

This biblical background provides the rationale for every word in Coppe's title. It is both first and second, because the book will be destroyed by fire; it is flying, because it is impossible to stop it and it goes everywhere, and it is on fire, both because of its own destruction and because of the judgement upon the land which it announces. Like John the Seer, Coppe wanted to record what the voices had said to him.

> And behold I writ, and lo a hand was sent to me, and a roll of a book was therein, which this fleshly hand would have put wings to, before the time. Whereupon it was snatched out of my hand, and the Roll thrust into my mouth; and I eat it up, and filled my bowels with it, where it was as bitter as worm-wood; and it lay broiling, and burning in my stomach, till I brought it forth in this form.
> And now I send it flying to thee. (1987, p. 18)

That is how it became 'A Fiery Flying Roll'.

The background is to be found in the same chapter of Revelation mentioned above.

> And I went unto the angel and said unto him, give me the little book. And he said unto me, Take and eat it up; and it shall make thy belly bitter, but it shall be in thy mouth as sweet as honey. And I took the little book out of the angel's hand, and ate it up; and it was in my mouth sweet as honey: and as soon as I had eaten it, my belly was bitter. And he said unto me, Thou must prophesy again before many peoples, and nations, and tongues, and kings. (vv. 10.9–11)

As the message to the Church that was neither hot nor cold but only lukewarm was vomited from the mouth of the risen Christ (Rev. 3.16 KJV) so Abiezer Coppe, inspired by the prophets of the Old and New Testaments, brought up from his stomach his message to the victorious Puritan churches of Cromwell's England.

David Brainerd (1718–47): The exclusive Church and otherness

Sometime in May 1745 David Brainerd, a Presbyterian minister aged 27, was returning from a visit to Shamokin, an Indian town on the Susquehanna in western Pennsylvania, when he had an unusual meeting.

On the 8 September 1742 the New York Committee of the Scottish Society for the Propagation of Christian Knowledge had recommended to its headquarters in Edinburgh that Brainerd should be appointed as a missionary to the American Indians, usually known today as the native people of America. In March

1743 he was directed to join the Reverend John Sergeant, who had established a mission among the Indians at Stockbridge, about 18 miles north-east of Albany in New York state. Sergeant had been working in this area since 1734 (Grigg 2009, pp. 46, 49–50).

There had been missions among the native peoples of New England since the work of John Eliot (1604–90) had established the semi-independent Indians 'praying towns' (Tinker 1993, p. 22). Interest in such missions had increased since 1713, when the Treaty of Utrecht brought peace between France and England. Not only was the frontier more secure; there was an increasing desire to form a Protestant community in the North Atlantic, in which the converted Indians would be included.

For some time David Brainerd had wanted to leave New England to work with the native people in the Delaware River Valley of Pennsylvania. His opportunity came when the SSPCK gave him permission to leave Stockbridge, transferring his work to Pennsylvania. Although he had already been licensed as a preacher he had not yet been ordained. This took place in New York on 11 and 12 June 1744 (Grigg 2009, p. 74).

Brainerd had already spent a couple of weeks with the few remaining Indian families in the valley, and after his ordination he decided to attempt the longer journey further west through wild, rugged country to the Susquehanna River. It was returning from his second visit to this area a year later that he had the strange encounter.[6]

'When I was in these parts in May last', he writes in his journal from 21 September,

> I had an opportunity of learning many of the notions and customs of the Indians, as well as of observing many of their practices: I then travelling more than an hundred and thirty miles upon the river above the English settlements; and having in that journey a view of some persons of seven or eight distinct tribes, speaking so many different languages. But of all the sights I ever saw among them, or indeed anywhere else, none appeared so frightful or so near akin to what is usually imagined of infernal powers; none ever excited such images of terror in my mind, as the appearance of one who was a devout and zealous reformer, or rather restorer, of what he supposed was the ancient religion of the Indians. (Edwards 1985, p. 329)[7]

Anthropologists today would describe this man as a shaman, traditional healer, spiritual leader, visionary, one who had power to bring together the human and the divine worlds (Craffert 2008, pp. 135–68). Due perhaps to the upheavals in traditional life caused by the white settlers, the destruction of the hunting grounds, the disillusionment created by many broken treaties and the distraction caused by alcoholism a new wave of spiritual insight, mysticism and prophetic renewal was taking place amongst the native peoples in the 1740s and 50s along the north-eastern frontier (Merritt 2003, pp. 89–128). But whereas

---

6 For accounts of this meeting see Pointer 2007, pp. 117–18 and Grigg 2009, pp. 83–4.

7 Edwards published the diary in 1749. The background of the diary and the manuscript tradition is discussed in the editor's introduction on pp. 1–85.

most members of this movement were political figures calling upon the scattered tribes to organize for resistance, the man described by David Brainerd was more of a religious reformer and a mystic. What startled Brainerd was the impact of the appearance of the shaman before there had been a chance to find out what he wanted or what he stood for.

> He made his appearance in his pontifical garb, which was a coat of bears' skins, dressed with the hair on, and hanging down to his toes, a pair of bear skin stockings, and a great wooden face, painted the one half black, the other tawny, about the color of an Indian's skin, with an extravagant mouth, cut very much awry; the face fastened to a bearskin cap which was drawn over his head.

Brainerd was not alone, but was travelling with his Indian companion and interpreter Moses Tatamy on horseback. We do not know anything about the circumstances of the encounter, whether other Native American people were nearby or how far they had travelled from the nearest settlement. What was alarming, however, was not only the dress of the medicine man but the way he behaved.

> He advanced toward me with the instrument in his hand that he used for music in his idolatrous worship, which was a dry tortoiseshell, with some corn in it, and the neck of it drawn on to a piece of wood, which made a very convenient handle. As he came forward he beat his tune with the rattle, and danced with all his might, but did not suffer any part of his body, not so much as his fingers, to be seen: And no man would have guessed by his appearance and actions that he could have been a human creature, if they had not had some intimation of it otherways.

David Brainerd was born in the little town of Haddam on the banks of the Connecticut River, where he was one of several children of Hezekiah and Dorothy Brainerd. David's father died when he was only nine years old and his mother five years later. David went to stay with his aunt and her family in East Haddam, remaining there for four years. The Brainerd family had been comfortably well off and David inherited farmland when he was 18. New Haven was only about 30 miles away, and David decided to go to Yale to study for the ministry (Grigg 2009, pp. 29–31).

The Great Awakening, a revival of intense religious experience, was sweeping through New England in the late 1730s and 40s having begun in Northampton, where Jonathan Edwards (1703–58) was the minister. David has left a vivid account of his personal conversion experience which took place when he was 21 bringing him into a deep personal devotion and confirming his calling to the Christian ministry. It is possible that his own religious experience of personal sin and of the presence of God through Jesus Christ helped him to recognize someone of real spiritual stature in the Native American prophet.[8] Nevertheless, it took some time to recognize these qualities.

---

8 For more details about Indian prophets of this period see Merritt 2003, pp. 84–5.

> When he came near me I could not but shrink away from him, although it was then noonday, and I knew who it was, his appearance and gestures were so prodigiously frightful!

It seems from this remark that Brainerd had either met the shaman before or was aware of his presence in the area, but he had not visited the home of the shaman before, and this was a rather shocking experience at first.

> He had a house consecrated to religious uses, with divers images cut out upon the several parts of it. I went in and found the ground beat almost as hard as a rock with their frequent dancing in it.

It was here that a memorable conversation took place. 'I discoursed with him about Christianity, and some of my discourse he seemed to like; but some of it he disliked entirely.'

His religion, the prophet said, had been taught him by God, and 'he never would turn from it, but wanted to find some that would join heartily with him in it; for the Indians, he said, were grown very degenerate and corrupt'.

Brainerd himself was, of course, recognizable as a holy man. The native people, whether they responded to his message or not, seemed to respect him and many seemed to recognize in him the spiritual fervour that marked the authentic person who was able to mediate between earth and heaven.[9] At any rate, the shaman seemed to be aware of this quality in him, because he apparently made an attempt to recruit him.

> He had thoughts, he said, of leaving all his friends and travelling abroad, in order to find some that would join with him; for he believed God had some good people somewhere that felt as he did.

The prophet now told David the story of his spiritual journey. Perhaps he was responding to the personal testimony David would have given him and was determined to match him story for story. There is no doubt that Brainerd was impressed by his story.

> He had not always, he said, felt as he now did, but had formerly been like the rest of the Indians, until about four or five years before that time [which would have roughly coincided with David Brainerd's own conversion experience]: Then, he said, his heart was very much distressed, so that he could not live among the Indians, but got away into the woods and lived alone for some months. At length, he says, God comforted his heart and showed him what he should do; and since that time he had known God and tried to serve him; and loved all men, be they who they would, so as he never did before. (Edwards 1985, pp. 329–30)

---

9 Sandra Gustafson (2000, pp. 81–2) suggests that Brainerd had adopted some of the styles of the Indian preachers in order to make his own message more acceptable to them. Richard Pointer (2007, p. 118) observes that Brainerd's own religious outlook would have prevented him from acknowledging this adaptation, even to himself.

There are some parallels between this and David Brainerd's own conversion experience. Brainerd said that a book by Solomon Stoddard (1643–1729) was 'in the hand of God . . . the happy means of my conversion' (Grigg 2009, p. 10). Stoddard had been the minister of the Northampton Congregational Church for 55 years and was succeeded by his grandson Jonathan Edwards. The book was *A Guide to Christ, or, The Way of Directing Souls that are under the Work of Conversion* (1714). Stoddard was an intermediate figure between Calvinist orthodoxy and modern evangelical Protestantism. Whereas classical Calvinism taught that since only God knows the number of the elect, it is impossible and irrelevant to try to ascertain the date or time of one's conversion. Stoddard, however, taught that there were various recognizable steps leading to the conversion experience which were a necessary prelude to Christian salvation and mature saving experience. Not only did he teach that conversion should be specific and datable, but it would be prefaced by a period of heightened awareness of one's helplessness and sin. During this time the sinner would feel acutely the danger in which stood his or her immortal soul. Following the crisis of conversion itself, which could only be granted by the grace of God, it was necessary that good works should follow, which would testify to the genuine nature of the conversion. Brainerd's own conversion followed this pattern as he described it and the experience of the prophet is not altogether dissimilar. Brainerd was not only impressed by the story but by the man's manner 'He treated me with uncommon courtesy, and seemed to be hearty in it' (Edwards 1985, p. 330). Brainerd made inquiry among the Indians who knew the prophet, or perhaps he had done so previously, which would be how he came to recognize him. He reports:

> I was told by the Indians that he opposed their drinking strong liquor with all his power; and if at any time he could not dissuade them from it, by all he could say, he would leave them and go crying into the woods.

Brainerd was particularly impressed by the reformer's independence of mind.

> It was manifest he had a set of religious notions that he had looked into for himself, and not taken for granted upon bare tradition; and he relished or disrelished whatever was spoken of a religious nature, according as it either agreed or disagreed with his standard.

The reforming sage used the standard of his own beliefs and conclusions to agree or disagree with Christianity as explained by David Brainerd. 'While I was discoursing he would sometimes say, "Now that I like: so God has taught me", etc. And some of his sentiments seemed very just.' There were disagreements, of course, but Brainerd reports them in a rather pensive reflective style without the sharpness of the evangelist who is in sole possession of the truth.

> Yet he utterly denied the being of a devil, and declared that there was no such a creature known among the Indians of old times, whose religion he supposed he was attempting to revive. He likewise told me that departed souls all went southward, and that the difference between the good and bad was this: that

the former were admitted into a beautiful town with spiritual walls, or walls agreeable to the nature of souls; and that the latter would forever hover round those walls, and in vain attempt to get in.

Brainerd concludes the description in the same reflective way:

He seemed to be sincere, honest and conscientious in his own way, and according to his own religious notions, which was more than I ever saw in any other pagan: And I perceived he was looked upon and derided amongst most of the Indians as a precise zealot that made a needless noise about religious matters.

The fact that the reformer was rejected by his own people and was suffering for his faith made a further appeal to Brainerd, who concluded: 'But I must say, there was something in his temper and disposition that looked more like true religion than anything I ever observed amongst other heathens.'

Although surprising in some ways, the interest that David Brainerd showed in the native prophet and his attitude toward him is not entirely uncharacteristic. As a student at Yale, Brainerd had been caught up in the excitement of the revivals that were sweeping across New England, which had aroused concern and even opposition from more conservative ministers. The pro-revival group had a tendency to be critical of ministers whom they regarded as unconverted. He had been expelled from Yale, and whatever the exact circumstances of his expulsion, it left him feeling bruised and rejected. It was also when he was at Yale that he had begun to cough up blood, because of the tuberculosis that killed him seven years later (Grigg 2009, pp. 14–22).

Many of the congregations in New England were divided over their attitudes to the awakening. During the months after he left Yale, before his mission to the Indians began, he was in effect an itinerant minister. As he visited the various congregations he tried to reconcile them. In a letter to a friend he said, 'God don't deal with all his children as with me' (p. 44). John Grigg, the most astute and scholarly of the Brainerd biographers, remarks that 'Brainerd's attitude may well have been rooted in a sense that the man's [the Indian prophet] spiritual journey was a legitimate quest for God', adding '[p]erhaps, in Brainerd's view, God was leading this man to himself down a different pathway that would eventually reach the same destination' (p. 84).

It is also possible that David Brainerd's acceptance of the prophet reflected a common attitude of the English settlers toward Native American religion. When Indian beliefs coincided with those of the Europeans, they were regarded as a confirmation coming from the heart of nature itself. There is a striking example of this in one of the sermons of Jonathan Edwards, delivered when Edwards was only 19 years old. The title of the sermon is 'The Importance of a Future State': one of the evidences of life after death, says Edwards, lies in the fact the great majority of humanity believes it, 'which plainly and evidently shows that the bare light of nature teaches them. How else should they all agree in it? Even the barbarously ignorant Indians here in America have light enough to believe *that*, for they do all believe it . . .' (Edwards 1992, p. 360). The editor comments: 'The English seem to have relished confirmations of the broad outlines of their religion by American Indians, as if Indian culture represented "natural" think-ing, somewhere between innate ideas and animal instinct' (p. 360, n. 4).[10]

This philosophical interpretation was not typical of the general approach of the colonial settlers toward the Indians, who were almost always regarded as lazy, undisciplined and uncivilized people who lived under the domain of Satan, worshipped idols, indulged in wicked and cruel festivals and were hostile to everything that Christianity stood for. If we combine this attitude with the Cal-vinist theology of New England, with its emphasis upon the reality of sin and the lost condition of all who rejected or were ignorant of Christ, Brainerd's attitude becomes more surprising. His theology would have told him that the Indian prophet who had heard the Christian gospel but had rejected it in favour of his own opinions was guilty of blasphemy and stood in imminent danger of hell fire. At every point of his diary, Brainerd would add a verse or two of Scripture, sometimes as confirmation of the truth of the biblical passage, but more frequently as a comment on the biblical character of his own actions. Yet in the presence of the Indian prophet it did not occur to Brainerd to refer to Acts 10.34–5: 'Of a truth I perceive that God is no respecter of persons: but in every nation he that feareth him, and worketh righteousness, is accepted with him.' Although he was unable to interpret his encounter with the shaman in the light of this passage, there can be little doubt that here we see one of the most exclusive forms of Christianity strangely open to otherness.[11]

David Livingstone (1813–73): The competitive Church and its rival

In his private journal for 12 October 1853 David Livingstone summarized a number of conversations he had had with rainmakers in southern Africa (Liv-ingstone 1960). Livingstone, then aged 40, had already been in southern Africa for more than ten years as a missionary of the London Missionary Society, which had been founded in 1795. This was his second major journey into cen-tral southern Africa, and he had reached the Zambezi River, which the local people called the Leeambye.

Christian missionaries had already been in dispute with African rainmakers for nearly 50 years. The first recorded encounter seems to be by the LMS mis-sionary J. T. van der Kemp in 1804. In a time of drought he had been approached by Chief Mgqika with a request to use his spiritual powers as a holy man to bring rain, since his own rainmakers had failed. The missionary insisted that only God could make rain, but that he would pray to God through Jesus Christ. The next day 'it pleased the Lord to give us a plentiful rain', and van der Kemp regarded this as a sign from God which would encourage the local people to embrace Christian faith (Chidester 1992, p. 40). David Chidester remarks that

---

10 On the other hand Richard Pointer (2007) emphasizes the indifference of both contem-porary preachers and subsequent historians toward the possibility of Indian influence.

11 Sandra Gustafson (2000, p. 88) draws attention to 'the resemblance between the awak-enings of the colonists and the Indians', which the Brainerd encounter suggests. She concludes: 'Perhaps most striking in Brainerd's description is his willingness to perceive the parallel between the New Lights and the nativists and then leave it alone, neither appropriated nor denounced, but respected as a discourse of spiritual revitalization.'

'[i]n this way, a Christian mission inserted itself into the local religious arena as an alternative "environmental religion", making contested claims on the rain as a symbol of religious truth, meaning, and power' (p. 40).

When there was a period of drought or when the local rainmakers failed to bring the rain, the missionaries interpreted this as a judgement from God upon the wickedness and unbelief of the people. Chidester quotes examples from 1826 and 1829. In that year William Shaw, a missionary with the Wesleyan Missionary Society (founded 1813), held a prayer meeting for rain when the traditional rainmakers had failed. When rain fell two weeks later, it was regarded as a confirmation of Christian ownership of the rain. When rain fell after the Sunday morning service in Natal, the missionary Joseph Jackson reported that the people said, 'our mouths are now stopped; we can answer you nothing; we see that God is, and that he hears prayers' (Etherington 1978, p. 52). Chidester describes this as a conflict over symbols, and in this way 'missionaries appropriated the African religious symbol of rain as a sign of their own exclusive, privileged religious authority and power' (1992, p. 40).

Georgina Endfield and David Nash have studied the conflicts of rain in the early days of south African missions in great detail, finding that '[m]any different missionaries consistently attacked rainmaking practices in order to nullify, dismantle, or undermine the religious authority of these revered specialists' (2002, p. 731).

They showed that the rainmakers counterattacked, blaming the arrival of the missionaries for the lack of rain. It was as if there were two 'environmental religions' in competition with one another. The missionaries seldom regarded the practices of rainmaking and other aspects of African ritual as indicating adaptation to local climatic conditions, or as examples of traditional knowledge, but on the whole the missionaries reported the actions of the rainmakers 'in a wholly negative sense, as a form of treachery and deceit rather than as a form of local knowledge' (p. 734).

Irrigation was important to the missionaries not only as a necessary development for building and maintaining local agricultural communities, and thus offering an alternative to the nomadic, hunter/gatherer life of the people, but in order to demonstrate Christian civilized control over water.

Against this background it is interesting to study the development of Livingstone's own approach to the question of African religions as symbolized in the control of rain. In a letter dated 14 April 1842 Livingstone refers in a lighthearted way to his irrigation works as making him a rainmaker. In conversation with one of the chiefs, he says: 'As I did not like to be behind my professional brethren, I declared I could make rain too, not, however, by enchantment like them, but by leading out their river for irrigation' (p. 736). Even the Chief's own doctor laughed heartily at this joke.

A year later, in 1843, Livingstone had to defend himself, because the local people were blaming the failure of the rain upon his own arrival. Commenting on this, he says that '[t]he people could not or would not perceive that the excuses he [the rainmaker] advanced were mere pretences . . . I was sorry to see my friends [the local African people] deceived by an imposter' (p. 732).

It is unusual to find such negative language on the part of Livingstone when describing the rainmakers, and one must remember that he was being attacked for the drought. It is characteristic of his practical approach to dig irrigation channels rather than get involved in an argument about the Christian rain God and the local customs.

The tone of the conversations he records ten years later on the Zambezi river is more like that of a conversation between equals. He did indeed treat them as his professional brethren. So that readers can judge this for themselves the whole of this fascinating exchange or series of exchanges is inserted.

Missionary (coming to a rain doctor who has a great number [of] bulbs, roots, plants, and pots and powders about him). Hail, Father! What are you doing with so many medicines?

Rain Doctor. I thank you, my son. I am charming the rain. We are killed by the Sun.

M. You can make rain then.

R.D. We need rain. Without it we have no milk, the cattle having no grass. We cannot get roots in the field either if the stalks are not brought to the surface by rain. Without it the women would hoe the gardens in vain, we should get no corn. We should perish if we had no rain.

M. As to the benefits of the rain you and I are of one mind, but I believe no one can make rain but God.

R.D. You water your garden by means of the river, but we who use no irrigation must make rain or we should get no corn. We have done it from time immemorial, and we know it is better to apply rain to the whole plant, than a little river water applied only to its root. You do according to the customs of your forefathers, and so do we. You don't need rain but we should die without it.

M. As to the benefits and good influences of the rain, and superiority over irrigation, we are perfectly agreed. That which I dispute is that your medicines have any influence on the rain whatever. God alone can make it.

R.D. I know that perfectly. God alone can make rain, my medicines don't make it. But he has given us the knowledge of certain plants and trees by which we pray to him to make rain for us. We charm the clouds, and He makes the rain for us.

M. But God has told us that there is only one way by which we can pray to him acceptably, viz. by Jesus Christ.

R.D. Truly. And he has told us differently. God has been very good to both white and black. To the white he has given the knowledge of guns, gunpowder, horses, and many other things which we know nothing about. He has given you wisdom too. We see it. To us blacks he has not been so liberal, but he has given us the knowledge of some things too, and the most important is that of certain trees and plants which we use to make rain. We have the knowledge of rain making, you have it not. Now we don't despise those things God has given you, though we are ignorant of them. Nor should you despise what he has given us, though you do not know nor understand them.

M. When did God give you the knowledge of rain making?

R.D. In the beginning, of old. When we first opened our eyes in the world, we found our fathers working with these medicines, they were taught them by their fathers, and so from the beginning, and we now do as they told us to do. We follow in their trail.

M. But God has given us his book, and that gives us correct information as to what he did. Our origin is the same, and in the book which never forgets we have what God revealed to our common ancestors, and he tells us that he has appointed seed time and harvest, summer and winter, and that he gives rain from heaven and fruitful seasons. And this he does to the good and the evil alike, and I think he would give you rain without any medicines. I don't despise your knowledge, I only believe you are mistaken, and should like you to make a trial. God will give us rain if we get it at all.

R.D. No he won't. He might to you white people, but not to us blacks to whom he has given the knowledge of his plants. He has no heart to us.

M. Have you ever tried?

R.D. How could we? We should starve. The town would become scattered. And whoever thought of trying starvation? We cannot buy corn as you do. We must grow it, and it is rain which causes it to spring up and yield.

M. But your medicines so frequently fail, and you never use them except at new and full moon, or when you see the clouds collecting.

R.D. Truly. And so it is with all medicines. We administer medicines to sick people and so do you, though people often die. If God does not please to heal, the patient dies. And so it is with the rain. We do not fail, but God refuses to give us rain. We have always made rain, it's our custom from of old.

M. I think you are wrong about the medicines. We apply them to animate, you to inanimate things. You often make a great smoke, and it never reaches the clouds which you say you are charming.

R.D. We apply medicines to everything, and if you wish us to throw aside our medicines why do you retain your own ?

M. I apply them to living beings, and see and know their effects. You make smoke and cause all the women of the town to pass through it. They feel no effect. You sprinkle all with medicines, no effect is visible, but effects are always visible from my medicines. I can foretell their effects. Can you tell us when we shall have rain?

R.D. There are defects in all medicines, but I see plainly you don't want rain. We do, and cannot do without it. If you make rain for us I shall let it alone.

M. I do wish rain most heartily, and I think your work tends to drive away rain and displease God. He wishes us to feel our dependence on Him alone, and though you say you pray to him all the women in the town believe that you make the rain. They call it your rain, and praise you for it instead of God.

R.D. Well, if you wish rain and pray to God for it, why does it not come? You fail as well as we.

M. We pray for it but do not make it. We leave it to his good pleasure to give or withhold it. You say you pray to him, but you believe you make it independent of him.

R. And so we do. We make it, and if people – witches – did not hinder us by their witchcraft you would soon see it.

M. Well, as you can make it will you make rain for me during the dry season, or on all the gardens now and not on mine? Or will you appoint any day within a fortnight in which it will rain?

M. Let us try our medicines. I shall foretell the effects of mine on any person or animal. Will you now cause the clouds to assemble?

R.D. I need one medicine for it which I will send for first.

M. If you really believed you could make rain, command the clouds, you would not be unwilling to try. I can never get you to make a trial. You wait till you see the clouds coming, then commence your incantations, so that no one can perceive whether your medicines have any effect. I think they have no effect.

R.D. No effect! Magala makapa. Whose rain was that which fell lately but mine? And by whom did the people eat corn for so many years? Who caught the clouds for them but me?

M. The rain was given by God, and would have fallen had you let your medicines alone.

R.D. Of course, and it is so with all medicines, people get well though they use no medicines. But I see you don't want rain, and your talk is just like that of all who talk on subjects they do not understand. Perhaps you are talking, perhaps not. To me you appear to be perfectly silent.

M. Remain well, my friend.

R.D. Depart pleasantly, Father. (Livingstone 1960, pp. 239–43)[12]

There are certainly some traces of competition or rivalry in this dialogue. The rainmaker, for instance, points to the origin of the knowledge of rainmaking in the ancient traditions of the African people, but the missionary points to the knowledge of God as revealed in the sacred literature of his people. There is a contest about the relative efficacy of the two traditions of medicine, and there is a trial when the missionary challenges the rainmaker to fix a date for the coming of the rain.

At the same time, the dialogue also shows a high degree of mutual respect. It often reads like two experts comparing their techniques and traditions. You do it according to the customs of your forefathers, and so do we. God has been very good to both people, but what God has given to the Africans is simply different from what God has given to the Europeans. Each tradition is to some degree ignorant of the other. Both the sets of techniques, whether praying in the name of Jesus Christ or charming the clouds, are known sometimes to fail. It is the rainmaker who is most ready to acknowledge the need for tolerance of the other and to demand mutual respect, although there is an implied challenge in his offer to abandon his techniques, if the missionary agrees to make rain, a challenge which Livingstone does not accept. Instead, the missionary relapses into the mutual accusation which was typical of the conflict between the two environmental religions when he says that the work of the rainmaker 'tends to drive away rain and displease God'.

---

12 There are various versions of this well-known conversation. A shortened form may be found in Comaroff and Comaroff 1991, pp. 210–11.

This use of reason marked by respect was typical of Livingstone's attitude to local culture. 'I exercise no authority but that of love and kindness' (p. 134). According to Livingstone, it was African society that was based upon force and compulsion. They were amazed when he proposed to persuade them by nothing but friendship and love (p. 155). This is in striking contrast with the general practice of the south African missions. David Chidester says:

> Most missionaries entered the mission field with the ideal of achieving conversions through persuasion. After some time in the field, however, nearly all turned to advocate various instruments of economic, social, political, or military coercion to create the necessary conditions for Christian conversion. (1992, p. 41)

It is not even clear to what extent Livingstone regarded individual conversion as being the principal purpose of his mission strategy. Nearly every conversion involved a switch in power from that of the Chief to that of the British culture and Government (p. 44). But Livingstone had frequently been attacked for his support for the freedom and independence of the African peoples (Ross 2002, pp. 67–77). His admiration for the Jesuit missions led him to see that '[t]he widespread diffusion of the Christian message laid the ground for long-term success on a large scale which concentration on immediate individual conversions did not' (p. 100).

Livingstone believed that by opening up central southern Africa to agriculture and commerce African people would achieve a greater degree of independence, wealth, and dignity, which would thus frustrate the growing slave trade which was encroaching both from the East and the West through the Portuguese and the Arabs (p. 62). To establish such an African civilization was his broad missionary strategy. This was not understood by most of the missionaries of his day and was later transformed into an imperialistic adventure (pp. 239–44). Livingstone's policy was consistent with his lifelong interest in other aspects of African culture, such as traditional healing which again distinguished him from most of his contemporary fellow missionaries.

Nevertheless, beneath the common courtesy and respect, there is a profound failure to understand each other. One of the differences between Livingstone and the African rainmakers was to do with incompatible concepts of materiality in the religious life.[13] As he approaches him, Livingstone observes that the rainmaker has 'a great number [of] bulbs, roots, plants, and pots & powders about him'. Certainly the missionaries used medicines, but '[w]e apply them to animate, you to inanimate things', categories which the traditional African world view would not have recognized (Livingstone 1960, pp. 239, 241). Livingstone's Protestant rejection of materiality was for him 'the proper mode of worship' involving only 'praying with them in our simple inexpensive form' (p. 226).

There was another kind of powerful knowledge Livingstone could have used in his debate with the rainmaker, and it is worth asking why he did not. He

---

13 For the anthropological concept of materiality, see Miller (ed.) 2005. Matthew Engelke (2007) brilliantly applies this to central southern Africa.

understood, in accordance with the scientific knowledge of his day, the meteo-rological conditions which would bring about rain. Consider this example:

> [T]here was a Halo of about 20° in diameter round the sun. I remarked to him after taking the observation, with the view of eliciting his opinion on the weather from the increased watery vapour in the atmosphere which such phenomena indicate, 'Does that Halo not foretell rain?' (pp. 225–6)

But the African friend refused to admit this, interpreting the phenomena in a purely religious and mythological way.

In parts of the country the bullocks were attacked by ticks, which could kill them. Livingstone explained this by 'a general benevolence of a great system in which each element had its part the influences of which, whether over rain or sea, can be ameliorated by human intervention'.

Here is another example of Livingstone's interest in scientific knowledge:

> Future missionaries will probably look on our attempts to stop rain making by asserting the impossibility of anyone making rain but God in another light than we do, for it is not impossible that power may be obtained over the clouds. An electrical machine attached to a kite will bring down rain from a cloud, and this may be so improved as to call down copious showers when needed. (p. 168)

It seems fair to ask why, when Livingstone was confronted by the rainmaking apparatus of the African shaman, he did not offer a rational reply in terms of recognizable meteorological phenomena which although not enabling him to cause rain yet might at least enable a degree of rational prediction. As if anticipating the question, Livingstone continues his previously quoted comment about the rainmaking kite by saying, 'we discourage the rain-doctor because in his work the people are led to give that honour to a knave which belongs to God only'.

There seem to be two possible interpretations of this remark.

1 Livingstone believed that it would be blasphemous for any human being to try to make rain.
2 Livingstone believed that although making rain in itself was not a religious problem, it would be blasphemous if such action drew away the adoration of the people from God to the human rainmaker.

It is clear that Livingstone did not believe (1) as we have seen, he had already contemplated the scientific possibility of making rain with perfect calmness. Turning to (2) why should Livingstone have thought that the rainmaker, who believed that it was God who sent the rain, intended to draw the adoration of the people toward himself? A certain amount of gratitude, even glorification, of the one who made rain in conditions of drought would be entirely understand-able. Livingstone himself was frequently addressed as Lord and given other hon-orific titles (Ross 2002, p. 89). Livingstone 'was every day shocked by being addressed' by the title of God (Blaikie 1910, p. 38).

Let us return to the famous dialogue once more. If he did not use scientific reasoning, how then and why did Livingstone try to undermine the claims of the rainmaker? His first counter assertion is the statement 'I believe no-one can make rain but God.' He appears to have suppressed his scientific knowledge that rain could at least be anticipated by observing the signs in the clouds and that one day it would be possible for people to make rain. The rainmaker ignores this reference to God and continues in a purely naturalistic manner 'you water your garden by means of the river, but we who use no irrigation must make rain': the implication is that each tradition uses natural methods and God does not come into it one way or another. This is supported by the way the rainmaker goes on to argue for the superiority of rain over irrigation. In reply Livingstone insists upon the relationship of cause to effect. 'That which I dispute is that your medicines have any influence on the rain whatever. God alone can make it.' Livingstone appears to introduce God immediately into the cause/effect sequence. He then refers to prayer, as a kind of equivalent to the medicines. Following a discussion about the comparative authority of the sources of 'correct information' Livingstone continues by saying that God 'tells us that he has appointed seed time and harvest, summer and winter, and that he gives rain from heaven and fruitful seasons . . . I think he would give you rain without any medicines'.

The point about the seasons is irrelevant since this is not under dispute. The salient feature continues to be Livingstone's insistence that 'God will give us rain'. There is then a discussion about observable consequences in which Livingstone draws parallels between the effects of the rainmaker's medicines and the effect of his own Western medical substances. The implication is that God remains within the sequence of natural causation, producing obvious effects as do the medicines, although admittedly being less predictable in order to protect the mystery of God's grace.

Livingstone now introduces this divine causality in a negative as well as a positive way: 'your work tends to drive away rain and displease God' he continues 'he wishes us to feel our dependence on him alone'. Was Livingstone suspicious then of every human attempt to increase control over the environment? As a trained and practising doctor it would appear not. Why then speak like this to the rainmaker? He accuses the rainmaker of trying to make the rain 'independent of him [God]', which is clearly unjust since the rainmaker has agreed earlier in the dialogue that it is only God who makes the rain. Livingstone shares with the rainmaker belief in the divine cause of rain.

There is, of course, plenty of biblical authority for the belief that God is the rain giver.

The LORD will open the heavens, the storehouse of his bounty and will send rain on your land . . . (Deut. 28.12)

He bestows rain on the earth; he sends water upon the countryside. (Job 5.10)

Do any of the worthless idols of the nations bring rain? Do the skies themselves send down showers? No, it is you, O LORD our God. (Jer. 14.22)

Just as God sends the rain God can also withhold it.

> I also withheld rain from you when the harvest was still three months away. I sent rain on one town but withheld it from another. One field had rain; another had none and dried up. (Amos 4.7)

> Then the LORD's anger will burn against you, and he will shut the heavens so that it will not rain . . . (Deut. 11.17)

Samuel (1 Sam. 12.17–18), Elijah (1 Kings 17.1) and Haggai (1.11) were all powerful rainmakers, and rain was given by God in response to prayer (1 Kings 8.35–36; Zech. 10.1).

Since his youth, Livingstone had been deeply interested in the relationship between science and Christian faith. But his mentor, the theologian philosopher scientist Thomas Dick (1774–1857) did not give him much help in sorting out the relation of the Bible and the developing science of meteorology. The creator God, said Thomas Dick, 'has not left himself without a witness to his beneficence in any age, "in his giving rain from heaven . . ."' (Dick 1831, p. 17).

According to William Blaikie, it was Livingstone's reading of Dick's *The Philosophy of a Future State*, 'which led him to Christ, but did not lead him away from science' (Blaikie 1910, p. 28).

It is possible that when Livingstone spoke of God giving the rain, he was simply referring to the general providential arrangement of creation. He refers to his general intention to teach the providence of God saying, 'I intend to commence with the goodness of God in giving iron' (1960, p. 60).

On the other hand, what are we to make of the following remark:

> Everything languishes during the intense heat; and successive droughts having only occurred since the gospel came to the Bakwains, I fear the effect will be detrimental. There is abundance of rain all around us. And yet we, who have our chief at our head in attachment to the gospel, receive not a drop. Has Satan power over the course of the winds and clouds? (p. 76)[14]

The more one sees of David Livingstone's scientific interests not only in the weather but in geology, botany, zoology, agriculture and many other disciplines the more surprising it is that he did not introduce such knowledge into his dealings with the rainmaker. At least three possibilities suggest themselves. First it is possible that in spite of having read Thomas Dick, Livingstone's appreciation of the difference between the scientific realms was still fairly simple. He was not philosophical in his approach to faith, and it seems possible that like many Christians in the mid nineteenth century he had kept his scientific and his religious/biblical knowledge in separate compartments.

---

14 It is curious to find this issue still debated today. Kevin Cain (2001) firmly believes, on the authority of Scripture, that God controls the weather, but denies that Satan has any part in it.

A second possibility is to do with the antithetical relationship between secular-ized Europe and the traditional religious life of Africa. Perhaps some Christian missionaries were reluctant to contribute to the decomposition of traditional faith, a process from which the churches in Britain had already been suffering. Perhaps there was a degree of reluctance about disenchanting the African imagi-nation, as it seemed to these Europeans of the industrial Enlightenment (Ustorf 1992; Comaroff and Comaroff 1991).

This leads to the third possibility, the resurgence of the missionary vocation of David Livingstone. It has often been said that the love of exploration, geog-raphy and the increase of scientific knowledge tended to prevail over his work as a missionary. Whatever truth there may be in this, it is not true of the dia-logue with the rainmaker. Here we see the missionary triumphing over the sci-ence educator. Although Livingstone made one or two experiments in science education as we have seen, there is no doubt that in general, particularly in the first half of his African years, he wanted to transfer the loyalties of the African people away from their traditional religions. In these rainmaking occupied a central place, as it also did in Christian faith. In spite of his respect for African religious customs and beliefs he had lapsed into the competition between the two environmental religions. When engaged in this contest, he was unable to think of the rain as a natural phenomenon but only as a religious power, which had to be broken by the living God. That is why science education would not have been relevant. In the dialogues between Livingstone and the rainmakers we catch a glimpse of the process whereby Christian faith became a religion amongst the religions, and found itself as Christianity in the confrontation with African traditional religion. Although there were so many moments in his heroic life when he expressed the spirit of Christian-ness, the dialogue with the rain-maker was not one of them.

We have seen how the prophetic Church was founded, and how it was almost lost. Can it be put together again? Can the fragments of the prophetic Church be restored so as to be meaningful today?

Part 3

The Recovery of the Prophetic Church

In Part 2 (Chapters 4–7), we considered some of the developments in the medieval and early modern Church, the legacies of which have made it difficult for Christian adults in the West today to recover the prophetic message of the Bible. In spite of this, that message was never completely lost, and it would have been possible to describe some of the sense of the medieval Church who kept the prophetic tradition alive. However, the remoteness of ancient Israel and the complexity of the various interpretations of the Gospels do raise a question about the viability of the prophetic tradition as an inspiration for the Church today.

In Chapter 8, I will describe the slow recovery of that tradition, which was hampered by the way that the Old Testament prophets continued to be interpreted as predicting the coming of Jesus Christ. I illustrate this tendency in the thought of Martin Luther and then I describe how nineteenth-century Old Testament scholarship began to hear the prophets in their own authentic voice. The remaining problem was to integrate the prophetic tradition into the life and thought of the modern Church. I select Walter Rauschenbusch and Max Weber as preparing the way for this in the thought of some of the more recent systematic theologians. In Chapter 9, I discuss the work of Paul Tillich. The way that Tillich included the prophetic tradition within his systematic thought and then began to put it into practice is an outstanding example of the contemporaneity of prophesy. Chapter 10 deals with Reinhold Niebuhr, whose approach to the prophetic Church is in some ways complementary to that of Tillich, especially in Niebuhr's earlier writings, although his later justification for the use of American nuclear weapons is more controversial.

8

Prophetic Theology from Martin Luther to Max Weber

Martin Luther (1483–1546)

If we wish to understand the place of prophecy in the Christian tradition we must understand the changing relationship between the Old Testament and the New, or between the Hebrew Bible and the Christian Testament. Put simply, the question is whether the Old Testament is to be interpreted in light of the New or whether the New Testament should be interpreted in light of the Old. If the Old Testament is consistently interpreted in light of the New Testament, the result is that the Old Testament is valued mainly because it foreshadows the New, because the overt meaning of the New Testament is regarded as being covert in the Old. Although the view that the Old Testament predicts current affairs is largely confined to some of the strands within conservative Christian faith, the belief that the prophets are of significance mainly because they are thought to have pointed toward the coming of Jesus Christ is still a widely held assumption. This way of understanding the prophets is not only authorized by the New Testament itself, but continued for many centuries to be the main way that the relationship between the Old Testament and the New was understood.

Let us take as an influential example Martin Luther's understanding of the Prophetic Books. Commenting on Amos 9.11, 'I will gather together the pieces of the tent of David which has fallen and rebuild it', Luther remarks that 'we must properly take this to mean the kingdom of Christ . . . In a wonderful way this is an elegant and beautiful prophecy' (1975, p. 189). It is a prediction of the coming of the Church and the preaching of the word among the Gentiles. Commenting on Amos 5.24, a verse which became famous during the American Civil Rights movement: 'But let justice roll on like a river and righteousness like a never failing stream', Luther says: 'It seems to me, then, that he is speaking about the Gospel which is going to be revealed through Christ' (p. 166). Another verse, which is frequently used by the Christian peace movements today, is Micah 4.3: 'They will beat their swords into ploughshares and their spears into pruning hooks. Nations shall not take up sword against nation, nor will they train for war anymore.'

Luther says Micah is 'speaking about the peace which the Word works in Christians who . . . have peace with all men' (p. 239). Referring to verse 7b, in the same chapter: 'And the LORD will reign over them on Mount Zion from this time forth', he says:

> Here is a clear and magnificent passage about the divinity of Christ . . . How else could He be the Lord and sit on the throne of His father David forever, except the people also be eternal? But He will not be eternal in a mortal or dead body, but in a body raised again and glorified. Here again the prophet includes the resurrection of the dead. (p. 241)

Luther thus finds the Christian doctrine of the general resurrection anticipated in this verse.

It is not surprising that Martin Luther regards Micah 5.2, about the ruler who shall come out of Bethlehem as a prediction: 'The Spirit of this prophet was great. He was able to define very precisely the place where Christ would be born' (von Ewald 1875–81, p. 247). Luther summarizes his general approach to the prophetic books in the following passage:

> Now all of them prophesied about the destruction of the old people and the bringing in of a new people, about the abolition of the external kingdom and the establishment of a new spiritual kingdom which would happen through Christ. You see, when the physical kingdom ended, the spiritual kingdom of Christ succeeded it. It was impossible for the external kingdom of the flesh to stand along with the spiritual kingdom. Therefore the external kingdom had to be abolished, and that was accomplished by the miraculous counsel of God when He caused His people to be carried off into captivity. (p. 207)

It was, however, necessary that a remnant should be saved because: 'there had been a promise that Christ would be born of these people' (p. 207). The Book of Micah is summarized by Luther as follows: 'He first rebukes the wicked way of life of the people and then passes over to the kingdom of Christ' (p. 268). So the threats and warnings apply to the contemporaries who are sinful people while the promises and comforts applied to those who have faith in Christ.

Nevertheless, sinful people are the same in all ages, and Luther is well aware of the attacks made by the prophets upon their own generation, and the analogy between these and the misdoings of his own age. Amos criticized the way the merchants did not sell the pure grain to the poor but mixed it with dust and sweeping from the floor, so that they may increase their profit. 'This is something which our own merchants do as well as all those who have things to sell' (p. 181). When Amos said, 'In that day shall the fair virgins and young men faint' (Amos 8.13), Luther makes the following remark:

> Up to now what have our universities throughout the world been except devourers of our finest youngsters? When they were sent away by their parents to learn godliness, to learn good skills in order to be able to serve in positions of leadership in the state, they learned nothing else but to excel in drinking and fornication. (p. 184)

Commenting on a passage in Micah, Luther says: 'There can hardly be anything more destructive in a state than this evil: namely, when the princes do not promote equal justice but allow money to overwhelm them so that they corrupt justice' (p. 233).

Luther regards the prophets as being forerunners of the Reformation of preachers of the word of God. Just as the prophets were opposed by religious leaders, so the preachers of the word are opposed by the pope and the princes. Just as the prophets attacked the sins of both rich and poor, people being much the same down the ages, the preachers of the word make similar protests about conditions of their own time. Luther is careful not to take the element of prediction too far, rejecting the more fanciful examples. Referring to the commentaries of Jerome, he remarks that: 'Jerome and other interpreters apply this to the Passion of Christ, but what they write is forced out of the text' (p. 246). Nevertheless, the contrast between the time of law and the time of grace, the external kingdom of God and the spiritual kingdom of Christ is the major thrust of Luther's interpretation. In spite of his robust and courageous attacks upon social injustice, he seldom allows the Hebrew prophets to speak with their own integrity. Nor could he do so, for not until the nineteenth century was it realized that the prophets should not be read in the light of the New Testament and Christian faith but only in the context of the ancient Middle East.

The nineteenth-century discovery of the prophets

It was through the historical and philological studies of Orientalists rather than theological study that the prophets began to be understood in their own context. Prominent in this scholarly movement was Heinrich von Ewald (1803–75), professor of Oriental languages in the University of Göttingen, and from 1841 professor of theology at Tübingen. It is said that his defence of liberty and democracy owed much to his understanding of the prophets (Blenkinsopp 1984, pp. 28–9).

In the English-speaking countries the work of George Adam Smith (1856–1942) was significant. In 1892, he became professor of Old Testament in Glasgow and in 1909 Principal of the University of Aberdeen. His *Book of the Twelve Prophets, Commonly Called the Minor* was published in two volumes in 1898, passing through many editions including a second revised edition in 1928.

Walter Rauschenbusch (1861–1918)

G. A. Smith was a major influence in the life of Walter Rauschenbusch. It was his work as pastor of the German Baptist Church in a disadvantaged part of New York City from 1886–1897 that alerted Rauschenbusch to the impact of the American financial/industrial system upon poor people. His interpretation of the mission of the Church in the context of the class stratification of American society became a major theme of his work as professor of church history in Rochester Theological Seminary from 1902–17. The teaching of Jesus about the kingdom of God had already been the inspiration for the founding of the Brotherhood of the Kingdom in 1892. The constitution of the association committed its members to: 'lay special stress on the social aims of Christianity and . . . endeavour to make Christ's teaching concerning wealth operative in the Church' (White and Hopkins 1976, p. 73; Curtis 1991, p. 109; Gorrell 1988, p. 18).

Emphasis upon the kingdom of God remained fundamental in the thinking of Rauschenbusch throughout his life. His influential *Christianity and the Social Crisis* (1912), which begins with three historical chapters, states that

> [t]he outcome of these first historical chapters is that the essential purpose of Christianity was to transform human society into the kingdom of God by regenerating all human relations and reconstituting them in accordance with the will of God. (p. xiii)

His familiarity with German Old Testament scholarship led Rauschenbusch to the origins of the kingdom of God in the Hebrew prophets. The introduction describes the prophets as 'an integral part of the thought-life of Christianity' (p. 2). It is impossible to understand Jesus without understanding how he was influenced by the prophets.

Rather than discussing the prophetic books one by one, Rauschenbusch tells us that he will select certain common features that are relevant to his main theme. The outstanding characteristic of the teaching of the prophets was that 'God demands righteousness and demands nothing but righteousness' (p. 4). The prophets represent the evolution of religion from an earlier stage when the purpose of religion was to placate God by sacrifice into a new kind of ethical faith. The prophets rejected the cult in favour of social relations. The Christian 'ceremonial system' (p. 7) does not differ essentially from that against which the prophets protested and if Christianity had followed the teaching of the prophets the accumulation of injustice in Western society might have been averted.

The second feature of the teaching of the prophets which impressed Rauschenbusch was that their emphasis was upon the ethics, not so much of private, but of public life; it was social rather than individual. In effect 'it meant politics in the name of God' (p. 8). The social crisis which was the subject of the book was the injustice created by great wealth and extreme poverty. Rauschenbusch had come to see that capital and labour represent two 'antagonistic classes' (p. xiv). The individualization of modern Western culture had combined with an emphasis upon personal religion and spiritual inwardness to create a climate in which it was difficult, if not impossible, for Americans to appreciate the huge collective forces which were driving wage labour into poverty.

The third aspect of the teaching of the prophets was that the scope of their work was national rather than individual. Their activities ranged from supporting revolutions to anointing kings. Only after the loss of the nation did the prophets turn to the cultivation of inner spirituality. Nevertheless, the sympathy of the prophets was entirely on the side of the poorer classes. The modern equivalent would be the proletarian immigrant workers in the great cities who had no share in the means of production. Jehovah was the vindicator of these voiceless classes. The chief duty of religious morality is to represent the rights of the helpless. The Bible speaks for the common people, and this is one of the features which marks it out as divinely inspired.

A parallel may be drawn, Rauschenbusch suggests, between the social development of ancient Israel and modern America. Both nations had their origins in societies without inherited aristocratic classes and feudal monarchies. The land had been distributed with more or less equal justice. Hebrew society acquired a monarchy and developed a class system which drove a wedge between the rich and the poor, but the prophets, especially Amos, drew upon the ancient democratic tradition. Amos was able to articulate the growing demand for justice, and in the United States today, Rauschenbusch observes, there is increasing resentment as the gulf between the rich and the poor becomes more and more obvious.

A difference between the religion of the prophets and the situation in modern America lay in attitudes toward the afterlife. In Christianity, faith in the future life has to some extent subdued the demand for social justice, whereas the prophets, who had no such belief, were able to concentrate on the lives of the people around them.

As Israel was caught up in the struggle between the empires of the Middle East, the prophets developed an international perspective. They asserted that 'Jehovah is fundamentally a god of righteousness, and a god of Israel only in so far as Israel was a nation of righteousness' (p. 25). This international perspective led the prophets to see that 'God moves on the plane of universal and ethical law' (p. 25).

When it became impossible to seek for national righteousness, because the nation had been destroyed, the concerns of the prophets became increasingly religious in the narrow sense. 'Thus the death-pangs of the national life were the birth-pangs of the personal religious life' (p. 28); in Ezekiel we see that holiness rather than justice has become central. 'The righteous nation was turned into a holy church' (p. 30). A certain concentration upon ritual and ceremony crept back into religion which Jesus, as the heir of the prophetic tradition, had to resist. Gradually the prophetic hope became the apocalyptic desperation.

Another parallel which struck Rauschenbusch was the fact that the true prophets were heavily outnumbered by the false, just as today there are many more preachers who 'act as eulogists of existing conditions' (p. 38). They proclaim a retreat into interior spirituality which is, in Rauschenbusch's view, derived from 'the feeblest and most decadent age of Hebrew thought' (p. 42). The question which faces the American republic is whether its inspiration should be drawn from this late period of individualism or from the social responsibility of the classical prophets. Those today who admire the rich rather than the poor, who put their faith in personal religion rather than public religion, will have the Hebrew prophets to contend with.

Max Weber (1854–1928)

In the meantime, on the other side of the Atlantic, a new and powerful contribution to understanding the prophetic tradition was taking shape. Just as development in the mid nineteenth century had not come from theology as much as from Oriental studies, so now it was the relatively young discipline of sociology that was to throw light on the prophetic tradition. Max Weber published a series of essays on the sociology of ancient Judaism in German in 1917–19. These articles were published as a book in 1921, and translated into English in 1952 under the title *Ancient Judaism*. Reinhold Niebuhr, a Lutheran pastor with a German background, was reading Weber during his Detroit ministry of the 1920s (Fox 1985, p. 102; Brown 2002, p. 32; Stone 2005, p. 25), while Paul Tillich, who did not come to the United States until 1933, was already familiar with Weber's work in the 1920s (Tillich 1968, pp. 270–71).

Weber traces the history of Hebrew prophecy back to the ecstatic figures who accompanied the armies of Israel into battle. These were like dervishes or inspired seers, whose singing, dancing and mantic speech encourage the warriors. When Israel became a monarchy, however, the prophet became the man of God, who was able to communicate the will of God to the holders of political power. Samuel may have been the first prophet whose prestige was such that he was able to do this. Elijah, however, delivered his oracles not only to the reigning powers but to the Israelite public. Magical elements are less prominent; the only source of Elijah's power was prayer. He was also the first who could be described as a prophet of doom.

As the tradition developed, the prophets became a bit like the intellectual leaders, whereas the earlier ecstatic divines tended to work in groups or bands, the later prophets were solitary figures. Weber says that they may also be called the 'demilitarized' prophets (1952, p. 112), because '[t]hey were no longer military dervishes and ecstatic therapeutics and rainmakers, but a stratum of literati and political ideologists' (p. 112). Traces of militaristic magic may still be found in both Elijah and Elisha, but in the later prophets, from Amos onwards, rational reforming tendencies prevail. It is significant, Weber thinks, that this kind of critical movement should have emerged on the fringes of the empires in the ancient Middle East: 'Rarely have entirely new religious conceptions originated in the respective centers of rational cultures' (p. 206). They tend to appear outside the great centres of political and intellectual life, because in the centres of power, reality is seldom questioned. It is only on the margin, where the impact of those great political cultures is felt acutely, that critical questions can arise: 'The possibility of questioning the meaning of the world presupposes the capacity to be astonished about the course of events' (p. 207). So the Yahweh of battles became the God of history, the Master of political destiny, from being a nature God and a tribal patron to being a God of ethical rationalism.

It was consistent with these origins, however, that free prophecy arose with a rising external danger to the country or with the threatened loss of the Hebrew monarchy. As the prestige of the kings diminished and the external dangers increased, so prophecy gained in power. The oracles of the prophets 'constitute the earliest known example of political pamphlet literature directly addressing itself to contemporaneous events' (p. 272).

In a sense, the prophets may be described as 'world-political demagogues and publicists' (p. 275). They were not political partisans because they were, in a certain sense, not interested in good citizenship in contrast to the philosophers of ancient Greece. The sole concern of the Hebrew prophets was faithful response to the demands and to the love of Yahweh.

We must not take them, however, to be popular democrats in the modern manner. With the possible exception of Ezekiel's vision of the new state, 'no prophet proclaimed a social–political program' (p. 278). In that sense the prophets were not champions of democratic ideals. Many of them, Amos apart, were aristocrats, appealing to the courtly and priestly leadership. Although all of the prophets continued to manifest ecstasy, they differed from the earlier ones in that they spoke not from their ecstasy but about it. Once they had grasped ecstatically the meaning of what they wanted to say they obtained clarity of mind through realizing the intentions of Yahweh: 'They did not seek ecstasy. It came to them' (p. 291).

Another distinguishing characteristic of these great prophets was their rejection of many royal policies. They maintained an attitude of cultural hostility, although they were often highly cultured people. Whereas the popular opinion, when faced with national disaster, was that the other gods were stronger or that Yahweh has ceased to care, the prophets maintained that Yahweh willed misfortune on his own people.

Moreover, Yahweh punished not only Israel who was within the covenant, but nations that had never been in the covenant. It was for breaking the covenants of brotherly responsibility that not only the ruling classes but the whole people came under condemnation. This presupposes the ancient solidarity of the tribal confederation, and the authority of the Decalogue. With the destruction of the temple and the state itself, the message of doom reached its climax, and the message of hope took its place. Hope had always been a feature of the prophetic message, since the preaching of doom was nearly always conditional as we see from the book of Jonah. The proclamation of doom was to some extent pedagogical.

The prophets of Israel were not mystics. There is no trace of a denial of the senses in order to lead to a richer inner life of the kind that is often found in oriental religion. The God of the prophets is not apprehended inwardly but ethically and always in action. There was no experience of oceanic bliss for the Hebrew prophets: 'Thus mystic possession of otherworldly godliness was rejected in favor of active service to the super-natural but, in principle understandable, god' (p. 315). There was no thought in the prophets of otherworldly salvation. Their thinking always remained solidly this worldly, even when the eschatological hope was expressed.

All of the prophets, in one way or another, dreamed of a kingdom of peace to come in the future, generally the rather near future. Nevertheless, it was the doom of Israel that confirmed the authenticity of the prophets and stamped their prestige upon the whole of the Old Testament.

> These giants cast their shadows through the millennia into the present, since this holy book of the Jews became a holy book of the Christians too, and since the entire interpretation of the mission of the Nazarene was primarily determined by the old promises to Israel. (p. 334)

This then was the situation of the prophetic tradition when it was inherited and transformed by two of the greatest theologians of the twentieth century.

9

The Prophetic Theology of Paul Tillich

The role of the prophet in the early work of Paul Tillich

Prophetic theology appears first in the work of Paul Tillich (1886–1965) in his rejection of religion, which is summed up in the last sentence of his 1919 essay 'God is known only through God!' (1973, p. 154). This emphasis upon the divine initiative had been a major theme of Karl Barth's commentary on the Epistle to the Romans that had been published the same year (Barth 1919). Tillich and Barth both reacted against the liberal theology of the nineteenth century that tended to regard religion as the finest flower of human culture and the outcome of a long process of increasing religious insight. Religion had become a sphere of human activity like art and science; religious activities distinguished from secular activities were being studied by the psychology and sociology of religion; people held religious beliefs alongside their other beliefs and God had become one reality beside others (Tillich 1973, p. 43). This quality of being 'alongside' may be described as the 'spatialization' (p. 13) of religion and of God. Religion had been deprived of its ultimacy, what Tillich was later to call its quality of 'ultimate concern'.

Against this conditioning or relativizing of God, Tillich described God as 'the Unconditional', while Karl Barth, who preferred biblical terminology, emphasized that God must always be Lord (p. 13). Tillich therefore concluded that '"Religion" is a derogatory term, indicating that inferior quality within religion which consists in its failure to go beyond the subject. In that case it is nothing more than a God-ward intention that does not have God, because God has not manifested himself within it' (p. 127).

It is religion itself that exposes the hollowness of its own intentions, and this is why, in the sentences just quoted, false religion is expressed in quotation marks in contrast to the Unconditioned which breaks through it. Paradoxically, it is religion itself that raises a protest against religion. Although true religion is generally hidden, it can break through in the form of mystical or prophetic opposition to false religion. When this happens it is a matter of grace, and the life-giving Spirit, of revelation and of salvation. Human religion at its best can prepare the way for these manifestations of the Unconditioned, but can also resist their appearances. One reason for this is that when the Unconditioned breaks through all human religious institutions are diminished. The danger is that 'the revelation of grace becomes a religion of the means of grace' (p. 147). True religion exists whenever the Unconditional is affirmed as the Unconditional, and religion is abolished through its presence. True religion, and thus the work of both mystic and prophet, can only be spoken of paradoxically for the true prophet is a product of culture as well as an expression of the Unconditioned breaking into culture. If one says 'God is' and means it literally, in the sense of a sentence with a subject and an object, then religion, false religion, triumphs and is on the way to atheism, but if 'God is' is said paradoxically, then perhaps language comes as close as it momentarily can to expressing the unconditioned (p. 141). Two tendencies in the cultural history of religion may be discerned: the sacramental and the theocratic. In both of these the Unconditioned may break through into history. The primal attitude of wonder towards the cosmos, a kind of primeval natural mysticism, becomes more specific, focusing upon particular objects, times or persons as bearers of holiness. 'These things and actions thereby receive a sacramental quality. Their significance depends upon the fact that in them, as finite, conditioned realities, the presence of the Unconditioned import of meaning is experienced' (p. 89).

Tillich does not use the concept of the theocratic in the political sense, in which a society might regard itself as being under the direct rule of God, but to refer to the critical aspect of religion in which the divine struggles against the demonic. Holiness itself possesses both divine and demonic elements, but as religion is purged by anti-demonic criticism, the divine emerges in its beauty, goodness and power. Theocratic tendencies may be brought to bear upon sacramentalism, when the latter becomes focused upon objects that are increasingly regarded as holy in themselves and no longer as expressions of the Unconditioned. But these two tendencies should not be too sharply divided; 'just as there is a theocratic element in the sacramental, so there is a sacramental element in the theocratic' (p. 89): the theocratic demand, the demand that God should be the Lord, must become concrete if it is to impinge upon human experience, and so it tends to take sacramental form, particularly in charismatic persons. Should this person or concrete form become domesticated by religion, theocratic criticism will again be brought to bear upon it.

One of the principal expressions of the theocratic is prophecy. 'The great powerful theocratic movements are borne by prophetic personalities' (p. 90). However, guided by theocratic criticism, the sacramental tendency may become more widely generalized, seeking for the holy beneath all specific holiness and so become mysticism. In the ecstasy of mysticism the unconditional is apprehended. If the theocratic finds expression in both, the mystic and the prophet, what is the difference between them? Mysticism deliberately remains attached to the sacramental attitude. It seeks for the ultimate as expressed in the sacraments: 'It does not participate in the theocratic struggle, even though it agrees in many ways with the theocratic criticism' (p. 90). The prophet, guided by the theocratic demand, becomes critical of myth and cult, whereas the mystic dwells profoundly in both myth and cult, seeking for the ecstasy of the divine presence within them. Mysticism is the enduring foundation of religion but the theocratic principle is at work in all the great reforming religious movements. As examples of these, Tillich refers to Jewish prophecy, early Christianity, Islam, some of the Christian sects and the Protestant Reformation, particularly the anti-iconographic aspects of Calvinism (p. 91). Through such movements 'the anti-demonic struggle is taken up, and the demand is raised for a just social order, an ethical form of personality, and a true knowledge of God' (p. 91).

Nevertheless, there is a danger in the theocratic demand. It may become harsh and unyielding. It may become a religion of law rather than of grace. It has a tendency to turn into secular ethics and to be ruled by obligation and duty rather than by freedom and love. Moreover, acutely aware of human failure and of the unconditional demand of God, it is prone to religious despair. These then, are the demonic temptations of the prophetic. This is why the prophetic must never lose vital contact with the sacramental. In culture as a whole these two tendencies are also found. Religious mysticism becomes pantheism and prophetic theocracy becomes rational enlightenment. When the two trends within religion and the two trends within culture harmonize in response to the Unconditioned, then we have the religion of grace and the humanizing of culture and the integration of culture and religion. Traces of such unification are found within all religions and all cultures. In Pauline Christianity, for example, the Spirit responds to the human longing for direct, ecstatic encounter with the holy. But it does not sink into disorder nor into the demonic subjective, because it is always linked with the 'theocratically exclusive symbol of the Christ' (p. 107). In other words, the mystical ecstasy of life in the Spirit is always maintained in ethical life and in public responsibility, because it is always the Spirit of Christ, and the Christ remains the one in whom prophetic demand and ecstatic encounter are united. The teachings of Jesus and the Spirit of Christ can never be separated.

Socialism as prophetic

Tillich became increasingly interested and involved in German politics during the 1920s, and by the time he was appointed professor of philosophy at Frankfurt in 1929 he was deeply engaged in an attempt to discover the human and religious significance of socialism. In 1926 he had developed his view of the *kairos* (1936, pp. 123–75), the critical moment in history when the Unconditional is about to break forth, this led him to his theory of expectation. Inspired by the visions of the Hebrew prophets and the kingdom of God the motif of expectation became one of the central features of his analysis of socialism. His writing of *The Socialist Decision* was complete by the end of 1932, and the book itself was published in early 1933. However, on 30 January 1933 Adolf Hitler came to power. The book was suppressed along with other socialist literature, and in a strange turn of fate most of the copies were destroyed in the warehouse in Potsdam in an Allied raid (1977 [1933], pp. xxiii–xxiv). In April 1933, Tillich, along with other Frankfurt intellectuals, was dismissed from his university post by the Nazis. In the following months, although Tillich travelled widely throughout Germany trying to discover a possible arena of work, it became more and more dangerous for him. He was offered a prestigious chair in theology at the University of Berlin by the Nazi education office on the condition that he should revoke and deny the argument of the book, but he refused. Shortly after, he left for the United States where Reinhold Niebuhr had invited him to lecture. The book, although stifled at its birth, became a symbol of resistance to Nazi ideology, and is today generally regarded as Tillich's most significant prophetic and political writing.

The politics of romantic nationalism that was rapidly growing in popularity and power drew its strength from the 'myth of origin' (p. 13). The most basic of these is the mythological quality attributed to the soil itself, which is associated with the myth of noble blood, the emphasis upon lineage leading back to the mother and father, to patriarchy and to the pure solidarity of the tribe. This then leads to a cyclic view of life in which the vegetation dies and rises again, and the imagination is dominated by space. Space exists beside other space and so this kind of mythology always leads to polytheism. To some extent modernity has fragmented the myths of origin, but romantic nationalism seeks to restore them, giving them spiritual, social and political presence. Criticism within romantic nationalism is only possible within the terms dictated by the myth of origin. When the myth takes the form of a single origin, then all must be included within the myth. The result is domination.

The principal challenge to the myth of origin comes from the prophetic tradition. The Jewish prophets fought explicitly against the myth of origin and the domination of space, and they conquered. The God of the prophets is not one who fuses with other Gods, but even more remarkably allows other gods to invade God's own land. This breaks the intimate connection between God and the soil. Time is elevated above space. It acquires a direction. 'Prophetism transforms the origin into the beginning of the historical process' (p. 21). Even the creation of the world becomes an historical act carried out by God in time. Thus, Old Testament prophetism represents the persistent struggle of the spirit of Judaism with the realities of Jewish national life. For reasons such as these, the Old Testament became no longer the book of the nation of Israel but a book for all humanity. The God of Israel becomes not only the judge of Israel, but the God and judge of the whole world. The New Testament continues the same prophetic protest against sacred tradition, sacred land and sacred empires, and the cross of Christ not only shatters the body of Jesus, but at the same time shatters the powers of romantic nationalism. The spirit of Judaism is the necessary and eternal enemy of political romanticism, and therefore anti-Semitism is an essential element in political romanticism. Prophetism itself, however, has a tendency to settle down into a new priesthood that turns the prophetic proclamation into a binding legal rule. This tendency can also be seen in the prophetic elements in early Christian faith. Both the Reformation and the Enlightenment were protests against the growing power of the myth of origins, but from different perspectives, religious and rational. In the history of class struggle, the rise of the bourgeoisie also represents a breaking with the tradition of soil and blood. The bourgeoisie emerged with revolutionary power determined to shape the world in accordance with their own interests.

The spirit and meaning of the prophetic tradition is today found hidden within socialism. The main purpose of *The Socialist Decision* is to reveal the religious depths of the socialist movement, and to show how socialism can only succeed in overcoming romantic nationalism if it grasps the significance of the prophetic quality within it. An important aspect of this lay in the spirit of expectation which is so typical of socialism: 'Socialism lifts up the symbol of expectation against the myth of origin and against the belief in harmony' (p. 101), which is an important aspect of the bourgeoisie principle. This element of expectation brings the socialist movement into an explicit relation with the prophetic tradition. This can be seen in the way that socialism developed out of the radical Christian sects, and they themselves were dependent upon the prophetic spirituality of early Christian faith. History strains toward the newness of life. When Christian faith became institutionalized in the Graeco-Roman world, this social and historical expectation was individualized and became an expression of the yearning for personal immortality. So, the radical ethical demand of prophecy was diverted toward the fate of the immortal soul in the next world. On the other hand, the ethical demand for social transformation expressed in the striving toward the renewal of the world must not be turned into a utopian hope. The expected deliverance will come, because it is promised; it is not dependent upon human activity. If it becomes a historical goal, it is bound to lead to disillusionment. Nevertheless, there is a prophetic demand as well as a prophetic hope. This demand requires a human response, human commitment to action. In the tension between these two poles, the promise bringing hope and the demand for action, lies the very essence of socialism. The demand is always focused upon a particular historic situation, a crisis which is discerned by the prophetic spirit. This moment is the *kairos*, the moment when the Unconditional breaks out in society in the form of the radically new. The central feature of this radically new demand is justice. This is why 'the prophets fought against the repression of the poor by the powerful, and threatened the whole people with destruction on account of such injustice' (p. 106). In the parables of Jesus we see the paradox of the kingdom. It is found in the everyday when the everyday becomes extraordinary; it is given in every moment, but there always remains the 'not yet'.

Marxism is the organized, theoretical expression of socialism. Tillich exposes the contradictions and inner tensions of Marxism, defending it at the same time from the many misunderstandings, sometimes deliberate, which have obscured its fundamental message of justice and hope. Many similarities between the prophetic tradition and Marxism may be found. For example, in both, one finds the idea that history moves forward toward its goal behind the backs, as it were, of the protagonists. The Hebrew prophets saw how the Gentile nations cannot but fulfil the purposes of Yahweh, whether they realize this or not. This can be compared with the belief of Karl Marx that capitalism, quite apart from its own self understanding and regardless of its intentions, was nevertheless a step on the way toward the classless society. This belief would never, however, be allowed to deprive human action of its urgency, for a human future achieved without human cooperation would be a future denying humanity itself. Only in a truly democratic society can all social groups cooperate toward the vision of a shared social justice, and in this lies the prophetic element of democracy itself.

One of the tasks of socialism, Tillich believed, was to call the churches to renew within themselves the prophetic element which is so central an aspect of Christian tradition. Socialism can do this by showing how religion itself has betrayed the sense of expectation which once it possessed. 'Socialism has to strengthen the prophetic as opposed to the priestly element in the churches' (p. 145). The Protestant churches, at least, may absorb the socialist principle in the form of the New Testament teaching about the *kairos*. *Chronos* is calendar time or clock time, but *kairos* is the crisis of revelation, the moment of insight when everything changes. Tillich looked for a new era of collaboration between socialism and the churches in which a new secular vocabulary would be charged with religious meaning, and at the same time the language of religion would be purged from its false consciousness to take on new political significance. These hopes would be fulfilled not first of all in universal humanity but in particular communities and nations, for the prophetic tradition, although it breaks the myth of origin, is not without a sense of continuity and is always a participant in the concrete problems of the people. Therefore, 'in accordance with the prophetic character of its expectations, socialism must place the people to which it belongs, and which it seeks to lead toward socialism, under the unconditional demand of justice . . .' (p. 151). 'Therefore prophetism alone truly serves the nation. It is the legitimate representative of the idea of the nation' (p. 152). But because prophetism also looks towards the universal horizon, the alien and the immigrant are also to be protected within the life of the nation in the name of the same demand for justice.

Although the complexities of Tillich's analysis are intended to bear upon the political situation in the Germany of his day and were quickly made obsolete by the Nazis, the book remains a classic study of the relation between religion and politics. His analysis of democracy under the conditions of capitalism has a sharp relevance to our own period. 'It is possible that democracy, though present in form, is in fact made inoperative by the ruling group. This is exactly the situation in a state based on a class system' (p. 142).

Six years earlier, Tillich had said that 'there can be no doubt that the capitalist form of economics has to the highest degree the supporting, creative and transforming character of the truly demonic, but it is just as true that this creative force is combined with a destructive one of horrible strength' (1936, pp. 119–20).

In 1936, Tillich, now in New York, published a reflection upon his life and work. In it, he says:

My preference for the Old Testament and the spirit of prophetic criticism and expectation has stayed with me, and through the bearing of this upon my political attitude it has become decisive for the shaping of my life and thought. (1936, p. 33)

Although Protestantism cannot be understood apart from the prophetic movement, it 'must exist in the constant tension between the sacramental and the prophetic, the constitutive and corrective element' (p. 27). Both sides of Protestantism need each other. Without prophetic criticism the sacramental would become far too independent and even demonic, and without the sacramental prophetic criticism would become empty and sterile.

Prophetic broadcasts

Although the Nazis immediately realized what he was saying, Tillich's 1933 advocacy of socialism did not refer to them by name. He soon had an opportunity for a more direct challenge. Between 1942 and 1944 he broadcast more than 100 pro-German but anti-Nazi addresses. These were broadcast from New York, via London to occupied Europe, and Tillich included Germany itself within occupied Europe. In these speeches we see the militant theologian at work, with the prophetic tradition as a significant part of his attack. Tillich treats the Nazis as violent intruders into the history and culture of Germany, having no rightful place in the spirit of the German people, and destined to pass away as the new Germany arose. He made a special effort to undermine anti-Semitism by hailing the Jews as 'the people of history, the people of the prophetic, future-judging spirit' (Stone and Weaver (eds) 1998, p. 14). The prophets had been as critical of the Jewish nation as they were of other nations, so the question which Jewish history asks us is whether any people should remain limited and bound to their national space and history, or whether they should break out of this and stretch beyond. Therefore to be true to their own nationality, the German people should rise up in resistance against Hitler. Any nation that resists justice is resisting God. '[N]owhere is the thought of justice more closely connected with the idea of God than in the religion of the prophets. For them, God is first, and above all, the God of justice' (p. 27).

Any nation that committed itself to injustice became by that very fact an enemy of God, and God would contest against that nation. The prophets knew that their own nation would perish if it ignored justice, and so the prophetic message today declares that Nazi Germany must perish. 'The National Socialists are fighting against the Old Testament, because they are fighting against the spirit of justice that speaks there against Jewish nationalism, just as it does against every other nationalism. Every nation that condemns justice is itself condemned' (p. 127).

True Germans should become like Jeremiah, lamenting the tragic and futile end of his own nation. Just as the ancient prophets saw the destruction of the cruel, oppressive cities of the ancient empires, Babylon, Nineveh and Roman, so God will judge the cruel and oppressive cities of Germany that have collaborated with the Nazis. To see these dreadful happenings as judgement was actually a sign of hope, because it meant that the wrongs which the Nazis had inflicted upon Germany and the world were being recognized as deserving punishment.

Tillich's opinion of the statement issued by the Moscow conference of November 1943 is particularly significant. The Declaration included a strong condemnation of the atrocities of the war, and Tillich comments: 'these words about the acts of the Nazis sound like prophetic speech, like words in which the conscience of the world is speaking' (p. 203).

For the first time the idea of crimes committed against humanity was outlined, and Tillich saw in this a universalizing of the prophetic spirit, hidden within the dawning ethical conscience of humanity. Perhaps the God who used the oppressive nations of the ancient world, without their knowledge or consent, will yet bring this legacy out of the horrors of the Nazi movement, the awakening of the conscience of the nations. A direct line leads from this to the Nuremburg Trials and to the Universal Declaration of Human Rights.

Prophecy and the 'Spiritual Presence'

Tillich's most comprehensive treatment of the prophetic is to be found in the third volume of his *Systematic Theology*. The Trinity provides the basic structure of the systematic theology, the first volume dealing with God the Father, the second with God the Son and the third with God the Holy Spirit. This represents a three-fold manifestation of God as creative power, saving love and ecstatic transformation. The basic form of the doctrine, in Tillich's view, is dialectical, moving from thesis to antithesis and then to a new realization or actualization in the synthesis. The basic movement is from God as the abyss or ground of being, to the form of the divine manifestation in Jesus as the Christ. This original, binary understanding of Christian faith gradually became Trinitarian, as the conviction that God was acting in Jesus as the Christ in the Church and in the lives of individuals took intellectual shape. This may be thought of as reflecting the dialectical nature of life itself in which life goes out from itself and returns to itself in process of continuing self-realization (1963, pp. 283–94).

The Spirit represents the ecstasy of life fusing with life, life transcending life or life greeting life.[1] If we were to use Tillich's earlier language we would say that God is the Unconditioned, Jesus as the Christ is the conditioned and the Spirit is the ecstasy with which the former breaks out in the latter. Similarly, we might say that the Spirit represents the point at which the Unconditional erupts into the surface of creation from the uncreated depths. We may compare Tillich's thought at this point with that of Augustine of Hippo, for whom the Spirit is the love that binds the father and son together. Love is the dynamic principle of Trinitarian unity. Tillich prefers to speak of life, and of ecstatic life, including both freedom and love within the character of life itself. In *ekstasis* life stands out from itself.

This Trinitarian theology and in particular this view of the ecstatic and life-giving Spirit is then related to the structure of human life. We have seen this again and again in Tillich's method: a combination of detailed scrutiny of various aspects of human self-awareness carried on in the light of imaginative insights or intuitions springing from Christian faith. '[T]he dimension of the spirit actualizes itself within the dynamics of self-awareness and under its biological conditions' (1963, p. 118). This may be experienced in the intellectual excitement of discovery, the solving of a mathematical problem, the outcome of a legal enquiry or in literary creation. 'It occurs in every prophetic pronouncement, every mystical contemplation, and every successful prayer' (p. 118). This is what the prophets were describing when they spoke of hearing the voice of God. The actual content of the proclamation of the prophets, like the content of the visions of the mystics, in whatever culture or religion they appear, is moulded by the tradition from which they arise. These would be different but the process would be similar. 'When God spoke to the prophets, he did not give them new words or new facts, but he put the facts known to them in the light of ultimate meaning and instructed them to speak out of this situation in the language they knew' (p. 127). This experience of contact between the self-transcending human spirit and the divine Spirit, the Spirit of God is called by Tillich 'the Spiritual Presence'.

However, human life is ambiguous in a way that mathematical structures are not. There is always, in human beings, emotional ambiguity, conflicting interests, and diversity of meanings. As we have already seen, the holy itself is ambiguous, taking either divine or demonic directions. When human beings or groups exalt themselves, their own persons, structures or meanings, claiming

---

1 This is why the whole of Part IV (pp. 11–294) of Tillich's *Systematic Theology* Vol. III is entitled 'Life and the Spirit'.

some kind of ultimacy, then the demonic has broken out in the midst of the Spiritual Presence. It is because of this contest with otherness in the form of the profane or the demonic that mysticism in the Western tradition has usually not taken as an ideal the absorption of the personality into the divine. 'In the religion of the Old Testament the divine Spirit does not eliminate centred selves . . . but it does sublimate them into states of mind which transcend their ordinary possibilities and which are not produced by their toil or good will' (p. 143). Rather, '[t]he Spirit grasps them and drives them to the heights of prophetic power' (p. 143). In prophetic religion, 'the Spiritual Presence is the presence of the God of humanity and justice' (p. 143). Therefore it follows that '[t]here is no pure Spiritual Presence where there is no humanity and justice' (p. 144).

The prophetic spirit is the spirit of resistance against profanization and demonization. A community may possess active or only latent Spiritual Presence, but in either case it is always vulnerable to these distortions. In the case of the community we call Church, the Spiritual Presence is such that it has the principle of resistance within itself and can be applied critically in moments of crisis. In principle, the Spiritual Presence makes of the Church a community of love. For this reason, the Church in its prophetic role must expose and attack those political, social and economic inequalities and forms of oppression and exploitation which destroy the potential for humanity in the individual and for justice in the group. One of the distinguishing features between a community which is active with the Spiritual Presence and one that is only latent is that in the former case the spirit of prophetic criticism rises up from within it, from the very centre of the tradition itself. The prophetic spirit struggles against the distortions of the religious tradition in the name of and for the sake of its true meaning. So it was that the criticisms offered by the prophets and apostles upon the spiritual communities of their day, far from offering injury to the communities, saved them. The Church as an active centre of Spiritual Presence may relate to it surrounding secular communities both through gradual penetration, which might be thought of as the priestly way, or through open criticism which may be described as the prophetic way. The churches must encourage such prophetic criticism of the negative features of the surrounding society, although they know that prophetic activity may not usher in the Spiritual Presence but can only prepare the way for it. This criticism may operate in both ways, not only from the Church to the world, but from the world to the Church. The latter direction may be described as a kind of latent or implicit prophetic activity, directed against '"holy injustice" and "saintly inhumanity"' (p. 214) of the Church. We may also describe this as a kind of unconscious prophetic activity or a prophetism in reverse. One of the duties of the Church in society is to safeguard the right and duty of its own prophetic mission in relation to the wider society. Society must come to recognize and to expect prophetic criticism from the Church.

Although the prophetic spirit was manifest with great effect at the time of the Reformation, it is not confined or restricted to any denomination. Every religion and every church may generate prophetic criticism, but it is also true that every religion and church has in some way or other betrayed it, and that goes for the churches of the Reformation as much as for any others. Wherever the prophetic spirit appears, however, it represents the victory of the Spiritual Presence over false religion.

One of the most important functions of the Hebrew prophets was to challenge the judges to be faithful to justice, even at the cost of being disloyal to their own social class interest. No law of either Church or state can claim ultimate status. But under the criticism of prophecy and infidelity to the inherent norms of justice itself laws may become morally purged and so come closer to theonomy, that is, the condition of being more open to the demands of ultimacy.

Prophecy and Jesus as the Christ

If the Spiritual Presence may draw near in any and every religious tradition, we must ask the question whether the demonic power of distorted religion has, at any point, been decisively broken. As a Christian theologian, Paul Tillich replies that this has happened in the prophetic tradition on the basis of which the event of Jesus as the Christ took place. The whole history of religion is the general presupposition and the prophetic tradition within Judaism is the particular basis for the appearance of this unique and final event. The coming of Jesus must not, however, be looked upon as the product of a process of historical development. Jesus as the Christ is not a horizontal event on the plane of history, but a vertical eruption in which the essence and the existence of being came together, forever reconciling in principle the alienation of life and leading to further eruptions of the Spiritual Presence. Although the prophetic tradition is the basis and part of the presupposition of Jesus as the Christ, Jesus himself is not revered only because of his words and deeds, which were of a prophetic nature, but because of the event of reconciliation which took place in him. Jesus as the Christ is the unique centre of historical and existential meaning because of what he was. The focus of Christian faith is thus not upon Jesus the human being, as was the case with the liberal theologians of the nineteenth century, but upon Jesus as the bearer of the new being. In the symbol of the kingdom of God, Tillich sees the Spiritual Presence as the consummation of history; at the same time the kingdom can be striven for and prophetically symbolized. Every human structure that tends away from tribalism and nationalism toward greater harmony and integration may be regarded as symbolic of the kingdom. Tillich even spoke of the 'ultimately prophetic character of the idea of empire' (p. 341) in the sense that in resistance to empire, groups tend to break away in tribal or national fragmentation. Had he been writing today Tillich would doubtless have spoken of globalization rather than of empire, and we may feel that his reference to empire is regrettable. Nevertheless, his thinking points the way toward globalization, and we see within that world-wide movement traces of both the Spiritual Presence and the demonic power of which he spoke.

Prophecy and the churches

These reflections led Tillich to emphasize the significance of the Old Testament in Christian faith: 'Without the Old Testament, Christianity relapses into the immaturities of the universal history of religion' (p. 365), and this includes relapsing into the religion of the Old Testament itself, which was, after all, the main target of prophetic criticism. The prophetic spirit is thus the spirit of hope. It may be latent or even actively repressed over long periods of history, but it is never altogether absent, and when the *kairos* comes, it will again rise to the surface. Wherever it appears, expectation of the coming kingdom of God is renewed, and the churches are once again awakened to their task of witnessing to its justice and its peace. Much accumulation of religious tradition may be necessary before the prophetic attack upon it will be stimulated and felt to be meaningful. This is why there is such a predominance of religious tradition compared with religious revolution. A living Church, nevertheless, will constantly rekindle the prophetic spirit, and in prophecy will find again its challenge and its hope.

10

The Prophetic Theology of Reinhold Niebuhr

The prophetic tradition in the thought of Reinhold Niebuhr (1892–1971)

Paul Tillich shared his interest in prophetic ministry with his slightly younger contemporary Reinhold Niebuhr. They were colleagues together in Union Theological Seminary in New York, where Tillich was professor from 1930–55 and Niebuhr from 1930–60. Both laid emphasis upon the public responsibilities of theology. But whereas the approach of Tillich was mainly philosophical, Niebuhr worked primarily in Christian social ethics with special reference to national and international questions. These interests led them both into a concern for the meaning of history. Tillich published *The Interpretation of History* in 1936, and *Beyond Tragedy: Essays on the Christian interpretation of history* by Reinhold Niebuhr appeared two years later. Whereas Tillich's social and theological interests were formed during the political upheavals in Germany between the two world wars, Niebuhr was deeply influenced by his experiences as a pastor in Detroit, home of the American automobile industry. Paul Tillich regarded history as having exercised prophetic judgement upon the Nazi regime and Niebuhr was concerned with the destiny of the United States of America as it rose to international leadership before and after the Second World War. To understand how these two Protestants interpreted prophetic religion one must reckon with the different context provided by the histories of Germany and America during the middle years of the twentieth century. Tillich as a German faced the history of a great cultural and theological tradition which had been captured by an evil power and practically destroyed in the vengeance that followed. Niebuhr, as an American, was interpreting the history of a great nation that had risen to world leadership and yet was caught in the ambiguities of power and justice.

During his earlier studies at Eden Theological Seminary Niebuhr had studied the Book of Amos, and in 1941 he said in a speech: 'All theology really begins with Amos' (quoted in Brown 2002, p. 15). No doubt, as Brown says, '[t]he lines of Niebuhr's mature achievement began to take shape during his early teaching years at Union Seminary' (p. 36). It is clear none the less that his interest in prophetic ministry went right back to the earliest days of his Detroit pastorate, probably inspired by his study of Amos at Eden.

Evidence for Niebuhr's early interest in the role of the prophet can be found in his published diary, *Leaves from the Notebook of a Tamed Cynic* (1990 [1929]), recording the impressions of his ministry in Detroit (1915–28). In 1915, at the age of 23, he was already ruefully comparing the routine nature of his ministry with the life of the prophets. 'The prophet speaks only when he is inspired. The parish preacher must speak whether he is inspired or not' (p. 12).

During the years that followed, we can trace the development of Niebuhr's liberal individual faith as it became more social in its orientation and more aware of the problems of social life. In 1923 he wrote of the possibility that the family might be 'a selfish unit in society' (p. 45). In 1924 he was thinking of ministry in terms of prophecy and its difficulties. 'I'm not surprised that most budding prophets are tamed in time to become harmless parish priests' (p. 47). Was it possible then for a parish minister to exercise a prophetic calling? Gradually he became aware of the possibility of becoming a prophet 'without being forced into itinerancy' (p. 48). His concept of this was of one who possessed a combination of the awe and mystery of the liturgy with an ethical insight into the problems of modern life so as to create a critical and reforming perspective (p. 49). This seems to have dawned upon him during a trip to England when, describing a visit to York Minster, he writes 'there are men here in England who preach prophetic sermons in cathedrals' (p. 50).

Another glimpse into what Niebuhr thought about prophetic ministry may be seen in his description of the life of a bishop who had recently died. The bishop had been a prophet, because he 'knew how to interpret the Christian religion so that it meant something in terms of an industrial civilization. His fearless protagonism of the cause of democracy in industry won him the respect and love of the workers of the city as no other churchman possessed it' (p. 60).

But to what extent did the conditions of modern society and of church life make effective prophecy possible? Niebuhr reflects that the ministry of the prophetic bishop 'didn't change the prevailing attitude of Detroit industry by a hair's breadth' (p. 60).

In the closing years of his Detroit ministry we see Niebuhr becoming more critical of the pious individualism which was characteristic of much Christian faith. 'One ought to strive for the reformation of society rather than one's own perfection' (p. 60). In 1925 he reflects on a church conference he had attended.

> The church conference begins and ends by attempting to arouse an emotion of the ideal, usually in terms of personal loyalty to the person of Jesus, but very little is done to attach the emotion to specific tasks and projects. Is the industrial life of our day unethical? Are nations imperialistic? (p. 62)

This prompts the further thought.

> Why doesn't the church offer specific suggestions for the application of a Christian ethic to the difficulties of our day? If that suggestion is made, the answer is that such a policy would breed contention. (p. 62)

Here and at several other places, Niebuhr refers to the resistance of congregations to such specific ethics, because of their vested interests. He now meditates upon the pedagogical aspects of prophetic ministry. One must try to avoid bitterness. Nevertheless: 'Better a warrior's grimness than the childish sentimentalities of people who are too ignorant or too selfish to bear the burdens of the world' (p. 72).

In 1926 he reflects:

> You can't rush into a congregation which has been fed from its very infancy on the individualistic ethic of Protestantism and which is immersed in a civilization where ethical individualism runs riot, and expect to develop a social conscience among the people in two weeks. (p. 85)

Can the Church be expected then to have any impact upon the reformation of society?

> The church is like the Red Cross service in war time. It keeps life from degenerating into a consistent inhumanity, but it does not materially alter the fact of the struggle itself. (p. 89)

In responding to a sermon that was nothing but 'a fulsome eulogy of Jesus' (p. 90), he remarks '[h]ow much easier it is to adore an ideal character than to emulate it!' (p. 90).

The young minister meditates on the significance of the stock exchange. How should Christians respond to 'the evils and the ethical problems of stock manipulation' (p. 101)? The problem of the churches' attitude towards racism begins to trouble him, and this leads him to wonder why people go to church at all.

> The church service is not an end in itself. Not even religion is an end in itself. If the church service does not attract people by the comfort and challenge it brings to them, we only postpone the evil day if we compel attendance by appealing to their sense of duty. (p. 134)

Jewish congregations, on the other hand, could be more interesting. There Niebuhr found an 'avowed devotion to the Hebrew prophets' and discovered that

> [t]here is at least a considerable appreciation of the genius of prophetic religion and some honest effort to apply the prophetic ideal to life. I am afraid that the individualistic traditions of Protestantism, and perhaps also the strong Pauline strain in Protestant theology, have obscured the social implications of Jesus' gospel much more than is the case in Jewish religion. (p. 147)

He summed up his response to Judaism with the comment '[t]he glory of their religion is that they are really not thinking so much of "salvation" as of a saved society' (p. 147).

To what extent is it possible for a Christian theologian to be both a philosopher and a prophet? 'Philosophers are not usually prophets. They are too reasonable and circumspect to create or preserve the prophetic vision' (p. 150).

It was with reflections of this kind that, after 13 years in local ministry, Niebuhr took up his post in Union Theological Seminary in New York City in 1928. His first important book was *Moral Man and Immoral Society* (1932), which has become a classic of Christian social ethics. He describes how he became critical of the economic ethic of self-reliance which teaches people how to be prosperous and which has led to an increase in middle-class complacency.

From Jewish and Catholic sources he had rediscovered the importance of the social fabric and had also been impressed by the work of Walter Rauschenbusch and other pioneers of the Social Gospel movement. However, Niebuhr rejected the confident optimism of the Social Gospel movement coming to believe that faith in the achievement of social progress was not only leading America into a false sense of pride but seriously misunderstood the Christian view of the corporate structure of sinfulness. This rejection of the liberal theology of the late nineteenth and early twentieth centuries was decisive for Niebuhr's theology, as it was, indeed, in the thought of Tillich also.

In order to show the relevance of the ancient prophets to the contemporary world, Tillich and Niebuhr looked for structures or patterns which they could find repeated in later history. They did this in characteristically different ways. For Tillich, it was a matter of the emergence again and again of fundamental ontological realities; for Niebuhr, it was to be found in certain historical developments, although he was at pains to deny that this was a matter of increasing human enlightenment. Increasingly he realized that the crux of the problem of the relationship between religion and politics lay in the way that the nation understood its god. This led Niebuhr into the character of tribalism, into the messianic as the exalted self-understanding of the tribe, and onto prophecy as providing a critique of both the tribe and its god.

The origins and limits of messianism

When David went up to battle, he took with him the ark of God. This reminds us, Niebuhr suggests, that battles always involve more than the physical strength of the opposing sides (1938, p. 51). The tribes take with them their ancient memories, and for every battle there is a god, or two gods. The gods of battle are both the glorification of the tribe, and they also point to something beyond the tribe, something to which the tribe itself owes obedience. In every one of these tribal gods there was a trace of transcendence, a hint of a lofty morality, something greater than the tribe:

He is the god of a particular culture in conflict with other cultures; the god of a particular type of human existence in conflict with other types of human life. Yet he is more than that; and it is by that *more* that he becomes an effective ally in the battle. For human beings who develop a life which involves more than existence do not fight well if they are not certain that more than existence is involved in the struggle. (pp. 53–4)

Thus the gods of the ark, the gods of battle, make each battle more terrible, because they involve the certainty that the struggle is for something beyond the tribe. It is something more valuable than the tribe itself. This certainty can lead to righteous fury and cruelty. So in the various battle gods we see a kind of inchoate monotheism, for the god of battles is not bound to the tribe; he is also the God of creation.

This is further illustrated by the fact that David, although he has been so faithful to the God of battles, was considered unworthy to build the temple.

'This God is not the ally of the nations but their judge and their redeemer' (p. 56). The way David solved this problem was not altogether satisfactory. David said, in effect, 'I am not good enough to build the temple, but "my son is young and tender." Let the temple be built by the purity of youth' (p. 56). Niebuhr regards this as the sectarian solution to the ambiguities of religion and religious conflict. In spite of the failings of our family it is still purer than anyone else. So it was that '[t]he symbol of the god of battles found a resting place in the temple dedicated to the God of peace' (pp. 62–3). The god of battle was thus subordinated to the universal God, but not wholly excluded.

When we come to the prophets of Israel, the national battle God was almost entirely excluded: 'Prophetic religion is more rigorous than priestly religion. It speaks an eternal "no" to all human pretensions. Priestly religion, on the other hand, appreciates what points to the eternal in all human values' (p. 63).

The religion of the priests is more dangerous, for there is a possibility that people will continue to adore the ark. The prophet is more iconoclastic, and yet there is a danger that the prophet will fail to appreciate the aspiration hidden within all culture.

In Niebuhr's later thought the God of battle was described as the Messiah of prophetic expectation. National religions begin as expressions of hope, the expectation of national triumph. All great empires believe that they represent the culmination of human culture. Niebuhr distinguishes three levels in this national messianism. First there is the 'egoistic-nationalistic element'. Secondly, there is an 'ethical-universalistic element', and in the third level we may talk of a 'supra-ethical religious element' (1943, p. 18). The first two levels are found earlier than the rise of Hebrew prophetism, in the religions of ancient Egypt, Babylon and Assyria. The first level is found in all imperial self-understanding. The more ethical type is found in the ideal of the shepherd king. This represents an advance over the earlier type because it is now recognized that corruptions in society are due to corruptions of power. This is why the strictures of the prophets at this level are directed against the rulers. 'It recognizes that injustice flows from the same source from which justice comes, from the historical organization of life' (p. 21).

The ideal of the messianic king, although sometimes an idealization of an earthly ruler, at its best has transcendent elements, recognizing that historical political power is unable to realize the messianic realm. All three levels are found in Hebrew prophecy, although the element of national messianism is never fully eliminated. In spite of this, the great achievement of Hebrew prophetism was that it gave an interpretation of history too profound to allow the illusions of an historical messiah king to bring about the desired realm of justice. The prophetic tradition increasingly universalized the messianic nationalism. The prophet Amos saw history 'not from the perspective of a nation but as a universal whole. And God is regarded as the sovereign of all peoples' (p. 24).

The important thing about the prophecies of Amos was not only their universalism, but the criticism of the optimistic character of so much messianic prophecy. Amos delivers a series of judgements against the nation of Israel. Although it had become a nation with a special sense of destiny, its pride in this calling must be humbled and punished. Thus, the prophetic movement is the 'beginning of revelation' (p. 25), for a transcendent God speaks from beyond all human achievement. '[F]or the first time, in the history of culture the eternal and divine is not regarded as the extension and fulfilment of the highest human possibilities . . .' (p. 25).

For Amos, it did not matter which nation was involved; each nation and the whole collection of nations stood under the judgement of God. This shows that the real problem of history is the proud pretension of all human endeavours. It is this that engulfs history in evil and sin.

The element of false confidence and optimism is never entirely extinguished in Israel. Even when prophecy gave way to apocalyptic, some of the writings were admittedly universal but others remained within the limits of messianic nationalism. In the New Testament, Peter was appalled at the idea that the newly recognized Messiah of Israel should suffer and die, and even after the resurrection, the disciples were still wondering when the kingdom would be established in Israel. The sense of imperial destiny continued to be a feature of the Christian empires of Europe, and it lives on still in America.

Niebuhr thus rejects the traditional interpretation of the Old Testament prophecies of Christ as predictions of the life and death of Jesus of Nazareth. He regards them rather as examples of a much older characteristic, both of individual nations and of great empires, namely, the interpretation of their own survival and grandeur as sponsored by God, a God who is created as the image of that national glory. This is seen today in the belief in 'the manifest destiny' of the United States. Niebuhr in this way was able to develop a critique of American power. First, such messianic self-understanding was a common weakness of all empires. Second, the pride implied by this was bound to be humbled by God. Third, optimistic messianic nationalism was opposed by prophetic faith.

The problem of messianism and its resolution

The prophetic movement of Israel was thus caught between promise and judgement. The promise was that goodness and power would be combined in the person of Messiah. In this way, the historic corruption of political power would be overcome, and justice would be realized. This was the messianic hope. On the other hand, there was the knowledge that all nations and peoples were involved in rebellion against the God of justice. All history stands under the judgement of God. 'Here the prophetic interpretation of history approaches the Christian doctrine of original sin' (p. 28). This, however, does not itself point to the problem. There is no doubt that the power of God is able to bring about the judgement. It is not a question of how good will overcome evil, of the vindication of the just and good among all nations. Hebrew faith 'was certain that the hidden sovereignty of God would guarantee the ultimate triumph of good over evil in history' (p. 33). This faith was not locked into an eternal struggle of good and evil with no certain outcome. The problem lay at a deeper level. 'The problem of the meaning of history according to prophetism is how history can be anything more than judgment' (p. 30).

Where can the divine mercy be found, which makes of history anything more than a series of judgements? Even the pacification of nature, as the wolf and the lamb lie down together, and the amelioration of injustice as the poor take the place of the unjust rich does not solve the problem. Does the divine have resources of mercy great enough 'to redeem as well as to judge' (p. 30)? The problem is how mercy will overcome the evil concealed even in the highest human good.

This leads to a deadlock in the significance of history itself. If judgement and mercy are at loggerheads, how can history have any final meaning? Even the more transcendent forms of later apocalypticism fail to meet this dilemma. For if the paradoxes of history are only resolved by a super-historical and super-natural Son of Man, who does not arise from history but puts an end to all history, does not history itself remain meaningless? In Niebuhr's view, the unre-solved problems of the prophetic movement found their answers in the person and work of Jesus Christ. Jesus transformed the nature of messiahship in the very process of fulfilling it, so that '[t]he Christ whom Christian faith accepts is the same Christ whom Messianism rejects, as not conforming to its expecta-tions' (p. 39).

In the first place, Jesus reforms prophetism from its legalistic aspects. The humane intentions of the Sabbath, for example, had become hidden in legalistic qualifications. Moreover, Jesus rejected the remains of nationalistic messianism by declaring that the temple was to become a house of prayer for all the nations. The problem of the overcoming of evil by good whilst at the same time recogniz-ing that even the good stand in need of mercy is also resolved in the teaching of Jesus. Those who appear to be highly moral are not accepted by God as much as the person who seeks humble forgiveness confessing his or her sins. In the parable of the sheep and the goats, those who are called into eternal life did not know that they were serving Christ in their deeds of mercy. The fundamental difference between the righteous and the sinful is not denied, but it is moved onto a higher plane where the apparently righteous do not know the true nature of their righteousness, nor do the evil perceive the inner character of what they have done. The most profound resolution of the limits of the prophetic tradi-tion, however, lies in the insight that Messiah must suffer.

> To declare, as Jesus does, that the Messiah, the representative of God, must suffer, is to make vicarious suffering the final revelation of meaning in his-tory. But it is the vicarious suffering of the representative of God, and not of some force in history, which finally clarifies the obscurities of history and discloses the sovereignty of God over history. (p. 46)

This may be interpreted in the liberal manner, whereby love is gradually pen-etrating and improving the world, or in a tragic sense, in that suffering love was crucified and pushed out of the world, and although it will win in the end, its historical experience is only of failure. Niebuhr rejects both these interpre-tations. Rather, we should understand that according to Christian faith, God takes human sin into God's own life and bears it. Thus 'the contradictions of history are not resolved in history; but they are only ultimately resolved on the level of the eternal and the divine' (p. 47). Nevertheless, 'God's mercy must make itself known in history, so that man in history may become fully conscious of his guilt and his redemption' (pp. 47–8).

God, the judge of evil, takes it upon God's own self in the person of Jesus Christ. This is the divine way of judging evil. So evil is condemned but the evil doers are redeemed. Niebuhr agrees that these resolutions of the prophetic dilemma are actually adumbrated in the prophetic literature of the Old Testament. God is shown there as always actively at work in history, and it is through the suffering servant of God that God's redemption is realized. The bringing together of the symbols of the suffering servant and the triumphant Son of Man in the New Testament makes these trends explicit. And yet the paradox remains. As suffering servant, God has acted, but as glorious Son of Man, God has still to act. Niebuhr lays emphasis upon the Second Coming of Christ as being essential to understanding the paradoxical condition of faith in history. 'The love which enters history as suffering love, must remain suffering love in history' (p. 50). The cross of Christ does not banish actual evil, and the New Testament makes it clear that both good and evil will increase as the end approaches. The Christian view of history is not one of gradual improvement, but of a constant struggle with ambiguity. The symbol of the antichrist 'refutes every modern liberal interpretation of history which identifies "progress" with the Kingdom of God' (p. 51, n. 1).

Niebuhr summarizes his view of Christian faith in relation to the prophetic tradition as follows:

> Its significance lies in its explicit formulation of the problem of life and history, as it was apprehended negatively in the prophetic interpretation of history and as it was positively affirmed in Jesus' reinterpretation of prophetic expectations. It is closely related to Jesus' insistence that the righteous are not righteous before the divine judgment; and to his conception of the suffering Messiah as a revelation of the justice and the mercy of God. (p. 131)

The continuing relevance of the prophetic tradition

Niebuhr not only created a prophetic theology of the Bible and of history, but for more than 30 years of public ministry he addressed the United States with his powerful blend of Christian faith and political realism. The combination of ethical challenge and sombre warning places him in the tradition of the American Jeremiad (Bercovitch 1978). If we take his published work as a whole, three themes predominate. First, there is a sustained effort to speak truth to power. Second, there is the belief that in addressing power, both national and international, the prophets of Israel are the originators and the best models. Third, there is the claim that the suffering love of God seen by faith in the cross of Christ presents a clue to the mystery of history, and this may become a source of hope. That hope, however, will never be free in this life from ambiguity.

Niebuhr had lived through the failure of the League of Nations to prevent the Second World War and was deeply interested in the possibilities of creating a new community of nations. He believed that such a community would arise because of the fear of anarchy, but it would also be limited by the pride of the powerful. These efforts at internationalism would have to be accompanied by a sense of universal, moral responsibility.

> The first religious apprehension of a universal and unlimited moral obliga-
> tion was achieved in prophetic monotheism, which was first expressed in the
> prophet Amos's conception of a universal history, over which the God of
> Israel presided as sovereign but of which the history of Israel was not the
> centre and end. (Niebuhr 1945, p. 106)

Modern technologies of transport and communication have made the emergence
of a world community more feasible, but technology itself will not enhance
international solidarity, because it is the rich and powerful nations who will
control the technology. 'For a long time to come the international community
will have few elements of inner cohesion, or benefit from the unity of a common
culture or tradition' (pp. 114–15). The limits of internationalism in the post-war
period were clearly seen by Niebuhr.

> The international politics of the coming decades will be dominated by great
> powers who will be able to prevent recalcitrance among the smaller nations,
> but who will have difficulty in keeping peace between each other because
> they will not have any authority above their own, powerful enough to bend
> or deflect their wills. (p. 116)

Niebuhr welcomed the United Nations, which was founded in 1948, but he
also saw that the hope of peace between the nations was balanced against the
fact that at more or less the same time the world was divided between two great
power blocs, each having the capability of destroying each other and themselves
in a nuclear holocaust. This illustrated his belief that in the drama of history,
good and evil possibilities develop together (1956, p. 219).

Much of Niebuhr's writing was directed toward the internal social and political problems of the United States, and the nature and efficacy of its international responsibilities. The essays in his collection *Reflections on the End of an
Era* (1937) deal with many of the great issues of the day including class conflict within America, the collision between Christian faith and communism, the
characteristics of capitalism, fascism and communism and the nature of bour-
geois individualism. Although some of the issues with which they deal are no
longer as relevant as they were in the late 1930s, they still read well, like long,
weighty editorials in a quality newspaper. In *The Irony of American History*
(1962) Niebuhr offers some of his most trenchant criticisms of America. He
describes the American dream as an example of the messianic destiny, which
nearly every nation attributes to itself at some time or another. Written at the
height of the Cold War, Niebuhr sees the nation he loves caught up in ironic
dilemmas it is unable to solve. It is ironic that a nation founded upon the ideals
of peace and democracy should now be forced to possess and possibly to use
weapons of mass destruction. It is ironic that a nation which arose as a rejection
of imperialism should find itself now accused of imperialism, and that a nation
which saw its wealth as a gift from God for the benefit of all peoples should now
be held in ill repute by the poor people of the world.

> The ironic elements in American history can be overcome, in short, only if
> American idealism comes to terms with the limits of all human striving, the

fragmentariness of all human wisdom, the precariousness of all historic con-
figurations of power, and the mixture of good and evil in all human virtue.
(p. 133)

All of these points are then illustrated by references to the Hebrew prophets
and the teachings of Jesus. The prophets 'regard nothing as absolutely secure
in human life and history; and believe that every desperate effort to establish
security will lead to heightened insecurity' (p. 159).

It is ironic that the prophet of ironic ambiguity should have left a heritage
which is itself ambiguous. Reinhold Niebuhr has been criticized for his support
for American imperialism and for his doctrine of necessary violence. Neil Elliott
thinks that a popular form of Niebuhr's theology led to discouragement in the
American churches about the efficacy of actions for peace and justice, and that
his emphasis upon the eschatological doctrine of the kingdom of God meant
that it was always out of reach (2008, p. 164). Too often, Elliott remarks, the
teaching of Niebuhr 'has served to insulate the doctrine of inevitable violence
and to legitimate inequalities of power and wealth from critique by the Christian gospel' (1995, p. 80). To some extent 'Niebuhr's Christian realism provided a theological rationale for US military interventions' (p. 80). While the
strength of these criticisms cannot be denied, it is also true that the naiveté of
much British political resistance could learn from Niebuhr's doctrine of collective and national sinfulness.

Reinhold Niebuhr as a Christian prophet

It is in his earlier work that the prophetic aspect of Niebuhr's thought is most
vividly expressed. We conclude by referring to one of his most powerful early
sermons entitled 'Transvaluation of Values' (1938, pp. 195–214). The sermon
is a denunciation of power and wealth based upon the comment made by Paul
to the Corinthian Christians, when he said:

> Not many of you were wise by human standards; not many were influential;
> not many were of noble birth. But God chose the foolish things of the world
> to shame the wise; God chose the weak things of the world to shame the
> strong. He chose the lowly things of this world and the despised things – and
> the things that are not – to nullify the things that are. (1 Cor. 1.26b–8)

The sermon anticipates the insights of liberation theology, although published
30 years before the earliest writings of the Latin American theologians.

> One of the most instructive facts of human history is that not the so-called
> impartial observers of justice and injustice are clearest in their condemnations
> of injustice but rather the poor victims of injustice. Thus the poor and oppressed
> must, through the physical knowledge of the pain they suffer, see some facts
> and pronounce some judgments which the wise cannot see. (1938, p. 209)

Niebuhr had been challenged by the thought of Friedrich Nietzsche, who had spoken with contempt about Christianity taking the values of the poor, the miserable and the weak and allowing them, through envy and resentment, to suck the strength from the aristocratic values of beauty and power thus, according to Nietzsche, turning society upside down and holding the human race back (Nietzsche 2007). Niebuhr, in his sermon, agrees that Christian faith has transfigured all these aristocratic values but rather than holding humanity back, he believes that this is the very call of the gospel which works in the world of human pride and sin representing the judgement and mercy of God.

Part 4

Towards the Prophetic Church

In Part 3, we saw how it is possible for the ancient prophetic tradition to be integrated into modern theological thought. Since then the theory and practice of nonviolent action in Mahatma Gandhi and Martin Luther King Jr have paved the way for contemporary prophetic praxis. It is true that social justice in the British churches, particularly in the Church of England, has drawn more upon the theology of the incarnation rather than of prophetic protest. In Britain today we are witnessing a significant coming together of these two traditions which promises to provide a rich resource for the prophetic Church.

In Chapter 11, I offer an overview of this theological development. It is a brief history of Christian faith seen from the perspective of the Western prophetic tradition, showing how this challenges globalization and late capitalism in both Britain and America. In Chapter 12, I return once more to the problems of Christian adult theological learning. I show how false dichotomies have marginalized the prophetic tradition of social justice, and I argue for a closer inclusion of the ethics of justice and peace into Christian spirituality. At the same time, this is an attempt to refocus Christian mission upon the kingdom of God. Finally, Chapter 13 presents 25 propositions for the reformation of theological education.

A Theory of Theological Development from the Perspective of Western Christian Faith

Introduction

The self-understanding of faith has passed through many revisions and development is particularly rapid during the present period of religious and economic globalization. Christian consciousness carries forward the impressions left by earlier experiences, and the natural tendency to conserve tends to retard recognition of these impressions, making it difficult for religion to fulfil its responsibilities toward the contemporary world.

A major impression upon Christian faith has been left by 1,700 years of residence within the political power, first of the Roman Empire and then of successive European Christian empires. Since the modern missionary movement took place during the period of European and American ascendancy, those forms of Christian faith received by the evangelized countries carry the marks of this geopolitical context. The task of disentangling Christian faith that comes to modern people with these many layers of earlier interpretations is complex and demands criteria historical, theological and ethical. The one who attempts such disentanglement also stands in a certain socio-political reality, and has to grapple with both conscious and unconscious vested interest. This demands a sophisticated theological approach to both false consciousness as a collective phenomenon and self-deception as a feature of individual life. Nevertheless, the legacy of faith and the suffering of the present world insist that the serious Christian make an effort in this direction. There is no pure essence of Christian faith. There is no simple, unmediated approach to the Bible. Naiveté only succeeds in leading us into a morass of unexamined presuppositions and leaves Christian faith without defence and without the analytic energy to tackle the problems of life and death today.

This chapter attempts to grasp this nettle through a combination of theological assertion and historical interpretation, commencing with a series of theological fundamentals springing from faith in God as the living God of Christian tradition.

Basic orientations

The Church is an instrument of Christian faith (Eph. 3.10). The Church is also part of Christian faith, since faith in the one, holy, catholic and apostolic Church is affirmed in the ancient creeds. However, when we are considering the role and prospects of a particular denomination, it is important to emphasize that the Church as a whole (and therefore the particular, historic denominations as well) does not live unto itself but is an instrument to further the mission of Christian faith in the world (2 Cor. 4.5). No specific denomination is essential to this task, and Christian faith will generate new movements from time to time to become new instruments of its own mission.

Christian faith is an instrument of the mission of God (Eph. 3.8–9). It is not the only such instrument. In spite of its unique characteristics and value, Christian faith does not live to and for itself, but is to be judged by its faithfulness to the mission of God (Rom. 11.21).

The mission of God is a mission of life for all human beings and for the whole creation (Gen. 2.9; Deut. 30.15; Ps. 36.9, 103.4; John 1.4, 10.10; Tit. 1.2). In Scripture God is shown to be opposed to every force and structure which frustrates life (Exod. 2.23–5; Rom. 1.18; Jam. 4.6). God is energetic in the pursuit of justice (Ps. 9.8; Isa. 11.4; Luke 1.52–3). God tears down the oppression, exploitation, greed and pride that oppose the fulfilment of God's mission (Ps. 146.7–9; Isa. 10.1–3; Mic. 2.9–3).

The special characteristic of the mission of God which found expression through Jesus was the inauguration of a community of inclusive love (Matt. 5.43–45; Luke 7.36–50; John 13.34). Jesus declared that the mission of God was to establish the rule of God in his words and actions (Mark 1.14–15; Luke 11.20). As prophet (Matt. 13.53–57), teacher (John 3.2) and Son of God (John 1.49) he opposed the social and physical distortions which were obstructing the appearance of the new community (Luke 6.6–10, 13.10–16). Faithful to the end, he sealed his witness with his blood (Mark 12.1–8, 14.24; Heb. 13.20). The Church flows from the life of Jesus (Acts 20.28; Rom. 5.10), a life laid down and restored (John 10.15–17), and through the Church the risen Christ continues his mission (Matt. 28.20; John 15.1–8). The mission of the Church is thus the same, by continuation, as that of Jesus Christ (Matt. 16.18; John 20.21; 2 Cor. 4.10), and the mission of Jesus is identical with but not the only form (Amos 9.7; Mal. 1.11; Acts 10.34–35) (Falk 1985) of the mission of God (Matt. 11.27; John 1.18).

In reflecting upon the God who is the ground and source of mission, the followers of Jesus affirmed faith in God as the one who sends the mission (Matt. 10.40; Acts 10.38), faith in Jesus as the one who was sent (John 5.36), and faith in the Holy Spirit who is the loving energy of the sending (Acts 2.33, 19.2–6). In this Trinitarian faith in the sender, the sent and the sending the Church finds the ground of its hope (Matt. 28.19–20; Rom. 8.16–17). This hope is made actual insofar as the disciples of Jesus, formed into the Church by the Holy Spirit (Rom. 5.5), are becoming the symbol of the community of inclusive love, and thus remain faithful to the mission of the Triune God (Eph. 2.13–18).

The mission in history

God acts through creating creativity (Hartshorne 1967, p. 26). The world that God created is not a static reality, emerging complete and entire. Rather, it is a dynamic, evolving world which carries the stamp of its originator in its endless innovation, novelty and change. Thus the mission of God in promoting life must be mediated through the dynamics, structures and vicissitudes of life itself (Tillich 1953, p. 162). By the same token, the meaning of the mission will be interpreted by human beings (1 Cor. 13.12; 2 Cor. 4.7), who are both the objects and the agents of the mission. This meaning will be distorted, misunderstood and contradicted. It will also be accepted, transformed and transforming.

The fulfilment of God's mission will be a renewed creation, when the liberty of the children of God will reach its glorious realization, along with the renewal of the created order (Rom. 8.21). This lies in the future. The God who originated the mission from the past is also the God who calls from the future (John 14.18; Rev. 1.8).

Since the mission is a proclamation and a demand for justice, it will be countered and opposed by injustice. The mission to actualize a community of universal love will be opposed by sectional interests and tribal loyalties (Erikson 1975, pp. 176–9; 1982, p. 95). The mission to establish a community of inclusive love will be opposed by selection, hierarchy, the setting of boundaries and limits, the distinction between us and them (Nipkow 2003, p. 193). The forces of opposition to God's mission are also dynamic, proactive, intelligent, forcing acceptance of their own will rather than the will of God (Rom. 7.21–3; Eph. 6.12), seeking life for themselves rather than life for all, building up structures, concentrated centres of hostility and opposition (Hinkelammert 1986, pp. 125–6), just as the mission of God builds up structures and powers of the life of love.

The prophetic and apostolic mission of the Church, the incarnated mission, will be subject to ambiguity and compromise (pp. 240–1). It will tend to be understood from the position in the life cycle (Fowler 1981; Oser and Gmünder 1991) and the place within the power structure (Metz 1981; Hull 1992) inhabited by those who seek to promote it. Moreover, those who benefit from the injustice in the world will not read the mission in the same way as those who suffer from the injustice (Lamb 1982; Schüttke-Scherle 1989). The meaning of the mission, which is the meaning of Christian faith and the nature of the Church, has become part of social memory. It has passed through the distortions and deceptions that are typical of the way that societies remember (Connerton 1989; Halbwachs 1992; Werbner (ed.) 1998). Each national or linguistic or ethnic group that comes into contact with the mission will understand it experientially within the confines of their own historical and geopolitical setting. In so far as the mission is made articulate in language and speech it will express the vested interests, the grammatical aggression by means of which each language subdues meaninglessness in the interests of those who are structured by that language (Foucault 1972; Pêcheux 1982; Derrida 1989). Religion itself will be found on both sides of the antitheses created by the mission (Baum 1975). There is no other way for the life of God to communicate with the spontaneous and developing character of created life than through these ambiguities.

The mission of God and Christian faith in Europe

Five hundred years of association with the European search for power have led to a huge expansion of Christian influence, but have also seriously compromised the Christian tradition insofar as it is a witness to and an agent of the mission of God. Those who inherit the results of these centuries of collaboration and protest tend to understand Christian faith from within this context. The contamination exists both objectively in that it has taken place and subjectively in the mental and spiritual lives of those who are its products (Comaroff and Comaroff 1991, 1992). Those who have been shaped by the European tradition of Christian faith find it hard to recognize its distorted character. This would mean perceiving distortion within themselves, and that implies some contrast or antithesis which would render the distortion visible.

Moreover, the process is itself highly ambiguous. As this ambiguity is realized, attitudes towards it are necessarily ambivalent. We do not know what would have become of Britain (to take an example of one significant European country) within the context of aggressive international competition if the theology of God's special covenant with Britain had not given the peoples of these Western European islands a sense of identity, confidence and purpose in the world (Drinnon 1980; Hughes and Allen 1988). If Britain had not received its vigorous sense of identity and national destiny from Christian faith, perhaps it would have got it somewhere else with profound consequences both for Britain and for Christian faith in Europe and the world.

When we read how Francis Drake and his sailors on their voyage around the world, anchoring off the Pacific coast of North America, went ashore, and going down on their knees sang Psalms, while pointing to the sky, in order to evangelize the group of native Californians who met them (Heizer 1947), we do not know whether to groan with embarrassment at this early example of the arrogance with which Europeans have treated native cultures (Berkhofer 1965, 1978; Swain and Bird-Rose (eds) 1988; Tinker 1993) or whether to admire the confidence and the courage that drove those isolated men in that tiny vessel across the unknown oceans of the world.

It is not our business to condemn previous generations, but it is our responsibility to understand ourselves in relation to them. The dramatic effects of Britain's appropriation of Christian tradition in the service of its newly discovered national enterprise demand our attention.

We have seen how when the colonization of North America was being undertaken in the early decades of the seventeenth century, the passages of Scripture that inspired the colonizers included Genesis 12.1: 'Now the LORD said unto Abram, "Go from your country and your kindred and your father's house to the land that I will show you. I will make of you a great nation, and I will bless you and make your name great"' (Symonds 1609), and Joshua 17.14–18, where the tribes of Joseph complained that too small a portion of land had been given them. Joshua told the tribes to go up into the land, cut down the forests 'cast out the Canaanites' and possess the land (Gray 1609). Here we find the seeds of that contempt for the so-called primitive and savage 'red Indians', an image of white supremacy and destiny which is still with us today.

By the end of the French wars of the early eighteenth century, Britain had emerged as a world power with a mission to spread political and economic enlightenment together with Christian civilization around the globe.

We have traced that mission in the hymns of Isaac Watts in whom the experiential theology of the Puritan tradition became the nationalistic theology of the Protestant empire.

It is a striking fact that in the approximately 600 hymns written by Isaac Watts, some 20 of which remain in the repertoire, there is hardly one dealing with the service of the Church to the community and the world. In these hymns, the congregation has become a world unto itself. Everything is reduced to worship. Indeed, there is nothing but doctrine and worship; the mission has been swallowed up by 'gospel', the repetitive celebration by the local congregation of its own intellectual and emotional life.

Between 1770 and 1850 the nation of commerce, agriculture and industry became the first capitalist country in the world (Macfie 1967; Viner 1972; Hirschman 1977; Smith 1993, 2002). The power of money, first located in the north Italian cities in the thirteenth and fourteenth centuries, moving to Portugal and Spain in the fifteenth and sixteenth centuries and to the Netherlands in the seventeenth century, now made its temporary home in London (Arrighi 1994). These years have been called 'the age of atonement', because not only was there an emphasis upon responsibility for one's debts and the need to repay them and so atone for one's financial mismanagement, but this was mirrored in a theology of the cross that interpreted the death of Christ as God's punishment for human sin, diverted away from the debtors themselves and inflicted upon the head of the innocent Jesus, thus maintaining confidence in the stability of the moral economy of the world (Hilton 1988; Selby 1997).

From approximately 1870 to 1914 the pound sterling ruled the world, and British theology reached its climax. In Victorian and Edwardian hymns we find the principal statements and popularizations of this theology. The military metaphors, often taken all too literally, the sense of weariness in the face of a surrounding world of evil, the concentration upon the glories of heaven, and the nostalgic recreation of a pastoral life, are the typical emphases that emerged (Tamke 1978; Adey 1988; Wolffe (ed.) 1997).

The present situation: first phase

This is the tradition of Christian faith which congregations and local churches in areas influenced by Europe have inherited. For more than four centuries, this theology was functioning. We may deplore it or we may admire it, but this theology did something. It gave a sense of identity, confidence and purpose (Wolffe 1994). Moreover, it played an important part in establishing Christian faith in almost every nation on earth (Stanley 1990). We may sometimes be embarrassed about how this took place, but without it Christian faith would not now be in such an advantageous position to influence the history of the world.

However, this faith is no longer functional. The theology of the Empire has outlived the Empire. The Empire has gone, but its theology lingers on. Much of the modern Church is like the Israelites, going into exile with a royal kingdom theology. Faith has become a remnant, far from the glories of its greatest achievements. How can the Lord's song be sung in a strange land? How can the imperial theology still be proclaimed in a post-imperial age? However, before describing in further detail the characteristics of the religious situation today, we must examine in greater detail the content of this received power-theology. In doing so, we shall notice that it is not a recent development. Christian faith has been the partner of imperial power ever since the conversion of Constantine and the adoption of Christian faith as the official religion of the Roman Empire (Kee 1982). The developments in Britain would not have been possible without a thousand years of preparation. Moreover, since this theology in the form we have received it was shaped by Britain's aspirations and Britain's place in the world, and since those aspirations were shared by other European nations, who sometimes had a similar place in the world, wished to have one (Christensen and Hutchison (eds) 1982), or were influenced by those who did so, the British theology has many links and parallels with theological developments in other European countries. Since Europeans exported this collaborative faith in the heyday of European power, from approximately 1800 to 1939, it is not surprising that Christians nurtured in the non-European world often bring back to Europe the faith which Europe had a century ago.

The principal features of this imperial faith as it is received today are as follows:

Sin

Sin is driven out of the actual, material world into pre-historical origins, provided with a sexual or mystical transmission and a post-mundane judgement.

God

The forward dynamic of Christian faith is denied as the God in front of us becomes the God above us. Metaphysics and its accompanying hierarchy takes the place of apocalyptic with its hope of transformation (Bloch 1986, 2009).

Jesus Christ

The teaching of Jesus is reduced to a comma in the Apostles' Creed. As with the doctrine of sin, so with the person and work of Jesus, everything has become either beginning (the Nativity), ending (the Crucifixion and Resurrection) or future (the Second Coming and the Last Judgement), but rarely focuses upon the words and deeds of Jesus. In some traditions, there is a kind of concentration upon Jesus which is almost unhealthy. Jesus is no longer conceived of within the Holy Trinity, but in a sort of isolation. When Christian faith interpreted Jesus as the Second Person of the Trinity, the effect was to relativize Jesus, to regard him as relative to the Father and the Spirit, and so to emphasize the place of Jesus Christ in the mission of the whole Godhead. When this is forgotten, it becomes easier to adore Jesus in a kind of erotic manner than to obey him. We gaze upon him but rarely follow after him. The Christian mission has been turned into a personality cult of Jesus.

Salvation

Salvation is conceived of in spiritual and eternal terms. It is realized in heaven or lost in hell. Salvation is individualized and interiorized.

The Church

The centre of the life of the Church has become worship. Because of the Church's concentration upon its own life and its isolation from the mission of God that called it into being, the Church itself becomes a fetish. The theology of justice and peace is replaced by an orifice theology concerned with what comes in or out of the bodily orifices (Douglas 1996): sex, speech and sacraments. As the Eucharist becomes intrinsic rather than instrumental, church life becomes trivialized.

The Christian life

The Christian faith is conceived of in terms of truth rather than action within the mission of God, through Jesus. This leads to a preoccupation with words, ideas, revelation and authority. The emotional repertoire of the Christian emphasizes guilt for oneself rather than anger on behalf of others, while deportment is characterized by niceness rather than by committed action.

The Bible

The Bible is read in the light of the above assumptions and may thus become incomprehensible, irrelevant, ritualized and boring.

Christian education

The Christian education of children often becomes merely moralistically biblical.

Other religions

As the mission of God against injustice and for a universal community of inclusion is minimized, the consciousness of Christians is nurtured into a competitive relationship with people from other faiths.

The present situation: second phase

Although the British power theology has lost its old function and remains only in a number of fetishized fragments, the powers opposing the mission of God continue to proliferate and strengthen. The power of money has moved not only from London to New York, but already has passed beyond the control of one of the world's last remaining independent states (the USA), into a globalized form, where it exercises greater authority than ever before (Wachtel 1990; Amin 1997; Martin and Schumann 1997). A money-curtain has been erected around the rich two-sevenths of the world, and the character of the Christian tradition continues to evolve within the perspectives of reality that life within this enclosure creates. Money is worshipped as God, and God is worshipped as money (Hull 1996, 1997a). The most energetic forms of the new power-and-money theology may be found in the United States, which as the most powerful nation in the world today is able to offer the context within which this sort of theology can still function (Stoll 1982; Diamond 1989; Barkun 1994). The contrast between the relative vigour of Christian faith in the United States and the languid, nostalgic and exhausted form which it often takes in Britain, is to be accounted for in terms of the different positions in the history of global economics occupied by these two nations.

We now see that the residue of the British imperial theology begins to take on a new function that is mainly unconscious. Since the fragments masquerade as genuine Christian faith, and are taken to be so by many British Christians, the mask of British theology now functions at least sometimes and to some extent as a protection against facing the reality of genuine encounter with the mission of God and its implications. This is actually a less healthy situation than the previous one. The relationship between the imperial theology and the place of Britain in the nineteenth-century world was positive – the two realities, faith and world were mutually supportive and this mutuality was consciously realized and spoken about.

Today, however, Christian faith as the remnant of a past reality has a negative relationship towards the modern world of capital and power. Rather than supporting the Church and the gospel in pursuing the mission of God, the theological fragments act as a kind of collective anaesthesia, existing in a dreamlike state of nostalgic self-deception. It functions in the service of the money-God to obstruct and prevent Christian faith from reclaiming its calling to serve the mission of God. It is because of this negative, substitutionary dream-like quality that contemporary Christian faith in Britain tends to become a fetish, whereas the genuinely functioning, living, imperial theology of a century ago was not a fetish but an ideology.

The theology of resistance

Did no one challenge the growth of the collaboration between the Christian faith in Britain and Britain's search for powerful identity? Yes, there were continual protests and challenges. One of the most striking movements of protest took place during the period 1630 to 1662, the period of the first British overseas colonies and the Civil War. The community at Little Gidding, gathered around Nicholas Ferrar (1592–1637) (Williams (ed.) 1970) and the leader of the Diggers' Movement, Gerrard Winstanley (c.1609–60) (Winstanley 1973; Bradstock 1997), are two outstanding examples. There are interesting parallels between Winstanley's theology and the Minjung and liberation theologies of South Korea and Latin America today.

The movement initiated by John Wesley (1703–91) in the eighteenth century can be interpreted as a massive popular protest on behalf of the poor and the marginalized, against the power theology that had been re-established early in the eighteenth century, following the upheavals of the previous period. Although the Arminianism of Wesley was not new, in its context it represented an explosion of energy for the inclusive community of universal love, the pursuit of which is the mission of God.

As one example of the later influence of Methodism as providing a counter-theology, we could consider the Methodist Movement for the rights of agricultural labourers in East Anglia between 1872 and 1896 (Scotland 1981). In their effort to articulate a gospel theology that would empower the labourers in their struggle, the Methodist preachers and organizers used the expression 'temporal salvation' as a limitation and criticism of 'eternal salvation', which was being used to defer the expectations of justice from this world to the next.

The next example of the protest theology of justice and human rights to be mentioned here is that of John William Colenso (1814–83), Bishop of Natal, who became famous for his courageous attempt to bring biblical study into line with nineteenth-century developments in the natural and social sciences. Even more significant, however, was his anthropological work, especially his re-statement of the purpose of Christian missions and his struggle on behalf of the rights of the black people of South Africa against the encroaching demands of British power. In spite of the opposition which his ministry aroused from his fellow bishops in southern Africa and England, John William Colenso may be regarded as a prophetic figure, one of the earliest champions of liberty and a precursor of liberation theology (Morris 1973; Parsons 1997).

Next, we must mention the Christian Socialist Movement associated with the names of Frederick Denison Maurice (1805–72), Charles Kingsley (1819–75), John Ruskin (1819–1900) and others. Maurice lost his Chair of Theology in King's College, London in 1853 because of his refusal to accept the doctrine of eternal punishment in hell, and he had a profound impact upon the emergence of a liberating political education for working people (Maurice 1968).

Finally, mention must be made of the various expressions of the 'everlasting Gospel' of the mission of God in our own century, including the work of Archbishop William Temple (1881–1944), especially his influence upon the creation of the Welfare State (1968). We should also consider the many movements for theological reform in recent decades (Ambler and Haslam (eds) 1980).

Contributions of enormous significance to the revitalization of Christian faith as an instrument of God's mission are being made today by new theological movements outside Europe: Latin American Liberation Theology, South Korean Minjung Theology, Indian Dalit Theology, while movements within the European and North American cultural circles, such as Black Theology and Feminist Theology, are making very important contributions to our general awareness of the inner nature and purpose of the Christian traditions in America and England, so virulent in the one, so decadent in the other.

In spite of their significance as examples of theology outside the European power-tradition, it is not possible to make a simple application of these non-European theologies to the situation in Europe. There is ample scope for renewal in the critical, protesting, prophetic theology which has always lived on in Europe itself. There is a need to develop these resources in order to recover a fresh sense of Christian mission in Britain today.

A reconstructed theological contribution to God's mission

I will now make some positive suggestions for the reconstruction of the aspects of the imperial theology noted above.

Sin

The traditional doctrine of sin, which concentrates upon the salvation and sanctification of the sinner, should be supported but qualified by a doctrine that places equal emphasis upon the sufferings of those who are the recipients and victims of sin. At present, the Christian approach towards evil in the world is lopsided in favour of forgiveness for the actors, rather than compensation and justice for the victims (Park 1993).

God

Increasingly God will be found not in the discussions about meaning that have characterized Western theological reflection, but through participation and involvement in theological action on behalf of the emerging community of inclusive love. God will become real, when the knowledge of God is pursued in the works of justice and peace (Jer. 22.14–16).

Jesus Christ

Rather than merely adoring Jesus, Christian education should encourage discipleship of him. The nations are to be instructed in the things that Jesus has taught (Matt. 28.20). The principle features of this teaching are the great reversal between the weak and the powerful, the rich and the poor and the breaking out everywhere of the community of inclusive love. The death of Jesus Christ will be understood as indicating and exemplifying the presence of God amidst human sufferings, and this will move Christian disciples towards the discovery of God in the midst of those who suffer. Moreover, Jesus died as a faithful witness to what he had taught and done. Thus his death sanctifies all the movements which seek to establish the community of inclusive love, the protest movements against oppression and injustice. Jesus is the archetype, representative and instigator of God's action for deliverance and is thus the founder and finisher of faith (Heb. 12.2). Jesus is the crucified people (Song 1996).

The Holy Trinity

The doctrine of the Holy Trinity will be seen as a witness and a symbol of the unfinished character of the Christian understanding of the community of inclusive love, since the full meaning of the Holy Trinity is still veiled in the future. Moreover, the perichoretic unity of the three persons will inspire and activate Christians into all forms of social solidarity. The Greek theologians of the fourth century spoke of the Holy Trinity as a perichoresis, an ecstatic circular dance. The Holy Trinity will be increasingly understood as the incorporation of human suffering into the divine experience and as thus motivating and justifying a similar involvement on the part of the Church. The essential openness of the Holy Trinity, as representing God's self-disclosure in history and for history, will initiate attitudes of openness towards other historical impressions of the Ultimate (Hull 1995).

Salvation

Salvation as the eternal well-being of the soul or person of the individual, will be modified and enriched by understanding salvation as everything which overcomes the powers which are hostile to the community of inclusive love, and everything which encourages the flourishing of human life and all life in creation (Jantzen 1998, pp. 156–70).

The Christian life

Justification by love will modify and enrich a one-sided emphasis upon justification by faith.

The Bible

As the ambiguity of the Bible is increasingly recognized, and its patriarchal assumptions are grappled with, the Bible will come to have a new relevance as conversation rather than as a reification of the word of God (Kwok 1995).

Other religions

Christian faith will be seen as the partner of God's other saving projects, and the futile and competitive relationships between the world religions that have characterized centuries of European domination will come to an end.

The interpretation of faith today

In seeking to interpret the meaning of contemporary faith in Britain it may be helpful to use as a model Sigmund Freud's theory of the interpretation of dreams (1991). As we have seen, the problem is that we are working in the context of a non-functioning post-imperial theology that is the implicit collaborator with the forces which oppose the emergence of the community of inclusive love. Freud distinguished the latent dream from the manifest dream and the later elaborated dream. The latent dream is the real dream, the dream which expresses the desires that are normally concealed and repressed. We may compare this with Britain's growing desire for identity, security and prosperity in the world.

The latent dream, however, remains latent; it is prevented from coming into the conscious life by the ideals of Christian faith, which resist the capitulation of the ego to such base desires, to those whose identity has been moulded by Christian faith and who wish to be consistent with it. The acknowledgement of such selfish desire would bring about a huge conflict in the mind. The manifest dream is the result, a combination of Christian fragments with more primal desires. This is the dream as we remember it upon waking up, our conscious self-understanding, the acceptable self. The older elements in the dream which served the primordial desires have been to some extent censored out, and one only remembers them along with the partly Christianized fragments. This is what we have left in the Christian religious folk-consciousness of Britain today. We will not be able to understand many contemporary manifestations of Christian consciousness, unless we realize that they are to be accounted for as the residual fragments of what was once the latent dream which has been partly repressed by contact with Christianity.

The censorship, which is the name Freud gave to the energies that prevent the latent dream from coming into consciousness, is the prophetic tradition of Christian faith which works against the collaboration of Christianity with tribal desire, a prophetic resistance which has never been entirely silenced. However, those early voices of protest and opposition were operating without the assistance of the social sciences. Before Christian theology had received the penetrating illuminations offered by Karl Marx, Friedrich Nietzsche, Sigmund Freud, Ernst Bloch, Paul Ricœur, Michel Foucault, Jacques Derrida and many others, it was more difficult for Christians (even under the pressures of modernity) to understand, analyse and respond to the driving forces behind and beneath the religious surface of Britain. Their attention was, on the whole, fastened upon the content of faith rather than its processes and its functions.

Finally, the dream that is the product of what Freud called secondary elaboration is the dream as we describe it to others, or perhaps to ourselves. The incoherent fragments of the manifest dream are bound together into a more-or-less coherent narrative, the mysterious gaps left by the censorship are smoothed over with little explanatory phrases and the result is a kind of story. As the unity of the latent dream was disrupted by the challenge of a Christian faith dedicated to justice, the latent dream was fragmented, driven into the unconscious, and what remained were fragments, the manifest dream of certain aspects of post-imperial Christian consciousness. Finally, these fragments were synthesized, systematized, and fused together again in a coherent narrative which became the dream of secondary elaboration, e.g. the hymns of Isaac Watts or the prosperity gospel of contemporary Christian life in wealthy countries. We may find this secondary elaboration in many contemporary sermons and prayers since it represents the sedimented Christian consciousness of 500 years of power.

Educational practice for the reconstruction of relevant Christian consciousness today must confront the problems of self-deception, both individual and collective. In the short-term, modifying the money-curtain may appear to be contrary to British and European interests. This is only one example of the ways in which moving Britain towards a historic mission on behalf of suffering humanity in order to establish an ecumenical community of justice and reconciliation may be seen to be contrary to British interests. Since it is difficult to combine this insight with one's continued self-respect and moral integrity, the mechanisms of self-deception are in continual use. This is particularly true for people within the Christian tradition, for whom the options of a hardened secularized hedonism or a defiant hypocrisy are not so easily available. Self-deception is one of the ways that communities try to forget, and the Church as the custodian of the subversive memory of Jesus (Metz 1980, pp. 88–99) must always struggle against its own self-deception.

This means that Christian education, whether for ministry or for lay discipleship, must reappraise the history of theology in Europe and North America. This can best be done within the context of the social sciences, for the character of this theological tradition can only be understood in relationship to the geo-political and social/economic situation of Britain, in Europe and the world, and is fundamental to the re-education of faith (Hull 2002). By way of contrast, the emerging non-European theologies should also be studied. These should not be added to the theological curriculum as a special study, but should be thoroughly integrated into the study of systematic, biblical and historical theology.

A central place must be given in this reconstruction to the study of sin, qualified and enriched as described above, because this represents the Church's struggle to comprehend and oppose the structures of evil. The re-education of faith has been seriously hampered by a deficient doctrine of sin. This action/study will involve evaluation and participant action in the realities of such sin, as expressed through poverty, the oppression of children and women, and racism, both in Britain and abroad.

The hymn books must be purged of the relics of the Victorian theology of power, such as 'Hark how the heavenly anthem drowns, all music but its own.' This represents the British theology of power. The gospel of redeeming love does not drown out all music but its own, since it does not seek to oppress and dominate. The music of God is a receptive, listening harmony that penetrates and elevates all the music of the world. On the other hand, churches must avoid the dangers of the Jesus-fetish music as well. Christian education must learn to read the Bible again as representing the cry of the oppressed people and as God's redemptive action on their behalf.

Finally, the theological re-education of the churches cannot be done through talking, words and study. Only through thoughtful participation in action on behalf of the community of inclusive love will the dreaming theology of the post-imperial Church be dissipated.

Conclusions

The Christian tradition in Europe and North America today faces a critical choice. The medieval concept of Christendom was replaced by the modern concept of Christianity. This was an understanding of the Christian tradition as being a systematic structure of belief forming a world religion in competitive relations with other similar religious systems. As such, Christianity was para-phenomenal, being the reified expression on the plane of ideas of the emerging global competition between Europe and the rest of the world. The period of Christianity is now coming to an end. The future lies with what we might call

Christian-ness (Panikkar 1988), a revival of ethical discipleship to Jesus inspired by biblical faith in God as sender, sent and sending, the Triune God in redemptive action on behalf of God's world. However, the passage of Christianity into Christian-ness is not uncontested. A shrewd and hardened form of Christianity is also emerging. This adopts even more competitive and rigid forms of life as its dreamlike facade is unmasked. We may describe this as Christian religionism (Hull 1996a), and it serves the money-God, just as Christian-ness serves the living God.

Is there a future for the Church? There will continue to be a future for the Church as the instrument of Christian faith as long as the Church is true to the Christian faith and Christian faith is faithful to the mission of God. However, one might imagine another future for the Church, a future in which it becomes the shrewd and hardened collaborator with the powers of financial oppression. Then the Church would no longer be the Church.

12

Towards a Theology of Prophetic Action

In the first part of this chapter I will outline a biblical theology of Christian action. In the second part I will approach the same subject from the point of view of Christian spirituality and personal discipleship. At the end of each part I will briefly discuss some possible objections.

Mission-shaped and kingdom-focused

Elsewhere, I have distinguished between a church-shaped mission and a mission-shaped Church (2006). This refers to the difference between a mission which is essentially shaped by the interests and concerns of the Christian churches and a Church which, forgetful of itself, is ready to perceive and respond to the mission of God. The expression 'kingdom-focused' refers to the focus of the Church's activity as being not upon itself but upon the coming of the Kingdom of God. The expression 'kingdom of God' refers to that heavenly and earthly reality in which the purposes of God are realized. It also refers to the teaching of Jesus and the proclamation of the early Church, and it is also a symbol of the utopian future.[1] Christian faith is best understood in its messianic aspect as an agent of the now and future kingdom and Church as an agent of Christian faith for the same ultimate purpose. In this sequence, only the kingdom of God, which is the object of the mission of God, is self-authenticating; both Christian faith and Church are instrumental to the kingdom.

It is often said that Christian faith invites us into a double relationship, one vertical and the other horizontal. The vertical is said to be our individual or collective relationship to God, while the horizontal is said to represent our relationship with each other (Gnanakan 1993, p. 208).[2] It is sometimes said that the vertical empowers the horizontal, or motivates it, as is suggested by the rather old-fashioned expression 'social responsibility' that indicates that the Church in its vertical relation to God must not forget that it also has a responsibility to others. I have even heard preachers use the shape of the cross to illustrate this

---

1 Paul Tillich interprets the kingdom of God and eternal life as the two symbols of Christian hope (1963, pp. 297–9).

2 Gnanakan rightly emphasizes that '[a] righteous vertical relationship is demonstrated in righteous horizontal relationships' (1993, p. 92), but he continues: 'Reconciliation must begin with the vertical dimension, with people made right with God'(p. 147), thus indicating his failure to grasp the radical nature of horizontal transcendence. Gnanakan's source for this distinction is Visser't Hooft, 'The Mandate of the Ecumenical Movement', Stockholm 1925 reprinted in Goodall (ed) 1968, pp. 313–23.

idea. The vertical arm, it is said, points heavenward, while the outstretched arms embrace all humanity. It is something like this that stands behind the concept of a church-shaped mission, where the Church has become the location for a vertical transcendence, or the guardian of an other-worldly revelation, so that the horizontal dimension becomes an extra, albeit a necessary, one.[3] I shall offer a reconstruction of this duality in order to provide a more secure focus upon the kingdom of God leading to a genuinely mission-shaped Church.

Knowledge of God in the Bible

The biblical revelation announces the good news that the vertical has been collapsed into the horizontal. In other words, biblical faith in its prophetic form, that tradition which is most significant for the mission of God, transforms the experience of transcendence from the remote to the near, from the abstract to the concrete.

We may distinguish between three kinds of transcendence: vertical transcendence, horizontal transcendence and future transcendence. Vertical transcendence is hierarchical. Like Jack's beanstalk or Jacob's ladder it creates two worlds, an earthly one and a superior, spiritual one. Horizontal transcendence means that we are confronted by absolute otherness, by the presence of the other person, the fellow human being, whose need places upon me an unqualified demand such that in that demand I find myself in the presence of God. The third kind, the transcendence of futurity, means that beyond the need of the brother or sister before whom I stand there lies, outside my reach, beyond my grasp, the brothers of that brother, and the sisters of that sister, stretching out to the whole of humanity and indeed to all creation now and to come. In this understanding of future transcendence, God is the lure of history, the One who calls to me from the far side of the horizon. The Bible tells the story of the God who came down to earth, the One who became God-with-us, in such a way that the transcendence of height has become transmuted into that of presence, in horizontality, and into the extension of the horizontal into the horizon, the future of the coming kingdom of God.

The answer given by Jesus to the question about which was the greatest commandment was '"You must love the Lord your God with all your heart, all your soul, and all your mind." This is the first and greatest commandment. A second is equally important: "Love your neighbour as yourself"' (Matt. 22.37–39, NLT). Most of the English translations render verse 39 as 'the second is like it'. The word translated 'equally important' or 'alongside it' (*The Message*) is *homoia*. This is the word attributed to John the Baptist, when he said that the person who had two tunics should share with the person who had none and

---

3 Willem Visser't Hooft was seeking for the right balance between the two dimensions when he said 'The whole secret of the Christian faith is that it is man-centred [*sic*] because it is God-centred. We cannot speak of Christ as the man for others without speaking of him as the man who came from God and who lived for God' (1968, p. 318), but Jesus Christ was a man, a human person and in that person we see God. Thus the whole secret of Christian faith is that it is God-centred because it is person-centred.

the one who has food should do 'the same'. The first husband of the woman referred to in Matthew 22.23–33 died, and the second, third and all the rest did 'the same'. This is the paradox of the two great commandments, one is 'greatest' yet the other is 'the same'. How can this paradox be resolved?

Perhaps someone might wonder why the text does not read *homooia* (of the same substance), bearing in mind the distinction between *homoousion* and *homoiousion*, which became so significant in the fourth century. At that time, in the debate between Arianism and what was becoming orthodoxy, *homoousion* came to mean that which is numerically or ontologically identical, whereas *homoiousion* was regarded as meaning only similar. This is why *homoousion* emerged as the orthodox description of the relation between the Father and the Son. But this distinction only emerged in the course of the controversy, to meet a particular conceptual crisis; before this, the two words were virtually identical in their meaning.[4]

The word *homoousia* is not found in the New Testament, and it would have made no sense to have used it in the later meaning it came to have, in any of the passages we are discussing.[5] The lawyer who was told to go and do *homoia*, the same kind of thing, could not do exactly the same unless he waited by the Jericho road for a Samaritan to be mugged in identical circumstances. The third brother could not die with exactly the same death as the second simply because he was the third and not the second. But they both died, and their deaths were the same. If we introduce the later distinction, we may say that the love of the transcendent is not ontologically identical with the love of the immediate, just as the love of ultimacy is not identical with the love of penultimacy, but since one is the way to the other, since one is fulfilled in the other, they are tantamount to the same thing. In practice, for all intents and purposes, they are the same.[6]

Thus the paradox is resolved: the first commandment is ultimately the greatest, but for all practical purposes, the second is the same. The vertical has no independent existence as far as human beings are concerned; it has conceptual but not practical independence. Indeed it is only approached by that which is similar to it. Nevertheless, the ultimate remains greatest.[7]

---

4 Lampe (1961) refers to Athanasius using the word *homoios* to assert the likeness of the humanity of Christ to that of general humanity (p. 954) and also points out that the use of the word was attacked on the grounds that the 'distinction between Father and Son is thereby abolished' and that as late as the first century one word was being used to explain the other.

5 Note that the word *homoousion* is not listed in Liddell and Scott 1968.

6 Liddell and Scott (1968, p. 1224) indicate that *homoios* meant having the same rank or station and refers to Plotinus in the third century CE using the word to describe angles which were equal. It is also used in mathematics to describe the square of a number as being the product of two equal factors.

7 Karl Barth has an extensive discussion of the meaning of the two great commandments in his *Church Dogmatics* I.2 (1956, pp. 381–454). Although a quick reading might suggest that my interpretation is more radical than that of Barth, a careful study of these pages shows that Barth rejects the idea that the vertical is completely collapsed into the horizontal mainly because '[w]e cannot believe in our neighbour', and thus it would be misleading '[t]o confuse or confound the two demands' (p. 413). Moreover, Barth's eschatological interpretation means that love of the neighbour takes place in this world whereas love of God is eternal. However, love of the neighbour is 'the inevitable outward side of that which inwardly is love to God'

The origins of the prophetic tradition

In this teaching Jesus stands squarely in the prophetic tradition. In the Hebrew Bible there is to be no image or likeness made of God (Exod. 20.4) and yet God made human beings in God's own image and likeness (Gen. 1.27). Does this mean that human beings are to be worshipped as God? Or that images of the human may be objects of worship? Certainly not! Then how are we to explain the paradox? There could be no independent image of God precisely, because the revelation of God came only through the human other (Miranda 1977, pp. 36–44). Nor could images of the human be made for worship, for what had become holy was not the image of the human but the image of God in the human such that God was available in no other form or image save through God's image in the human. God had become present only through inter-subjectivity, and through inter-subjectivity qualified in a particular manner, the way of justice.

Thus over and over again, the God of the Bible is described as the God who loves justice.

'The LORD is known by his justice.' (Ps. 9.16)
'The LORD is righteous; he loves justice.' (Ps. 11.7)
'The LORD works righteousness and justice for all that are oppressed.' (Ps. 103.6)

The references to God as the God of justice not only refer to the character of God, but to what God does and thus to where and how God is to be found and served. The Bible does not merely announce an abstract ethical quality in God, but reveals a God who executes justice and who requires justice.

It is sometimes said that the first part of the Decalogue (Exod. 20.3–11) represents the human duty toward God while the second part (Exod. 20.12–17) is duty to our fellow humans. But this must surely be to divide where no division is to be found. The whole of the two tables is based upon its preface, in which God is the redeeming and liberating Saviour, who brought Israel up out of Egypt, out of slavery (Exod. 20.2). It is as the emancipator of slaves that God graciously gives the covenant (Brueggemann 1997, p. 25).

The popular impression that the Ten Commandments are a series of abstract demands rather than a consequence of the mercy of the liberating God may have been affected by the fact that in the 1662 *Book of Common Prayer* the text is introduced by the words 'God spake these words, and said, I am the Lord thy God: Thou shalt have none other gods but me' (p.237), thus omitting the crucial words, 'which have brought thee out of the land of Egypt, out of the house of bondage'.[8]

(p. 412) and 'we cannot love God, without this loving, as it were, manifesting itself' (p. 413). In this comment 'this love' refers to love of the neighbour. This is quite consistent with my own comment 'the vertical has no independent existence as far as human beings are concerned', i.e. as far as our lives in this world are to be lived.

8 In the 1926 revision of the Prayer Book the words were still omitted, but in the *Alternative Service Book* (1980), there is an alternative which places the words 'who brought you out of the land of Egypt, out of the house of bondage' in brackets, a feature which is also found in *Common Worship*. The effect of this is to minimize the role of the liberating God and to emphasize God as the general law-giver.

In the Deuteronomic version of the origin of the Decalogue its ethical foundation is emphasized. This is done through declaring the character of God as the lover of foreigners.

> For the LORD your God is God of gods and Lord of lords, the great God, mighty and awesome, who shows no partiality and accepts no bribes. He defends the cause of the fatherless and the widow, and loves the alien, giving him food and clothing. And you are to love those who are aliens, for you yourselves were aliens in Egypt. (Deut. 10.17–19)

The implication of our own liberation is to set others free; indeed, it is through recognizing the demand of the oppressed other that God, the great God, is both recognized and obeyed. If God is not worshipped in this way, God becomes just another religious idol, but God is to be worshipped in this way and thus there can be no making of graven images.

Whenever the cult of worship and sacrifice tried to approach God without passing through the demand of the other for justice, it was regarded by the prophets as being blasphemous and an insult to God.

> I can't stand your religious meetings.
> I'm fed up with your conferences and conventions.
> I want nothing to do with your religion projects,
> your pretentious slogans and goals.
> I'm sick of your fund-raising schemes,
> your public relations and image making.
> I've had all I can take of your noisy ego-music.
> When was the last time you sang to me?
> Do you know what I want?
> I want justice—oceans of it.
> I want fairness—rivers of it.
> That's what I want. That's all I want. (Amos 5.21–24, *The Message*)

Isaiah shows us that when the vertical is honoured apart from the horizontal, it becomes trivial and corrupt.

> 'The multitude of your sacrifices –
> what are they to me?' says the Lord.
> 'I have more than enough of burnt offerings,
> of rams and the fat of fattened animals;
> I have no pleasure
> in the blood of bulls and lambs and goats.
>
> When you come to appear before me,
> who has asked this of you,
> this trampling of my courts?
>
> Stop bringing meaningless offerings!
> Your incense is detestable to me.

New Moons, Sabbaths and convocations –
I cannot bear your evil assemblies.

Your New Moon festivals and your appointed feasts
my soul hates.
They have become a burden to me;
I am weary of bearing them.

When you spread out your hands in prayer,
I will hide my eyes from you;
even if you offer many prayers,
I will not listen.
Your hands are full of blood;

wash and make yourselves clean.
Take your evil deeds
out of my sight!
Stop doing wrong,

learn to do right!
Seek justice,
encourage the oppressed.
Defend the cause of the fatherless,
plead the case of the widow.' (Isa. 1.11–17)

In Hosea we find the same bold affirmation. Reading the book as a whole, it
could be said that Hosea teaches that the vertical has become corrupt because
the horizontal has been ignored; it could also be said that the way to the vertical has been blocked by failure to observe justice in the horizontal. Israel has
become faithless in her religious life in that the character of the covenant God
has not been acknowledged.

For I desire mercy, not sacrifice,
and acknowledgment of God rather than burnt offerings. (Hos. 6.6)

They will not pour out wine offerings to the Lord,
nor will their sacrifices please him.
Such sacrifices will be to them like the bread of mourners;
all who eat them will be unclean.
This food will be for themselves;
it will not come into the temple of the Lord. (Hos. 9.4)

Sow for yourselves righteousness,
reap the fruit of unfailing love,
and break up your unploughed ground;
for it is time to seek the Lord,
until he comes
and showers righteousness on you. (Hos. 10.12)

It might appear that the teaching of the prophets was no more than the demand for a balance between the vertical and the horizontal and a claim that without a just dealing with the horizontal the vertical would be imperfect. The truth of inter-subjective transcendence, however, is more radical.

> The rubric of covenant thus requires a departure from the more conventional philosophical categories of immanence and transcendence and the entire Cartesian temptation to dualism, for covenant is not balancing of transcendence and immanence, but is a complete rejection of a dualism that is too tidy and free of risk (Brueggemann 1997, p. 30).

One of the clearest statements of the knowledge of God in the whole Bible is in Jeremiah 22.15–16. The prophet is attacking the luxurious lifestyle of the king, and comparing him unfavourably with his father, the great and good king Josiah.

> 'Does it make you a king
> to have more and more cedar?
> Did not your father have food and drink?
> He did what was right and just,
> so all went well with him.
>
> He defended the cause of the poor and needy,
> and so all went well.
> Is that not what it means to know me?'
> declares the Lord.

This, the prophet says, is what it is to know God: to defend the oppressed and the helpless.

> Note well these lines do not say that judging the poor and needy is the cause and knowing Yahweh the consequence; nor, conversely, that judging the poor and needy is the consequence and knowing Yahweh the cause. Rather the two are equated. (p. 613)

We may conclude that the prophetic tradition attacked a religion-shaped mission in the name of a mission-shaped, or a kingdom of God-shaped religion.

Jesus and the prophetic tradition

The same teaching is typical of Jesus. Access to the vertical is impossible unless the horizontal is first recognized.

> Therefore, if you are offering your gift at the altar and there remember that your brother has something against you, leave your gift there in front of the altar. First go and be reconciled to your brother; then come and offer your gift. (Matt. 5.23–24)

There is no point in worshipping God if you are not at peace with your brother or sister. Human reconciliation is a condition of access to the divine. There is no point in praying for forgiveness unless we forgive others.

> Forgive us our debts,
> as we also have forgiven our debtors. (Matt. 6.12)

> This is how my heavenly Father will treat each of you unless you forgive your brother from your heart. (Matt. 18.35)

There is a precise reciprocity between the human and the divine. Forgive us as we forgive. Of course, God remains God, and sometimes the ultimate breaks through disregarding the failure of the penultimate. Jesus prayed that God would forgive those who nailed him to the cross not because they had forgiven him, but because they did not know what they were doing. But in all ordinary human relations, divine/human similarity is the rule of grace.

It is through the demand for justice that the kingdom is declared (Luke 4.18–19). The central theme of the teaching of Jesus, the great reversal, announces the blessing upon the poor and the disaster to fall upon the rich (6.20–6). He fulfilled the spirit of what Mary had sung about, by casting down the mighty from their seats, filling the hungry with good things, and sending the rich empty away (1.52–3). Jesus interpreted the meaning of following him as consisting of a life lived within the sphere of the great reversal, the demand for justice in inter-human relations. The rich young ruler went away sorrowful when Jesus invited him to get rid of his possessions in favour of the poor (18.18–26). Jesus makes radical and concrete the commandments of the law and then interprets their meaning as relationship to himself, but only when the demands of inter-subjectivity have been recognized. In the same way, Zacchaeus, confronted by the gracious acceptance of Jesus, put right the injustices that he had carried out in his professional conduct (19.1–10). There is a contrast between the man who brought Jesus to his home having recognized his social obligations and the man who went away sorrowful to his own home, not able to accept the demands of radical discipleship.

Typical of the prophetic understanding of God was the scribe of Mark 12, who responded to the reply of Jesus about the greatest commandment.

> 'Well said, teacher,' the man replied. 'You are right in saying that God is one and there is no other but him. To love him with all your heart, with all your understanding and with all your strength, and to love your neighbour as yourself is more important than all burnt offerings and sacrifices.' (Mark 12.32–33)

In Matthew's Gospel, the prophetic principal that mercy is better than sacrifice is twice referred to. In Matthew 9.17, Jesus defends his ministry to the marginalized by referring to it, and in Matthew 12.7 he defends his disciples against the demands of religious legalism.

In discussing the God of the Hebrew Bible, we saw how in the absence of God, justice, extended to the image of God in the other person, became the way of

God. At first, in the Garden of Eden, God came visiting like a friend, but after the murder of Cain the resumption of human trust became the principal direction of the will of God and this, as we have seen, implied the absence of the explicit image of God. So it is in the New Testament as well. The truth that the biblical God is known in inter-subjectivity reaches its fulfilment in the person of Jesus Christ, in relation with whom his first followers found God (John 20.28, 1.1; Mark 1.1). When God was found in the face of Jesus Christ it was not the supreme anomaly of biblical religion but its epitome, it encapsulates all the other tendencies.

In the absence of Jesus, he is to be found through the open acceptance and reception of others. 'Whoever receives a child in my name receives me' (Matt. 18.5). The way to Jesus Christ is through an open reception offered to children, and the whole logic of the inter-subjective structure is brought out clearly in the parallel in Mark and Luke: 'Whoever receives a child like this in my name receives me; and whoever receives me, receives not me but the One who sent me' (Mark 9.37; Luke 9.48). In Luke 10.16 the logic is the same although the interpersonal direction is reversed, now the reference is not to receiving but to being received: 'He who listens to you listens to me; he who rejects you rejects me; but he who rejects me rejects him who sent me.' In Matthew an additional mediation is introduced, that of the angel who represents the child before God, but the logic is the same, since God remains the Father of Jesus, and access is through a child. 'See that you do not look down on one of these little ones. For I tell you that their angels in heaven always see the face of my Father in heaven' (Matt. 18.10). The disciples of Jesus are to find him again and again in the face of human deprivation and poverty, wherever there is human loneliness or sickness, there he is to be found (Matt. 25.37–40). The remarkable thing about this last saying is that access to Jesus Christ is secure through the needy other even in ignorance thus the cognitive aspect of recognition is transmuted into ethical action.

This is the essential message of the Minjung theology of South Korea. As Professor Kim of the South Korean Church said to a group of people invited to meet him in Birmingham some years ago, 'This is the teaching of the Minjung theology: Jesus Christ was born among the poor. If you would find him, there you must seek him.'

This meaning of the absence and the presence of Jesus continues throughout the rest of the New Testament. Examples may be found in 1 John 3.17, 3.18, 4.20–21; James 1.27, 2.14–16, 3.9, 5.4. It is worth pointing out that in James 2.8 the commandment which Jesus described as being equivalent to the love of God is described as 'the royal law', and that this central tradition of the New Testament is squarely in the prophetic tradition as illustrated by the anti-iconic reference in James 3.9.

The transcendence of otherness

Let us return for a moment to the saying by Jesus about the greatest commandment and the one like it. Jesus says that we are to love our neighbour not as the neighbour loves us but as we love ourselves. The relationship between love of self and love of neighbour is not reciprocal but parallel; nor does the text say that we are to love our neighbour in so far as our neighbour loves God, nor in so far as we ourselves love God. The commandment places upon each one of us an unqualified, one-directional, non-theological obligation. It is in these characteristics that transcendence is to be found. Emmanuel Levinas puts it like this. '[T]he idea-of-the-Infinite-in-me – or my relation to God – comes to me in the concreteness of my relation to the other . . . in the sociality which is my responsibility for the neighbor' (1998, p. xiv).

Levinas goes on to say that we certainly will not discover it by looking upon the human face as some kind of emblem or picture of divine creativity. Nevertheless, it is when I contemplate the origin of this that 'the word God comes to the tip of one's tongue', and it is in this sense that the idea of the infinite is placed within me as a prophetic event, that is, because my responsibility to the other is unqualified and is not reciprocal (p. xv). Levinas concludes 'responsibility for the Other is transcendence' (p. 13).

Because I am placed under the command of the infinite which comes to me through otherness, I am not free to decide whether or not I shall respond. Responsibility for the other is not a product of my freedom. I am thus hostage to the other. In the same way, we are not to have the luxury of choice as to which neighbour we will select for the exercise of our responsibility. I do not designate the neighbour for whom I will be responsible, but I say, '[H]ere I am' (p. 72).

This, of course, is not a proof of God's existence. It is not a proof of anything. It is a trace of ultimacy found in the penultimate. 'Our relation to God is itself real only as it shows itself in relation to our neighbours' (MacMurray 1965, p. 72).

Modernity and the loss of biblical otherness

It is easy to see why the significance of this biblical tradition has been so misunderstood and minimized in our culture. Possessive individualism (Macpherson 1964), which has been the central characteristic of the Western worldview since the seventeenth century, tends to exaggerate the character of human beings as consuming units, and the place of mutuality has been overtaken by an emphasis upon the interior life, heightened by the continually growing expectation of freedom and multiple choice.

It is true that the modern status of human rights has been enormously important in the protection of the vulnerable and of all citizens in the presence of the state and other powers, but this theology of the covenant does not refer to the other as having rights but to myself as placed under a responsibility of guardianship for my fellow human being. True, conservative newspapers are fond of saying, rather resentfully, that we have emphasized rights at the expense of responsibilities, but they are always speaking of the responsibilities of the other upon whom rights have been conferred, not of my unqualified responsibility to the other in a realm which transcends rights. Levinas sums this up by saying that in this way one is 'ousted from his interiority as an ego' (1998, p. 73). Is it any surprise that in a society built upon the stimulation of the consuming ego, such an ethic is seldom heard? In such an ethic the identity of the self does not reside in possessions. 'Then he said to them, "Watch out! Be on your guard against all kinds of greed; life does not consist in an abundance of possessions"' (Luke

12.15). So Levinas remarks to listen to the cry of the desolate is to 'walk among reasons that "reason" does not know' (p. 77). I am torn out of my habitat, stripped of my comfort zone by the fact that I am not innocent of what happens to my neighbour.

We see then that the logic of the word God implies ethical intentionality on my part. This is not in the first place an intention to worship God because one must resort 'to the notion of a horizontal religion, abiding on man's earth, and which ought to be substituted for the vertical one which departs for the Heavens in order to refer to the world' (p. 105).

It is important to recognize that in this horizontal relationship, the space between, or the distance, is always preserved whereas if I love myself in the neighbour this distance disappears. The parallelism of self and other implies relationship not fusion. This has the effect of making religion objective. After all, interiority can only be memory, given the 'darkness of the lived moment' (Bloch 1986 vol. 3, p 1178), and if I live for my inner Christian experience I am involved in a kind of religious memorial reconstruction, but if I acknowledge the intentionality of faith in God toward the human other, I am dragged out of my feelings and memories, out of the salvation of my soul into my love for my brother and sister. Moreover, to realize the full force of this it is necessary to grasp the fact that it goes beyond dialogue (Levinas 1969, pp. 68–9). I am responsible for the other whether or not the other is interested in or capable of dialogue with me. This is clearly evident in the Christian concept of love, and at this point I part company with Levinas, whose concept of love seems to be embedded within friendship, with associations of fecundity and the erotic. The divine love which was poured out upon us in that while we were still sinners Christ died for us is not a matter of friendship, but of the God who loves even when love is not returned (Rom. 5.8; 1 John 4.10) (1969, pp. 254–5, 270–3).[9]

The mission of God is therefore to restore the brokenness of the body of humanity and to renew the face of the earth. Of this mission Israel was to be an agent, a chosen vessel, to be a light to the nations. Again and again, however, Israel assumed that it was the object of God's mission. This is why the Deuteronomist had to remind the people that they had not been chosen because they were a great and mighty people but because they were the 'smallest of all nations' (Deut. 7.7). Similarly, Amos had to warn the people of Israel that they were in danger of exaggerating the significance of their own salvation history.

'Are not you Israelites
the same to me as the Cushites?'
declares the Lord.
'Did I not bring Israel up from Egypt,
the Philistines from Caphtor
and the Arameans from Kir?' (Amos 9.7)

The history of Israel shows a tendency to change emphasis between the tribalism of Gideon and Ezra and the universalism of Ruth and Jonah. This tendency

---

9 On the other hand, Levinas also speaks of '[t]he imperative of gratuitous love, which comes to me from the face of another' (1998, p. ix).

to replace the mission of God by the welfare of the nation led finally to the destruction of the temple and of the state. That destruction was repeated in the destruction of the body of Jesus upon the cross and the total elimination of Jerusalem. It was out of these tendencies toward idolatrous self-absorption and the destruction that followed that Christian faith emerged as a new vehicle for the universal restoration, the establishment of the kingdom of God on earth as it is in heaven. The destruction and consequent absence of Jesus is referred to in John 16.7: 'But very truly I tell you, it is for your good that I am going away. Unless I go away, the Advocate will not come to you; but if I go, I will send him to you'; and 'Therefore from now on we recognize no one according to the flesh; even though we have known Christ according to the flesh, yet now we know Him in this way no longer' (2 Cor. 5.16).

Christian faith institutionalized within churches and denominations is not immune from the tendency toward self-absorption. Again and again Christian history shows that Christians have consciously or unconsciously turned away from the mission of God for justice and peace toward the propagation of their own tribalistic religion, or Christian faith has been identified with the interest of Christians and the welfare of the Church. So powerful is this tendency that it is possible to lose sight of the mission of God almost entirely and to replace it with the notion of ecclesiastical expansion. These experiences give a new and more disturbing meaning to the saying of the apostle that we preach not ourselves but Jesus Christ and him crucified.

While it is possible to divide people in Britain into the churched and the unchurched, and to see it as the principal purpose of mission to transfer as many people as possible from the latter category to the former, this distinction is not fundamental to the mission of God. If we take the biblical prophetic tradition seriously, we must say that a more fundamental distinction in the sight of God is between the rich and the poor, those at home and the aliens, those who seek for selfish power and those who set out to serve their neighbours, those who in the name of the national interest are ready to renew nuclear weapons and those who seek for peace and equality between the nations. Where do we look today to find the great reversal of which Jesus spoke? How can it be that the mission of God who wills that all people should be saved has been turned into a competitive ideology and an institution with the same survival instincts as any other institution?

So profoundly has our understanding of Christian faith been contaminated by our culture of individualism, money and power, and by the replacement of the Church as agent by the Church as object, that a biblical theology of the mission of God must give rise to many questions.

What is the difference between the approach outlined here and social and political service? Are not peace and justice issues the responsibility of secular professions and of society as a whole? Should not the Church let them get on with it and concentrate on what we do uniquely, proclaim Jesus Christ?

It is no doubt true that anyone who struggles for justice, peace and the integrity of creation is a partner of the mission, and should be encouraged. What matters is not being different but getting on with the job. When Jesus confronted the claim that his exorcisms were done in the name of Beelzebub (Luke 11.15), in his reply he asked them by what authority their own people were doing the same (11.19). Similarly, when the disciples reported that they had found someone casting out demons who was not a member of their group, and they had tried to stop him, Jesus had said, 'Forbid him not, for whoever is not against us is on our side' (Mark 9.38–40). An exorcism is an exorcism no matter who does it, and a pain relieved is a pain relieved.

Nevertheless, the presence and activities of the Church are different in several important ways. When the relief of suffering is done in the name of Christ, it becomes significant of something greater. In other words, Christian faith places the elements of individual and communal reform in a wider pattern of interpretation. This context is provided by Christian faith itself, which gives to the acting parties the vision of a whole historic destiny, in which God is working out the purpose and meaning of creation itself. Such an interpretation sustains meaning and hope in the most hopeless situation, and this gives to the Christian working for the coming of God's kingdom a strength and an endurance, a joy that others must find elsewhere, if at all. Thus the Christian may glimpse the transcendent beyond the other, and the ultimate future of transcendent otherness, while the secular person may not have such imaginative resources of interpretation to inspire and strengthen.

Secondly, the churches must exercise an influence upon secular society by occupying a significant place in civil society, and by the insistence on ethical and humane standards maintain a constant pressure on public life. This we may describe as the prophetic function of the Church.

Moreover, if the churches withdraw into purely religious activity (as the secular world would see it) and only preach Christ without lifting a finger to alleviate human suffering, our message will become mere words. We will lose the respect of the public even more thoroughly, and we will be in flagrant disobedience to Scripture.

Nothing in this discussion implies that the Church will not go on preaching Christ. In the context of striving for the kingdom of God, such preaching, which will expose the faith, hope and love which inspire us, will have much more credibility, and is more likely to draw people into the relevance of faith.

Moreover, proclaiming and working for the kingdom is not the only thing Christian life offers. There is still what Bonhoeffer described as 'the secret discipline', there is still worship, the study and interpretation of the Scriptures, the intellectual life of theology, the pastoral care of congregations, the carrying out of the rituals of the life cycle. However, in the context of mission as the kingdom of God, all these other activities take on a new urgency and relevance.

Jesus as Saviour and Lord

Although at first sight this might seem to be an example of the vertical, it is clear that in the days of his ministry, relationship with God through Jesus was the supreme example of prophetic horizontality. In these days of the Church, when Jesus is seated at the right hand of God in glory, he is to be found through human otherness, as we have seen.

Nevertheless, it is true that the prophetic tradition may be placed side by side with other traditions such as the mystical, the charismatic and the sacramental.

The prophetic tradition has been emphasized here, because it is the one most relevant to the mission of God. If we are to mould the life of our churches upon the mission of God, it is to the prophetic tradition that we must turn.

This is made all the more important because Christ-mysticism, when it takes an exclusively vertical form or is preoccupied with Jesus as with an imaginary friend, is in danger today of becoming a kind of erotic spirituality in which it is easier to adore Jesus than to follow him. This erotic fascination, so neatly summed up in the comment 'Jesus is my girlfriend' has many of the features of a fetish.[10] This danger is implicit in the remark made by a preacher at a recent Good Friday morning service, who said, 'I have nothing against social justice, but the heart of the Christian faith is personal devotion to Jesus.' This is indeed the case, but what the preacher has forgotten is that we are to find Jesus through human otherness, and any religious experience of which Jesus is the content but which is isolated from obligation to the human other quickly degenerates into a kind of self-congratulatory spiritual self-enclosure. One can see this clearly in so many of the hymns about this kind of Christian experience, in which the believer's feelings of happiness, satisfaction and security have become the focus of faith. Such 'Happy Christians' need to hear again the words of the prophet James who says that without ethical commitment, faith is meaningless.

On the question of an exclusively vertical relationship to God it might be thought that prayer represents such a relationship. Relationship to God, however, does not arise as an act of pure revelation, but is formed out of the way our concept of God has been fashioned in all the relationships of life especially our relationship to our parents in our childhood. Prayer itself is modelled upon our experience of conversation with others, and in speaking to God we cannot help but bring into that speaking all the meanings of conversation we have acquired in our lives. The accumulated factors which lead to the formation of the concept of God, and the concept of talking to God may be described as the God-image within us. If prayer is naively addressed to God, it is necessarily addressed to the God-image within us, and psychoanalytic object-relations theory and attachment theory have helped us to realize the process whereby the God-image is created (Rizzuto 1979; McDargh 1983). It is necessarily formed through absorption and projection of traces of God as perceived or imagined in other people, so even in direct prayer, we are in a bundle of life with others.

Whether in sophisticated prayer it is possible consciously to pass through the other to the infinite, I cannot tell. This would mean approaching the God beyond God in earthly human experience, but I am sure that such communion with God, if it can be known, would be in love, and love of God is only formed and expressed through love to others. When we pray, it is in the company of the communion of saints.

A great deal of contemporary theology and practice of mission is couched in terms of church growth. The emphasis in the present chapter, however, is not upon church growth but on the function of the Church. It is understandable that those who love the Church and who may be employed by various church institutions would regard it as their duty to secure the growth of the Church, and would argue not unreasonably that the functions of the Church cannot be carried out if the Church itself should shrink to vanishing point. If, as the theologians from Asia, Africa and Latin America are always telling us, God becomes real in the pursuit of justice, we need have no fears for the Church once it pursues the mission of God along prophetic lines. When the Church forgets its true calling, any growth will be ambiguous, but when the Church fulfils its function its health, relevance and possibly its growth will follow. Church growth, in other words, is a by-product of church function.

In the Eucharist, the person of Jesus Christ is reconstructed in memory and becomes a presence that is at least symbolic. Because of this way of memorializing Jesus, the presence of Jesus in his mission as the one who being sent also sends us transforms the Lord's Supper into an impetus for the mission of God. Being a communion, most usually taken together, and being a sacrament of reconciliation, it has powerful elements of prophetic faith. The broken bread brings us into a single body as we eat it, meaning that in the body of Christ we become his body, the reconstructed social body. This is also why the sacrament is essentially inclusive, and should be open to all, so representing and creating that universal fellowship which is the objective of the mission of God.

The distinction between the churched and the unchurched may not be a fundamental distinction recognized by the mission of God, but does it have any significance at all? For those who believe in one holy and apostolic Church the distinction must always have some significance, but we should also remember that the God of the Bible says in Isaiah 65.1: 'I revealed myself to those who did not ask for me; I was found by those who did not seek me. To a nation that did not call on my name, I said, "Here am I, here am I."' I also remember the words of Paul when addressing the Greeks: God 'is not far from each one of us. For in him we live and move and have our being' (Acts 17.27–28), in the idea that 'the word is near you, it is on your lips and in your heart' (Rom. 10.8), and that Christ is 'the logos that enlightens every human being' (John 1.9).

Only one way to walk with God

As a teenage Christian, I always felt uncomfortable when we sang the hymn by William Cowper, published in the *Olney Hymn Book* in 1779, that begins 'O for a closer walk with God'. The poet had, it seemed to me, committed or perhaps we should say that he had indulged in some sin which, or so he thought, had caused the Holy Spirit to depart from him, leaving 'an aching void the world can never fill'. The sin was not named, but I was pretty sure it had something to do with sex. When one announced a hatred of it, the holy dove would return. But how could one hate sex? This threw me (and I am sure the same has been felt by many others) into a desperate collision course between faith in God and on the other hand the attractiveness of one of life's most exciting options. This struggle culminates in the third verse, when the singer cries out:

The dearest idol I have known,
What e'er that idol be,
Help me to tear it from thy throne
and worship only thee.

I now believe that these adolescent agonies were induced by a spirituality of inwardness in which emotional satisfaction and religious demands were opposed to one another in such a way as to make it quite impossible for one to realize what it might be to walk closely with God.

Not until my adult life, and indeed my later adulthood, did I gradually realize that I had been duped by a spirituality that had made me insensitive to the world's sufferings, had given me the idea that my feelings were the most important thing in being Christian, which had created a psychological tension that afflicted my life for several years.

All this time, the Bible itself was telling me how to walk closely with God, but I was unable to hear it. This was not only because of the preoccupation with my inner life and my struggles of conscience, which had given me a misguided concept of purity, but a kind of inability to penetrate the veil which hung between me and the Bible.

The veil was the image left on the imagination of the Church by its struggle for legitimation during its first few centuries.

Walking with God

When the Old Testament speaks of walking with God in the sense of pursuing a certain way of life, the reference is usually to obediently observing the laws and commandments of God. In Deuteronomy the giving of the Decalogue concludes with the following exhortation.

> So be careful to do what the Lord your God has commanded you; do not turn aside to the right or to the left. Walk in obedience to all that the Lord your God has commanded you, so that you may live and prosper and prolong your days in the land that you will possess. (Deut. 5.32–3)

Similar expressions are found in Deuteronomy 8.6, 11.22, 19.9, 26.17, 28.9 and 30.16. This ideal of the religious life is summed up in Deuteronomy 10.12–13:

> And now, Israel, what does the Lord your God ask of you but to fear the Lord your God, to walk in obedience to him, to love him, to serve the Lord your God with all your heart and with all your soul, and to observe the Lord's commands and decrees that I am giving you today for your own good?

To keep God's commandments is to walk in justice because 'The Lord loves righteousness and justice; the earth is full of his unfailing love' (Ps. 33.5), and 'And the heavens proclaim his righteousness, for he is a God of justice' (Ps. 50.6). Walking with God in this way is to know God for 'The Lord is known by his acts of justice' (Ps. 9.16).

This is why those who follow the way of the Lord are said to walk in justice: 'he is a shield to those whose walk is blameless, for he guards the course of the just and protects the way of his faithful ones' (Prov. 2.7b–8). In Proverbs, wisdom calls out 'I walk in the way of righteousness, along the paths of justice' (8.20). And if you follow wisdom, 'Thus you will walk in the ways of the just and keep to the paths of the righteous' (2.20). This is why those who seek an end to warfare and for peace between the nations are described as walking in the light of the Lord.

> He will judge between the nations as arbiter among many peoples.
> They will beat their swords into mattocks
> And their spears into pruning-knives;
> Nation will not lift sword against nation
> Nor ever again be trained for war.
> Come, people of Jacob,
> Let us walk in the light of the Lord. (Isa. 2.4–5)

The whole teaching of the Hebrew Bible on what it is to walk with God is summed up in Micah 6.8, 'He has shown all you people what is good. And what does the Lord require of you? To act justly and to love mercy and to walk humbly with your God.'

In the New Testament letters, the verb *peripateo*, which literally means 'walk', is frequently used to describe the way of life expected of Christian disciples. In many of the modern translations, however, this rather beautiful, concrete image, with its hint of making steady progress on the journey, is rendered by expressions such as living or even simply doing. So the King James Bible, the Authorized Version, translated Ephesians 4.1 'I therefore, the prisoner of the Lord, beseech you that ye walk worthy of the vocation wherewith ye are called', whereas today's New International Version says: 'As a prisoner for the Lord, then, I urge you to live a life worthy of the calling you have received.' Similarly, the AV of Ephesians 2.10 reads: 'For we are his workmanship, created in Christ Jesus unto good works, which God hath before ordained that we should walk in them.' But the TNIV has: 'For we are God's handiwork, created in Christ Jesus to do good works, which God prepared in advance for us to do.'

In order to highlight the metaphor of walking we will take further illustrations from the AV. To walk with God through Christ is to live the ethical life, characterized by honesty, sincerity, acts of mercy, and above all by love. 'Let us walk honestly, as in the day; not in rioting and drunkenness, not in chambering and wantonness, not in strife and envying' (Rom. 13.13). Christians 'have renounced the hidden things of dishonesty, not walking in craftiness, nor handling the word of God deceitfully; but by manifestation of the truth commending ourselves to every man's conscience in the sight of God' (2 Cor. 4.2). This walking is an imitation of Christ: 'As ye have therefore received Christ Jesus the Lord, so walk ye in him' (Col. 2.6), and its climax is love: 'And walk in love, as Christ also hath loved us' (Eph. 5.2). This love continues and enriches the Old Testament walking in obedience to the Lord, so that 'Love worketh no ill to his neighbour: therefore love is the fulfilling of the law' (Rom. 13.10), and 'And this is love: that we walk in obedience to his commands. As you have heard from the beginning, his command is that you walk in love' (2 John 1.6).

It is clear that to walk with God, to be in a state of steady fellowship with God through Jesus Christ according to the Bible, is essentially a horizontal relationship. God is loved through the neighbour, and obedience to God is shown through seeking after justice for others. Any personal or direct relation with God must be on the far side of that walking, not on this side. It is not a matter of loving God first and then as an outcome loving our neighbour but rather the biblical model is that as we love the neighbour and seek justice for him and her, our love to God finds concrete expression, is enriched, and finds a closeness with God who has commanded us so to walk. This is to be in Christ, to walk the way of Jesus Christ, to seek to live as he did, the man for others. But if someone believes that he or she is walking with God and neglects the ethical, interpersonal character of this walking, such a person has a faith that is dead.

We must ask how it came about that the plain teaching of the Bible appears to have been lost, to some extent, and the inter-personal relationship was turned into an introspective one, as we saw in the famous hymn 'O for a Closer Walk with God'.

The struggle for Christian legitimacy

Nearly all the authors of the New Testament were Jews, and they were caught up in a dispute about their legitimacy as inheritors of the traditions of Israel, and about their claim that the crucified Jesus was the promised Messiah (Barrett 1963, p. 2). Early Christian faith was a form of Judaism (Dunn 2006, p. 156) at a time when there were many groups claiming the right to be true Jews, and the issue hung on an interpretation of the Jewish Scriptures.[1] Christians tried to prove that their faith, although new, was not a novelty. That mattered a great deal in a society in which antiquity was a mark of authenticity. The classical world valued antiquity highly, as can be illustrated by the disputes about the relative chronology of Greek and Hebrew culture and law (Clement of Alexandria 1991 Book I, Chaps 21, 25 and 29).

One of the things the Jews, gathered in Jerusalem for the feast of Pentecost, found impressive about the speech of Peter was his claim that '[t]his is what was promised by the prophets' (Acts 2.16). The criterion of quality was prediction, and every aspect of the birth, life, death and resurrection of Jesus Christ was soon found to have been predicted. So the use of parables by Jesus had been foretold (Matt. 13.14, 35); his miracles were anticipated (8.17), even the soldiers throwing dice for his clothes were fulfilling Scripture (John 19.24). This element of foretelling gave an air of normality, of expectation, to what otherwise must have seemed claims of enormous originality. To those who knew their Bibles, the message proclaimed, even the resurrection of Christ need come

---

1 James Dunn discusses this dispute about the nature of true Judaism (2006, pp. 185–214). His conclusion is that 'the real issue was, and still is, *which of the two chief strands emerging from second Temple Judaism was being truer to the original and most characteristic impulse of God's call and gifts*' (p. 214; Dunn's italics).

as no surprise (Acts 2.27). These things had to be, and to recognize this necessity was to be converted to Christian faith (Luke 24.25–34; Acts 8.30–38).[2]

In spite of the urgency of the demand for legitimation, significant traces of the character of the God of Israel do remain in the Gospels, and perhaps particularly in the Gospel of Luke. The concern of Luke for the marginalized and the outcast seems to have made him more ready to hear the message of the Bible (Luke 1.52–3), as it then was, or maybe it was the other way round: Luke's deep knowledge and love for the Bible made him more open to the cry of the outcast (4.18, 19.10, 19.20). Perhaps this might have been expected of Matthew's Gospel as well, and we do find many examples of it in Matthew, but on the whole the concern of Matthew to give a theological rationale for the emergence of the Gentile Church in which strong Jewish elements remained proved the stronger motive (Bosch 1991, pp. 56–83; Harris 2004, pp. 37–69; Senior and Stuhlmueller 1983, pp. 233–54).

There is some evidence that at least some elements within the later first-century Church were well aware of the way that foretelling was taking the place of forth-telling in the understanding of the Bible. One example of this may be found in the story of the rich man and Lazarus (Luke 16.19–31). This passage is often read under the influence of John 5.46, 'If you believe Moses, you would believe me, for he wrote about me', but there is no Christological element in the Lukan story. The rich man had completely ignored the presence of Lazarus although the destitute man was sitting at his very gate.[3] Perhaps he had never even noticed Lazarus was there. He was punished in the next life, because he had not listened to the voice of the poor. He now wants to warn his family about the dangers of the fiery torment, but Abraham's reply is: 'They have Moses and the Prophets, let them listen to them' (Luke 16.29). They were to listen to the judgment of God upon those who failed to hear the cry of the destitute.[4] The one who returns from the dead is the poor man Lazarus, but even when the poor

---

2 This is not to deny that Jesus himself may have interpreted his mission in the light of the Hebrew Scriptures. The point is, however, that the pressure of claim and counter-claim encouraged latter development of this tendency.

3 W. Manson (1930, pp. 190–2) agrees that the parable has to do with the failure of the wealthy to heed 'the ethical demands made by the Law and the prophets', and that the rich man 'is condemned for his refusal to shew mercy and justice'. He goes on to suggest that the poor man 'is saved by his righteousness'. Manson rightly emphasizes the contrast between the destitute poor and the selfish rich and that what the rich fail to hear is the ethical teaching of the law and the prophets, but he makes a mistake in thinking that the poor man is saved by his righteousness. Manson suggests that the reference to the resurrection means that 'if the Jews had really listened to Moses and the prophets, they would not have denied the Resurrection'. The point, however, is that if they had listened to Moses and the prophets they would not have denied the cry of the poor.

4 The contrast between the rich and poor classes is seldom perceived by the commentators, who tend to give the contrast a moral rather than an economic significance. Even Marshall (1978, p. 632), who sees this, takes it back again very quickly, 'the poor man is not specifically stated to be righteous or pious, but this is perhaps to be deduced from his name and from Luke's general equation of poverty and piety'. Nolland (1993, pp. 831–3) is one of the few who realizes that 'the rich man was doing no more than living out the life of his class'. Nolland concludes that '[t]he parable suggests that there is a profound challenge to the social status quo to be found in the law and the prophets'.

rise up against them, the rich cannot perceive the justice of God (Job 20.19–27). The Christian readers of Luke's Gospel might have seen this as a reference to the resurrection of Jesus. The idea, however, is not that the resurrection of Christ was foretold in Moses and the Prophets, but that if you ignore the claims of justice, you will still do so even as a Christian believing in the resurrection. Christ's resurrection inaugurated the kingdom of God, and the great reversal spoken by Jesus was now in full force, but to those who do not pay attention to the God of justice the resurrection becomes just a sensational nature miracle.

The need to establish worthy credentials did not cease when Christian faith was clearly distinguishable from Judaism, but continued with even greater vigour, because it had become an important aspect of a struggle between what had, by the middle of the second century, become two religions. This can be seen very clearly in the works of Justin Martyr in the middle of the second century, where the details of the life of Jesus are proven by prophecy.[5]

The result of this long drawn out situation of rivalry was that the meaning of the Old Testament, as it came to be known, for the New Testament was that of promise and fulfilment. The two covenants were related as type and ante-type, as looking forward and as realizing that vision of the future (Smalley 1963, pp. 11–12). What was concealed in the old is revealed in the new, covert in the first, overt in the second.[6] The Old Testament became preliminary, and so the foundations of a theology of supersession were laid. The message of the Law and the Prophets could no longer be heard in its own integrity but only as a foreshadowing of Christian faith.

This way of approaching the Old Testament continued throughout the Middle Ages and became even more prominent during the Reformation. Martin Luther's Christ-centred interpretation of the Old Testament led to him dismissing everything that was not clearly to do with Jesus Christ.[7] He rejected the apostolic authority of James, because '[h]e names Christ several times; however he teaches nothing about him, but only speaks of general faith in God' (1960, p. 396).

This approach to the first covenant is still driven home every time audiences hear Handel's Messiah. There is a messianic strand running through parts of the Old Testament, but this is by no means its major theme. Not until the twentieth-century theologies of the Old Testament by Eichrodt (1961, 1967), von Rad (1962, 1965), and above all Walter Brueggemann (1997) was the message of the Hebrew Scriptures heard in its own characteristic voice.

We must ask, then, about the nature and purposes of the God of Israel. What makes Yahweh god-like is the fact that God 'loves justice' (Ps. 99.4), not that Justice is a quality outside Yahweh to which Yahweh conforms, but justice is the very nature of Yahweh 'For I, the Lord, love Justice' (Isa. 61.8). In ancient Israel justice was not so much an abstract ideal to which the legal code should adhere as the principle characteristic in the personal life of God,

---

5 Justin Martyr. *I Apology* 31–53. Kelly (1963, p. 46) describes how Tertullian 'ransacks the Old Testament' for predictions of Jesus Christ.

6 'So the Old Testament first comes forth as a type, and the New Testament follows as the true reality' (Luther 1961, p. 254).

7 'To Him Scripture must bear witness, for it is given solely for His sake' (Luther 1972, p. 343).

a characteristic which must be shared by those who desire to walk in covenant with God (von Rad 1962, pp. 94–5, 370–83). The main concern of God is to establish a community of inclusion, where the aliens and strangers will be welcomed, and where unprotected sectors of society will be guaranteed security and welfare. Because God loves justice, God is known in the works of justice, since in performing such actions, the likeness of God is appropriated. 'The God with whom the people of Israel make a covenant is regarded as the source and foundation of justice and that is his first form of action' (Epsztein 1986, p. 139). Moreover, it is only possible to walk closely with God by means of following justice in the community. Referring to the philosophy of Emmanuel Levinas, Leon Epsztein says, 'Relations with the divine . . . pass through relations among human beings and coincide with social justice: that is the whole spirit of the Jewish Bible' (p. 140).

Although interpersonal, the justice demanded by God in the Bible does not relate mainly to individuals. 'The tradition of justice concerns the political-economic life of the community and urges drastic transformative and rehabilitative activity' (Brueggemann 1997, p. 193). God 'defends the cause of the fatherless and the widow, and loves the foreigners residing among you, giving them food and clothing' (Deut. 10.18).

In the work of Jesus Christ we see a similar proclamation of inclusion of the marginalized, liberation of the oppressed, and announcement of the coming of the reign of God. In that kingdom, ethnic and social barriers will be broken down, and religion will be fulfilled in mercy and love.

The early Christian community could not continue the same embodiment of social justice as the prophets of Israel proclaimed, and we may suggest several reasons for this. In the first place, as a small and threatened community, the Christians of the first century, and indeed, of the first three centuries, were in no position to create the social conditions leading to justice. Israel had been a state, but Christian faith was not embodied in a state until it became the official religion of the Roman Empire in the fifth century. By then, the state was as resistant to Christian faith as the Hebrew kingdoms had been resistant to the message of the prophets.

The second reason why the Church did not sustain the same interest in social justice as the ideals of the Old Testament was that the return of Christ and the end of the age was anticipated. Hence the advice of Paul that slaves should not seek their freedom, nor married partners separate from their partners, for the end was at hand (1 Cor. 7.5, 17–31). So not only did the early Church have no power to abolish slavery; they had no real motivation either. Jesus would look after all that when he came, which would be soon. The mission policy of the early Church has been described as 'filling the ark' (Spencer 2007, p. 46). The whole effort was devoted to snatching at least some from the wreck of society.

The third reason was that the early Church was naturally preoccupied by its own struggle for survival, not so much in the presence of a hostile state, as in relation to the Jewish tradition out of which it was only slowly emerging. The Old Testament, as we have seen, was called into the service of this ideological crisis, and it never emerged. It was in the interests of a Church that had entered into the power of the state to collaborate with that state in creating empire. So the demand for justice became the desire to extend the Christian empire.

Biblical theology of mission

When the Church of today considers the meaning of its biblical roots for its contemporary mission, its view is still clouded by its interpretation of the Old Testament as predictive or at least preliminary. An example of this influence may be found in the various books that deal with the biblical theology of mission. These mostly interpret the mission theology of the Old Testament as consisting in the self-understanding of ancient Israel toward the Gentile world. We find discussions about the universal blessing that Abraham's faith would bring to the nations, and about the degree to which the ethno-centricity of ancient Israel was qualified by some readiness to see the God of Israel at work beyond the borders of Palestine. So the books of Jonah and Ruth are often regarded as indicating an openness to foreign mission, but the book of Ezra is an example of exclusive identity. Such descriptions often conclude with an account of the missionary work of the Jewish Diaspora throughout the Graeco-Roman world, which became one of the opportunities of the Christian mission that succeeded it.

Even David Bosch, perhaps the most influential scholar of mission in the twentieth century, makes no direct reference to the mission of the Old Testament, but concentrates upon mission *in* the Old Testament, i.e. the degree to which ancient Israel engaged in mission. In spite of this, Bosch is confident that 'the Old Testament is fundamental to the understanding of mission in the New' (Bosch 1991, p. 17), but he seems to see this mainly in the revelation of God as the One who acts and whose actions offer a promise for the future. He refers to the essential character of the covenant between Israel and God as meaning that 'Israel is to serve the marginal in its midst: the orphan, the widow, the poor, and the stranger' (p. 18), but he does not appear to recognize this as the fundamental implication of the Old Testament for the historic mission of the Christian faith. Perhaps this is why in the 519 pages of his book, less than four are immediately concerned with mission in the Old Testament.

To take another example, the work of the Dutch missiologist Johannes Blauw (1962) when preparing his survey for the World Council of Churches, was mainly concerned with the extent to which the Old Testament offered a universal picture of the grace of God. He deals with the call of God to all nations according to Genesis 1–11 and shows how this gave a universalizing direction to Israel's self-understanding.

One of the authors that deals with the ethics of the Old Testament as a basis for Christian mission is Carroll Stuhlmueller. Oddly enough, what she derives from the Old Testament is not justice but violence. Having decided that '[w]e cannot deny inspiration to the "violent passages" and still uphold the overall inspiration of the Old Testament. Nor can we relegate the statements about war and struggle to a few isolated and minimally inspired passages', she concludes: 'Violence ought to be considered a charism or gift put to the service of God's people and God's providential plan, just as truly as any other quality, like pacifism or prayer' (Senior and Stuhlmueller 1983, p. 43). Such treatments of the mission of Israel and how it prepared the way for Christian mission may be surprising in some cases and convincing in others, but they miss the vital question as to what the mission of the Old Testament, as the word of God, is for the contemporary world.

Social justice or a personal relationship with Jesus Christ?

How far much contemporary Christian discipleship has wandered from the biblical model of walking with God may be seen in the comment made by a minister of a church in the West Midlands, referred to earlier in this chapter. During
his Good Friday sermon in 2007, he said: 'I have nothing against social justice,
but the heart of the Christian faith is a personal relationship with Jesus Christ.'
This remarkable comment could be reversed, and would still be just as true and
just as false. 'I have nothing against a personal relationship with Jesus Christ,
but the heart of the Christian faith is social justice.' Although this inversion has
the advantage of highlighting the choice which the preacher presented to his
congregation, it is no nearer to describing Christian discipleship. Whether we
preserve the original or invert it, the error remains. It resides in the little word
'but'. This contrasts features of Christian living that should be brought together,
not as alternatives, but as part and parcel of new life in the Spirit of Christ. The
truth is that if we have a personal relationship with Jesus Christ it should, to be
consistent, result in a commitment to neighbourly love, in short to social justice.
This consistency or mutual implication is so complete that it does not matter
which way round the emphasis is placed. The works of justice and love lead us
to Jesus Christ, and faith in Jesus Christ leads us to the works of justice and
love, where 'leads' means 'implies' and 'is equivalent to'.

That this conclusion follows from the very nature of justification by faith is set
out clearly by Karl Barth. Here is what he says about the righteousness of God:

> In this connexion it is important to notice that the people to whom God
> in His righteousness turns as helper and Saviour is everywhere in the Old
> Testament [the] harassed and oppressed people of Israel, which, powerless in
> itself, has no rights, and is delivered over to the superior force of its enemies;
> and in Israel it is especially the poor, the widows and orphans, the weak and
> defenceless. (1957, p. 386)

Thus Barth argues that God as the Saviour of those who cannot save themselves
has a preferential option for the poor. He continues:

> For this reason the human righteousness required by God and established in
> obedience – the righteousness which according to Amos 5:24 should pour
> down as a mighty stream – has necessarily the character of a vindication
> of right in favour of the threatened innocent, the oppressed poor, widows,
> orphans and aliens. (p. 386)

The righteousness of God is shown by the pouring out of God's justice in favour
of those who are denied it.

> For this reason, in the relations and events in the life of His people, God
> always takes His stand unconditionally and passionately on this side and on
> this side alone: against the lofty and on behalf of the lowly; against those who
> already enjoy right and privilege and on behalf of those who are denied it and
> deprived of it. (p. 386)

It is in the very nature of God to justify those who are oppressed by the powerful.

> God's righteousness, the faithfulness in which He is true to Himself, is disclosed as help and salvation, as a saving divine intervention for man directed only to the poor, the wretched and the helpless as such, while with the rich and the full and the secure as such, according to His very nature He can have nothing to do. (p. 387)

Barth then applies this to the condition of all people before God and so to the doctrine of salvation that relies on faith in the justice of God before whom we have nothing to offer and no ground of goodness of our own upon which to stand. However, Barth does not forget the political implications of the doctrine:

> [T]here follows from this character of faith a political attitude, decisively determined by the fact that man is made responsible to all those who are poor and wretched in his eyes, that he is summoned on his part to espouse the cause of those who suffer wrong. Why? Because in them it is manifested to him what he himself is in the sight of God. (p. 387)

In this remarkable manner, Barth draws out the political implications of salvation by faith alone. The Protestant principle is also a political principal of justice for the excluded. Barth specifically refers to both James and Luke in this connexion, contrary to Martin Luther, who did not seem to draw out of the doctrine of justification by faith this kind of social implication. Barth concludes this part of the discussion as follows:

> The man who lives by the faith that this is true stands under a political responsibility. He knows that the right, that every real claim which one man has against another or others, enjoys the special protection of the God of grace. As surely as he himself lives by the grace of God he cannot evade this claim. He cannot avoid the question of human rights. He can only will and affirm a state which is based on justice. By any other political attitude he rejects the divine justification. (p. 387)

Thus the righteousness and the mercy of God are united. In fidelity to his own nature as a God of justice, God helps those who cannot help themselves. In his justice, he supports the poor with mercy and grace. Only by extending grace to those who have nothing to offer can God be true to his own nature as a righteous god. Thus it is that, in Jesus Christ, God offers that which is worthy of God, God's own grace poured out upon the lost and the excluded, and accepts them all in God's own justice, a justice that rejoices in accepting those who are lost. Jesus is true to the nature of God. And so becomes the righteousness of God for us.

Alternatives to walking with God

Much of the life and practice of the contemporary Church has, as remarked above, wandered far from the biblical model. Some of the alternatives that take its place may be mentioned here.

Words of faith without faithful actions

Some Christians are so divorced from the real world into which they are invited to walk with God that they attach an almost magical quality to the mere words that announce the salvation of God through Christ. People are invited to give credence to these words, and this is described as conversion. One may, in faith, have a personal relation with Jesus, but there is only one way to be sure in faith that this is not the product of self-deception. This is how we know that we love God, because we love others. This is the fruit which indicates the nature of the tree; this is the walking with God which is true to the God and Father of our Lord Jesus Christ. Any other claim to personal relation with Jesus fails in both the love of God and the love of the neighbour to which Jesus gave commandments, for faith without action is dead. Walking with God through Christ describes a steady, consistent way of life lived in obedience to the life and death of the incarnate Lord, and not an isolated sitting before his imagined presence. Such an escape too easily leads to a Christian life more or less entirely preoccupied by feelings of blessedness. However, blessed it is not, taken in itself, to be described as walking with God because it lacks obedience.

Kingdom of God words without kingdom of God actions

This tendency is certainly getting closer to walking with God, but it falls short, because it also stops short at words. The words are the words of Christian justice and peace, but they are only words. I give two examples of this. First, when churches pass resolutions urging certain reforms or policies, if the state or the other authorities addressed ignore them, it often seems that nothing further takes place. The brave resolution remains only words: words that seem to express a will, but the will disappears when the words are ignored. Second, in church services, when prayers are offered in support of the suffering people of the world, but nothing else happens, it is to be feared that the prayers are not so much the inspiration of action but the opposite. Surely such prayers, in which we ask God to do this and that, but take no actions in the Spirit of God to bring about the desired outcome, are almost blasphemous in their emptiness.

Uninterpreted actions

If apparently kingdom of God activities are performed but remain uninterpreted by kingdom of God words and gospel words, once again, actions and words have become divorced. We are to pray to be one so that the world may know, to let our light shine before people that they may give glory to God (John 17.21; Matt. 5.16). Actions without words are certainly to be preferred to no actions at all, but they are not examples of walking with God unless God through Christ is acknowledged. Otherwise, what we have may be a good works ethic but not a gospel ethic.

Here then we have a criterion for assessing those new expressions that claim to be, or hope that they might be, fresh expressions of Christian faith, ecclesial structure or mission. Do the Christians involved in the fresh expression make a habit of walking with God? Do the structures make the mission of God visible? And if not, how is this to be brought about? There are many religions and many varieties of religious experience, some of which may have as their content the Christian symbols, but if we want to walk with God, the God of the Bible, there is only one way.

In order to promote this and to restore the prophetic Church, the theological education of clergy must be strengthened. The final chapter of this study sets out some principles for this task.

13

Theological Education for a Prophetic Church

The teaching of Christian mission

Recent developments in understanding the mission of the Church are reflected in the historiography of mission. The multi-volume work by Kenneth Scott Latourette (1938–45) is confident in tracing a record of continual growth, and even as late as 1986 Stephen Neill and Owen Chadwick could say that 'Christianity alone has succeeded in making itself a universal religion' (1986, p. 14), Christianity 'was to become the faith of all mankind' (p. 16). We may contrast this untroubled interpretation with the views of Jean Comby, who says that '[t]he historical church does not have a monopoly of signs and realizations of the kingdom' (1996, p. 176). He continues: 'Since there are many ways of bearing witness to the gospel, we can understand that the number of conversions can no longer be the criterion of the authenticity and effectiveness of witness.' The magisterial work of David Bosch (1991) replaces the history of expansion with a succession of theological models, creating the expectation of further paradigm shifts. The British missiologist Stephen Spencer (2007) adopts a somewhat similar approach using Weberian types instead of Kuhnian paradigms, arranging them in a sequence suggesting similar radical transformations. The most widely read recent major English textbook in this area, by the American Catholic missiologists Stephen Bevans and Roger Schroeder (2004), reassures us that there are continuities across the centuries, and escapes from the history of an expanding European Christendom by giving us a global and a less patriarchal perspective. Andrew Walls abandons the expansionist view for a theory of adaptability in which the centre of the Christian world has continually moved and is still doing so (2002).

One of the problems faced by contemporary missiologists is the very diversity of the concept of 'mission'. Is it, in effect, simply evangelization, is it the expansion of Christianity by whatever means, or is it some wider participation in the purposes of God? What significance should be attached to the distinction between Church and kingdom? And to what extent should the radical interpretations of the mission of Jesus (e.g. Myers 1988) suggest a completely new approach?

Mission and ministerial training

All of this is having some impact upon theological education, and in particular the training of Christian ministers. The same issues which are revealed in the historiographical changes above are at work in the British churches where the impact of pluralism, secularity and diverse spiritualities are amongst the factors requiring ministerial candidates to study mission. Much seminary training has returned to an emphasis upon evangelism, in spite of the relatively unsuccessful Decade of Evangelism (1990–2000) (Francis and Roberts 2009, pp. 67–81), and the problem of semantic emptiness in a society where Christian language has largely ceased to function.

In guiding the Church toward a new focus upon mission, the Anglican Consultative Council in 1984 drew up a statement for the worldwide Anglican Communion, and the bishops of the Lambeth Conference adopted it in 1988. The statement set out Five Marks of Mission, and these were adopted by the General Synod of the Church of England in 1996 and revised in 2012. They are as follows:

1   To proclaim the Good News of the kingdom.
2   To teach, baptize and nurture new believers.
3   To respond to human need by loving service.
4   To seek to transform unjust structures of society, to challenge violence of every kind and to pursue peace and reconciliation.
5   To strive to safeguard the integrity of creation and to sustain the life of the earth.

Although the Five Marks continue to act as a sort of ideal check list, the actual policies and practice of the Church of England have been influenced by a report entitled *Mission-Shaped Church* presented to the Archbishops Council, a senior body of the Church of England in 2004. Unfortunately, this report did not seek to represent the full range of the Five Marks, but concentrated rather upon revision of the parochial structure and the emergence of fresh expressions of church life. This has tended to focus on the second of the Marks, and says virtually nothing about the Fourth and Fifth Marks. This has led to my criticism that the report offered the Church not so much a mission-shaped Church as a church-shaped mission (Hull 2006), and few subsequent developments have encouraged me to revise this view (2008, 2009).

In this emphasis, the report of 2004 did reflect the interests of the local churches since generally it would be true to say that congregations find the first three Marks more comfortable than the last two. It is easy to see why. The First Mark, to proclaim the kingdom, is a general catch-all that can mean what you want; the Second Mark, encouraging discipleship of Jesus, is in the interests of local churches, since it is often interpreted as increasing church membership, and the Third, the stretching out to the community in loving care, is very natural for most churches. The final two Marks are the difficult ones. Achieving them is not evidently in the immediate interest of a local congregation; the issues are more abstract, and intrinsically controversial. What are 'unjust structures'? What makes them unjust? How can structures, as distinct from persons, be unjust? How can such structures be identified, and what is the process of their transformation? These are difficult questions, but, in spite of this, there is a theological literature on them (e.g. Delgado 2007; Myers and Lattea (eds) 1996; Wink 1992).

The final Mark, about protecting the environment, is probably more approachable. The churches have made huge strides in directing their congregations towards climate change, and there is a growing sense that this is part of a Christian duty towards the planet and its life (Church of England 2009).

The Anglican tradition and the teaching of social justice

Although the origins of modern Anglican concern for social justice may be traced back as far as the writings of Samuel Taylor Coleridge (Jones 1968, p. 48), it did not become prominent in Church and nation until the Christian Socialist Movement in the middle years of the nineteenth century, associated with F. D. Maurice, John Ludlow and Charles Kingsley (Raven 1920). However, there does not seem to have been much impact on the training of clergy before the closing decades of the century. B. F. Westcott, soon after his appointment as Bishop of Durham, wrote in a letter that 'all candidates for Holy Orders take CSU [Christian Social Union] lessons in social responsibility' (Jones 1968, p. 180; Reckitt 1947, pp. 65–93). It was argued by Richard Mudie-Smith that '[n]othing has so alienated the people . . . as the age-long opposition of the churches to their most elementary rights' (1904, quoted in Jones 1968, p. 59).

One of the principal theological emphases of the Christian Socialist Movement was the corporate nature of the Eucharist, and the implications of this for the training of clergy were quite clear. Stewart Headlam (1847–1924) believed that '[i]t becomes impossible for a priest who knows what the Lord's Supper means, not to take a part to the best of his power in every work of political and/or social emancipation' (Jones 1968, p. 160). The influence of this social theology upon the churches was substantial. Between 1889 and 1913 there were 53 bishops appointed in the Church of England, and no less than 16 were members of the Christian Social Union (p. 164), which had been founded in 1899 and had among its members Henry Scott Holland, Charles Gore and B. F. Westcott.

The 1908 Lambeth Conference was dominated by the concerns of social theology (p. 214), which reached its climax in the COPEC conference held in Birmingham in 1923 with the future Archbishop of Canterbury William Temple in the chair (Phillips 1996, p. 109). The socialist theology movement may be said to have achieved its greatest success with the creation of the Welfare State after the Second World War, and it certainly does not occupy a place in the thinking of the Church of England today comparable to its influence in 1910. The work of Kenneth Leach stands out as a beacon of this tradition in the period from the 1970s to the 1990s (Leech 1981, 1992, 1992a). But it is too important to be entirely lost. The deep roots of Anglican theology in the incarnation, the Trinity and the sacramental life of the Church are too rich and relevant not to encourage a revival of social commitment. In a very small way, and with some differences in emphasis, this is perhaps beginning to take place in The Queen's Foundation.

Social justice and clergy training in The Queen's Foundation

Since September 2008 all ministerial students coming to train at The Queen's Foundation for Ecumenical Theological Education in Birmingham, England, are asked to indicate what they will do to incorporate social justice into their preparation for ordination. This is looked upon as an aspect of theological competence and supported by modules in Christian Mission, Black Theology, Feminist Theology, Bible and Liberation, God in the Marketplace and many others. The social justice activities themselves, however, are not usually part of the formal curriculum, but are regarded as complementary ministerial training, a bit like being attached to a congregation or taking part in daily chapel worship. Provided it is thought through from a theological point of view, the Foundation does not mind what students do to meet this obligation, but they must do something. To help them in this, and to provide a forum for planning and education, the Centre for Ministerial Formation (one of the several centres in the institution and the one responsible for ministerial training) has created a Social Justice Committee.

Fifteen criteria for the approval of social actions have been drawn up (Appendix 1). These are not without potential controversy, and it might be asked whether it is the official policy of the institution to press local coffee shops to adopt fairly traded products or to urge the British government not to renew the Trident nuclear missiles. The view taken in response to these concerns is to point out that when a student minister preaches in a nearby church as part of his or her training, not everything that is said represents the opinion of the Foundation, although the student does represent the Foundation in the sense that he or she is there officially as a trainee. Similarly, students may take part in an anti-nuclear weapons protest, and do so with the official approval of the Foundation, but only in so far as the Foundation acknowledges that the activity is an appropriate aspect of training. As an institution in law, no view has been adopted on the actual question at issue. Having said this, however, it is very important for the mission of the Church that such prophetic actions should be conducted in the name of the entire congregation or institution. Duncan Forrester wisely remarks:

> I find quite unconvincing the argument that while the generation and sustaining of vision and the pronouncement of general principles may be the proper function of public theology and the Church, prophecy and dealing with specific issues are not a responsibility of the Church as a whole, or of representative church leaders, but should be left to the occasional interventions of individuals. (2000, p. 151)

The activities that have been undertaken may be divided into those that have taken place on the campus and those that have occurred outside. We have prepared a shoe rack containing 23 pairs of children's shoes, each pair standing for 1,000 children who have died that day from preventable causes. This was to express our support for the Ecumenical Advocacy Campaign of the World Council of Churches programme to draw attention to shortages of food. The shoe stand was formally presented in chapel, and then moved around the campus, spending a week or two in the various teaching rooms. Students took part in the 32 day fast of solidarity with the 32 most heavily indebted countries of the world, each student electing to fast for a day in sympathy with one country. Perhaps the most successful on-campus activity has been the postcard avalanche. Hundreds of campaigning post cards were collected from various agencies, and over a period of three weeks, students were invited to sign and post these in support of the various campaigns. Outside the campus, we have revived the concept of liturgical lamentations as a public symbol. For two years we marked the anniversary of the commencement of the Iraq war with a solemn procession in the city centre. Accompanied by a drum, the names of some of those killed in the war, both British and Iraqi, were called out accompanied by reading from the Lamentations of Jeremiah. For several years running groups of students and staff have sung anti-consumerist carols in the central shopping area in the weeks leading up to Christmas.

But the most dramatic events have been conducted at military sites associated with nuclear weapons. Three of our people were arrested when a party of nearly 30 from four theological colleges went to take part in the protest against the nuclear submarine base at Faslane in the Clyde (Jones and Hammersley 2009), and twice we have witnessed at the gates of the Atomic Weapons Establishment near Aldermaston near Reading. For several years we have used prayer vigils or acts of public worship to witness against the making of military drones in the West Midlands. These events have had a deep impact on all who took part.[1]

Our two most difficult problems are in overcoming the fear which prevents people from taking part, and the question of whether candidates will be able to lead their future congregations into such activity once they have been ordained and have left their training behind them. Already signs are appearing to suggest that some churches are changing.

Creating a new branch of Practical Theology

The first influential theologian to include Practical Theology in a course of theological studies was Friedrich Schleiermacher (1768–1834), but he did not extend it beyond training for church leadership (1966). The subject of Practical Theology was the Church and its efficiency. Practical theologians on the Continent in the late nineteenth century regarded the subject as dealing with practical aspects of ordained ministry. The gradual move from concentration upon the Church to concentration upon society in the light of a theology of sociology was greatly influenced by Johannes Baptist Metz (1928–). This implied the inclusion of lay people within the scope of the discipline. When in the 1960s and 70s there were serious attempts to overcome the older church-centred approach, the concept of the kingdom of God became very important. The task of Practical Theology was increasingly understood as all attempts to realize the kingdom.

---

1 Illustrated reports on many of these activities may be found at http://www.queens.ac.uk/ordination/prophetic.php.

Gerben Heitink, the author of the most authoritative contemporary manual of Practical Theology, says that the subject implies both the theory and practice of theology, that is, it is a theory of Christian action.

> [T]his term implies that any involvement with this discipline cannot be limited to an understanding and explanation of the praxis of believing and of 'being church,' but must also have as its purpose to influence and change this praxis. (1999, p. 6)

He adds: 'Thus the exercise of practical theology does not have the church, but rather society, as its horizon' (p. 9).

According to Heitink the main disciplines in Practical Theology are liturgy, homiletics, catechetics and ethics. He suggests in addition poimenics (shepherding or pastoral care) (p. 49) (shepherding or pastoral care) and deaconology 'defined as the theory of the service to humankind and society through compassion and justice' (p. 251). It is time now to add a new discipline: prophetics. This would be the theory and practice of the Church's counter-cultural protest in the service of the kingdom of God. To create and act upon such a theology must now become one of the central purposes of the teaching and practice of Christian mission.

Training for Christian leadership

The prophetic Church needs prophetic leadership. This is unlikely to be achieved without substantial developments in the training and education of clergy and lay people. Suggestions about this will be set out in the form of 25 propositions, each with a brief explanation. The propositions are divided into four groups: the nature of theological education (seven propositions), theological education for mission (seven propositions), theological education for evangelism (seven propositions), and finally, theological education for ministry (four propositions).

A   The nature of theological education

1   *The purpose of theological education is not to understand the world but to change it so as to reduce human suffering in the name of Jesus Christ.*

The final proposition of Karl Marx in his *Theses on Feuerbach* is: 'The philosophers have only interpreted the world, in various ways; the point is to change it' (Marx 1977, p. 158; see also Hull 1997b). This can be adapted so as to become the basic orientation for all theological education for Christian discipleship and vocation. It may or may not apply to the study of theology as a university discipline, but it is foundational for theological education in the Church (Hull 1994, pp. 253–4). Although it received its classical philosophical formulation in the work of Marx, a not dissimilar point is made by Paul in Romans 12.1–2, 'Therefore, I urge you, brothers and sisters, in view of God's mercy, to offer your bodies as a living sacrifice, holy and pleasing to God – this is your true and proper worship.

Do not conform to the pattern of this world, but be transformed by the renewing of your mind. Then you will be able to test and approve what God's will is – his good, pleasing and perfect will.' The renewal of the mind is intimately linked with the presentation of the body. Mental transformation is always embodied (Lakoff and Johnson 1999). One cannot acquire theology by thinking about it; one must do it. Marx introduced his theses by saying that the main defect of much philosophizing is that it 'is conceived only in the form of the object or of contemplation, but not as sensuous human activity, practice, not subjectively' (Marx 1977, p. 156).[2] In other words, mental (and we might say 'spiritual') contemplation is insufficient if the content of contemplation is objectified so that it is 'out there' or subjectified, so that it becomes merely existential; spirituality is projected from the body and is an extension of the body but it does not leave the body behind, for the person remains integrated (Hull 2003/4). Without extending theology into action, the study of theology remains dislocated or ineffective.

2 In order to change the world, it is necessary to understand it.

Christian faith is, in effect, a massive attempt to understand and to change the world. Study of Christian faith enables people to understand the world better, but only if that study is geared towards understanding faith in its context in the world and studying the world itself that is the context of faith. This might be described as an incarnational theology or as a contextual theology. Study of Christian faith reveals its messianic or prophetic character. It surges forward to change the world (Bloch 2009). Otherwise, it is not even understood.

3 Understanding is only a necessary not a sufficient means to change.

Understanding the world in itself and through Christian faith are forms of interpretation requiring hermeneutics. Hermes brings messages from the divine realm to humans, but if the message is not acted upon, there has been no point in his journey. Commentators have sought to interpret Scripture, but without acting on it, interpretation is barren. Hermeneutics leaves the world just as it was before, except that it is understood better. Often this leads to no more than a more successful adaptation to what is better understood. The point, however, is to interpret so as to act for change. Jesus said, 'everyone who hears these words of mine and puts them into practice is like a wise man who built his house on the rock' (Matt. 7.24). 'Do not merely listen to the word, and so deceive yourselves. Do what it says' (Jam. 1.22). We are to be doers of the Word and not interpreters only.

---

2 Paul Steidl-Meier has expressed clearly the value of Karl Marx for the Christian educator, and his comment indicates exactly my own position: 'Marx was one of the greatest thinkers of the nineteenth century. Not to be able to learn from him would be strange indeed. But to identify Christian social ministry with Marxist programs is ingenuous, though in some ways it may be understandable. Learning from Marx does not commit us to Marxism any more than learning from Kant or Plato makes one a Kantian or Platonist' (1984, p. 157).

4 *In theological education, theological reflection is not enough.*

There are several models of reflection; the point, however, is whether they lead to change. Theological educators sometimes speak as if knowledge and reflection leading to understanding were enough. But they are not enough.

5 *Theological education may be compared to action research, the purpose of which is to transform professional practice from within.*

Action research takes place from within a situation in an attempt to bring about change (Townsend 2013). Every class in theological education is a little case of action research. If insights are acquired, they lead to repentance and to a change of will.

6 *Theological education is often too concerned with knowledge, and with the interpretation of knowledge, as a way of maturing the faith of students but mature Christian faith does not consist only in having personal maturity but in pursuing the mission of God for life.*

According to James Fowler, the highest stage of faith development is reached when faith is actualized or universalized (1981, pp. 199–201). Fritz Oser agrees that religious judgement matures, when God is found in solidarity with others with no reservation (Oser and Gmünder 1991, pp. 79–82). Faith matures, when beyond the God who meets our needs we encounter the God who calls us to our vocation.

7 *Theology is best understood as one of the emancipatory disciplines.*

Jürgen Habermas distinguishes the disciplines of measurement or prediction, the disciplines of interpretation or hermeneutics and the disciplines of emancipation through self-reflective critical knowledge (1972, pp. 308–11). Physics would be measurement, history would be interpretative, and political economics and psychoanalysis would be emancipatory. Theological education should become an emancipatory discipline, drawing upon Marxian social science to provide it with the analytic tools necessary to understand poverty, and upon theology for the inspiration of faith, hope and love.

B **Theological education for mission (see Board of Mission 2002)**

8 *Just as theology is an emancipatory discipline, so the mission of God is primarily emancipatory.*

This is because the mission is not the mission of the Church or the mission of Christian faith, but the mission of God. Individual Christians may take part in the mission of God as part of their personal discipleship but if their actions are to be part of the ministry of the Church, they must be authorized or sent by the Church, in the first place, through the local congregation (Avis 2005). The individual Christian is thus an agent of the local church.

9 The local churches are agents of the one, holy, catholic and apostolic Church.

Local congregations are not to be isolated, but must be in fellowship with other congregations. The local church does not live for itself, but for the wider mission of the one, holy, catholic and apostolic Church, and we might add, the wider prophetic Church.

10 The one, holy, catholic, apostolic and prophetic Church is an agent of the mission of God.

What is true for the local church is true of the Church as a whole. It does not live unto itself, it is not the object of its own existence. It is a project of the mission of God. The Church is an agent of the mission, a symbol of the mission and a foreshadowing of the mission, but it is not the mission itself.

11 God may have other saving projects.

There is nothing in Christian faith that requires Christians to believe that God might not have other saving projects. Indeed, such is probably the case. If music has or may have a redemptive power, an energy to transform life and relieve pain, then we may consider it to be an agent of the mission of God. The same is true of love at its best, and many other elevating and humanizing activities. It is probable that other religions may also be projects of God, although this is only a Christian way of putting it. The overflowing love of God offers a powerful suggestion that God may be active in places and through agencies unknown to us. The business of Christians is to encourage Christian faith to be faithful as an agent of the divine mission.

12 The goal of the mission of God is the reign or kingdom of God.

The Church, in acting as an agent of the mission, proclaims the mission of God by seeking to adumbrate the kingdom. This is the First Mark of Mission recognized by the Anglican Communion worldwide and by other churches: 'To proclaim the kingdom of God'. In this way the mission of God through the Church is identified with the mission of God through Jesus Christ.

13   *Emancipation can only be understood by being involved in eman-*
      cipation and seeking the emancipation of others.

The causes of suffering and oppression can be studied and, up to a point, understood. But not until the learners turn their learning into practice will the meaning of emancipation be truly understood.

14   *Both Church and society need emancipation, the former in order*
      to serve the latter.

The mission proceeds from Church to world and from world to Church, and
to both Church and world by the Spirit of God. The society in which we live
requires emancipation from the love of money, the pursuit of power and
from various forms of injustice, inequality, poverty, exclusion, militarism
and violence. The determination of specific emancipatory needs will vary
from one situation to another. The Church needs to be emancipated from
self-deception, salvation as merely interior and eschatological, enclosure
within the accumulated power of its past, and from its tendencies of exclusion and self-preoccupation.

C   Theological education for evangelism

15   *In Britain today many people are so alienated from the Church*
      and its message that the language of faith has become largely
      unintelligible and meaningless.

There are at least two possible responses to this. The first response would be
apologetics, i.e. to explain and defend the meaning of Christian faith in a per-
suasive manner. However, apologetics is aimed primarily at sceptics. Millions
of people in Britain today are not so much sceptical about the Christian faith
as indifferent to it. They simply do not see the relevance of Christian faith, and
therefore the question of its coherence and credibility does not arise. A second
response is therefore necessary, one that attempts to demonstrate the Christian
faith in action without in the first place using Christian words.

16   *Contemporary experience indicates that although some forms of*
      speech evangelism can be effective, accompanying signs are often
      necessary to make verbal witness credible.

No doubt sometimes conversations about Christian faith can be interesting
and attractive, and thoughtful people who are not Christians may be moved
by hearing sermons or reading books, but in general advocates of Christian
faith are more credible when they speak or write about some issue in life or

society that is acknowledged to be of wider significance. The contributors on BBC Radio 4's 'Thought for the Day' are more impressive when they refer sensibly to a public issue than when they merely advertise their religion. When the meaning and relevance of faith is demonstrated in speech or in practice, it may be called a 'sign'.

17 The need to support speech with signs is not a new development.

A feature of the Fourth Gospel is the many 'signs' that accompanied the words of Jesus. For example, the changing of the water into wine at the wedding at Cana is described as 'the first of the signs through which he revealed his glory' (John 2.11). And the book of Acts tells us that convincing signs accompanied the proclamation of the gospel: 'The apostles performed many signs and wonders among the people' (5.12).

18 What were impressive signs in the ancient Hellenistic world do not have the same meaning for most people in post-Enlightenment Europe.

A late addition to Mark's Gospel says that 'these signs will accompany those who believe: In my name they will drive out demons; they will speak in new tongues; they will pick up snakes with their hands; and when they drink deadly poison, it will not hurt them at all' (16.17–18). There are a small number of churches in the United States, mostly in the Appalachian Mountains, where poisonous snakes are handled as a form of Christian witness, but this practice has been declared illegal in most states following several deaths because of snake bite. There have also been Christians who have drunk poison to demonstrate their faith. Signs like these would strike most people as being indications of fanaticism and credulity rather than witnesses to faith. The same cannot be said of *glossolalia*, the ecstatic experience of speaking in tongues, which is much more widespread and is exhilarating for Christians who practise it. However, Paul was critical of its value as a public witness: 'Anyone who speaks in a tongue edifies themselves, but the one who prophesies edifies the church' (1 Cor. 14.4). Exorcism is recognized as being therapeutic in some cases by many mainstream churches, but it is seldom credible to modern Western people as an evidence of the truth of Christian faith, although it may still have a place in the worldview of other cultures.

19 Sign literalism is as inappropriate today as other forms of biblical literalism.

Even under the conditions of postmodernity, the witness of Christian faith is less credible because of various kinds of literalism which have an appeal to some Christians. We may describe this as a hermeneutic of the literal, and we may distinguish several forms of this. There are kinds of scientific and historical literalism which fail to recognize the nature of the biblical literature, and there is a kind of ethical literalism which makes selective use of biblical precepts to demand compliance from modern Christians. For example, in the nineteenth century there were Christians who defended slavery on the grounds that it was supported in the New Testament (which it is), and today there are some who believe that gay and lesbian relationships are forbidden in the New Testament, although this is less clear. We may also describe certain kinds of evangelism as being 'word literalism' or perhaps 'gospel literalism' that takes certain expressions used in the New Testament to describe Christian faith such as 'Jesus is the son of David' or 'Jesus was the promised messiah' or even 'Jesus died for our sins' and uses them today regardless of the fact that the meaning of such expressions lies deeply hidden in the first century. It is because the literalism of such expressions leads to a loss of meaning that the Church of England requires its ordained clergy to confess the faith of the Church, 'which faith the Church is called upon to proclaim afresh in each generation'. The same is true of those who believe that the signs which supported the proclamation of Christian faith in the first century are still the ones to be used today. This may be called 'sign literalism'.

Just as these various kinds of biblical literalism are mostly ineffective as advocacy for Christian faith today, the same may be said of the biblical signs. As we have shown with the examples above, it is necessary to explain these ancient practices and forms of speech so that we retain something of their original spirit or function, while interpreting them in ways that modern people can more easily understand. However, it is as true today as it was in the ancient world that speech alone is usually insufficient. Words must be accompanied by actions. But what actions? A biblical theology of prophetic signs should be reclaimed today in order to make proclamation credible.

20   *The Five Marks of Mission recognized by the Anglican Communion, the Methodist Church and other churches may be regarded as such signs.*

They are: (1) to proclaim the Good News of the kingdom; (2) to teach, baptize and nurture new believers; (3) to respond to human need by loving service; (4) to seek to transform unjust structures of society, to challenge violence of every kind and to pursue peace and reconciliation; and (5) to strive to safeguard the integrity of creation and to sustain the life of the earth. Thus the proclamation of the kingdom of God is an evangelical sign. The remaining statements are examples of how the kingdom of God is to be proclaimed in our generation. Perhaps the Second Mark might be regarded as speaking about discipleship, and the remaining three Marks would then be some of the ways in which discipleship is to be expressed today. Numbers 3 and 4 are closely connected, for if the Third Mark refers to the works of mercy and the Fourth Mark to the works of justice, reflection almost always shows us that when we ask why a work of mercy is necessary we are led to deeper sources of injustice in our society. It hardly needs to be said that the protection of the earth itself is a compelling aspect of discipleship with an obvious implication for witnessing. The meaning of the Five Marks is that when discipleship is expressed through relevant, contemporary action, and so proclaims the kingdom of God, evangelism is taking place.

Of course, none of this means that the Five Marks do not have their own integrity. They are to be pursued for their own sake. Evangelization, if it takes place and is effective, is an implication not a motivation.

21 *The Fourth Mark of Mission, seeking to identify, expose, embarrass and transform the unjust structures of society, may become a credible and impressive sign of the presence of the kingdom of God.*

This might be done through the public lamentation of the sorrow and loss caused by the unjust structures of power and violence, or it might take the form of resistance to torture, enslavement, poverty and weapons of mass destruction. The 'Walks of Witness' conducted by local churches on Good Friday should help onlookers to identify Christ crucified in the contemporary world and not only in the memory of the Church. Actions of this kind may be regarded as prophetic signs, since they carry forward into contemporary life the values and ideals which the prophets demanded. Through the creation of such signs the Church itself may become a symbol and a foretaste of the kingdom of God.

D   Theological education for ministry

22 *Theological formation of both lay people and clergy should be based on belief in the prophetic calling of all believers.*

'I wish that all the Lord's people were prophets and that the Lord would put his Spirit on them!' (Num. 11.29). 'I will pour out my Spirit on all people. Your sons and daughters will prophesy, your young men will see visions, your old men will dream dreams' (Acts 2.17), and so will your women, both young and old. It is true that the prophetic Church is not the only biblical model of the Church. We may consider also the Church as the Mystical Body of Christ and the Church as sacrament, however, because of the urgency of worldwide inequality, poverty and suffering, the special calling of the Church today is to prophetic.

23 *Theological courses and centres should do what they teach.*

Courses and institutions should be actively linked with Christian campaigning bodies, and should model for their students the churches which some day they will lead. Thus to teach and learn theology, theology must be put into practice.

24 *Worship is an essential preparation for the liberating action of
    God through faith, but it is only a preparation. If it becomes
    autonomous, it may acquire the qualities of a fetish.*

Because it is only part of a larger whole, the fetish may glow with a kind of fascinating energy but this numinous quality should be found wherever God is at
work in the world and not only in worship. Worship is a resource for mission,
not a substitute for it.

25 *Students should be placed in transformative situations on the
    frontier of the Church and society, and not only in existing
    congregations.*

In assessing the spirituality of students, greater attention should be paid to their
competence as agents of change and their understanding and practice of social
analysis, the social sciences, and the practice of prophetic protest.

Conclusion

Theological education has two moments: out of pain and into pain. First, it is
necessary to find a resolution to one's personal pain, for not until individual
static is less noisy can one hear the pain of the world. But if theological education and pastoral care do no more than enable people to be reconciled to their
own personal pain, we will be left with a more comfortable Church but not
a prophetic one. This is why the second step is necessary – to move into an
understanding and an experience of the mission of faith for the alleviation of
the suffering of the world.

Appendix 1

Criteria for Prophetic Action

The following set of criteria are used in The Queen's Foundation for Ecumenical Theological Education in Birmingham, England to assess suggestions that are brought forward by staff or students about actions to be taken in the course of theological education.

Preliminary

Does the proposed action recognize the distinction between the works of mercy (the Third Mark of Mission) and the works of justice (the Fourth Mark of Mission)?

SECTION 1: Faith and Faithfulness

Formation

1   Is participation in the proposed action likely to be effective as a contribution to ministerial formation?

Theology

2   To what extent can the proposed action be regarded as springing from or inspired by Christian faith and its biblical roots?

Worship

3   Will the proposed action spring from worship and will it return to influence subsequent worship?

SECTION 2: The Example of Others Present and Past

Church policy

4   Is the proposed activity consistent with the ethical pronouncements and policies of the churches?

Policies of NGOs

5   Would any of the major Christian or social justice campaigning organizations support the proposed action?

Cooperation

6   Does the proposed action offer possibilities for cooperation with people from other religions? Does it present possibilities for cooperation with atheists and other secular people? Does it offer opportunities for cooperation with staff and students from other theological colleges and courses?

History

7   Are there examples of previous church actions in this area or subject? If so, what can we learn from these activities?

SECTION 3:   Citizenship and the Law

Legality

8   Is the proposed action legal? If not, is it nevertheless consistent with the highest ideals of citizenship? If illegal, is it nevertheless ethically and theologically legitimate?

SECTION 4:   Ethical Considerations

Non-Violence

9   Will the proposed action be fully non-violent in its purposes and methods?

Collateral damage

10   Will the proposed activities cause unacceptable embarrassment, disadvantage or loss to bystanders, or others likely to be affected?

Self Interest

11   Does the proposed action involve our own interest?

SECTION 5:   Practical Considerations

Effectiveness

12   Is the proposed initiative likely to be effective as a step towards its own intrinsic objectives? If not, is it worth doing as a symbol of protest?

Resources

13   Is the proposed action practicable in terms of time, money and other resources?

SECTION 6:   Methodology

14   How many of the above criteria should be satisfied in a particular case?

Appendix 2

Annotated Bibliography for Chapter 3

There is so much literature relevant to Chapter 3 that I could have added a footnote to nearly every sentence. Rather than doing this, I have given footnotes only when a specific quotation is used. I hope this annotated bibliographical appendix will guide readers who want to pursue some of the lines of thought that I have suggested. It will also demonstrate that I have said nothing that I had not already received from the work of others.

I would first like to pay tribute to the authors of the three books which have done most to influence my thinking. They are:

Norman K. Gottwald, 1999, *The Tribes of Yahweh: A Sociology of the Religion of Liberated Israel*, Sheffield: Sheffield Academic Press, first published in 1979.

This is a seminal book of biblical sociology, demonstrating the close connection between faith in God and a social structure of justice and peace as well as explaining why this connection is so little realized. Gottwald provides an essential background for understanding the teaching of Jesus about the kingdom of God.

Roland Boer (ed.), 2002, *Tracking 'The Tribes of Yahweh': On the Trail of a Classic*, London: Sheffield Academic Press.

A useful collection of articles dealing with the history, influence and Marxist ideology of the classic book by Gottwald.

Fernando Belo, 1981, *A Materialist Reading of the Gospel of Mark*, Maryknoll, NY: Orbis Books.

Although the complexity of structural Marxism makes this a difficult book to read, it is ground-breaking in its emphasis upon the actual conditions of first-century Palestine.

Ched Myers, 2008, *Binding the Strong Man,* Maryknoll, NY: Orbis Books, first published in 1988.

This is a foundational text for those interested in the social and political conditions of the life of Jesus. It is particularly important for uncovering the social class perspective of the modern reader.

Two additional books from Ched Myers apply his theology of Mark's Gospel to Christian lifestyle. They are challenging, but the American context of the examples means that they are not quite so relevant for Britain:

Ched Myers, 1994, *Who Will Roll Away the Stone?: Discipleship Queries for First World Christians*, Maryknoll, NY: Orbis Books.

Ched Myers and Karen Lattea (eds), 1996, *Say to this Mountain: Mark's Story of Discipleship*, Maryknoll, NY: Orbis Books.

Historical studies

Recent studies of the Roman Empire have tended to move away from topics such as the Roman army and legal system and have highlighted the social and ideological techniques used to control conquered populations:

Neil Elliott, 2000, 'Paul and the Politics of Empire: Problems and Prospects', in Richard A. Horsley (ed.), *Paul and Politics*, Harrisburg, PA: Trinity Press International, pp. 18–19.

Klaus Wengst, 1987, *Pax Romana and the Peace of Jesus Christ*, translated by John Bowden, London: SCM Press.

Several studies have concentrated upon Roman control through the patronage system:

Efrairn Agosto, 2004, 'Patronage and Commendation, Imperial and Anti Imperial', in Richard A. Horsley (ed.), *Paul and the Roman Imperial Order*, Harrisburg, PA: Trinity Press International, pp. 103–23.

Peter Garnsey and Richard Saller, 1997, 'Patronal Power Relations', in Richard A. Horsley (ed.), *Paul and Empire: Religion and Power in Roman Imperial Society*, Harrisburg, PA: TPI, pp. 96–103.

Such studies help us to understand the relationships between the high priestly families, the Herodians and Rome.

Yizhar Hirschfeld, 1997, 'Jewish Rural Settlement in Judaea in the Early Roman Period', in Susan E. Alcock (ed.), *The Early Roman Empire in the East*, Oxford: Oxbow, 1997, pp. 72–88.
Hirschfeld gives interesting archaeological background on the situation in Judea and Galilee at the time when the Synoptic Gospels were written.

Rodney Stark, 2007, *Cities of God: The Real Story of How Christianity Became an Urban Movement and Conquered Rome*, New York: HarperCollins.
Stark describes life in the cities of the early Empire.

Many studies of the Gospels and Paul in recent years have sought to interpret them against the imperial background. Warren Carter invites us to hear the Gospels as they might have been heard originally:

Matthew and Empire: Initial Explorations, 2001, Harrisburg, PA: Trinity Press.

The Roman Empire and the New Testament: An Essential Guide, 2006, Abingdon Essential Guides, Nashville, TN: Abingdon.

John and Empire: Initial Explorations, 2008, London: T&T Clark.

Anthropology, sociology and economics

John Milbank is sceptical about the usefulness of social science perspectives on the Bible: *Theology and Social Theory: Beyond Secular Reason*, 1990, Oxford: Blackwell.

Nevertheless, as my choice of books already indicates, I believe that contributions from sociologists, anthropologists and economists have shed much light on the background and meaning of the Gospels.

John H. Kautsky, 1997, *The Politics of Aristocratic Empires*, New Brunswick, NJ: Transaction Publishers.

Kautsky helps us to understand the social and political structure of the Roman Empire and to appreciate the huge gulf between the peasantry and the aristocracy in ancient Palestine. I found it illuminating to read Josephus *The Antiquities of the Jews* in the light of Kautsky. The admiration of Josephus for aristocratic government is an important theme in his history of ancient Israel, which is almost entirely confined to the rivalries and wars between the aristocratic elites of the ancient Eastern Mediterranean.

Since the early 1990s Bruce J. Malina has been studying the Gospels with the help of the sociology of Mediterranean culture. Interpretation of many of the sayings of Jesus has been enriched by his work on the honour code.

Social Science Commentary on the Synoptic Gospels, 1992, Minneapolis: Fortress (with Richard L. Rohrbaugh).

Windows on the World of Jesus: Time Travel to Ancient Judea, 1993, Louisville, KY: Westminster/John Knox Press.

The Social World of Jesus and the Gospels, 1996, London: Routledge.

The Social Gospel of Jesus: The Kingdom of God in Mediterranean Perspective, 2001, Minneapolis: Fortress.

The Social Setting of Jesus and the Gospels, 2002, Minneapolis: Fortress Press.

Pieter F. Craffert applies the anthropology of the shaman in traditional societies to Jesus of Nazareth: *The Life of a Galilean Shaman: Jesus of Nazareth in Anthropological-Historical Perspective*, 2008, Eugene, OR: Cascade.

The anthropologist Mary Douglas has written a brilliant book on Leviticus, *Leviticus as Literature*, 2000, Oxford: Oxford University Press, which has helped me to clarify the mission of Jesus and the demand for ritual purity.

Social history

Willy Schottroff and Wolfgang Stegemann (eds), 1984, *God of the Lowly: Socio-Historical Interpretations of the Bible*, Maryknoll, NY: Orbis.

Ekkehard W. Stegemann and Wolfgang Stegemann, 1999, *The Jesus Movement: A Social History of its First Century*, translated by O.C. Dean, Edinburgh: T&T Clark.

Robert L. Webb, 2006, *John the Baptiser and Prophet: A Socio-Historical Study*, Eugene, OR: Wipf & Stock.

It is often those who are themselves engaged in political controversy who have emphasized the political nature of the mission of Jesus. Andre Trocmé, a French Protestant pastor, turned his village into a refuge for Jewish families fleeing from the Nazis. An advocate of non-violent methods of resistance, his work has been inspirational for many later authors:

Jesus and the Nonviolent Revolution, 2003, ed. Charles E. Moore, Maryknoll, NY: Orbis.

Howard Thurman, 1981, *Jesus and the Disinherited*, Richmond, IN: Friends United Press.
Thurman interprets Jesus in the light of the struggle for African–American rights in the United States.

Obery M. Hendricks, 2006, *The Politics of Jesus: Rediscovering the True Revolutionary Nature of the Teachings of Jesus and How They Have Been Corrupted*, New York: Three Leaves Press.
Hendricks contrasts the non-violent methods of Jesus with the so-called Christian claims of American Presidents Ronald Reagan and George W. Bush.
An influential addition to the study of the non-violent protest movements of Jesus is: Walter Wink, 2003, *Jesus and Non-Violence: A Third Way*, Minneapolis: Fortress.

New Testament Studies

Turning to authors who can be described as mainly New Testament specialists, one of the most plausible alternatives to interpreting Jesus as a social and political prophet is to see him as an apocalyptic prophet, i.e. someone less concerned about the social and economic situation of the people around him than preoccupied with a powerful belief in the approaching end of history:

Dale Allison, 1998, *Jesus of Nazareth: Millenarian Prophet*, Minneapolis: Fortress.

Bart D. Ehrman, 1999, *Jesus: Apocalyptic Prophet of the New Millennium*, Oxford: Oxford University Press.

Some New Testament specialists interpret the prophetic work of Jesus mainly in terms of the similarities between his prophetic signs or actions and those of the Old Testament prophets:

C. H. Dodd, 1930, 'Jesus as Teacher and Prophet', in G. K. A. Bell and Adolf Deissmann (eds), *Mysterium Christi: Christological Studies by British and German Theologians*, London: Longmans, Green, pp. 53–66.

Morna Hooker, 1997, *The Signs of a Prophet: The Prophetic Actions of Jesus*, London: SCM Press.

However, many socio-political studies enable us to see that the understanding of Jesus as prophet involves the whole of his work:

Douglas Oakman, 2008, *Jesus and the Peasants,* Eugene, OR: Cascade Books.

Douglas Oakman, 2012, *The Political Aims of Jesus*, Minneapolis: Fortress.

Marcus Borg has explained the political nature of many of the religious controversies of Jesus:

Conflict, Holiness and Politics in the Teachings of Jesus, 1984, Toronto: Edwin Mellen.

But Paula Fredriksen takes a different point of view:

Jesus of Nazareth, King of the Jews: A Jewish Life and the Emergence of Christianity, 2000, London: Macmillan.

Richard Horsley has written extensively on the social and political background of Palestine in the time of Jesus, emphasizing Jesus as a reformer of Galilean village society and one in conflict with the powers:

Jesus and the Spiral of Violence: Popular Jewish Resistance in Roman Palestine, 1993, Minneapolis: Fortress Press.

Sociology and the Jesus Movement, 1994, New York: Continuum.

Jesus and Empire: The Kingdom of God and the New World Disorder, 2003, Minneapolis: Fortress Press.

Jesus in Context: Power, People and Performance, 2008, Minneapolis: Fortress Press.

Jesus and the Powers: Conflict, Covenant and the Hope of the Poor, 2010, Minneapolis: Fortress Press.

The Prophet Jesus and the Renewal of Israel: Moving beyond a Diversionary Debate, 2012, Grand Rapids: Eerdmans.

The parables of Jesus have been reimagined in their original context in a brilliant work by Luise Schottroff:

The Parables of Jesus, 2006, Minneapolis: Fortress.

William Herzog had already done something similar, interpreting some of the parables as examples of Paulo Freire's pedagogy of the oppressed in:

Parables as Subversive Speech, 1994, Louisville, KY: Westminster John Knox.

I owe a particular debt to his *Jesus, Justice, and the Reign of God: A Ministry of Liberation*, 2000, Louisville, KY: Westminster John Knox, which is one of the finest contributions made to Gospel scholarship in recent years.

Also important is his *Prophet and Teacher: An Introduction to the Historical Jesus*, 2005, Louisville, KY: Westminster John Knox.

Marxism and the Bible

Finally, I would like to acknowledge my debt to Marxist interpretations of the Bible. The authors I have read vary in their attitude to Marxism. Some are secular ideological Marxists, some are Christian Marxists and others are biblical scholars who have been influenced by the materialist outlook. I have already mentioned Fernando Belo.

Michel Clevenot, *Materialist Approaches to the Bible*, 1985, Maryknoll, NY: Orbis is really a simplified version of Belo applied to the Bible as a whole.

George Pixley came independently to much the same view as Gottwald on the kingdom of God, but applies it vigorously to the message of Jesus in *God's Kingdom*, 1981, London: SCM Press.

One of the most readable and influential accounts of the work of Jesus is Milan MacHovec, 1976, *A Marxist Looks at Jesus*, London: Darton, Longman and Todd. The original title of this book before it was translated from the German was *Jesus for Atheists*, which is a much better name for the book.

There is a similar problem with Jose Miranda, 1977, *Marx and the Bible: A Critique of the Philosophy of Oppression,* London: SCM Press. Miranda is a Latin American liberation theologian like Pixley, but his book is not really about Marx and the Bible. It is an important scholarly contribution to the meaning of the Bible as a whole, emphasizing its social and political significance.

Roland Boer has made outstanding contributions with his scholarly reviews of the literature in *Marxist Criticism of the Bible: A Critical Introduction to Marxist Literary Theory and the Bible*, 2003, London: Continuum.

If it is true, as I have suggested, that Christology has to some extent concealed the prophetic work of Jesus, it is Marxist admiration for Jesus which has restored it.

Acknowledgements

Chapter 7 is based upon two periodical articles: 'From Experiential Educator to Nationalist Theologian: the Hymns of Isaac Watts', *Panorama: International Journal of Comparative Religious Education and Values*, Vol. 14, No. 1, Summer 2002, pp. 91–106, and 'Isaac Watts and the Origins of British Imperial Theology', *International Congregational Journal*, Vol. 4, No. 2, February 2005, pp. 59–79.

Chapter 12 is based upon 'Christian Education and the Reconstruction of Christian Faith', in Marian de Souza, Gloria Durka, Kathleen Engebretson, Robert Jackson and Andrew McGrady (eds), 2006, *International Handbook of the Religious, Moral and Spiritual Dimensions in Education,* Dordrecht, The Netherlands: Springer, pp. 23–40.

Chapter 13 is based upon 'Mission Shaped and Kingdom Focused?', in Steven Croft (ed.), 2008, *Mission-shaped Questions: Defining issues for today's Church*, London: Church House Publishing: and 'Only One Way to Walk With God', in Louise Nelstrop, Martyn Percy (eds), 2009, *Evaluating Fresh Expressions: Explorations of the Emerging Church*, London: SCM Press, pp. 105–21.

Bibliography

Lionel Adey, 1988, *Class and Idol in the English Hymn*, Vancouver, BC: University of British Columbia Press.

Efrairn Agosto, 2004, 'Patronage and Commendation, Imperial and Anti-Imperial', in Richard A. Horsley (ed.), *Paul and the Roman Imperial Order*, Harrisburg, PA: Trinity Press International.

Joe Aldred, 2005, *Respect: Understanding British Caribbean Christianity*, Peterborough: Epworth.

Dale Allison, 1998, *Jesus of Nazareth: Millenarian Prophet*, Minneapolis: Fortress.

Dale C. Allison, 2010, 'Ezekiel, UFOs and the Nation of Islam', in Paul Joyce and Andrew Mein (eds), *After Ezekiel: Essays on the Reception of a Difficult Prophet*, London: Continuum, pp. 247–57.

R. Ambler and J. Haslam (eds), 1980, *Agenda for Prophets: Towards a Political Theology of Britain*, London: Bowerdean Press.

S. Amin, 1997, *Capitalism in the Age of Globalization: The Management of Contemporary Society*, London: Zed Books.

Yairah Amit, 2006, 'The Role of Prophecy and Prophets in the Chronicler's World', in Michael H. Floyd and Robert D. Haak (eds), *Prophets, Prophecy and Prophetic Texts in Second Temple Judaism*, London: T&T Clark, pp. 80–101.

Allan Anderson, 2007, *Spreading Fires: The Missionary Nature of Early Pentecostalism*, London: SCM Press.

David Armitage, 2000, *The Ideological Origins of the British Empire*, Cambridge: Cambridge University Press.

Karen Armstrong, 1988, *Holy War: The Crusades and their Impact on Today's World*, London: Macmillan.

G. Arrighi, 1994, *The Long Twentieth Century: Money, Power and the Origins of Our Times*, London: Verso.

Assize of Clarendon, 1186, http://www.fordham.edu/halsall/source/aclarendon.html.

Paul Avis, 2005, *A Ministry Shaped by Mission*, London: T&T Clark.

William Barclay, 1958, *The Mind of St Paul*, London: Collins.

M. Barkun, 1994, *Religion and the Racist Right: The Origins of the Christian Identity Movement*, London: University of North Carolina Press.

C. K. Barrett, 1963, 'The Bible in the New Testament Period', in D. E. Nineham, *The Church's Use of the Bible: Past and Present*, London: SPCK, pp. 1–24.

Karl Barth, 1919, *Der Römerbrief* [ET 1933].

Karl Barth, 1956, *Church Dogmatics I.2: The Doctrine of the Word of God*, Edinburgh: T&T Clark.

Karl Barth, 1957, *Church Dogmatics II.1: The Doctrine of God*, Edinburgh: T&T Clark.

Roland Barthes, 1977, 'Death of the Author', in *Image–Music–Text: Essays Selected and Translated by Stephen Heath*, London: Fontana, pp. 142–8.

John Barton, 2003, *Understanding Old Testament Ethics: Approaches and Explorations*, London: Westminster John Knox.

G. Baum, 1975, *Religion and Alienation: A Theological Reading of Sociology*, New York: Paulist Press.

Gerlinde Baumann, 2001, 'Prophetic Objections to YHWH as the Violent Husband of Israel: Reinterpretations of the Prophetic Marriage Metaphor in Second Isaiah (Isaiah 40–55)', in Athalya Brenner (ed.), *Prophets and Daniel*, Sheffield: Sheffield Academic Press, pp. 88–120.

Richard Baxter, 1662, *The Saints' Everlasting Rest: Or a Treatise of the Blessed State of the Saints*, 9th ed., London.

Hilary McD. Beckles, 1998, 'The Hub of Empire: The Caribbean and Britain in the Seventeenth Century', in Nicholas Canny (ed.), *The Origins of Empire: British Overseas Enterprise to the Close of the Seventeenth Century*, Oxford: Oxford University Press, pp. 218–39.

Fernando Belo, 1981, *A Materialist Reading of the Gospel of Mark*, Maryknoll: Orbis Books.

Arthur Christopher Benson, 1900, *Life of Edward White Benson Volume I*, London: Macmillan.

George Benson, 1609, *A Sermon Preached at Paul's Cross 7th May 1609*, London.

Sacvan Bercovitch, 1978, *The American Jeremiad*, Madison, WI: University of Wisconsin Press.

Peter L. Berger, 1980, *The Heretical Imperative: Contemporary Possibilities of Religious Affirmation*, London: Collins.

R. F. Berkhofer, 1965, *Salvation and the Savage: An Analysis of Protestant Missions and American Indian Responses 1787–1862*, Lexington, KT: University of Kentucky Press.

R. F. Berkhofer, 1978, *The White Man's Indian: Images of the American Indian from Columbus to the Present*, New York: Knopf.

Bernard of Clairvaux, *In Praise of the New Knighthood*, http://www.the-orb.net/encyclop/religion/monastic/bernard.html.

Bernard of Clairvaux, *Sermons on the Song of Songs*, http://www.pathsoflove.com/bernard/songofsongs/sermon64.html.

Bernard of Clairvaux, 1953, *The Letters of St. Bernard of Clairvaux*, translated by Bruno Scott James, London: Burns Oates.

Daniel Berrigan, 1996, *Isaiah: Spirit of Courage, Gift of Tears*, Minneapolis: Fortress.

Daniel Berrigan, 1997, *Ezekiel Vision in the Dust*, Maryknoll: Orbis.

Daniel Berrigan, 1998, *Daniel Under the Siege of the Divine*, Farmington, Sussex: The Plough.

Daniel Berrigan, 1999, *Jeremiah: The World, the Wound of God*, Minneapolis: Fortress.

Daniel Berrigan, 2008, *The Kings and Their Gods: The Pathology of Power*, Grand Rapids: Eerdmans.

Stephen B. Bevans and Roger P. Schroeder, 2004, *Constants in Context: A Theology of Mission for Today*, Maryknoll: Orbis.

William Garden Blaikie, 1910, *The Personal Life of David Livingstone*, London: John Murray.

Johannes Blauw, 1962, *The Missionary Nature of the Church: A Survey of the Biblical Theology of Mission*, London: Lutterworth Press.

Joseph Blenkinsopp, 1984, *A History of Prophecy in Israel: From the Settlement in the Land to the Hellenistic Period*, London: SPCK.

Joseph Blenkinsopp, 1995, *Sage, Priest, Prophet: Religious and Intellectual Leadership in Ancient Israel*, Louisville, KY: Westminster John Knox.

Joseph Blenkinsopp, 1996, *A History of Prophecy in Israel* (revised and enlarged edition), Louisville, KY: Westminster John Knox.

Ernst Bloch, 1986, *The Principle of Hope* (vol. 3), Oxford: Basil Blackwell.

Ernst Bloch, 2009, *Atheism in Christianity: The Religion of the Exodus and the Kingdom*, London: Verso.

Marc Block, 1973, *The Royal Touch, Sacred Monarchy and Scrofula in England and France*, London: Routledge, Keegan and Paul.

Board of Mission of the Archbishops' Council, 2002, *Presence and Prophecy: A Heart for Mission in Theological Education*, London: Church House Publishing.

Roland Boer (ed.), 2002, *Tracking 'The Tribes of Yahweh': On the Trail of a Classic*, London: Sheffield Academic Press.

Roland Boer, 2003, *Marxist Criticism of the Bible: A Critical Introduction to Marxist Literary Theory and the Bible*, London: Continuum.

The Book of Common Prayer, Cambridge: Cambridge University Press.

Marcus Borg, 1984, *Conflict, Holiness and Politics in the Teachings of Jesus*, Toronto: Edwin Mellen.

David J. Bosch, 1991, *Transforming Mission: Paradigm Shifts in the Theology of Mission*, Maryknoll: Orbis.

Andrew Bradstock, 1997, *Faith in the Revolution: The Political Theologies of Müntzer and Winstanley*, London: SPCK.

Andrew Bradstock, 2011, *Radical Religion in Cromwell's England: A Concise History from the English Civil War to the End of the Commonwealth*, London: I. B. Tauris.

John Brewer, 1989, *The Sinews of Power: War, Money and the English State 1688–1783*, London: Unwin Hymen.

Charles Brown, 2002, *Niebuhr and His Age: Reinhold Niebuhr's Prophetic Role and Legacy*, Harrisburg, PA: Trinity Press.

Walter Brueggemann, 1968, *Tradition for Crisis: a Study in Hosea*, Atlanta: John Knox.

Walter Brueggemann, 1992, *The Prophetic Imagination*, London: SCM Press.

Walter Brueggemann, 1992a, *Hopeful Imagination: Prophetic Voices in Exile*, London: SCM Press.

Walter Brueggemann, 1994, *A Social Reading of the Old Testament: Prophetic Approaches to Israel's Communal Life*, Minneapolis: Fortress Press.

Walter Brueggemann, 1997, *Theology of the Old Testament: Testimony, Dispute, Advocacy*, Minneapolis: Fortress.

Walter Brueggemann, 1998, *Isaiah 1–39*, Louisville, KY: Westminster John Knox.

Walter Brueggemann, 1998a, *Isaiah 40–66*, Louisville, KY: Westminster John Knox.

Walter Brueggemann, 2000, *Texts that Linger, Words that Explode: Listening to Prophetic Voices*, Minneapolis: Fortress.

Walter Brueggemann, 2006, *Like Fire in the Bones: Listening for the Prophetic Word in Jeremiah*, Minneapolis: Fortress.

Martin Buber, 1949, *The Prophetic Faith*, New York: Macmillan.

David Burr, 2001, *The Spiritual Franciscans: From Protest to Persecution in the Century after Saint Francis*, Philadelphia: Pennsylvania State University Press.

Manas Buthelezi, 1986, 'The Church as a Prophetic Sign', in Gennadios Limouris (ed.), *Church, Kingdom, World: The Church as Mystery and Prophetic Sign*, Geneva: World Council of Churches, pp. 138–44.

Nicholas P. Canny, 1998, 'The Ideology of English Colonization from Ireland to America', in David Armitage (ed.), *Theories of Empire 1450–1800*, Aldershot: Ashgate Publishing, pp. 179–202.

Nicholas Canny, 1998a, 'The Origins of Empire: An Introduction', in Nicholas Canny (ed.), *The Origins of Empire: British Overseas Enterprise to the Close of the Seventeenth Century*, Oxford: Oxford University Press, pp. 124–47.

Robert Carroll, 1979, *When Prophecy Failed: Reactions and Responses to Failure in the Old Testament Prophetic Traditions*, London: SCM Press.

William C. Carroll, 1996, *Fat King, Lean Beggar: Representations of Poverty in the Age of Shakespeare*, London: Cornell University Press.

Warren Carter, 2001, *Matthew and Empire: Initial Explorations*, Harrisburg, PA: Trinity Press International.

Bartolomé de las Casas, 1992, *Witness: Writings of Bartolome de Las Casas*, edited and translated by George Sanderlin, Maryknoll: Orbis.

John K. Chance, 1989, *Conquest of the Sierra: Spaniards and Indians in Colonial Oaxaca*, London: University of Oklahoma Press.

Kevin Cain, 2001, 'Who makes it rain? A question of biblical authority', *Evangelical Missions Quarterly* 37:3, pp. 320–7.

William Carey, 1792, *An Enquiry into the Obligations of Christians, to Use Means for the Conversion of the Heathens*, http://www.gutenberg.org/files/11449/11449-h/11449-h.htm.

Warren Carter, 2006, *The Roman Empire and the New Testament: An Essential Guide*, Abingdon Essential Guides, Nashville, TN: Abingdon.

Warren Carter, 2008, *John and Empire: Initial Explorations*, London: T&T Clark.

David Chidester, 1992, *Religions of South Africa*, London: Routledge.

Brevard Childs, 1979, *Introduction to the Old Testament as Scripture*, London: SCM Press.

Brevard Childs, 2004, *The Struggle to Understand Isaiah as Christian Scripture*, Grand Rapids: Eerdmans.

T. Christensen and W. R. Hutchison (eds), 1982, *Missionary Ideologies in the Imperialist Era, 1880–1920*, Aarhus, Denmark: Aros.

Eric Christiansen, 1997, *The Northern Crusades*, London: Penguin.

Church of England, 2009, *Church and Earth 2009–2016: The Church of England's Seven-Year Plan on Climate Change and the Environment*, London: Church House Publishing.

Tony Claydon and Ian McBride, 1998, 'The trials of the chosen peoples: recent interpretations of protestantism and national identity in Britain and Ireland', in Tony Claydon and Ian McBride (eds), *Protestantism and National Identity: Britain and Ireland, c.1650–c.1850*, Cambridge: Cambridge University Press, pp. 3–29.

Clement of Alexandria, 1991, *Stromateis: Books 1–3*, Washington DC: Catholic University of America Press.

Michel Clevenot, 1985, *Materialist Approaches to the Bible*, Maryknoll: Orbis.

Hywel Clifford, 2010, 'Deutero-Isaiah and Monotheism', in John Day (ed.) *Prophecy and the Prophets in Ancient Israel*, London: Continuum, pp. 267–89.

Hywel Clifford, 2010a, 'Amos in Wellhausen's Prolegomena', in Anselm C. Hagedorn and Andrew Mein (eds), *Aspects of Amos: Exegesis and Interpretation*, London: Continuum, pp. 141–56.

Charles Lloyd Cohen, 1986, *God's Caress: the Psychology of Puritan Religious Experience*, Oxford: Oxford University Press.

Penny J. Cole, 1991, *The Preaching of the Crusades to the Holy Land, 1095–1270*, Cambridge, MA: The Medieval Academy of America.

Penny Cole, 2013, *The Preaching of the Crusades to the Holy Land 1095–1270*, Kalamazoo, MI: Medieval Academy of America.

John J. Collins, 2010, 'The Sign of Immanuel', in John Day (ed.), *Prophecy and the Prophets in Ancient Israel*, London: Continuum, pp. 225–44.

Patrick Collinson, 1988, *The Birth Pangs of Protestant England: Religious and Cultural Change in the 16th and 17th Centuries*, London: Macmillan.

Patrick Collinson, 2002, 'John Fox and National Consciousness', in Christopher Highley and John N. King (eds), *John Foxe and His World*, Aldershot: Ashgate, pp. 10–34.

Jean Comby, 1996, *How to Understand the History of Christian Mission*, London: SCM Press.

Jean Comaroff and John Comaroff, 1991, *Of Revelation and Revolution, Vol. 1. Christianity, Colonialism, and Consciousness in South Africa*, London: University of Chicago Press.

Jean Comaroff and John Comaroff, 1992, *Ethnography and the Historical Imagination*, Oxford: Westview Press.

P. Connerton, 1989, *How Societies Remember*, Cambridge: Cambridge University Press.

Thomas Cooper, 1615, *The blessing of Japheth proving the gathering of the gentiles and the final conversion of the Jews*, London.

Patrick Copland, 1619, *Letter to Master Adrian Jabobson Hulsebus*, printed London: 1622.

Patrick Copland, 1622, *Virginia's God be thanked or, a sermon of thanksgiving for the happy success of the affairs in Virginia this last year*, London.

Abiezer Coppe, 1987, *Selected Writings*, edited with an introduction by Andrew Hopton, London: Aporia Press.

Abiezer Coppe, 2011 [1649], *Some Sweet Sips of Some Spirituall Wine, Sweetly and Freely Dropping from One Cluster of Grapes*, EEBO Editions.

Miles Coverdale, 1535, *Goostly psalmes and spirituall songes drawen out of the Holy Scripture*, London.

F. Crace, 1878, *Dyeing and Calico Printing: Including an Account of the Most Recent Improvements in the Manufacture and Use of Aniline Colours*, Manchester: Palmer and Howe.

Richard Crakanthorpe, 1608, *A Sermon . . . Preached at Paul's Cross 24th March 1608*.

Pieter F. Craffert, 2008, *The Life of a Galilean Shaman: Jesus of Nazareth in Anthropological–Historical Perspective*, Eugene, OR: Cascade.

Graham Cray, 2004, *Mission-Shaped Church: Church Planting and Fresh Expressions of Church in a Changing Context*, London: Church House Publishing.

Robert Crowley, 1549, *The Psalter of David Newely Translated into Englysh Metre*, London.

Susan Curtis, 1991, *A Consuming Faith: The Social Gospel and Modern American Culture*, London: Johns Hopkins University Press.

Arthur Paul Davis, 1948, *Isaac Watts, his Life and Works*, 8th edition, London: Independent Press.

Sharon Delgado, 2007, *Shaking the Gates of Hell: Faith-led Resistance to Corporate Globalization*, Minneapolis: Fortress Press.

Katharine J. Dell, 2011, 'Amos and the Earthquake: Judgment as Natural Disaster', in Anselm C. Hagedorn and Andrew Mein (eds), *Aspects of Amos: Exegesis and Interpretation*, London: Continuum, pp. 1–14.

Carol J. Dempsey, 2000, *The Prophets: A Liberation-Critical Reading*, Minneapolis: Fortress.

Carol J. Dempsey, 2010, *Isaiah: God's Poet of Light*, St. Louis: Chalice Press.

J. Derrida, 1998, *Of Grammatology*, Baltimore, MD: Johns Hopkins University Press.

S. Diamond, 1989, *Spiritual Warfare: The Politics of the Christian Right*, London: Pluto Press.

Thomas Dick, 1831, *The Philosophy of a Future State*, New York: R. Schoyer.

Dictatus Papae, http://www.fordham.edu/halsall/source/g7-dictpap.html.

The Dictionary of National Biography (1909), vol. xx, 2nd edn, London: Smith, Elder, and Co.

C. H. Dodd, 1930, 'Jesus as Teacher and Prophet', in G. K. A. Bell and Adolf Deissmann (eds), *Mysterium Christi: Christological Studies by British and German Theologians*, London: Longmans, Green.

H. H. Dodwell (ed.), 1929, *British India, 1497–1858* [The Cambridge History of India Vol. 5], Cambridge: Cambridge University Press.

Mary Douglas, 1996, *Natural Symbols: Explorations in Cosmology*, London: Routledge.

Mary Douglas, 2000, *Leviticus as Literature*, Oxford: Oxford University Press.

Richard Drinnon, 1980, *Facing West: The Metaphysics of Indian-hating and Empire-building*, London: New English Library.

James D. G. Dunn, 2006, *The Partings of the Ways: Between Christianity and Judaism and their Significance for the Character of Christianity*, 2nd edn, London: SCM Press.

Richard Eburne, 1624, *A Plaine Pathway to Plantations: A Discourse in General Concerning the Plantation of our English People in other Countrie*, London.

Peter W. Edbury, 1998, *The Conquest of Jerusalem and the Third Crusade*, Aldershot: Ashgate.

Jonathan Edwards, 1985, *The Life of David Brainerd,* ed. Norman Pettit, London: Yale University Press.

Jonathan Edwards, 1992, *Sermons and Discourses: 1720–1723*, ed. Wilson H. Kimnach, London: Yale University Press.

Bart D. Ehrman, 1999, *Jesus: Apocalyptic Prophet of the New Millennium*, Oxford: Oxford University Press.

Walther Eichrodt, 1961 and 1967, *Theology of the Old Testament*, 2 vols, London: SCM Press.

Howard Eilburg-Schwartz, 1994, *God's Phallus and other Problems for Men and Monotheism*, Boston: Beacon Press.

Neil Elliott, 1995, *Liberating Paul: The Justice of God and the Politics of the Apostle*, Sheffield: Sheffield Academic Press.

Neil Elliott, 2000, 'Paul and the Politics of Empire: Problems and Prospects', in Richard A. Horsley (ed.), *Paul and Politics*, Harrisburg, PA: Trinity Press International, pp. 18–19.

Neil Elliott, 2008, *The Arrogance of Nations: Reading Romans in the Shadow of Empire*, Minneapolis: Fortress Press.

G. H. Endfield and D. J. Nash, 2002, 'Missionaries and Morals: Climatic Discourse in Nineteenth-Century Central Southern Africa', *Annals of the Association of American Geographers* 92:4, pp. 727–42.

Matthew Eric Engelke, 2007, *A Problem of Presence: Beyond Scripture in an African Church*, London: University of California Press.

Leon Epsztein, 1986, *Social Justice in the Ancient Near East and the People of the Bible*, London: SCM Press.

Eric H. Erikson, 1975, *Life History and the Historical Moment*, New York: Norton.

Eric H. Erikson, 1982, *The Life Cycle Completed: A Review*, New York: Norton.

Harry Escott, 1962, *Isaac Watts, Hymnographer: A Study of the Beginnings, Development and Philosophy of the English Hymn*, London: Independent Press.

Norman Etherington, 1978, *Preachers, Peasants and Politics in Southeast Africa 1835–1880: African Christian Communities in Natal, Pondoland and Zululand*, London: Royal Historical Society.

Eusebius of Caesarea, 1989, *The History of the Church from Christ to Constantine*, revised and edited with a new introduction by Andrew Louth, Harmondsworth: Penguin Books.

Eusebius of Caesarea, 1999, *The Life of Constantine*, Introduction, translation and commentary by Avril Cameron and Stuart G. Hall, Oxford: Clarendon Press.

Georg Heinrich August von Ewald, 1875–81, *Commentary on the Prophets of the Old Testament,* tr. J. Frederic Smith, 5 vols, London: William and Norgate.

Z. W. Falk, 1985, 'From east to west my name is lauded among the nations', in J. Hick and H. Askari (eds), *The Experience of Religious Diversity*, Aldershot: Gower, pp. 25–33.

John Featley, 1629, *A Sermon Preached to the Nobly Deserving Gentlemen, Sir Thomas Warner and the rest of his Company Bound to the West Indies for their Farewell*, London.

Leon Festinger, 1956, *When Prophecy Fails*, New York: Harper and Row.

Leon Festinger, 1957, *A Theory of Cognitive Dissonance*, Evanston, IL: Row, Peterson.

Andrew Fitzmaurice, 2000, '"Every man, that prints, adventures": the Rhetoric of the Virginia Company Sermons', in Lori Anne Ferrell and Peter McCullough (eds), *The English Sermon Revised: Religion, Literature and History 1600–1750*, Manchester: Manchester University Press, pp. 24–42.

Josephus Flavius, 2009, *The Antiquities of the Jews*, tr. William Whiston, Bel Air, CA Wilder Publications.

Richard Fletcher, 1997, *The Conversion of Europe: From Paganism to Christianity 371–1386 AD*, London: Fontana.

Michael Floyd and Robert D. Haak (eds), 2005, *Prophets, Prophecy, and Prophetic Texts in Second Temple Judaism*, London: T&T Clark.

Alan Forey, 1992, *The Military Orders: From the Twelfth to the Early Fourteenth Centuries*, Basingstoke: Macmillan.

Michel Foucault, 1972, *The Archaeology of Knowledge*, London: Tavistock.

Fourth Lateran Council, http://www.fordham.edu/halsall/basis/lateran4.html.

Duncan B. Forrester, 2000, *Truthful Action: Explorations in Practical Theology*, Edinburgh: T&T Clark.

J. W. Fowler, 1981, *Stages of Faith: The Psychology of Human Development and the Quest for Meaning*, San Francisco: Harper & Row.

Richard Wightman Fox, 1985, *Reinhold Niebuhr: a Biography*, New York: Pantheon.

Leslie J. Francis and Carol Roberts, 2009, 'Growth or Decline in the Church of England during the Decade of Evangelism: Did the Churchmanship of the Bishop Matter?', *Journal of Contemporary Religion* 24:1, pp. 67–81.

Paula Fredriksen, 2000, *Jesus of Nazareth, King of the Jews: A Jewish Life and the Emergence of Christianity*, London: Macmillan.

S. Freud, 1991, *The Interpretation of Dreams*, Harmondsworth: Penguin.

Hans-Georg Gadamer, 1989, *Truth and Method*, London: Sheed & Ward.

Frederick Gaiser, 2003, 'Why does it rain? A biblical case study in divine causality', *Horizons in Biblical Theology* 25:1, pp. 1–18.

Gesta Francorum, http://www.fordham.edu/halsall/source/urban2-5vers.html#gesta.

Peter Garnsey and Richard Saller, 1997, 'Patronal Power Relations', in Richard A. Horsley (ed.), *Paul and Empire: Religion and Power in Roman Imperial Society*, Harrisburg, PA: TPI.

R. H. Glover, 1924, *The Progress of World-wide Missions*, London: James Clarke & Co.

T. R. Glover, 1941, *The Mind of St Paul*, London: Humphrey Milford.

Ken Gnanakan, 1993, *Kingdom Concerns, A Biblical Theology of Mission Today*, Leicester: Inter Varsity Press.

Norman Goodall (ed.), 1968, *The Uppsala Report 1968*, Geneva: World Council of Churches.

Donald K. Gorrell, 1988, *The Age of Social Responsibility: The Social Gospel in the Progressive Era 1900–1920*, Macon, GA: Mercer University Press.

Norman Gottwald, 1964, *All the Kingdoms of the Earth: Israelite Prophecy and International Relations in the Ancient Near East*, London: Harper and Row.

Norman Gottwald, 1999, *The Tribes of Yahweh: A Sociology of the Religion of Liberated Israel*, Sheffield: Sheffield Academic Press.

M. D. Goulder, 1990, *The Prayers of David (Psalms 51–72): Studies in the Psalter II*, Sheffield: JSOT Press.

Lester L. Grabbe, 2010, 'Shaman, Preacher, or Spirit Medium? The Israelite Prophet in the Light of Anthropological Models', in John Day (ed.) *Prophecy and the Prophets in Ancient Israel*, London: Continuum, pp. 117–32.

Robert Gray, 1609, *A Good Speed to Virginia*, London, http://digital.lib.lehigh.edu/trial/justification/jamestown/essay/4/.

Ole Peter Grell, 1991, Jonathan I. Israel and Nicholas Tyacke (eds), *From Persecution to Toleration: The Glorious Revolution and Religion in England*, Oxford: Clarendon Press.

John A. Grigg, 2009, *The Lives of David Brainerd: The Making of an American Evangelical Icon*, Oxford: Oxford University Press.

Sandra Gustafson, 2000, *Eloquence is Power: Oratory and Performance in Early America*, Chapel Hill, NC: University of North Carolina Press.

Samuel Guye and Henri Michel, 1971, *Time and Space: Measuring Instruments from the 15th to the 19th Century*, tr. Diana Dolan, London: Pall Mall Press.

Jürgen Habermas, 1972, *Knowledge and Human Interests*, London: Heinemann.

M. Halbwachs, 1992, *On Collective Memory*, London: University of Chicago Press.

R. Geoffrey Harris, 2004, *Mission in the Gospels*, Peterborough: Epworth.

Peter Harrison, 1990, *Religion and the Religions in the English Enlightenment*, Cambridge: Cambridge University Press.

C. A. Hartshorne, 1967, *A Natural Theology for Our Time*, La Salle, IL: Open Court.

Ragnhild Hatton, 1978, *George I, Elector and King*, London: Thames and Hudson.

Nicholas Healy, 2000, *Church, World and the Christian Life: Practical–Prophetic Ecclesiology*, Cambridge: Cambridge University Press.

Gerben Heitink, 1999, *Practical Theology: History; Theory; Action Domains: Manual for Practical Theology*, Cambridge: Eerdmans.

R. F. Heizer, 1947, *Francis Drake and the California Indians, 1579*, Berkeley, CA: University of California Press.

Obery M. Hendricks, 2006, *The Politics of Jesus: Rediscovering the True Revolutionary Nature of the Teachings of Jesus and How They Have Been Corrupted*, New York: Three Leaves Press.

Matthew Henry, 1960, *Matthew Henry's Commentary on the Whole Bible in One Volume: Genesis to Revelation*, ed. Leslie F. Church, London: Marshall, Morgan and Scott.

William Herzog, 1994, *Parables as Subversive Speech*, Louisville, KY: Westminster John Knox.

William Herzog, 2000, *Jesus, Justice, and the Reign of God: A Ministry of Liberation*, Louisville, KY: Westminster John Knox.

William Herzog, 2005, *Prophet and Teacher: An Introduction to the Historical Jesus*, Louisville, KY: Westminster John Knox.

Abraham J. Heschel, 2007, *The Prophets: Two Volumes in One*, Peabody MA: Hendrickson.

Clifford and Monica Hill, 1990, *. . . And They Shall Prophesy: The New Prophetic Movement in the Church Today*, London: Marshall Pickering.

Boyd Hilton, 1988, *The Age of Atonement: The Influence of Evangelicalism on Social and Economic Thought, 1795–1865*, Oxford: Clarendon Press.

Geoffrey Hindley, 2003, *The Crusades: A History of Armed Pilgrimage and Holy War*, London: Constable.

F. J. Hinkelammert, 1986, *The Ideological Weapons of Death: A Theological Critique of Capitalism*, Maryknoll: Orbis.

Yizhar Hirschfeld, 1997, 'Jewish Rural Settlement in Judaea in the Early Roman Period', in Susan E. Alcock (ed.), *The Early Roman Empire in the East*, Oxford: Oxbow.

A. O. Hirschman, 1977, *The Passions and the Interests: Political Arguments for Capitalism before its Triumph*, Princeton: Princeton University Press.

Christopher Hodgkins, 2002, *Reforming Colonialism: Protestant Colonialism and Conscience in British Literature*, London: University of Missouri Press.

Willem Visser't Hooft, 1968, 'The Mandate of the Ecumenical Movement', Stockholm 1925, reprinted in Norman Goodall (ed.), 1968, *The Uppsala Report 1968*, Geneva: World Council of Churches, pp. 313–23.

Morna Hooker, 1997, *The Signs of a Prophet: The Prophetic Actions of Jesus*, London: SCM Press.

Richard A. Horsley, 1993, *Jesus and the Spiral of Violence: Popular Jewish Resistance in Roman Palestine*, Minneapolis: Fortress Press.

Richard A. Horsley, 1994, *Sociology and the Jesus Movement*, New York: Continuum.

Richard A. Horsley, 2003, *Jesus and Empire: The Kingdom of God and the New World Disorder*, Minneapolis: Fortress Press.

Richard A. Horsley, 2008, *Jesus in Context: Power, People and Performance*, Minneapolis: Fortress Press.

Richard A. Horsley, 2010, *Jesus and the Powers: Conflict, Covenant and the Hope of the Poor*, Minneapolis: Fortress Press.

Richard A. Horsley, 2012, *The Prophet Jesus and the Renewal of Israel: Moving beyond a Diversionary Debate*, Grand Rapids: Eerdmans.

John Howe, 1863, 'Funeral Sermons', in *The Works of John Howe*, vol. VI, London: The Religious Tract Society.

John Hoyles, 1971, *The Waning of the Renaissance 1641–1740: Studies in the Thought and Poetry of Henry More, John Norris and Isaac Watts*, The Hague: Martinus Nijhoff.

R. T. Hughes and C. L. Allen, 1988, *Illusions of Innocence: Protestant Primitivism in America, 1630–1875*, London: University of Chicago Press.

John M. Hull, 1984, 'What Is Theology of Education?', in John M. Hull, *Studies in Religion and Education*, London: The Falmer Press, pp. 253–4.

John M. Hull, 1985, *What Prevents Christian Adults from Learning?*, London: SCM Press.

John M. Hull, 1990, *Touching the Rock: An Experience of Blindness*, London: SPCK.

John M. Hull, 1992, 'Human Development and Capitalist Society', in J. W. Fowler, K. E. Nipkow and F. Schweitzer (eds), *Stages of Faith and Religious Development*, London: SCM, pp. 209–23.

John M. Hull, 1995, *The Holy Trinity and Christian Education in a Pluralist World*, London: National Society/Church House Publishing.

John M. Hull, 1996, 'Christian education in a capitalist society: Money and God', in D. Ford and D. L. Stamp (eds), *Essentials of Christian Community: Essays in Honour of Daniel W. Hardy*, Edinburgh: T&T Clark, pp. 241–52.

John M. Hull, 1996a, 'A Critique of Christian Religionism in Recent British Education', in J. Astley and L. J. Francis (eds), *Christian Theology and Religious Education: Connections and Contradictions*, London: SPCK, pp. 140–64.

John M. Hull, 1997, *On Sight and Insight: A Journey into the World of Blindness*, Oxford: One World Books.

John M. Hull, 1997a, 'Christian Education: Sufficient or Necessary? (2) The Necessity of Christian Education', *Epworth Review* 24(2), pp. 38–46.

John M. Hull, 1997b, 'Karl Marx on Capital: Some Implications for Christian Adult Education', *Modern Believing* 38:1, pp. 22–31.

John M. Hull, 1999, 'Bargaining with God: Religious Development and Economic Socialization', *Journal of Psychology and Theology* 27:3, pp. 241–9.

John M. Hull, 2001, *In the Beginning There was Darkness: A Blind Person's Conversations with the Bible*, London: SCM Press.

John M. Hull, 2002, 'Understanding Contemporary European Religious Consciousness: An Approach through Geo-politics', *Panorama: International Journal of Comparative Religious Education and Values* 14(2), pp. 123–40.

John M. Hull, 2003/4, 'Is there a Spirituality of Money?', *World Religions in Education* [Shap Working Party]: *Wealth and Poverty*, pp. 81–4.

John M. Hull, 2006, *Mission-Shaped Church: A Theological Response*, London: SCM Press.

Peter Jackson, 2009, *The Seventh Crusade 1244–1254: Sources and Documents*, Aldershot: Ashgate.

Grace M. Jantzen, 1998, *Becoming Divine: Towards a Feminist Philosophy of Religion*, Manchester: Manchester University Press.

Peter d'A. Jones, 1968, *The Christian Socialist Revival, 1877–1914: Religion, Class, and Social Conscience in Late-Victorian England*, Princeton: Princeton University Press.

Ian Jones and Peter Hammersley, 2009, 'Social Protest as Formation for Prophetic Ministry: An Experiment in Transformative Theological Education', *Journal of Adult Theological Education* 6:2, pp. 176–93.

Henry Kamen, 1998, *The Spanish Inquisition: An Historical Revision*, London: Phoenix Giant.

John H. Kautsky, 1997, *The Politics of Aristocratic Empires*, New Brunswick, NJ: Transaction Publishers.

Benjamin Z. Kedar, 1984, *Crusade and Mission: European Approaches toward the Muslims*, Princeton: Princeton University Press.

Alistair Kee, 1982, *Constantine Vs Christ, the Triumph of Ideology*, London: SCM Press.

N. H. Keeble, 1987, *The Literary Culture of Nonconformity in Later Seventeenth-Century England*, Leicester: Leicester University Press.

J. N. D. Kelly, 1963, 'The Bible and the Latin Fathers', in D. E. Nineham (ed.), *The Church's Use of the Bible: Past and Present*, London: SPCK, pp. 41–56.

Neil Kendrick, John Brewer and J. H. Plumb, 1983, *The Birth of a Consumer Society: the Commercialization of Eighteenth Century England*, London: Hutchinson.

Ann Kibbey, 1986, *The Representation of Material Shapes: A Study of Rhetoric, Prejudice and Violence*, Cambridge: Cambridge University Press.

Colin Kidd, 1999, *British Identities before Nationalism: Ethnicity and Nationhood in the Atlantic World, 1600–1800*, Cambridge: Cambridge University Press.

Kwok Pui-Lan, 1995, *Discovering the Bible in the Non-biblical World*, Maryknoll: Orbis.

Tim LaHaye and Jerry B. Jenkins, 1995, *Left Behind: A Novel of the Earth's Last Days*, Carol Stream, IL: Tyndale House Publishers.

George Lakoff and Marc Johnson, 1999, *Philosophy in the Flesh: The Embodied Mind and its Challenge to Western Thought*, New York: Basic Books.

M. L. Lamb, 1982, *Solidarity with Victims: Toward a Theology of Social Transformation*, New York: Crossroad.

G. W. Lampe, 1961, *A Patristic Greek Lexicon*, Oxford: Clarendon.

Francis Landy, 2011, *Hosea*, 2nd edn, Sheffield: Sheffield Phoenix.

Jaime Lara, 2010, 'Half-way between Genesis and Apocalypse: Ezekiel as Message and Proof for New World Converts', in Paul Joyce and Andrew Mein (eds), *After Ezekiel: Essays on the Reception of a Difficult Prophet*, London: Continuum, pp.137–57.

Kenneth Scott Latourette, 1938–45, *A History of the Expansion of Christianity*, London: Eyre and Spottiswoode.

Kenneth Leech, 1981, *The Social God*, London: Sheldon Press.

Kenneth Leech, 1992, *The Eye of the Storm: Spiritual Resources for the Pursuit of Justice*, London: Darton, Longman and Todd.

Kenneth Leech, 1992a, *Subversive Orthodoxy: Traditional Faith and Radical Commitment*, Toronto: Anglican Book Centre.

Hervé Legrand, 1986, 'A Response to "The Church as a Prophetic Sign"', in Gennadios Limouris (ed.), *Church, Kingdom, World: The Church as Mystery and Prophetic Sign*, Geneva: World Council of Churches, pp. 145–51.

Emmanuel Levinas, 1969, *Totality and Infinity: An Essay on Exteriority*, Pittsburgh: Duquesne.

Emmanuel Levinas, 1998, *Of God Who Comes to Mind*, Redwood City, CA: Stanford University Press.

Henry George Liddell, Robert Scott and Henry Stuart Jones (eds), 1968, *A Greek-English Lexicon* (9th edition), Oxford: Clarendon Press.

Walter H. Lim, 1998, *The Arts of Empire: The Poetics of Colonialism from Raleigh to Milton*, London: Associated University Press.

Hal Lindsey and Carole C. Carlson, 1970, *The Late, Great Planet Earth*, Grand Rapids, MI: Zondervan.

James Linville, 2008, *Amos and the Cosmic Imagination*, Aldershot: Ashgate.

David Livingstone, 1960, *Livingstone's Private Journals 1851–1853*, ed. I. Schapera, London: Chatto and Windus.

J. Courtenay Locke (ed.), 1930, *The First Englishmen in India: Letters and Narratives of Sundry Elizabethans Written by Themselves*, London: George Routledge and Sons.

Martin Luther, 1960, *Luther's Works*, vol. 35, ed. by E. T. Bachman, Philadelphia: Fortress Press.

Martin Luther, 1961, *Luther's Work*, vol. 37, ed. Robert Fischer, Philadelphia: Fortress Press.

Martin Luther, 1972, *Luther's Works*, vol. 15, ed. Jaroslav Pelikan, St. Louis, MO: Concordia.

Martin Luther, 1975, *Luther's Works*, vol. 18, ed. Hilton C. Oswald, St. Louis, MO: Concordia.

Millar MacLure, 1958, *The Paul's Cross Sermons 1534–1642*, London: Oxford University Press.

A. L. Macfie, 1967, *The Individual in Society: Papers on Adam Smith*, London: Allen & Unwin.

Milan MacHovec, 1976, *A Marxist Looks at Jesus*, London: Darton, Longman and Todd.

Bruce J. Malina and Richard L. Rohrbaugh, 1992, *Social Science Commentary on the Synoptic Gospels*, Minneapolis: Fortress.

Bruce J. Malina, 1993, *Windows on the World of Jesus: Time Travel to Ancient Judea*, Louisville, KY: Westminster/John Knox Press.

Bruce J. Malina, 1996, *The Social World of Jesus and the Gospels*, London: Routledge.

Bruce J. Malina, 2001, *The Social Gospel of Jesus: The Kingdom of God in Mediterranean Perspective*, Minneapolis: Fortress.

Bruce J. Malina, 2002, *The Social Setting of Jesus and the Gospels*, Minneapolis: Fortress Press.

John MacMurray, 1965, *Search for Reality in Religion*, London: Friends Home Service Committee.

C. B. Macpherson, 1964, *The Political Theory of Possessive Individualism*, Oxford: Oxford University Press.

Christoph Maier, 1994, *Preaching the Crusades: Mendicant Friars and the Cross in the Thirteenth Century*, Cambridge: Cambridge University Press.

Bernard Manning, 1942, *The Hymns of Wesley and Watts: Five Informal Papers*, London: Epworth Press.

William Manson, 1930, *The Gospel of Luke*, London: Hodder and Stoughton.

Hilary Marlow, 2009, *Biblical Prophets and Contemporary Environmental Ethics: Re-Reading Amos, Hosea, and First Isaiah*, Oxford: Oxford University Press.

I. Howard Marshall, 1978, *The Gospel of Luke: A Commentary on the Greek Text*, Exeter: Paternoster Press.

H.-P. Martin and H. Schumann, 1997, *The Global Trap: Globalization and the Assault on Prosperity and Democracy*, London: Zed Books.

Karl Marx, 1977, 'Theses on Feuerbach', in David McLellan (ed.), *Karl Marx: Selected Writings*, Oxford: Oxford University Press, pp. 156–8.

Frederick Denison Maurice, 1871, *Prophets and Kings of the Old Testament*, 3rd edn, London: Macmillan.

Frederick Denison Maurice, 1968, *Learning and Working*, Oxford: Oxford University Press.

P. E. McCollough, 2004, Art. Daniel Price, *Oxford Dictionary of National Biography*, Oxford University Press [http://www.oxforddnb.com/view/article/22745/2004–09].

Richard C. McCoy, 2002, *Alterations of State: Sacred Kingship in the English Reformation*, New York: Columbia University Press.

John McDargh, 1983, *Psychoanalytic Object Relations Theory and the Study of Religion: on Faith and the Imaging of God*, Lanham, MD: University Press of America.

Nicholas McDowell, 2003, *The English Radical Imagination: Culture, Religion, and Revolution, 1630–1660*, Oxford: Clarendon.

Michael McGiffert, 1981, 'William Tyndale's Conception of Covenant', *Journal of Ecclesiastical History* 32:2, pp.167–84.

John W. McKenna, 1982, 'How God became an Englishman', in Delloyd J. Guth and John W. McKenna (eds), *Tudor Rule and Revolution: Essays presented to G. R. Elton*, Cambridge: Cambridge University Press, pp. 25–43.

Andrew Mein, 2010, 'The Radical Amos in Savonarola's Florence', in Anselm C. Hagedorn and Andrew Mein (eds), *Aspects of Amos: Exegesis and Interpretation*, London: Continuum, pp. 117–40.

Andrew Mein, 2011, 'Ezekiel's Women in Christian Interpretation', in Paul Joyce and Andrew Mein (eds), *After Ezekiel: Essays on the Reception of a Difficult Prophet*, London: Continuum, pp. 159–83.

W. W. Meissner, 1995, *Thy Kingdom Come: Psychoanalytic Perspectives on the Messiah and the Millennium*, Kansas City, KS: Sheed and Ward.

Jane Merritt, 2003, *At the Crossroads: Indians and Empires on a Mid-Atlantic Frontier, 1700–1763*, London: University of North Carolina Press.

Johannes Baptist Metz, 1980, *Faith in History and Society: Toward a Practical Fundamental Theology*, London: Burns & Oates.

Johannes Baptist Metz, 1981, *The Emergent Church: The Future of Christianity in a Postbourgeois World*, London: SCM.

John Milbank, 1990, *Theology and Social Theory: Beyond Secular Reason*, Oxford: Blackwell.

Daniel Miller (ed.), 2005, *Materiality*, London: Duke University Press.

Jose P. Miranda, 1977, *Marx and the Bible: A Critique of the Philosophy of Oppression*, London: SCM.

R. I. Moore, 1987, *The Formation of a Persecuting Society: Authority and Deviance in Western Europe 950–1250*, Oxford: Blackwell.

J. Morris, 1973, *Heaven's Command: An Imperial Progress*, London: Faber & Faber.

A. L. Morton, 1982, 'Abiezer Coppe', in Richard L. Greaves and Robert Zaller (eds), *Biographical Dictionary of British Radicals in the Seventeenth Century, Vol. 1*, Brighton: Harvester Press, pp. 173–4.

Sharon Moughtin-Mumby, 2010, '"A Man and his Father Go to Naarah in order to Defile my Holy Name!": Rereading Amos 2.6–8', in Anselm C. Hagedorn and Andrew Mein (eds), *Aspects of Amos: Exegesis and Interpretation*, London: Continuum, pp. 59–80.

Steve Moyise, 2010, 'Ezekiel and the Book of Revelation', in Paul Joyce and Andrew Mein (eds), *After Ezekiel: Essays on the Reception of a Difficult Prophet*, London: Continuum, pp. 45–58.

Richard Mudie-Smith (ed.), 1904, *The Religious Life of London*, London: Hodder & Stoughton.

Ched Myers, 1988, *Binding the Strong Man: a Political Reading of Mark's Story of Jesus*, Maryknoll: Orbis.

Ched Myers and Karen Lattea (eds), 1996, *Say to this Mountain: Mark's Story of Discipleship*, Maryknoll: Orbis Books.

Ched Myers, 1994, *Who Will Roll Away the Stone?: Discipleship Queries for First World Christians*, Maryknoll: Orbis Books.

Stephen Neill, 1986, *A History of Christian Missions*, 2nd rev. edn, ed. Owen Chadwick, Harmondsworth: Penguin.

Sharon Nepstad, 2008, *Religion and War Resistance in the Plowshares Movement*, Cambridge: Cambridge University Press.

Helen J. Nicholson, 1997, *The Chronicle of the Third Crusade: a translation of the Itinerarium peregrinorum et gesta Regis Ricardi*, Aldershot: Ashgate.

Reinhold Niebuhr, 1932, *Moral Man and Immoral Society: a Study in Ethics and Politics*, New York: Scribner.

Reinhold Niebuhr, 1937, *Reflections on the End of an Era*, London: Charles Scribner.

Reinhold Niebuhr, 1938, *Beyond Tragedy: Essays on the Christian Interpretation of History*, London: Nisbet.

Reinhold Niebuhr, 1943, *The Nature and Destiny of Man, Vol II Human Destiny*, London: Nisbet.

Reinhold Niebuhr, 1945, *The Children of Light and the Children of Darkness: A Vindication of Democracy and a Critique of its Traditional Defenders*, London: Nisbet.

Reinhold Niebuhr, 1949, *Faith and History: A Comparison of the Christian and Modern Views of History*, London: Nisbet.

Reinhold Niebuhr, 1956, *The Self and the Dramas of History*, London: Faber & Faber.

Reinhold Niebuhr, 1962, *The Irony of American History*, New York: Charles Scribner.

Reinhold Niebuhr, 1990 [1929], *Leaves from the Notebook of a Tamed Cynic*, Louisville, KN: Westminster/John Knox Press.

Friedrich Wilhelm Nietzsche, 2007, *The Antichrist*, Sioux Falls, SD: Nuvision Publications.

K. E. Nipkow, 2003, *God, Human Nature and Education for Peace: New Approaches to Moral and Religious Maturity*, Aldershot: Ashgate.

Martii Nissinen, 2003, *Prophets and Prophecy in the Ancient Near East*, Atlanta: Society of Biblical Literature.

Martii Nissinen, 2010, 'Comparing Prophetic Sources: Principles and a Test Case', in John Day (ed.), *Prophecy and The Prophets in Ancient Israel: Proceedings of the Oxford Old Testament Seminar*, London: T&T Clark, pp. 3–24.

John Nolland, 1993, *Luke 9.21–18.34*, Word Biblical Commentary vol. 35B, Dallas: Word Books.

Douglas Oakman, 2008, *Jesus and the Peasants*, Eugene, OR: Cascade Books.

Douglas Oakman, 2012, *The Political Aims of Jesus*, Minneapolis: Fortress.

Julia O'Brien, 2008, *Challenging Prophetic Metaphor: Theology and Ideology in the Prophets*, London: Westminster John Knox.

Jane Ohlmeyer, 1998, '"Civilizinge of those Rude Parts": Colonization within Britain and Ireland, 1580s–1640s', in Nicholas Canny (ed.), *The Origins of Empire: British Overseas Enterprise to the Close of the Seventeenth Century*, Oxford: Oxford University Press, pp. 124–47.

A. W. R. E. Okines, 2004, 'Why Was There So Little Government Reaction to the Gunpowder Plot?', *Journal of Ecclesiastical History* 55:2, pp. 275–92.

F. Oser and P. Gmünder, 1991, *Religious Judgement: A Developmental Approach*, Birmingham, AL: Religious Education Press.

Thomas Overholt, 1989, *Channels of Prophecy: The Social Dynamics of Prophetic Activity*, Eugene, OR: Wipf and Stock.

Anthony Pagden, 1995, *'Lords of All the World': Ideologies of Empire in Spain, Britain and France c.1500–c.1800*, London: Yale University Press.

Anthony Pagden, 1998, 'The Struggle for Legitimacy and the Image of Empire in the Atlantic to *c.*1700', in Nicholas Canny (ed.), *The Origins of Empire: British Overseas Enterprise to the Close of the Seventeenth Century*, Oxford: Oxford University Press, pp. 34–54.

Raimundo Panikkar, 1988, 'The Jordan, the Tiber and the Ganges: Three kairological moments of Christic self-consciousness', in J. Hick and P. Knitter (eds), *The Myth of Christian Uniqueness*, London: SCM Press, pp. 89–116.

S. Park, 1993, *The Wounded Heart of God: The Asian Idea of Han and the Christian Doctrine of Sin*, Nashville, TN: Abingdon Press.

John Parker, 1978, 'Religion and the Virginia Company 1609–10', in K. R. Andrews, N. P. Canny and P. E. H. Hair (eds), *The Westward Enterprise: English Activities in Ireland, the Atlantic and America 1480–1650*, Liverpool: Liverpool University Press, pp. 245–70.

G. Parsons, 1997, 'Rethinking the missionary position: Bishop Colenso of Natal', in J. Wolffe (ed.), *Religion in Victorian Britain, Vol. 5. Culture and Empire*, Manchester: Manchester University Press, pp. 135–75.

John Patrick, 1698, *The Psalms of David in Metre Fitted to the Tunes Used in Parish-Churches*, London.

M. Pêcheux, 1982, *Language, Semantics and Ideology: Stating the Obvious*, London: Macmillan.

Mark Pegg, 2008, *A Most Holy War: The Albigensian Crusade and the Battle for Christendom*, Oxford: Oxford University Press.

Paul T. Phillips, 1996, *A Kingdom on Earth: Anglo-American Social Christianity 1880–1940*, University Park, PA: Pennsylvania State University Press.

George Pixley, 1981, *God's Kingdom*, London: SCM Press.

Steven Pincus, 1998, 'To protect English liberties: the English nationalist revolution of 1688–1689', in Tony Claydon and Ian McBride (eds), *Protestantism and National Identity: Britain and Ireland, c.1650–c.1850*, Cambridge: Cambridge University Press, pp. 75–104.

Richard Pointer, 2007, *Encounters of the Spirit: Native Americans and European Colonial Religion*, Bloomington, IN: Indiana University Press.

Daniel Price, 1609, *Saul's Prohibition Stayed. Or the apprehension, and examination of Saul, and the inditement of all that persecute Christ, with a reproof of those that traduce the honourable plantation of Virginia*, London.

Gerhard von Rad, 1962 and 1965, *Old Testament theology*, 2 vols, Edinburgh: Oliver & Boyd.

Ian Randall and David Hilborn, 2001, *One Body in Christ: The History and Significance of the Evangelical Alliance*, Carlisle: Paternoster.

Walter Rauschenbusch, 1912, *Christianity and the Social Crisis*, New York: Associate Press.

Charles E. Raven, 1920, *Christian Socialism 1848–1854*, London: Macmillan.

Maurice B. Reckitt, 1947, *Maurice to Temple: A Century of the Social Movement in the Church of England*, London: Faber and Faber.

Helmut Reich, 1990, 'The Relation between Science and Theology: The case for complementarity revisited', *Zygon* 25:4, pp. 369–90.

David J. Reimer, 2010, 'Interpersonal Forgiveness and the Hebrew Prophets', in John Day (ed.), *Prophecy and The Prophets in Ancient Israel: Proceedings of the Oxford Old Testament Seminar*, London: T&T Clark, pp. 81–97.

J. S. Richardson, 1998, 'Imperium Romanum: Empire and the Language of Power', in David Armitage (ed.), *Theories of Empire 1450–1800*, Aldershot: Ashgate Publishing, pp. 1–9.

Jonathan Riley-Smith and Louise Riley-Smith, 1981, *The Crusades: Idea and Reality 1095–1274*, London: Edward Arnold.

Jonathan Riley-Smith, 1993, *The First Crusade and the Idea of Crusading*, London: Atholone.

Jonathan Riley-Smith, 2009, *What were the Crusades?*, 4th edn, London: Macmillan.

Isabel Rivers, 1991, *Reason, Grace and Sentiment: a Study of the Language of Religion and Ethics in England 1660–1780*, I. *Whichcote to Wesley*, Cambridge: Cambridge University Press.

Ana-Maria Rizzuto, 1979, *The Birth of the Living God: a Psychoanalytic Study*, Chicago: University of Chicago Press.

Robert the Monk's History of the First Crusade, 2005, tr. Carol Sweetenham, Aldershot: Ashgate.

Charles Henry Robinson, 1915, *History of Christian Missions*, Edinburgh: T&T Clark.

Stuart Robinson, 1969, *A History of Dyed Textiles*, London: Studio Vista.

Andrew C. Ross, 2002, *David Livingstone: Mission and Empire*, London: Hambledon and London.

D. Brent Sandy, 2002, *Plowshares and Pruning Hooks: Rethinking the Language of Biblical Prophecy and Apocalyptic*, Downers Grove, IL: InterVarsity Press.

John Sawyer, 1996, *The Fifth Gospel: Isaiah in the History of Christianity*, Cambridge: Cambridge University Press.

John Sawyer, 2010, 'Ezekiel in the History of Christianity', in Paul Joyce and Andrew Mein (eds), *After Ezekiel: Essays on the Reception of a Difficult Prophet*, London: Continuum, pp. 1–9.

Jane Sayers, 1994, *Innocent III: Leader of Europe 1198–1216*, London: Longman.

Friedrich Schleiermacher, 1966, *A Brief Outline on the Study of Theology*, Richmond, VA: John Knox Press.

Luise Schottroff, 2006, *The Parables of Jesus*, Minneapolis: Fortress.

Willy Schottroff and Wolfgang Stegemann (eds), 1984, *God of the Lowly: Socio-Historical Interpretations of the Bible*, Maryknoll: Orbis.

P. Schüttke-Scherle, 1989, *From Contextual to Ecumenical Theology?: A Dialogue between Minjung Theology and 'Theology after Auschwitz'*, Frankfurt: Peter Lang.

N. Scotland, 1981, *Methodism and the Revolt of the Field: A Study of the Methodist Contribution to Agricultural Trade Unionism in East Anglia 1872–96*, Gloucester: Sutton.

Peter Selby, 1997, *Grace and Mortgage: The Language of Faith and the Debt of the World*, London: Darton, Longman and Todd.

Donald Senior and Carroll Stuhlmueller, 1983, *Biblical Foundations for Mission*, Maryknoll: Orbis.

T. Drorah Setel, 1985, 'Prophets and Pornography: Female Sexual Imagery in Hosea', in Letty M. Russell (ed.), *Feminist Interpretation of the Bible*, London: Westminster John Knox, pp. 86–95.

Elizabeth Siberry, 1985, *Criticism of Crusading 1095–1274*, Oxford: Clarendon Press.

Paul Slack, 1990, *The English Poor Law 1531–1782*, London: Macmillan.

Beryl Smalley, 1963, 'The Bible in the Middle Ages', in D. E. Nineham (ed.), *The Church's Use of the Bible: Past and Present*, London: SPCK, pp. 57–71.

Adam Smith, 1993, *An Enquiry into the Nature and Causes of the Wealth of Nations*, New York: Modern Library.

Adam Smith, 2002, *The Theory of Moral Sentiments*, Cambridge: Cambridge University Press.

George Adam Smith, 1928, *The Book of the Twelve Prophets, Commonly Called the Minor*, London: Hodder and Stoughton.

C.-S. Song, 1996, *Jesus, the Crucified People*, Minneapolis: Fortress Press.

The Song of the Cathar Wars: a History of the Albigensian Crusade, 1996, translated with an Introduction by Janet Shirley, Aldershot: Ashgate.

Stephen Spencer, 2007, *SCM Study Guide to Christian Mission*, London: SCM.

Baruch Spinoza, 2001, *Theological-Political Treatise*, tr. Samuel Shirley, Cambridge: Hackett Publishing.

Brian Stanley, 1990, *The Bible and the Flag: Protestant Missions and British Imperialism in the Nineteenth and Twentieth Centuries*, Leicester: Apollos.

Rodney Stark, 2007, *Cities of God: The Real Story of How Christianity Became an Urban Movement and Conquered Rome*, New York: HarperCollins.

Ekkehard W. Stegemann and Wolfgang Stegemann, 1999, *The Jesus Movement: A Social History of its First Century*, tr. O. C. Dean, Edinburgh: T&T Clark.

Paul Steidl-Meier, 1984, *Social Justice Ministry: Foundations and Concerns*, New York: Le Jacq Publishing.

Thomas Sternhold, John Hopkins, and others, 1649, *The whole Book of Psalms Collected into English meter*, London.

Donald Stoll, 1982, *Fishers of Men or Founders of Empire?: The Wycliffe Bible Translators in Latin America*, London: Zed Books.

Ronald H. Stone, 2005, *Prophetic Realism: Beyond Militarism and Pacifism in an Age of Terror*, London: T&T Clark.

Ronald H. Stone and Matthew Lon Weaver (eds), 1998, *Against the Third Reich: Paul Tillich's Wartime Addresses to Nazi Germany*, Louisville, KY: Westminster John Knox Press.

Jacob Stromberg, 2011, *An Introduction to the Study of Isaiah*, London: T&T Clark.

Mark Sturge, 2005, *Look what the Lord has Done!: An Exploration of Black Christian Faith in Britain*, Milton Keynes: Scripture Union.

Jonathon Sumption, 1978, *The Albigensian Crusade*, London: Faber.

Tony Swain and Deborah Bird-Rose (eds), 1988, *Aboriginal Australians and Christian Missions: Ethnographic and Historical Studies*, Adelaide: South Australian College of Advanced Education.

William Symonds, 1605, *Pisgah Evangelica, by the method of Revelation*, London.

William Symonds, 1609, *Virginia: A sermon preached at Whitechapel in the presence of many honorable and worshipful adventurers and planters for Virginia 25th April 1609 published for the benefit and use of the colony planted and to be planted there and for the advancement of their Christian purpose*, London, http://eebo.chadwyck.com/home.

S. S. Tamke, 1978, *Make a Joyful Noise unto the Lord: Hymns as a Reflection of Victorian Social Attitudes*, Athens, OH: Ohio University Press.

N. Tate and N. Brady, 1696, *A New Version of the Psalms of David Fitted to the Tunes Used in the Churches*, London.

William Temple, 1965, *Christianity and the Social Order*, Harmondsworth: Penguin.

Howard Thurman, 1981, *Jesus and the Disinherited*, Richmond, IN: Friends United Press.

Paul Tillich, 1936, *The Interpretation of History*, London: Scribner's.

Paul Tillich, 1951, *The Protestant Era*, London: Nisbet.

Paul Tillich, 1953, *Systematic Theology* Volume 1, Welwyn: Nisbet.

Paul Tillich, 1955, *Biblical Religion and the Search for Ultimate Reality*, London: James Nisbet.

Paul Tillich, 1963, *Systematic Theology* Volume III, Chicago: University of Chicago Press.

Paul Tillich, 1965, *Ultimate Concern: Dialogues with Students*, London: SCM Press.

Paul Tillich, 1968, *A History of Christian Thought*, London: SCM Press.

Paul Tillich, 1973, *What is Religion?*, New York: Harper.

Paul Tillich, 1977 [1933], *The Socialist Decision*, New York: Harper & Row.

Paul Tillich, 1998, *Against the Third Reich*, Louisville, KY: Westminster John Knox.

Glen Tinder, 1991, *The Political Meaning of Christianity: The Prophetic Stance, an Interpretation*, San Francisco: HarperCollins.

George E. Tinker, 1993, *Missionary Conquest: The Gospel and Native American Cultural Genocide*, Minneapolis: Fortress Press.

Andrew J. Townsend, 2013, *Action Research: The Challenges of Understanding and Changing Practice*, Maidenhead: McGraw-Hill/Open University Press.

Andre Trocmé, 2003, *Jesus and the Nonviolent Revolution*, ed. Charles E. Moore, Maryknoll: Orbis.

Nicolas Tyacke, 1987, *Anti-Calvinists: The rise of English Arminianism c.1590–1640*, Oxford: Clarendon Press.

Christopher Tyerman, 1988, *England and the Crusades 1095–1588*, Chicago: University of Chicago Press.

Christopher Tyerman, 2004, *Fighting for Christendom: Holy War and the Crusades*, Oxford: Oxford University Press.

Robert Tynley, 1609, *Two Learned Sermons*, London.

Werner Ustorf, 1992, *Christianised Africa – De-Christianised Europe?: Missionary Enquiries into the Polycentric Epoch of Christian History*, Seoul: Tyrannus.

C. H. Vellacott, 1912, 'Textiles', in William Page (ed.), *A History of the County of Hampshire & Isle of Wight*, Vol. V (The Victoria History of the Counties of England), London, pp. 475–89.

J. Viner, 1972, *The Role of Providence in the Social Order*, Philadelphia: American Philosophical Society.

H. M. Wachtel, 1990, *The Money Mandarins: The Making of a Supranational Economic Order*, London: Pluto Press.

Andrew Walls, 2002, *The Cross-cultural Process in Christian History: Studies in the Transmission and Appropriation of Faith*, Edinburgh: T&T Clark.

J. R. Watson, 1999, *The English Hymn: a Critical and Historical Study*, Oxford: Clarendon Press.

Isaac Watts, 1705, *Hymns and Spiritual Songs*.

Isaac Watts, 1706, *Horae Lyricae: Peoms, chiefly of the Lyric Kind, in Two Books*, London, 1706. Second edition 1709 in three books. See also the 1837 edition with a memoir by Robert Southey, London.

Isaac Watts, 1715, *Divine Songs attempted in easy language for the use of Children*.

Isaac Watts, 1719, *The Psalms of David Imitated in the Language of the New Testament, and apply'd to the Christian State and Worship*, London. Later editions 1765 and 1782 and in *The Poetical Works of Isaac Watts: with the life of the Author* (Cooke's edition, London, 1802).

Isaac Watts, 1810 [1753], *The Works of the Reverend and Learned Isaac Watts, D. D.*, D. Jennings and P. Doddridge [eds]; 6 vols; London: J. Barfield.

John F. Walvoord, 2001, *Prophecy in the New Millennium: A Fresh Look at Future Events*, Grand Rapids, MI: Kregel Publications.

Robert L. Webb, 1991, *John the Baptizer and Prophet: A socio-historical study*, Sheffield: Sheffield Academic Press.

Max Weber, 1952, *Ancient Judaism*, London: Allen & Unwin.

Renita J. Weems, 1995, *Battered Love: Marriage, Sex and Violence in the Hebrew Prophets*, Minneapolis: Fortress Press.

Julius Wellhausen, 1885, *Prolegomena to the History of Israel*, tr. J. Sutherland Black, Edinburgh: Adam & Charles Black.

R. Werbner (ed.), 1998, *Memory and the Postcolony: African Anthropology and the Critique of Power*, London: Zed Books.

Klaus Wengst, 1987, *Pax Romana and the Peace of Jesus Christ*, tr. John Bowden, London: SCM Press.

Alexander Whitaker, 1613, *Good news from Virginia: sent to the Council and Company of Virginia resident in England from Alexander Whitaker, the Minister of Henrico in Virginia wherein also is a Narration of the present State of that Country and our Colonies there. Perused and published by direction from that Council and the Preface prefixed of some matters touching that Plantation very requisite to be made known*, London.

Ronald C. White, Jr and C. Howard Hopkins, 1976, *The Social Gospel: Religion and Reform in Changing America*, Philadelphia: Temple University Press.

Alvin M. Williams (ed.), 1970, *Conversations at Little Gidding*, Cambridge: Cambridge University Press.

Arthur H. Williamson, 1996, 'George Buchanan, Civic Virtue and Commerce: European Imperialism and its Sixteenth-Century Critics', *Scottish Historical Review* LXXV, pp. 237ff.

Walter Wink, 1992, *Engaging the Powers: Discernment and Resistance in a World of Domination*, Minneapolis: Fortress Press.

Walter Wink, 2003, *Jesus and Non-Violence: A Third Way*, Minneapolis: Fortress.

G. Winstanley, 1973, *The Law of Freedom and Other Writings*, ed. Christopher Hill, Harmondsworth: Penguin.

Eric R. Wolf, 1997, *Europe and the People without History*, Berkeley, CA: University of California Press.

J. Wolffe, 1994, *God and Greater Britain: Religion and National Life in Britain and Ireland 1843–1945*, London: Routledge.

J. Wolffe, 1997, '"Praise to the holiest in the height": Hymns and Church Music', in J. Wolffe (ed.), *Religion in Victorian Britain: Vol. 5: Culture and Empire*, Manchester: Manchester University Press, pp. 59–99.

Lewis B. Wright, 1943, *Religion and Empire: The Links between Piety and Commerce in British Expansion 1558–1625*, Chapel Hill, NC: University of North Carolina Press.

Bernard R. Youngman, 1956, *The Palestine of Jesus*, London: Hilton Educational.

Index of Biblical References

16.8	63	24.14	101
16.17–18	245	25.14–30	61
		25.35–45	60
Matthew		25.37–40	217
Book of	9, 15	26.52	57
1	15	28	92
1.22–3	9	28.19–20	196
1.23	15	28.20	47, 196, 204
2.2	56		
2.3	57	**Micah**	
2.12	57	Book of	32, 164
5.16	233	2	35
5.23–24	215	2.1	35
5.43–45	196	2.1–2	32
6.9–13	60	2.1–3	196
6.12	216	2.2	35
6.24	58	2.5	35
7.24	241	2.9	35
8.17	226	3.1–3	32
9.13	54	3.5–7	36
9.17	216	3.11	36
9.20	53	4.3	32, 163
10.40	196	4.3–4	36
11.11	47	4.4	32
11.27	196	4.6–7	32
11.30	60	4.7b	163–164
12.7	54, 216	5.2	164
13.14	226	5.10	36
13.35	226	6.8	225
13.44	56	7.1–6	27
13.53–57	196	7.3	32
13.57	47	7.5	27
16.18	196	7.5–6	32
16.29	86	7.7	27
16.33	92		
17.24–27	57	**Numbers**	
18.5	217	Book of	50
18.10	217	11.29	247
18.35	216	19.11	53
20.1–16	61	22.4–6	10
20.14	61		
21.15	111	**Philemon**	
22.23–33	211	1.11	106
22.37–39	210		
22.39	210	**Proverbs**	
23.37	47	2.7b–8	225
23.37–38	57	2.20	225
24	101	8.20	225

Index of Names and Subjects